# Boldness Be My Friend

Richard Pape was born and bred in Yorkshire, where he worked on the *Yorkshire Post*. He learned to fly privately in the 1930s and joined the RAF at the outbreak of war. His wartime experiences are the subject of this book.

After the war he wandered restlessly around the world and recorded his adventures in a succession of books. In 1955 he became the first man to drive from within the Arctic Circle to Cape Town. In 1958 he broke many motoring records in North America, and in 1959 he lived in Antarctica.

In 1962 he met Group Captain Leonard Cheshire, VC, OM, DSO, DFC, and in 1964 helped to found a Cheshire Home for incurably sick children in Papua New Guinea. There he met and married Helen Prouting, a lawyer working for the then Australian Administration of that Territory. They are at present living in Canberra, Australia.

Richard Pape holds the Military Medal, the Polish Air Force Eagle, the coveted Dutch Order of Merit, the National Resistance Commemoration Cross of the Netherlands and the USA Antarctic Service Medal.

D1392888

*Available in the same series*

**THE NAKED ISLAND**
Russell Braddon

**NANCY WAKE**
Russell Braddon

**THE LAST ENEMY**
Richard Hillary

**COCKLESHELL HEROES**
C. E. Lucas-Phillips

**THE WHITE RABBIT**
Bruce Marshall

**ARNHEM**
Major-General R. E. Urquhart

**THE DAM BUSTERS**
Paul Brickhill

**HISTORY OF THE SECOND WORLD WAR**
B. H. Liddell Hart

TRUE STORIES OF WORLD WAR II

# Boldness Be My Friend

Richard Pape

*Revised, expanded and updated edition*

**Pan Books**
London, Sydney and Auckland

First published in Great Britain 1953 by Elek Books Ltd
This revised, expanded and updated edition
first published in Great Britain 1984 by Granada Publishing
This edition published 1989 by Pan Books Ltd
Cavaye Place, London SW10 9PG
9 8 7 6 5 4 3 2 1
© Richard Pape 1953, 1984

ISBN 0 330 31021 6

Printed and bound in Great Britain by
Richard Clay Ltd, Bungay, Suffolk

DEDICATED TO
*Helen, my wife,*
*without whose insistence,*
*encouragement and criticism*
*this revised version of*
Boldness Be My Friend *would*
*not have been written*

# Contents

| | | |
|---|---|---|
| | Author's Note | 9 |
| | Ackowledgements | 12 |
| 1 | Realities of War | 15 |
| 2 | Flying with a Bomber's Moon | 37 |
| 3 | Special Mission Berlin | 54 |
| 4 | Hunted in Holland | 63 |
| 5 | The Dutch Underground | 78 |
| 6 | The Price of Treachery | 100 |
| 7 | Prisoner in Germany | 113 |
| 8 | Plotting Escape | 138 |
| 9 | A Polish Coal-mine | 159 |
| 10 | Escape in Poland | 172 |
| 11 | Nunnery to Dungeon | 186 |
| 12 | Gestapo Torture – and German Friends | 196 |
| 13 | Postscript to Poland | 211 |
| 14 | Flight from Czechoslovakia | 218 |
| 15 | Rings of Conspiracy | 258 |
| 16 | Breslau Intrigue | 281 |
| 17 | Obersalzberg – Berchtesgaden | 306 |
| 18 | Crisis to Crisis | 333 |
| 19 | The Bleak Baltic | 350 |
| 20 | Breaking Covert | 375 |
| 21 | Swing of Destiny | 393 |
| | Conclusion | 406 |
| | Appendix A: Foreword to the First Edition by Lord Tedder | 421 |
| | Appendix B: Introduction to the First Edition by Sir Archibald McIndoe | 422 |
| | Maps | 423 |

# Author's Note

This is a completely revised, expanded and updated version of my first book, published over thirty years ago. It has a totally new face, it is woven in a very different way and, above all, it contains hitherto unpublished facts which could not be told earlier.

The present narration has been built out of research long after the war was over, and memory of dramatic and dangerous endeavours and personal fortunes. Facts verified from records, in many instances unavailable to me thirty years ago, enable me to set down anew a running tale of ferocious situations and dark, sinister events in Hitler's Occupied Europe.

Interwoven with my personal tale are the histories and fates of many memorable resistance workers met in wartime in enslaved Holland, Poland, Czechoslovakia – also loyalist Germans rigidly opposed to the Nazi regime. I reveal some of the pathos and terror suffered by many. I seek to point up the courage and honour which no degree of brutal oppression was able to destroy. Much of what is told is not only personal testimony of my own experiences but intendedly a moving picture of fantastic Polish and other underground workers and their brilliant achievements. In this category of achievements was their manipulating of my visit in 1943, under masquerade as a Yugoslav stonemason, to Hitler's sacred Obersalzberg in Berchtesgaden Territory.

Writing the first edition of *Boldness Be My Friend* was one of the most difficult things I had to deal with. It was impossible to offer full and (as time proved) invariably accurate information. Many sources I would have liked to have tapped lay sealed behind the Iron Curtain. It will be remembered, too, that in the early post-war years there seemed a very real prospect of imminent war, again over the same ground. Within the nature of security limits, extreme caution and secrecy were vital especially relating to Polish underground organizations and activities relevant to the political and military problems affecting the gallant people of Eastern Europe. Over intervening years I avoided the challenge of writing about personal involvement in the Obersalzberg operation. A curious aversion and ambivalence were experienced. I was worried about likely repercussions upon Polish friends, also German collaborators. My fears were heightened upon learning of the terrible fate which had overtaken my escape-friend, Mieteck, which is related in this book.

When I wrote the first edition of this book in 1950, I was living in Johannesburg, South Africa. A measure of information came to me of the fates of Dutch resistance colleagues, who like myself had suffered Gestapo arrest. It was not until after the book was published in 1953, and upon my return to Holland, that I learned the full extent of the tragedy and heroism which had lain in my wake. At this later date it is possible to interweave our stories.

It is true that the book became overnight a best-seller. Much of the credit for its success must go to brave and magnificently unselfish people who assisted me in the resistance movements. Again, much of the instant acceptance of the book may be attributed to a Foreword by Lord Tedder, GCB, Marshal of the Royal Air Force and Deputy Supreme Commander of the Allied Expeditionary Force under General Eisenhower (see Appendix A). An Introduction by Sir Archibald McIndoe, CBE, the famous Royal Air Force plastic surgeon, gave further endorsement to the book (see Appendix B). I was highly honoured that men of such distinction subscribed their names to my story. Sir Archibald I knew well, but Lord Tedder I had not met. When in time I did meet Lord Tedder, an easy, strong bond of friendship and affection developed between us. Both he and Sir Archibald McIndoe were to have considerable influence in my post-war adventures. They were among the very few possessed of the genuine inside view concerning my underground activities against the enemy. Both of them totally honoured and respected my oaths of secrecy to the Polish underground organization.

Time hurries from us. I believe my tale should now be told, even though so long after the war has ended. Here then is a faithful human-interest pilgrimage. Perhaps even, in part, an historical record.

Richard B. Pape

# Acknowledgements

I wish to express my thanks to the following institutions and individuals for help in the preparation of this narrative. Various sources of information are mentioned in page footnotes, considered necessary as part of the integral story. If I have failed to trace or thank any copyright holders, so many years after the events this book portrays, I hope they will forgive me. I gratefully acknowledge such references and important contributions, also those which were freely given. Any errors concerning the cast who played out the resistance drama in Hitler's Occupied Europe are my own.

Dr James H. McCauley of Canberra, Australia, for continuing assistance and co-operation during the writing of this book

Dianne Dowling for assistance in preparation of manuscript for press

Ministry of Defence, England
Public Records Office, England
Imperial War Museum, England
The Royal Air Force Museum, England
Comité International de la Croix Rouge, Switzerland
Bundesarchiv – Militärarchiv, Freiburg, W. Germany
Stadtverwaltung (Stadarchiv), Koblenz, W. Germany
Hotel-Pension Turken, Berchtesgaden, Austria
The Reverend W. H. Pape, Bibelschüle Brake, Lemgo, W. Germany

The Australian War Memorial, Canberra

Polish Ex-Servicemen's Association in Britain and Australia

Army Records Office, England

The Royal Aero Club, England

609 West Riding of Yorkshire, Auxiliary Air Force Association

The Yorkshire Aeroplane Club, Yeadon, England

*The Story of 609 Squadron*, by Frank H. Ziegler

The Yorkshire Conservative Newspaper Co. Ltd, England

*The Yorkshire Post, Two Centuries*, by M. A. Gibbs and F. Beckwith

Polish Tourist Information Centre, England

Australian Army Central Records Office

Calvary Hospital, Wellington, New Zealand

*Polish SOE and the Allies*, by Joseph Garlinski

A. Czeczowickza (formerly of Partschendorf, Czechoslovakia), England

In Canberra, the Embassies of the Federal Republic of Germany, Austria, France, the Netherlands, Norway and the United States of America

Mieczyslaw Borodej, Poland

Eric Hudson, my brother-in-law, England, for loyal co-operation over the years

Royal Air Force Joint School of Photography, particularly Flt Lt G. H. Parry and D. H. Newham.

Mrs Theo Kyle, Auckland, New Zealand

Wallace Crighton-Brown, Nelson, New Zealand

Group Captain Leonard Cheshire, VC, DSO, DFC

Air-Vice Marshal J. Cox, CB, OBE, DFC, Royal Air Force (Rtd)

Hugh V. Clarke, former Director of Information and Public Relations, Department of External Territories, Canberra

Rear Admiral George J. Dufek, former Commander US Naval Support Force Antarctica

Allan Kent, former war correspondent, *Toronto Telegram*, Canada

Royal Netherlands Archives, The Hague, Holland

*RAF Flying Review*, England

Dr J. F. Ryan, FRACR, The Royal Australian College of Radiologists

Pam Langford (née Worrall), Sydney, Australia.

R. B. P.

# CHAPTER 1
## Realities of War

I was well prepared for war by 1939. Working for six years with the Yorkshire Conservative Newspaper Company in Leeds, I came under the strong influence of its political policy. Expressed in its newspapers, *The Yorkshire Post*, *The Yorkshire Evening Post* and *The Leeds Mercury*, its allegiance was Conservative and its policy outspokenly anti-appeasement of Adolf Hitler, anti-Nazism and anti-fascism. I grew into the bloodstream of those newspapers. I was in an atmosphere to feel the urgency, the certainty that war would not disperse before a drifting line of least resistance.

For most of my years with the company, I held a senior position in the Publicity Department which catered for the needs of the three newspapers. It was creative, challenging work and was where my abilities belonged. I had tried my hand at news gathering but my editor considered I lacked the temperament to become an efficient and dedicated reporter. I happily agreed for I disliked irregular hours which interfered with my sporting activities. In passing, I must say that field sports and the sustained tensions of rock climbing forged strengths to prove their worth in war, sustaining me through hardships and dangers demanding all the toughness, ingenuity, physical and nervous endurance I could possibly muster. I could never have moved and survived as I did without the hammerings I took on the playing fields of Yorkshire.

But newspaperdom was the hub of my existence. Influences I encountered there were to have tremendous bearing upon me in war. I learned the newspapers' racing code. In due course when a captive in Germany, I used it, embarking on coding operations with my former chief of the Publicity Department, Alfred Willcox, and under the auspices of the War Office. Over a hundred messages of military intelligence reached him and our code, modified over the years, was never detected. In the immediate pre-war years, *The Leeds Mercury* organized conducted tours for its readers and I was fortunate to accompany many to the Continent. Given every encouragement for advancement, I heeded the advice of my topmost seniors to learn German, at least to a reasonable level of fluency. This was to prove of incalculable value during three years of captivity in German Occupied Europe. In short, gaining knowledge on a variety of methods and subjects associated with my newspaper training came to my aid in extraordinary and unenvisaged ways. To this too was allied pre-war flying training and experience in aerial photography.

Looking back, it was all part of a strange inevitability with war looming on the horizon. In 1937, I became a member of 609 West Riding Bomber Squadron of the Royal Auxiliary Air Force. The squadron had come into existence the year previously, a month before Hitler's army marched into the Rhineland. In those days it was approaching the impossible to gain acceptance as a trainee pilot, but thanks again to my association with the newspapers, and particularly the influence certain of their directors had with the squadron, I was enlisted as an aerial photographer. Every weekend became devoted to intensive training. Using the superb F24 camera, flying in Hawker Hart aircraft, I became skilled in the practice and knowledge of photographic techniques, target finding, pinpointing and allied navigation.

Again in the curious inevitability of direction, in 1938 I was led into a preliminary exercise in Intelligence gathering. Nazi euphoria was rising as Chamberlain struck his matches of appeasement around the bulb of Hitler's war-making thermometer. Like the rest of the general public, I had no idea of the friction existing between British Intelligence organizations and Chamberlain who regarded spying in peacetime as dishonourable. Alarmed at Britain's unpreparedness for a war which they saw as certain, Intelligence Services were largely compelled to go underground and much of what they so vitally accomplished was kept hidden from Chamberlain and like detractors.

British Intelligence Services were on the lookout for men and women in specialized business concerns, the sciences and the arts to be recruited as amateur operators in undercover work. In my publicity duties for the Tours Department of *The Leeds Mercury*, I often met a Mr King, an executive of Ponds, the British cosmetics concern. We got along well and eventually I learned he was interested in far more than preserving English complexions. King was a scout for likely recruits for the Intelligence game – for civilians of the right fibre, loyalty and education. I was viewed as suitable material – a skilled photographer, with good knowledge of German, experience in aviation, background of foreign travel and an adventurous frame of mind. I was subsequently approached by a Major Shelley, purportedly a representative of a British chemical company with international ramifications.

I admit to a smattering of pride in being one of those singled out for secret work. I had a perfect 'cover', obtaining material for organized tours. Under false identity I travelled to Koblenz with two genuine representatives of travel agencies, Messrs Chapman and Cadwallader. They too played roles in the Intelligence community. We stayed in the fashionable Riesenfürstenhof Hotel located on the southern peninsula where the Moselle River joins the Rhine. I carried Leica camera equipment and a very neat miniature camera which could be used effectively in artificial light using fast film. Intelligence in Britain had learned of a small group of Himmler's SS officers (Scholtzstaffe – Black Shirts, later known as the Death Head Brigade and to murder in millions) who were billeted in the hotel and wearing plain clothes. It was also learned that in the event of war the large, dignified hotel would be immediately requisitioned as a centre for control of the Rhineland. In such an event it would represent a positive target for RAF destruction. Opposite the hotel, on the rocky heights above the other bank of the Rhine, was the Ehrenbreitsein Fortress. Dating from AD 950, it had developed over the centuries to become known as the 'Gibraltar of the Rhine'. Here parties of the plain-clothed SS officers paid daily visits; it was also known that chemicals of some kind were being stockpiled within its precincts.

Suffice to say, I secretly photographed many of the SS fraternity both inside and out of doors. From the rocky heights of the fortress, I plotted compass bearings for possible aerial attack on the hotel. As for the fortress, it was under high security and it was impossible for me to discover what went on inside. Towards the end of my stay my companions warned me I was under surveillance. I applied acting, false clues and extreme caution thereafter. Nevertheless, I was required to visit a nearby police station to account for my Leica – the police pretext for questioning me being that a similar camera had been reported stolen from the hotel. My 'cover' stood the test. If I returned to England unscathed, I did learn the smell of fear, comparative whiff though it was. I was also aware that Intelligence operations are risky and unpredictable enterprises, that the most brilliant planning is no guarantee of success. Most vitally, the pre-war visit to Koblenz was an unforgettable experience in discovering and trusting a sixth-sense warning of danger. How often I was to need it in the years ahead!

As for the Riesenfürstenhof Hotel, it was destroyed in an Allied bombing raid during the war and has never been rebuilt. Whether my information played any part, I know not.

In December 1938, 609 West Riding Bomber Squadron, Royal Auxiliary Air Force was suddenly restructured, changing from Bomber to Fighter Command. Hawker Hinds were replaced with Spitfires. My days of flying in a rear cockpit with the F24 camera were over. If war came quickly I had no intention of being swept into it as a photographer, so I resigned from the squadron. A new mood of apprehension was stirring throughout the nation which had embarked on all-out rearmament. Fired with an urgency to become a pilot, I began private tuition with Captain Henry V. Worrall, DSC and Bar, and Croix de Guerre. Worrall, an Australian, was the chief flying instructor of the Yorkshire Aeroplane Club which shared the same flying field at Yeadon with 609 Squadron. I could not have wished for a more skilled aviator to be my instructor. After the First World War in which he distinguished himself with the Royal Naval Air Service, taking part in the attack on the German cruiser *Goeben* at Gallipoli, he became a test pilot. He did the first test flight on the 'Airspeed Envoy', designed by Neville Shute Norway and A. H. Tiltman. He also went as co-pilot to Sir Allan Cobham on a history-making flight to Cape Town. Obtaining my 'A' licence and Royal Aero Club Aviator's certificate I spent all available time flying solo. It was an expensive pursuit until, almost at the last hour, Worrall had me made a member of the newly formed Civil Air Guard, when a proportion of my flying time was paid for by Air Ministry. Conditions applied. In the event of war I would promptly become part of the Royal Air Force.

After I had acquired my pilot's licence, the unsettling quality of the news worsened, and one seemed unable to focus steadily on anything. Young men like myself were suspended in restlessness, impatient for an end to uncertainty, either to be freed to get on with careers or go into the trade of war which, it was generally considered, would be short and swift. On 23 August 1939, Germany signed a pact with Russia containing a secret clause for the division of Poland. Two days later Britain, no longer falsely hopeful, signed a Mutual Assistance Treaty with Poland.

War at last! The announcement of 3 September 1939 brought a sense of relief with the long uncertainty over. I may have harboured ideas of becoming a fighter-pilot 'ace' and returning to the newspapers to find the grass greener for promotion. I was strangely unwilling to face axioms of war dangers, death or mutilation, that skilful German fliers would be bent upon my destruction, just as I visualized shooting them down with daring and ease. After flying over Britain's verdant countryside, carefree and unmolested, to contemplate bursting flak shells, tracer-laced skies, death in a matter of seconds seemed elusive and silly and caused me no distress. As for becoming a prisoner of war the idea was too remotely beyond likelihood to deserve a thought. Like most of those preparing to go off, my belief in survival seemed like a guaranteed inheritance, a feeling of almost superhuman consolation. Most fighting men may attune imagination to believing in superiority in cheating death – until really mixed up with shot and shell when imagination parts company with fact. Inexplicably, some are consistently lucky in physical peril and all I can say is, I was one of them.

I became a permanent member of the RAF for the duration on 13 September 1939. Unknown to me at the time, this was twenty-five years to the day since my father had enlisted and, as he had been, I was twenty-three. My father was first in action in Gallipoli, returning to France as a machine-gunner. Later he transferred to the Royal Tank Corps and was twice wounded.

My first posting was to Cardington, where nine years earlier the R101 airship had slipped its moorings on its ill-fated maiden flight. Airships had significance for me. My Grandfather Pape had been a design engineer of the rival R100. Many long hours I had spent with him in his study where he had fascinating models of the R100 and its cross-sections. I had shared something of his pride when it had proved a success, and of his bitterness at its being scrapped. God only knew what fate lay ahead of me now, with that first intake of some hundreds of men anxious to fly against the enemy. I waited with nervous excitement upon the decision as to my disposal. When it came, it was astonishing. I had hoped to be back in a cockpit in next to no time; instead, with six others I was posted to a newly formed officer-cadet training wing at Cambridge University. Where I had expected favoured treatment, my flying licence now seemed to clog advancement. The truth was, we had to curb impatience while flying-training channels were being established.

I occupied delightful rooms in Memorial Court, Clare College, looking out on immaculate lawns. Forty officer-cadets occupied the court, a wing of Clare added after the First World War. Clare dates from the fourteenth century and retains a medieval air of aloofness, a peculiar dignity where the past keeps continuity with the future, yet with a mysterious, communicable atmosphere of the real English character over the ages. Its dining-hall is venerable, with stained-glass windows, high vaulted ceiling and timbers mellowed by age. At a table where I sat with pilot trainee Frank Dimblebee, we carved our initials among those of scholars long since gone. I wondered if I were carving my own last memorial.

We studied under lecturers at various of the colleges. Examinations were frequent and tough. After each, some of our fellows departed and I surely would have been among them but for Grandfather Pape's past tutoring of

me in mathematics. It was the time of the 'Phoney War' or
'Sitzkreig' and, as month followed month, we chafed at
cloistered inaction, growing browned off even with pub-
crawling in the evenings. Interest revived somewhat when
we were taken a number of times to a building where I lay
on a platform with a bombsight, some thirty feet up, while
on to a screen below a cine projector beamed night views of
enemy land areas, or daylight panoramas of ocean wastes
whereupon to locate enemy pocket battleships. With the
simulator producing flak bursts, probing searchlights,
blanketing cloud and alarming noises and the 'pilot' taking
evasive action throwing me off course, I had to navigate to
target and aim for bombing. Uncannily real, it gave the
vivid impression that bomber missions would be damned
hazardous and uncomfortable. To hell with lumbering
bombers, I thought – a single-seater fighter was infinitely
safer and made more sense.

The Phoney War lasted nine months, six of which I
spent at Cambridge, if praying and beseeching to get to
flying school. Winter passed by. Civilians and servicemen
became casual with the 'Bore War'. My pay was far less
than my newspaper salary and I sank the last of my savings
in golf and rounds of pubs. I vehemently resisted suggestions to forget about Fighter Command and think about
training as a pilot for Bomber Command. It was mooted I
be dispatched to Canada for special training in view of a
secret new four-engined bomber which was in an advanced
stage of production. What I and my colleagues did not
know was the grim extent of disasters befalling RAF
bombers through navigational failure, and the desperate
need to revise training and devise new aids to accuracy. In
strongly rejecting any suggestion of Canada, I told the
Cambridge selection committee I'd fight for England from
England; I'd quit and join a tank unit before I'd be
relegated to train for a so-called four-engined bomber not

even in existence! What the hell had happened to flying-training schools in Britain?

On 10 May 1940 Germany broke the Phoney War stalemate, striking 'like lightning in the night' into Holland, Belgium and France. The light mood in Britain went out. Churchill became Prime Minister and promised, four-square, a long, bitter, hard road ahead. Suddenly, on 20 May, my stalemate ended. My resistance against bombers prevailed and I was posted to an Advanced Flying-Training School in Wiltshire.

Blazing for action, it was with a sense of frustrating rebuff that I found myself assigned to a flying instructor who, after Captain Worrall, I considered the essence of timidity and nervous flying ability. On the Western Front, the British Army and sections of Belgian and French forces were being squeezed down a corridor to the back door at Dunkirk. I was furious that the war would be over while I wasted time doing hours of straight and level flying, dainty turns, take-offs and landings. I was astonished at the small numbers undergoing flying tuition and a complete lack of action-packed training when a hell-for-leather war was in progress and every hour and every qualified pilot counted. From the start I had taken an aggressive stand against my instructor. Unable to contain myself any longer, I determined to show him what aerobatics were all about and I put the kite through its paces. There was a hell of a to-do. Brought up before the CO I was brusquely told I would learn to fly the RAF way or not at all. Fortunately a chief instructor arrived from Central Flying School. He took me up to 6,000 feet and said, 'Right, now give me hell.' I really took the brakes off and gave a model performance.

I was on my way again to another flying-training centre, but was taken aback when it proved to be a small RAF unit using the testing field and facilities adjacent to the Bristol Aeroplane Company at Filton, Gloucestershire. Here the brilliant Beaufighter was going through early trials, and the factories there were also in full production of the new 1,800-hp radial engines to power the Stirling – to be Britain's prototype four-engined bomber. Indicative of the factories' importance, Spitfires were dispersed about the flying field at a time when the evacuation of the armies at Dunkirk was commencing and every fighter which could possibly be spared was needed over its beaches.

It was an odd posting. I was billeted in a private home in the suburb of Patchway, with a widow and her daughter-in-law. The son/husband was with the Army across the Channel. It was strange being in a private home at·that time, in personal contact with the suffering known to families as they waited, taut and hoping for news of their men. The two women were distraught. I was put into a milieu I would not have known living with men in a barrack, where sentiment and spiritual understanding had little room to manoeuvre. Over a few days, I saw the young wife take on the look of middle age; the mother's face became a stoic mask through which neither shade of despair nor glint of hope dared appear. I had more time for observing than I wished, for my training was suspended while instructors were caught up in the evacuation effort. In the end, when over 300,000 exhausted soldiers had been plucked from Dunkirk, news came that the son/husband was back in England, shaken but otherwise undamaged.

I resumed flying, but something had happened I would never have believed. Piloting had become boring. I was impatient with slow training, and felt pushed aside, useless in the past crisis. An unvoiced undercurrent of fear for Britain's survival was about. Churchill asserted that the only weapon remaining for Britain to hit back with was Bomber Command. Realistic analysis of what German bombers had accomplished in the name of Nazi splendour in Warsaw, Rotterdam and Dunkirk brought home that for one possible enemy killed in an individual combat, I could better give vent to anger by unleashing tons of bombs on Germany. Lurking in my mind also was a fear. Nearing my mid-twenties, I might be judged too old for fighter combat. A cheerless lull followed Dunkirk. I was not to know it would last only a month before the start of the greatest battle of Britain and, with the shortage of pilots the biggest worry, I might have been at the controls of a fighter in action sooner than I imagined. Before then, however, two incidents in quick succession settled my future.

The first involved a fair young maiden, flying boots and a cow. I was friendly with 'Jason', a young Spitfire pilot enamoured of a Land Army girl, Fay, who worked on a farm at nearby Horseferry. She bemoaned her tea ration and cold, wet feet. With gallantry to the rescue, sundry pounds of tea and smallest-size fur-lined flying boots were 'acquired' from RAF Stores. I flew with Jason in a Miles Master aircraft which he flew in liaison with other units. Taking off, we found the farm where Fay had pegged out a white sheet in a field. Something went wrong with our run-up to target, for when I dropped the tea-loaded boots lashed together, instead of them hitting the bull's-eye, they clouted a placidly grazing cow. It streaked off like a greyhound. If Fay dissuaded an angry farmer with a bruised cow from reporting the matter, alas, she confided in her loquacious friend, Dianne, who was very friendly with Perry, my flying instructor. Dianne's obvious liking for me, too, produced in Perry a constrained hostility towards me. Jason and I were in direst danger of being court-martialled and were possibly saved by the desperate shortage of pilots and, as we thought, by the incident not being officially recorded. After the publication of the first edition of this book in 1953, the RAF Club in Piccadilly gave me a reception presided over by Lord Tedder. I recall him lighting his pipe, then grinning at me. 'By the way, Pape, what happened to the boots you pinched to bomb a cow?'

I was in decided disfavour with instructor Perry when the second incident followed. At a little, club-like pub one evening, I criticized RAF training and foolishly boasted that when flying before the war, I had taught myself to side-slip, stall and, from about ten feet above the ground, drop, bounce, swing across wind and stop in a minimum distance for tight emergency. Perry was sceptical. Two things I overlooked: we carried on drinking too late into the dawn, and it was ten months since I had done the stunt, having been taught the technique by Captain Worrall. My optical focus was all to pot when I took off solo next morning, and my stomach was very peculiar. Foolish braggadocio would not let me cry off. If human fallibility is the very essence of the colour of life, I certainly blotched my record with a huge 'black'. Coming in to land I was vehemently confident, slipping down smoothly, so I thought, and cut the throttle. The engine, not according to rules, also cut and refused to burst instantly into song. Certainly not at my sagacious best, I had misjudged my height, as if fooled by a bifocal divide. Powerless to zoom out of trouble, the machine seemed to stand still in a most unusual way until gravity laughed and dropped me vertically with a mighty thud on the grass. If I was somewhat jarred the undercart was not damaged, but my sorry performance was viewed by two senior officers who had just arrived to put the instructors themselves through their periodic testings. My pilot career was brought into disreputable collapse. I was grounded, I was dressed down; my defence of faulty mechanical maintenance was swept aside. I was not amenable to discipline. Recommendation for a commission from Cambridge was scrubbed. When all seemed lost, the very best occurred. I was to be transferred for training in Bomber Command to an intensive naviga-

tional course in Scotland. Some comment was made about
my colour of hair and expected impetuosity. A legacy from
a blond father and a golden-red-haired mother was my
thatch of vivid red hair.

It was the right slot for me and, had I not been so self-
willed, I might have found it earlier. Miraculously, it was
exactly what I wanted, and my exit from Fighter Command
I never regretted for many reasons, not the least being the
conviction that, knowing my temperament, I would never
have survived the war as a fighter pilot. Policy towards
navigational training had changed since the beginning of
the war when mathematical wizardry had been looked
upon as the predominant requisite. Tragic losses and
abortive missions had forced a rethinking on the high
mathematical standard I had been required to reach at Cambridge. At No. 1 Air Navigational School, at Prestwick,
I was instructed in navigation and meteorology with
emphasis shifted to a reasonable knowledge of mathematics,
while stressing accuracy and efficiency. Essentially allied
were team spirit and character, the ability to avoid panic
and stark fear, to keep a cool, rational head in the most
terrifying conditions of vicious war and savage weather,
plus mental and physical endurance for long gruelling
hours in the sky. Experience had proved that some men,
though brilliant mathematicians, had gone to pieces under
stress. Once courage failed and the mind became bewildered, disaster and death loomed large for the precious
aircraft and its crew.

For training, no more testing a place could have been
found than Scotland with its islands and ragged coastline,
and the vast, lonely area across the sea to Ulster, where
fearful weather had a villainous habit of erupting without
notice. I trained for three months with some splendid
young fellows; most of them died before the end of 1942.
Exchanging individual piloting for the bondage of a crew

dependent upon every calculation I made radically changed me. I was braced by a kind of covenanting fervour to austere self-discipline. Being cooped up for hours in an alien sky, rendering each other service, developed a high consciousness of a communal code of honour. Guiding an aircraft in the early part of the war was purely a case of dead reckoning, assisted by taking astro-sights of the pole star and others – provided the damned heavenly bodies were visible. Radar-based inventions were to come into being, but these sophisticated devices for transmitting a beam for aircraft to follow to the target and home were only in the planning stage before I was out of the flying war.

With the perversity of war, I collected my first wound from the fire of friend. Evidence remains as a ridged scar at the back of my head. With a newly trained pilot I took off from Prestwick in perfect visibility on a flight plan crossing to Northern Ireland where the weather, with its eternal hatred of predictability, maintained tradition. Near Donegal Bay the beauteous day fused with menacing sheets of black cloud and sent runners to lie in wait as a curtain of grey with blasts of drizzle off the west coast of Scotland. As we passed over a convoy of merchant ships under naval escort heading for the Firth of Clyde, a frigate flickered demand for identification. I signalled back with the Aldis lamp then, unfortunately, fired the wrong colours from the Very-cartridge gun in the roof. The correct colours of the hour had changed minutes earlier. No quarter from the Navy when sneaking German reconnaissance aircraft were in the sky! We heard thud, thud, thud on our port quarter and stared in stupefaction at black puffs. We went into a frame-shaking dive and weaved landwards. With temporary loss of vision in swirling greyness, suddenly out of the vapours loomed Ailsa Craig, a cone-shaped islet of bald granite rising abruptly from the sea to 1,114 feet. I was well aware of this phenomenon reaching upwards like a mailed

fist at the approach to the Firth and usually gave it and its
cranky air currents a wide berth. Down at about 500 feet I
screamed, 'Pull out! Swing starboard!' The black shape
rushed towards us. My pilot heaved out of the dive and
into a split turn. I was hurtled backwards, striking my head
on a steel plate. I was knocked out cold. A day later, I
awoke as if with a massive hangover through which I
registered painfully a chorus of birds and glistening
sunshine beyond the windows. A medical orderly spoke in
Scottish brogue. 'Are you hungry?'

I groaned. 'Feed the bloody birds and shut the bastards
up.'

'Och, mon, they're singing because it's such a lovely
day.'

'To hell with the weather. Clear off. Go and saw down
Ailsa Craig!'

Ever since that little skirmish with the Royal Navy I
have doubted its restraint of the traditional shot across the
bows and have suspected that those dauntless sea-dogs, in
defence of their homeland, would fire first and ask
questions of the corpses afterwards.

While in our remoteness in Scotland, the Battle of
Britain had been won in the south but we had no illusions
of how touch-and-go it had been. I was saddened but proud
to learn that a journalist colleague on *The Yorkshire Post*
had perished as one of the famous 'few' in the battle. He
was Flight-Lieutenant John Dundas, DFC and Bar (the
latter awarded posthumously). He too was a member of
609 Auxiliary Air Force Squadron before the war and
together we would leave the newspaper office on a Friday
evening for weekend training with the close-knit brotherhood of Yorkshiremen. John Dundas was an intellectual
and aristocrat, related to the Marquess of Zetland and
Viscount Halifax, and was destined to become the most
acknowledged warrior of 609 Squadron. He shot down

Major Helmuth Wick, Commander of the Richthofen Fighter Geschwader and Germany's highest scoring 'ace' of the time, who was credited with fifty-six victories, one fewer than Adolf Galland, the idolized top German 'ace' of the war. Dundas had at least $13\frac{1}{2}$ victories and four probables.

After the Luftwaffe's losses in the battle, Germany ended its daylight raids to concentrate on night raids for the following year. The blitz of cities intended to reduce Britain to its knees began, and Britain, its Commonwealth and Empire stood alone with Germany thrusting at the heart. Even while the Nazis raved, 'Surrender or face destruction', and some French believed the British would have their necks wrung like chickens, the British people, battered but angered, were proving they could 'take it' at home, but were demanding reprisal. Proof that we could hit back, however weakly as a beginning, occurred on the night of 25 August 1940. Eighty Hampden and Wellington bombers set out to strike at Berlin for the first time in history. Fitted with extra fuel tanks, just enough to get them there and back without navigational error or severe headwinds, even though only twenty-nine reached Berlin and unleashed a mere twenty-two tons of bombs, they were enough to shock the German nation and blow Goering's boast that no British bomber would ever violate the sacred German capital. Further attacks were made by 7 September 1940, which was the night the Luftwaffe began its first mass raids on London – a night I have always had terrible cause to remember. I had my first experience at the receiving end of bombs, learning at first hand what I would be inflicting upon others.

Chance took me into the East End of London that night and Fate brought me out, physically unscathed, from the midst of the eight-hour-long waves of attack which caused Goering to gloat, 'London is in flames'. I was on my way to

Marazion, opposite St Michael's Mount in Cornwall, for a
short leave with my godmother and her husband, the
Reverend Arthur Hosken, known as the 'sporting parson
of Penzance'. The Mount was within his parish and many a
time I walked there with him, across the rocky path at low
tide. I loved Marazion. In September 1940 it was an
anachronistically peaceful part of England when Germany
had thousands of barges massed in Channel ports for
operation 'Sealion', the invasion of Britain. On the train
from Scotland, I sat next to a Regular RAF sergeant of
ground staff whom I recall as Harry Pilkinson or Parkinson.
We had quite a few beers over which he told me he was on
compassionate leave to help his mother, crippled father and
teenage sister pack and move out of the East End. He felt
it something of a miracle that he had found jobs for his
mother and sister in a canteen and a cottage to rent in a
village near his RAF station in Yorkshire.

It was late afternoon when we alighted at King's Cross
Station. There was a sinister, dreadful fear in the air about
what was happening. Intense bombing of the Thames-side
dockland was under way. The area was blazing furiously
and we saw bombers high up like glistening gnats, their
drone mingling with the sharp crackle of anti-aircraft fire
and the crump of bombs in the distance towards the East
End. Harry's immediate desperation struck some chord,
prompting me to offer to lend a hand to get his family away
from that stricken zone that night. He grabbed at my
offer. We took a taxi to Endsleigh Gardens Hotel where I
signed in and left my bag, then continued to his district
about ten miles away. We were set down in a main
thoroughfare. The driver refused to venture into the maze
of narrow streets during a raid. Columns of black smoke
rose from bombed buildings in the vicinity, and the
burning dockland in the close distance cast a wavering,
pallid, red glow beneath the clouds in the fading light. I

tautened whenever I heard a crashing explosion uncomfortably close. We turned into Harry's street. It was narrow, about a quarter-mile long with compacted rows of unpretentious terrace houses facing each other, typical of London's poorer area. We passed a smouldering gap in the line of houses. Air-raid wardens were working feverishly. People were being bandaged and carried away on stretchers. A stench of creeping gas was offensive. The road had became an unimaginable spectacle of broken glass and debris. But nothing seemed to matter except to reach Harry's people.

I met a real cockney family for the first time. They were vociferous, their patriotism, endurance and still their humour deeply moving. In the downstairs living-room the father was in a wheelchair; the mother and daughter usually pushed him to a communal shelter when air-raid sirens sounded. This evening they were waiting for Harry. It was useless trying to convince myself I had no fear in the presence of a cripple and two women who barely flinched at tremendous explosions and distinct reverberations. I had an imperilled sense of claustrophobia, wanting nothing but for us to get out. Came a lull in the bombing. They insisted we sit to a quick meal. I had a gripping, ugly fear the Luftwaffe would resume. It did, in less than thirty minutes.

Harry and I were roping a suitcase when the sirens howled and, before we could have finished our task, a scream of bombs came over the rooftop followed by deafening explosions and blinding flashes from the street behind. Violent explosions came one after another at close range. There was nothing we could do but lie flat, face down on the floor, and wait for the end – or we knew not what. The high-pitched whine of bombs again passed over and houses straight across the road in front were blown to pieces. To describe that mind-shattering explosion is impossible. Our small house heaved, the front door and windows blew in, glass flew everywhere, smoke, acrid fumes and the stench of cordite belched through the openings. The dwellings opposite had disappeared into rubble with flames leaping high, casting grim shadows and weird lights into the living-room. The old man, lying on a mattress under the table, screamed a torrent of curses against the Hun and to this day I picture his wife crouching over him, her face frozen, eyes staring as if carved in stone. Harry and I leaped to our feet, seeming to know at the same moment we had to get out fast to the nearest shelter.

He said, 'I'll try to get an ambulance or someone with a stretcher for Dad. We'll carry the cases.'

I stopped him. 'I'll go. You stay with your family!'

'I'll come with you,' his sister almost begged, 'I know the district.'

'No, stay with your mother. I'll get something.' I rushed out, impelled by a certainty of finding an ambulance or some uniformed personnel, but the street was lifeless except for spluttering incendiary bombs. I raced on. Close to the end were two new, ominous gaps facing each other. Flames leaped and linked under swirls of black smoke and floating ash. Just before I reached a broad cross-thoroughfare, jumping over and dodging smouldering debris, a series of tremendous flashes and explosions burst over the area around the corner ahead to my right. The earth trembled. So did I. Christ! I had just missed it by seconds. I suppressed a desire to scream or vomit, seeing houses gutted, burning, splintered. Stick after stick of bombs criss-crossed that flaming area. I leaned weakly against iron railings, scarcely believing such a grievous scene. 'I give up. Bugger it!' I was absolutely convinced the war was at an end. We would never win. No one could withstand this attack. It was terrible. No transport could get through; enlisting any aid was out of the question. For what seemed an eternity, I was the only living being in that devil's inferno. Fire stung my face, acrid smoke dried my throat, sparks cascaded in all directions. Eventually, as if conjured up in a magical play, air-raid wardens materialized, looking vacant, almost stupid, as if searching for an answer beyond understanding. People began rushing from houses, careering about like maddened animals. Men and women passed me in terror and piercing screams added to the insane cacophony of war from so many nerve-racking sources. I was abruptly elbowed by a uniformed man wearing a tin hat. 'Clear off, take cover!' Then observing my uniform, 'Get moving, son, we can't afford to lose you chaps.'

Disregarding his directions to a shelter below a church, I retraced down Harry's street, avoiding the gaps still spurting flames. The shriek of bombs came behind me. I threw myself flat on the road. They passed over so close I felt I could have reached out and touched them. A direct hit was scored beyond, on my right – straight opposite the smoking wreckage which had faced Harry's house! I knew absolutely, before I reached there, my new-found cockney friends had gone for ever. Their mortal remains were somewhere below that ghastly flaming mass.

I hurried past. Just beyond, I paced up and down . . . up and down. A trembling seized me. No other living soul was about. It was useless staying. There was nothing I could do for anyone. I made off, threading through endless, empty, ill-lit streets, away from the swirling fires of dockland and the East End. Hatless – I had lost my cap – dishevelled, sooty, oddly I craved food. My pace was erratic: rapid, trudging, sometimes stopping in bewildered disbelief, saying to myself, 'You lucky bastard!' Occasionally I asked direction from men who moved like black beetles in the gloomy streets, or glimpses of the dome of St Paul's guided me like a beacon. I was sure the cathedral was aflame within; the dome was glistening crimson, or pulsating, dull red through vapoury veils, like a monument of wounded pride. I recall coming to Cheapside, Blackfriars and finally Victoria Embankment. Searchlights waved like giant rapiers across the sky, bursting anti-aircraft shells gave a pyrotechnic display, a German raider corkscrewed downwards on fire. Looking upon the Thames was comforting for it seemed a reassurance that my standing luck would see me through. The Embankment was alive with traffic – an occasional clanging fire engine and a train of cars, ambulances, buses, moving eastwards and coming back with the injured; in the dim-lit interiors of the vehicles I glimpsed white-uniformed nurses.

When I trudged on, I came upon a truck half-way up on the pavement. A stocky man was struggling in the weak light of a torch to change a flat tyre. I gave him a hand and he introduced himself as 'Cabbage' Cudlipp. He carted produce to hotels and restaurants in the central city from Covent Garden where he had been heading when, as he put it, 'It was just my bleedin' luck to get a pierced "blimp" on a night like this. Gawd, would I like to smash that bloody Hitler's face in for that lot!' and he waved towards the distant, crimson glow.

Cabbage was kindness itself. Asking why I was abroad at that now early morning hour, I told him what had happened. He drove me to the rear of the Savoy Hotel, left me in the truck while he nipped in to see a chum in the kitchen and returned to present me with a paper bag of food and a flask of brandy. He then went miles out of his way to take me to Endsleigh Gardens. I was rocking on my feet. 'Thanks, Cabbage, look after yourself.'

'No worries about me, laddie. I was the luckiest devil in the last war – years of it, in and out of the trenches and not as much as a "Blighty". I'd say you've got the same sort of luck. Now get into that grub and have a good sleep.' He let in the clutch. 'Bless you laddies. Good morning.'

That night in London was the prelude to a week of mass bombings at the end of which Goering could boast 14,000 killed and 25,000 wounded. It long haunted me that Harry might have been the one to survive, or his sister along with me. I was left with a mysterious conviction I would never be killed by a bomb. There were to be other times when I had narrow squeaks under enemy bombing, and ironically under Allies' bombs – Russian in Lithuania, British in Berlin and American in Leipzig. It is not for me to posture as an armchair theorist and go over moral issues underlying the task of bomber crews fulfilling routine duty in the huge, impersonal machine of war. I considered myself privileged, in a curious way, experiencing the merciless murder and mass destruction in the East End raid. It made a far deeper incision in my mind than when I had distant views of Swansea and Cardiff under heaving seas of flame. Those remote conflagrations stirred me to anger but the personal impact of the London experience instilled intense bitterness which, together with anger, forged a vicious will to resist and revenge. Yet, it is true, in every raid when I pressed the 'tit' and let my bombs fall free, I had stirrings of conscience; memory fused with realistic imagining of what I could be causing. I would infinitely have preferred a detached, objective attitude. In the event it made no difference in my bellicose actions, for with Hitlerism intent upon smashing my country there was no acceptable, patriotically honourable choice. I had no anger against ordinary enemy civilians, but I had to oppose harbouring disturbing considerations of a moral or intellectual nature (as did many aircrews, Allied and German), in the interests of practical aggressive values of aerial warfare – not to mention enthusiasm for keeping oneself alive. For Hitler, Goering and the Nazis, I had ferocious hatred.

My leave in Cornwall was overshadowed by the shock in the East End. I spoke of what had happened but neither my godmother nor her husband preached or probed my thinking; except, when seeing me off at Penzance, Arthur walked alongside the train as it ground into movement and simply said, 'Good luck, Dick. Try to keep faith. It's an anvil which has worn out many hammers.'

# CHAPTER 2

# Flying with a Bomber's Moon

From Scotland, I went to a bombing and gunnery school in South Wales, and trained in single-engined Fairey Battles, a breed of aircraft withdrawn from front-line service after proving no match for Bf109 German fighters in the Battle of France. It was not until 1942 that bomb-aimers were added to crews to relieve navigators in their many constant and exacting tasks. In 1940, however, bomb-aiming was the second most important responsibility of a navigator – ahead of being also stand-in pilot, emergency wireless operator and air-gunner if necessary. Training was relentless. The urgency for vast improvement was evident from the mounting sacrifices of planes and aircrews, out of all proportion to the damage being inflicted on the enemy. The War Cabinet had been shocked to learn that of 6,000 sorties, 4,000 crews had not bombed their targets or pressed home their attack. Not one aircraft in three had bombed within five miles of a designated target, sticks of bombs had been as much as ten miles apart in opposite directions, and a great percentage had exploded in open country. I also acquired great respect for air-gunners. In 1940, tail gunners were having a rough time. We knew of macabre expressions among ground crews of how they carried the poor bastards away in bucketfuls and hosed out the gore from the revolving turrets. I had once revelled in aerobatics, but now having to fire machine-guns at a target drogue towed behind another aircraft, while my pilot put me into aerobatic positions, had none of the old joys. To hell with being a gunner!

At that Stormy Down bombing school in Wales, when

our country was doggedly on the defensive with bombs thundering down on our cities, my colleagues and I fretted and fumed at still not being in combat. Since Scotland days, we had matured suddenly to a stoic gravity, losing much of our sparkle or rhetorical turn of youth. Yet, for all our will to heap upon German heads a multiple-measure for measure, as Churchill vowed we would, we were only too conscious of the hardships and dangers we would shortly face as replacement crews. Far from starry-eyed, we had a particular dread of daylight raids, knowing something of the appalling losses they were causing to Bomber Command. It thus came as a lift to morale when we learned of their suspension and a switch to night bombing. This decision followed a raid of 18 December 1940 when two-thirds of the twenty-two Wellingtons sent to attack shipping at Wilhelmshaven went down, most in flames over the target area. Fifty top-class crewmen perished for no appreciable gain. When my turn came, I would fly under cover of darkness.

Next came an Operational Training Unit in Hertford-shire. Now I was verging on the real thing. Snow covered the face of England in a winter the like of which the country had not seen for years when I went off for the first time over enemy-held territory. It had a phoney aspect, for our loads were bundles of propaganda leaflets, 'Luftpost', known to crews as 'bumph' – the missions were termed 'soft' raids and looked upon as exercises for 'blooding' crews. The enemy did not reply with paper bullets or tomfoolery flak, and I certainly became aware that even on the paper-runs life's duration could be as brief as a passing train. Dutifully on that first raid, we untied the bundles and threw the leaflets out by the armful until our tail gunner howled, 'Christ! We look as if we're towing a white streamer a quarter of a mile long!' The ghostly trail in the moonlight was an open invitation to German night-

fighters to follow up. Thereafter, we booted them out as
bundles to drop like blocks of granite, and bawdily vied
with each other in conjuring up fornicating or ludicrous
scenes whereupon they might crash. As far as I was
concerned, fluttering down bumph with notions of stirring
victorious Germans to rebellion seemed as improbable as
finding fairies in the bottom of my beer mug. I was
conciliatory towards dropping forged ration cards for
disruption of the German economy, or leaflets urging
enslaved allies to resist, but distinctly nervous about
carting 'razzles' to the Black Forest where research
establishments were thought to be hidden away. Razzles
were six-inch-square, celluloid folders containing packs of
phosphorus in damp cotton wool which when dried would
ignite, set ablaze the forest and hopefully burn the Jerries
out like mice from a cornfield. I loathed the infernal
devices. Only one needed to burst into flame aloft to mean
fiery 'curtains' for the crew.

I narrowly missed ending up in a blazing pyre returning
from my last bumph raid. Near the French coast a brace of
Messerschmitts pounced on our Wellington. Tracers
seemed to crawl up to glint past the fuselage like silver
darts, flowing towards us in a slow, graceful, inward-
turning curve. We dived into swirling cloud vapour. It was
like being plucked into a mother's arms for consoling titty.
No doubt scared as hell and faking nonchalance, a voice
burst into croaky song over the intercom:

> 'I didn't want to join the Air Force,
> I didn't want my bollocks shot away,
> I'd rather hang around
> Piccadilly Underground,
> Living on the earnings of a high-born lady.'

Leaving the protective cloud behind, we slanted towards
the English Channel and again were attacked by a fighter.

Its fire ripped fabric and shattered rib structure of our fuselage, then inexplicably the attacker sheered off. Almost home, we spotted a companion Wellington a short distance ahead, clearly defined in the moonlight. The flare path at our base was temporarily lit to allow our companion to approach and land. Circling to await our turn to get down, suddenly a Ju88 appeared from nowhere and bored down, pouring out dead-straight lines of tracers to send our companion Wellington crashing in a mass of flames. It was a numbing, agonizing experience to see six friends die on our doorstep, and realize how closely it might have been ourselves. It was regular practice for Ju88s to follow our aircraft home and swoop to kill at the landing approach. Had we not been able to dawdle a while in that cloud cover, we could easily have been in the lead. It was not the last time I would ask myself, 'Why those poor bastards and not me?'

Now a fully qualified navigator, I was posted on 14 April 1941 to No. 15 Squadron, 'Oxford's Own' of motto 'Aim Sure', based at Wyton in Huntingdonshire. I arrived at the squadron when it was being equipped with the first four-engined bombers of the war, the new 'Short Stirling'. It was the second squadron to be so, with No. 7 at Oakington the first by a few weeks. Throughout the war Germany was never to have a four-engined bomber, a visionary defect it was to regret. I was thrilled and proud, for it was the zenith for navigators of the day to be selected to guide these 'miracle' monsters which, Churchill proclaimed, would deliver 'shattering strokes of retributive justice' to the Third Reich. Only twenty-one Stirlings had been delivered to squadrons in that first quarter of 1941 and they were drifting off the production line at about one a week. Each Stirling represented a vastly expensive machine; precious too were its eight highly trained crewmen. I considered myself lucky being chosen to guide the ultimate in RAF

bombers of the day. Vividly I recall my introduction to the
87-foot-long giant. There was nothing like it at the time.
Landing wheels were almost my height, and the bomb-
aimer's window twenty-five feet up under the nose. I was
soon to find out that the incredibly high undercarriage,
necessitated by mid-mounted wings, resulted in a dangerous
side-swing on take-off unless the pilot was very skilled. In
fact, on the maiden flight of the breed the undercarriage
had collapsed in full view of high-ranking air staff.

Access to this hulk was via a ladder near the tail.
Entering a Stirling for the first time should have been a
triumphant moment; instead, I felt a strange agitation as if
I was a Jonah entering the fearsome insides of a whale, with
elusive, gloomy thoughts. I had flown in many types of
aircraft but had never been attacked by similar doubts. It
seemed impossible it would ever get off the ground, and
many did not. Ascending the narrow fuselage tunnel, its
sides crammed with engineering equipment and devices, I
reached my navigational table behind the pilot's seat.
Peering rearwards down the sloping passage, with no end in
sight, the thought struck like a bullet: how the hell do I
make a quick exit in emergency? 'Forget the rear door,' I
was told, 'even if you reach it and jump, you'll be sucked
smack-bang into the elevator assembly.' The rear-gunner
could swing his turret and drop out; for the others it meant
reaching short steps down to the bomb-aimer's window
which opened up to form an escape hatch. I was learning
why the Stirling became known as the 'Flying Coffin' or, to
those steady-nerved, uncannily eye-sighted Aussie and
Kiwi air-gunners on the squadron, the 'Flying Shithouse',
its stark, oblong fuselage stirring memories of the sentry-
box type of 'loo' familiar in their rural scenes back home –
which most of them were never to see again. Incredibly,
among the endless modifications delaying the advent of the
Stirling since its conception in 1936, its wing span had been

shortened purely to fit into the 100-foot-wide RAF
hangars. The result was to reduce its ceiling seriously.
While it was supposed to be able to reach 14,000 feet, I
never flew in one with a bomb load above 12,000 feet. It
was a marksman's dream for the superb accuracy of
German anti-aircraft batteries. Equally farcical, officialdom
had insisted the fuselage cross-section be governed by the
standard size of RAF packing cases. The much-vaunted
Stirling was mainly a failure and disappointment from the
start. Flying in this clumsy, ugly giant, dragging itself tail-
down through the skies when striving to gain height with a
bomb load, its crew members realized death was always a
close neighbour. Small wonder it earns minimal mention in
accounts of aerial warfare, as if the mistake is buried in
haste. Nor has one survived to this day, even as a museum
piece.

In fairness, outstanding virtues of the Stirling were its
ability to withstand tremendous punishment and stagger
home on two engines, which I soon appreciated. In the five
months I was with 15 Squadron, I took part in nine major
sorties, just short of the average survival rate for Stirling
crews of the day. When so many aircraft failed to return, a
few tough operational flights made us 'old hands', and
much time was devoted in flights over Britain to training
new arrivals. We did not operate as did our successors of
1942 onwards, when the 'heavies' to come – Manchesters,
Halifaxes and Lancasters – formed aerial armadas, flying in
vast, regimented bomber streams and employing navigational radar devices and electronic aids unknown to us.
There was an aura of skilled amateurism and independence
about our night operations. Given a designated target, the
pilot and I were left to choose our way there and back.
Loyalties and personalities of well-chosen crew members
played an enormous role. In particular a highly personal
relationship of co-operation existed between pilot and

navigator. It was essential for each to esteem the other's qualities with cordiality and utter trust, no matter how tough the going. Propaganda in that early phase tended to make Stirling crews into a new breed of glamour boys, the cream of the cream of Bomber Command. Public adulation was embarrassing but, knowing as we did that our lives were calculable in weeks, we took advantage of free beers from admirers in pubs, not to mention appreciating the gleams which came into the eyes of the female element, the WAAFs on the squadron. While in no way underrating the courage and achievements of later bomber stream fliers who woefully dubbed themselves 'the poor bloody infantry of the air', I still find an odd fascination of aloofness in knowing I belonged to the wartime era when so much was left to the discretion of pilot and navigator. At that period, dead-reckoning navigation was something of an art in which competence conferred prestige, if – inversely – it meant selection for more hazardous missions and possible hastening towards doom.

Setting out for a raid on Cologne one night, I was wagered a magnum of champagne if I hit its cathedral in retaliation for the destruction of Coventry Cathedral. I aimed with deliberate, risky, time-wasting precision until I had it square in my sights, but all claim to the champagne went flat when my photographs revealed our stick of bombs had missed by about 150 yards and worse (or better) had failed to explode. Like some uncanny rebuke, tired and shaky after return to base and debriefing, I had just thrown myself on my bed, boots and all, when I heard the characteristic, unsynchronized drone of a German aircraft's engine – then the shrieking onrush of a bomb. My room was at the end of the upper floor of a concrete barrack housing about 100 aircrew. A 500-kilogram bomb, mercifully with delayed fuse, hurtled past my end wall. It plunged deep into the ground before exploding, flinging

tons of earth upwards to crash on the flat roof over my
head. A yawning crater outside reached just short of the
wall. Had the German bomb-aimer varied a fraction of a
second, all the King's men may never have put me together
again, or many others in that barrack. Thoroughly shaken,
tending to feel I had been picked on, I cleared off, swearing
furiously as I cycled away to Huntingdon in the early light.
There an elderly Miss Standen and her sister lived at
Chiswick House, its doors ever open to nervy fliers seeking
an atmosphere of sanity. It was always the same in those
days when losses were frighteningly high. Always the same
anxious, fearful question after an operation. 'Did Bill,
Tubby, Stinker and Dick return all right?' A silence, and
then a queer, hesitant reply, 'Only Stinker and Dick.'
Adjusting to empty beds, or empty chairs in the mess after
a raid, we accepted to a great degree we were all at the
mercy of Luck.

The F24 camera was back in my life. It was regarded as a
'box of gold' and certainly curbed 'shooting a line' about
reaching the target and bombing prowess. Night raids
meant carrying long cylinders of photoflash flares which
were timed to drop with the release of bombs. The
cylinders were dangerous things to carry when bursting,
perforating red-hot flak was all about the aircraft. Just how
precious this equipment was at the time has since been
described to me by Flight Lieutenant G. H. Parry of the
RAF's Joint School of Photography. He wrote (in 1979):

the very limited number of night cameras and 8″ photoflashes
made it necessary to confine the equipment to selected crews
only . . . With the development of the night bomber offensive,
the need for night photographs became urgent and improvements
were made in the night photographic assembly during 1941 . . .
With a [new type] control, the opening of the shutter was delayed
until 5 seconds before the flash explosion was due, thus the effect
of searchlights and other light sources was reduced to a great
extent . . . Coincidentally, I was stationed at Wyton when Nos

15 and 40 Squadrons were operating there in 1940/41 and often met returning crews with their night cameras at the satellite aerodrome at Alconbury. It could well have been that our paths crossed.

It could indeed. I was taking off from Alconbury's grassy field and on return, while the crew waited in our transport vehicle, I had to stand by the camera until its magazines were collected and I had given details of usage and any faults. It was a dicey business hanging around, as Parry said:

We were often caught in the open with 'Jerry' following our bombers home and dropping bombs and strafing the airfield. While I was clutching the grass, I never quite knew whether I should leave my helmet on my head or place it over my posterior. They were certainly exciting times.

One night, with the F24 set in the nose compartment of Stirling N6030P, I set out for Frankfurt, the target an engineering complex within a wide loop of the River Main. While we were approaching from the south, following the Rhine, suddenly all hell came up and we flew into a wall of exploding steel. A Wellington and a Whitley blew up into crimson balls within our sight ahead. Our 'kite' was riddled as if glowing, red-white sparrows with steel snouts had burst in and gone mad. In the midst of a flak barrage the entire synchronization of my body and mind seemed to be faulty, aberrant, with crashing explosions, thunderous roar of four great engines, ricochet of metal on metal, shrapnel bursting into the fuselage, whizzing past and out again. We were carrying fewer high explosives than usual but a devil of a lot more incendiaries and those damnable magnesium cylinders. If vitally hit with flak we could go to kingdom come like those unlucky bastards we'd just seen go up. As I recall, our pilot, Flying Officer Boggis, was hit in the arm by shrapnel but able to carry on as we lurched and bucked.

I was thinking, 'Bugger this for a joke,' when he yelled out
to me in the bomb-well, 'For Christ's sake, drop your shit
anywhere and let's get to hell out!' The concentrated
barrage worsened. It was certain death to press on. I let
everything go from somewhere above the junction of the
Rhine and Main. Next day, the CO called me in to 'tear a
strip' I thought, for ducking the target. Instead he was
elated. 'Good show, Pape! You straddled a bridge to
perfection. First-rate control of nerves. Next time you
perform as well, I'll recommend you for a "gong".'

'Thank you, sir,' I said, but thought, 'Balls, I never saw a
bloody bridge. Too damned scared to notice anything. I
just pressed the tit.'

When Hitler made his fatal mistake in attacking Russia on
22 June 1941, the news of the Titans locked in battle sent
us into paroxysms of boozy elation, toasting the Russian
Air Force. Morale soared with the expectation that some at
least of the Luftwaffe's night-fighter units which were
increasingly plaguing us would be withdrawn for combat
on the Eastern Front. Enthusiasm was short-lived for
within a week the Luftwaffe was dealing such devastating
blows that the Russian Air Force was rapidly caving in.
Stalin urgently exhorted Churchill to recommence an RAF
bomber offensive by daylight, to draw back German
fighters and relieve the unbearable pressure on his Front.
Churchill agreed to a temporary resumption of daylights,
using Stirlings and the Blenheim light bomber. Under
heavy fighter escort, the Stirlings were to make short-haul
raids on strategic targets in France but the unfortunate,
outclassed Blenheims were to strike at more distant targets
inside Germany, unescorted, owing to the limited range of
Spitfires. As if admitting the Blenheim crews were sacrificial
offerings, Churchill toured some of their stations appealing
to them to 'strive mightily', saying, 'I am relying on you to

help Russia in this way, and so help us all in the long run.'

Taking myself back to those days, a fearful unease still creeps over me. We knew daylights had been suspended as being virtually suicidal and futile. I was damned nervous as we trooped into the briefing-room for our first daylight on 7 July 1941. 'Stalin's stooges', the crews cynically dubbed themselves. Stirlings were to fly in close arrow-head formations of threes, combining their defensive armament. The target was marshalling yards at Hazebrouck, France. No margin for error. Careless aiming could send down massive destruction upon friendly civilians. A master bomb-aimer in the leading aircraft would give the order, whereupon all three bomb-aimers were to release a total of eighteen tons of blast and destruction simultaneously. Impressing obedience, the master bomb-aimer said, 'When I give the order, I want all to go down like this,' and he opened his fist to send a handful of ball bearings clanking into a metal bucket.

I flew in machine N6030C with twenty-four 500-pound bombs. We took off mid-morning and droned away to rendezvous over the south coast with 200 Spitfires. It was heart-warming, thrilling, as the fighter swarm packed about us, tier upon tier forming what became known as a 'beehive'. Among that escort were Battle of Britain aces: Johnny Johnson, Douglas Bader, 'Sailor' Malan, 'Cocky' Dundas (brother of my newspaper colleague) and others of like calibre. Messerschmitt Bf109s and 110s waited until we got through the coastal flak over France, and then pounced. Droves of them were spread out against the blue sky. With astonishing speed, the beehive broke up. It was a breathtaking spectacle to see the Spitfires streaking outwards, upwards, diving from seemingly nowhere to intercept and engage. Pilot-to-pilot contests raged as fighters zoomed, twisted and wheeled and all attempts of the Messerschmitts to hurtle at us for a kill were thwarted.

Action was swift, too overwhelming to take in more than gasping mental-breaths of the mad whirlwind of furious engagements and tumult of air battle. Vapour trails criss-crossed, crimson and orange flashes darted from guns, red lines of tracers created weird arcs, and machines went down trailing black ribbons of smoke. In flashing, distant tangles, I could not distinguish friend from foe. Parachutes blossomed and I still see four appearing one after the other, precisely timed as for an air pageant, slipping lazily as if down the edge of an invisible ruler. The worst image in memory still to spy on me and along with other images often to make sleep perfidious, is of snarling fighters sweeping past us spitting cannon shells or bullets, friend and foe alike.

As we throbbed slowly on and before I descended to my bomb-sight, the fighters, just as surprisingly and suddenly as the beehive had broken up, receded farther and farther into the infinity of the heavens, continuing their personal savagings as distant dots. We seemed to be left terribly, nakedly alone. Then we realized the Messerschmitts had sheered away to allow their ack-ack to open up. My tongue stuck to my palate as a confusion of bursting shells boxed us in, causing our Stirling to sway to concussion . . . a matter of time, the end was inevitable. Yet, wondrously, the encircling black puffs ceased, if only to signal a prowling 109 to attack. It dived from an oblique frontal angle making straight for our leading Stirling. 'Christ!' I thought. 'This is it.' If the leader and its bombs went up, our whole close formation would be blasted to smithereens. But we were not as alone as we thought. A blessed Spitfire must still have been covering us. It dived almost vertically, beautifully on the mark. Pieces flew off the 109 as it reeled into a spin, belching black smoke. The Spitfire zoomed upwards. An avenging 109 streaked in pursuit . . . a burst of cannon-fire . . . our gallant defender gushed out orange flame and gyrated crazily earthwards. It stirred in me a feeling of awful, personal loss.

The ack-ack resumed. Confronted by the perilous situation of a cluster of even more black puffs ahead, our master bomb-aimer steered our formation some degrees off what had been a perfect approach to target. Lying over my bomb-sight, my eyes riveted on ground dispositions, it appeared well-nigh impossible to regain our approach unless we circled and risked running up again. The deadly holocaust of anti-aircraft fire imposed enormous strain but we kept formation and swung obediently to port for rectification. We straightened out for the marshalling yards but I knew instinctively it was going to be a miss. 'Release,' came the terse command. Almost paralysed with dread, I watched the bombs go down, seeming to float at first, then gracefully dip to fall as a shoal. Official records say: 'the bombs were seen to fall 200 yards to the south', and records of the fighter escort agree. I do not know what our photographs revealed, but I feel sure the reports were over-kind to our skill by perhaps half a mile. God knows how many French people perished.

Our formation opened up on the homeward run, each for itself. Still harassed dangerously by fighters and flak, I caught sight of our leader going into a diving turn, slewing earthwards towards the French coast. I felt a quick fear it had been hit. Wrenching my eyes away from its diminishing silhouette, I had a second shock; our other Stirling was sliding towards the English Channel, like a giant eagle descending with peculiar imperturbability, leaving a lazy thread of smoke. A howling sound on our radio link-up made it impossible to communicate. We put our nose down and tore at full bore for the flat coastline. Onwards over an angry sea, we deprived a pursuing Messerschmitt of whatever possible advantage by weaving in harum-scarum fashion as close as we dared to heaving white crests between which deep black troughs opened up like mocking burial trenches. Racing over the Channel still remains a strange and terrible experience and the crossing never seemed so interminable or empty. Nor have I been so seasick in my life. We arrived at base sweaty, shaking and sickened. When someone said, 'Roast pork on the menu,' I really wanted to die.

An air of secrecy always surrounded the fates of non-returning bombers, but word seeped along that one of our three had ditched in the sea and the other, badly mauled, had struggled to Manston in the south. With the best will in the world, I could not master recurrent bouts of shaking which beset me that afternoon as I rested on my bed. In the evening, we were assembled to learn we would fly again next morning; our target, steelworks in Lille, and I might be master bomb-aimer. To my utter embarrassment, the shakes chose that moment to return. The briefing officer focused on me. 'Good God,' he exclaimed, 'not another one!' I was unaware that two who had flown that morning had been sedated by the medical officer, experienced crewmen though they were. It was not cowardice, not a question of quitting. I railed at the very thought of going LMF (lack of moral fibre), with all its attendant humiliation and disgrace. Fear of the white feather was greater than the dread of facing death. I well knew courage was control of fear; that the bravest people experience fear when in a whirlpool of doubts and forebodings, when not at grips with something objectively definite, when physical courage was not called into action. I had found that fear ceased when I ceased to care, resigning myself in the face of known perils, viewing even certain death with indifference. But I had watched our bombs fall away over Hazebrouck and knew that we must have ploughed a grievous furrow among friendly civilians.

I said I would fly on any missions over Germany. I would

continue to fly daylights over France, but I could not
guarantee hitting the target. If I could not get it smack-on
in my sights, I would not give the order to 'release'. I
would turn away and dump our bombs in the sea. With the
benefit of hindsight, I know I was right and have never
regretted speaking up as I did. Our bomb-sights, though
modified from 1914–18, were still inaccurate and inordinately complicated; our bombs frequently unreliable.
Exceptional luck and almost psychic capacity were needed
for pin-point bombing, even assuming an uninterrupted,
straight and steady run-up to target, and hard-hitting
German flak certainly had something to say about that. I
am pretty certain that my spiritless attitude resulted in
another scrubbing of recommendation for commission, but
shattered hopes did not worry me as against shattered
French bodies in a built-up area of Lille. To my infinite
relief and that of the others who had taken part in the morning raid, we were stood down for a few days, and we
embarked on a boozy belt-up of Cambridge pubs. The three
Stirlings which went to Lille encountered murderously
accurate flak; every machine was peppered, riddled and
ripped, so severely mauled that when our turn came again
and we were told our target, our reaction – steel-tipped
though we considered our nerves after our diversion – was,
'Oh shit, Lille again.' It was packed with anti-aircraft guns.
If I remember correctly, leaflets were dropped before these
'circus' raids, as they were called, to warn French civilians
to keep clear of targets. Of course they put the enemy on
notice, but that was what it was all about, building up
pressure in the west . . . we bombers were decoy ducks to
get the enemy eagles into the sky.

Mid-morning on 11 July 1941, we took off for the Fives-
Lille Steel Works. With the beehive stacked about us as we
droned beyond the coastal flak of France, again our escort
scattered. Once more we witnessed that awe-inspiring

spectacle: aggressive, harrying Spitfires tangling with Messerschmitts in running dog-fights, vapour trails, stabbing flames, aircraft flicking out of control, gyrating, streaking black smoke. Repeating their tactics, the Messerschmitts drew the Spitfires away while ground batteries opened up. Shells crashed round us with sickening concussion as we coursed on, filled with confusion and anger, knowing the gunners had the bead on us. With fear that quickens the heartbeat and can make a trembling body of the bravest, the strain almost amounted to a death wish, to get it over, the final knock-out blow. I am sure every man in our lumbering arrow-head was certain he was lost. The only defence was to open up the formation and independently dive for it. The formation did neither, advancing almost wing-tip to wing-tip for the bombing run, but Lille was still some distance away. Unless a miracle happened to make the Jerry gunners take their paws off us, we would never survive the barrage.

Then befell the most fantastic piece of fortunate fate. A freak thunderstorm broke loose, which by any rare chance seemed impossible when ten minutes earlier we had been flying in sunny blue sky. With speed and force the weather gods became our friends. Lightning gashed the sky, thunder roared like the heartiest, ironic laughter, the sky darkened in one hysterical stride and blinding rain obliterated everything, lashing with musical joy against the perspex of the cabin. Nothing conveys the balm of relief in the stiff RAF record: 'Thunderstorm over target, so secondary target at Hazebrouck Marshalling Yards attacked. Direct hits were obtained by at least two of the three sticks on yards and on the station.'

One more daylight to St Omer, and I got away with it again unscathed. Then to our relief, daylights were abandoned as far too costly in men and machines. One of the most daring 'circus' raids had been by fifteen Blenheims on Bremen, Germany's second largest home port. Led by an Australian, Wing Commander Hughie Edwards, DFC, these outmoded machines had made a hazardous low-level approach across 150 miles of German territory and through awesome defences over the port. Two machines crashed over the dock area, two disappeared and the rest staggered home with many wounded; the majority of the machines were so badly shot up they never flew again. Edwards was awarded the Victoria Cross and was later to become the first flier of the war to win 'the big three' (VC, DSO, DFC), equalled only by Guy Gibson and Leonard Cheshire. But highly trained crews were too few to be flung as offerings to the deities of war.

# CHAPTER 3
## Special Mission Berlin

Back to night operations. Chances of longevity heightened – a prospect I viewed with excited desirability as I had fallen genuinely in love for the first time. Soon after joining the squadron I met 'Blondie'. She was twenty-three, pretty, with a sweet nature that combined delightfully with a lively mind and creative intelligence; from the outset our association developed rapidly, genuinely appealing to each other in heart and mind. She came of a middle-class family akin to my own. On other stations I had taken out WAAFs lightheartedly and hopefully, but my affair with Blondie was never a half-joke.

I had survived seven operational raids; the first six were considered most risky in a crewman's life. Then I was told of a special mission to Berlin and the more I learned of it, the greater grew my impatience to get airborne; in some mysterious, vital way, impulses suggested I had found a challenge I had long been seeking. In Britain responsibility for anti-aircraft defences rested with the Army, but in Germany, when Goering had won control of the Air Force from the Army in 1935, he had taken anti-aircraft defences for himself as well. Since the first bombing of Berlin, a year had passed during which new defence measures for the German capital had been initiated, embracing the latest in technological developments. A secret headquarters was created close to one of Goering's residences; a centre for radar and predictor control for massive anti-aircraft and searchlight defences. British Intelligence remained aware of progress, and by mid-1941 it was decided to probe from the air for this nerve centre.

Together with an RAF Regular, Flight Lieutenant Wallace Terry, I studied in secret everything relevant to the target. Terry was an unflappable, skilful pilot of exceptional eye and nerve. I had flown as a navigator with many fine pilots but never had I found myself woven so readily into mutual trust as with him. Thirty-five years later, I had a revitalized appreciation of Terry's calibre as a man and pilot. For this, I am indebted to Air Vice Marshal Joe Cox, CB, OBE, DFC (the man responsible for putting Douglas Bader, the legless pilot, back into the sky at the outbreak of war). Joe Cox and his wife were visiting Canberra in 1976 when their hostess handed him a copy of *Boldness Be My Friend*, saying I lived a few streets away. Cox was so delighted to find my references to Wallace Terry that he called upon me and I learned of their hair-raising experiences over Heliopolis in April 1940. At that time, Cox was a Squadron Leader with Central Flying School (CFS) at Upavon, UK, when he went out to Egypt and Iraq to ascertain why pilots were killing themselves on take-offs in Blenheims – a problem fortunately solved.

Terry at the time was with 216 Squadron based at Heliopolis when by chance Cox met him in the bar at Groppi's in Cairo and learned of the near-tragedy when Terry was flying a party of Army officers from Iraq to Egypt in a Bristol Bombay Freighter. One officer became violently airsick and dashed for the toilet at the rear of the passenger compartment, followed by three others, anxious to help. The weight of the four at the rear so upset the aircraft's centre of gravity (C. of G.) that it went into a series of flick stalls, so violent that footprints were later found on the roof of the passenger cabin. Somehow Terry brought the machine under control. As CFS was preparing 'Handling Notes' for the Bristol Bombay at the time, Cox asked Terry to go up with him to demonstrate what had happened. Cox said:

It was brave of him to agree, having had that awful experience. Naturally I got clearance from the Squadron Commanding Officer (216) before I flew the Bristol Bombay with *his* pilots, all (19 of them, I think) volunteers. Nothing happened when I put the first pilot passenger into the toilet. The aircraft 'pitched' a little when the second one went in, and more still when the third joined them, but I could still control the aircraft. I let Wallace Terry 'feel' her and he agreed, so I put the fourth in with the other three, then my scheme succeeded beyond my wildest dreams. The aircraft's nose whipped violently and uncontrollably upwards then over to the right. Fortunately Terry and I succeeded in preventing her going on her back and eventually got her level and brought the nose down only to discover that when it came back on the horizon it carried on down in a steep dive! We could not get her out. Terry shouted (the door to the cabin was behind him) to the pilot passengers to 'come forward'. He and I had given up and were holding our hands across our heads waiting for the crash. The pilot passengers (whose clothes were badly damaged and some of them cut about the legs) responded magnificently and pulled (crawled) themselves forward so much so that to the amazement of Terry and myself the aircraft came out of the dive at 400 feet. I flew around for a bit to let my heart settle down, then landed the aircraft back at Heliopolis. All of us got down to preparing a load sheet and we discovered that when the four Army officers (pilot passengers) were in the toilet together, the C. of G was 18 inches aft of maximum safe! No wonder the Bristol Bombay 'stood on its tail'.

(Out of this came the 'invention' of the load sheet, a compulsory document completed by every transport pilot – civil or military – prior to take-off to ensure proper distribution of load.)

This was Wallace Terry with whom I was selected to fly. Patiently we worked over maps and photographs until a small triangle of woodland on the north-western reaches, beyond the mass of Berlin, became ingrained upon the mind's eye. The environs we marked into categories for possible bombing runs from any point of the compass as might suit our purpose. With barest warning, we set off for the 1,200-mile round-trip on the night of 2–3 September

1941. Meteorological predictions were for excellent conditions; bright moonlight. We were allowed a great deal of
freedom as a lone roamer to follow our individual line in
the sky and to decide our run-up; probable night-fighters
and flak opposition, we were given to understand, would
be hectic around such a master-brain complex. A fleet of
bombers went ahead to fan out over the capital, activate
flak and searchlight batteries and, as far as possible, detract
from us. Our mission, independent of the main force, was
in the nature of an exploratory raid, to have a good look
and return with reliable photographs as a prelude to large-
scale onslaughts. It would rest with the skipper and me to
put our bombs to best use, preferably aiming into the
centre of the triangle of forest.

Terry did not question my change of course, to fly south
of Wittenberge and, skirting Berlin, meeting only moderate
flak, to make for its north-western forest belt. Our advance
bombers, across the central regions of the city, drew up a
terrific screen of bursting shells and bluish streams of
supporting searchlights as we hunted for our target. It was
glorious moonlight, making it amazingly easy locating the
triangular forest. A couple of dummy runs to test wind
speed and direction: almost impossible to believe, not a
light, not a shot came up at us. Surely they must know a
lone British plane was on the hunt? The silence was
uncanny. Either our Intelligence had been misled, or the
Germans were deliberately not advertising the forest's
secret. I called to Terry, 'I'm set for the run. As soon as
I've bombed, shove the nose down and beat it for home.'

Co-operating to a nicety, we ran-up from the north-east.
The bombs exploded in a line of tiny red spurts, straddling
the forest's centre. What happened then over Berlin was
totally unexpected. As if with the flick of a switch, that
devastating wall of fire power which had seemed to run for
miles vanished and every searchlight went dead!

'Bloody phenomenal!' I yelled.

'Hit something damned vital,' Terry called back.

Tracking over thickly populated areas of southern Berlin without any interference made the minutes seem endless; in fact the defence impotence lasted about seven minutes. We received a monstrous shock as it all switched on again and we found ourselves in the clutches of a vicious box-barrage and coning searchlights of freakish accuracy. Terry's virtuosity cleared us of the blinding lights and flak pattering against the wildly weaving machine. I recall my CSC (course and speed calculator) being dashed from my hand a few inches from my chest by a whizzing chunk of metal. Bereft of my navigational aid, I settled down to dead reckoning to get us home. Only then, I became aware of a prickling in the centre of my forehead. I was astonished to find a gash in my flying helmet; a piece of shrapnel, its force fortunately absorbed by the leather, had cut through and stopped at the bone. I prised it out of my forehead with my penknife and turned over on my table a tiny piece of German metal. It was insignificant in itself, about the size of a shirt-button, flat and razor-edged, yet my heart thumped. I had always optimistically assured myself, 'it can never happen to me'. I have never forgotten my bewilderment of the moment, if I have since derived understanding: 'The wounded soldier [I was barely in the category] has just visualized danger in a new and very personal way. It has been brought home to him as never before that he is not a spectator but a bit of the target . . . there is a welling up of the instinct of self-preservation.'*

My thoughts flashed to the WAAF I was longing to marry. Blondie had left the day before the raid for a week's leave, home to her parents. I had met her parents several times and we got along famously. Blondie was to confide

* Lord Moran, *The Anatomy of Courage* (Constable, London, 1966).

that she was two months' pregnant. Banns were to be put up in her village church and we would marry as soon as possible. After the rootless, unsettled pattern of my life, and probably its present hazards, I yearned to settle down and make a success of our lives. I had no misgivings; she was the girl for me and I considered myself wonderfully fortunate to have such a fascinating person reciprocating my feelings.

'Top brass' was jubilant when our photographs of the triangular forest were processed. Given thirty-six-hour leave passes, Terry and I donned civvies and headed for Cambridge to get nicely plastered. We patted ourselves on the back; obviously the raid had been a dramatic success. We made up our minds to quit after completing our present tours (thirty sorties) and apply for instructors' postings with some flying unit. I would not continue to subject Blondie to the fearful tensions she gamefully covered up every time I set off on a raid – as did so many wives and sweethearts of men who flew into danger. Wallace Terry, too, was seriously attached to a splendid young woman.

I was at a Huntingdon bus stop to meet Blondie on the morning of 7 September and overjoyed to learn of her parents' affectionate reaction. We were to visit them the following weekend, leave permitting, to arrange our wedding. We returned to the squadron utterly happy, with plans to dine out that night to celebrate. There was no suggestion of operational flying; the weather was poor with a darkening canopy of cloud.

It was all a short, lovely dream. That afternoon aircrews were called for briefing. It came as a thunderbolt – a special raid on Berlin that night by over 300 bombers from various squadrons. Wallace Terry and I received independent orders for a second lone sortie over the same triangular forest and were warned to expect real opposition this time.

Most of the route would be above blankets of cloud with little view of the ground, which meant dead reckoning at its very best. There should be reasonable moonlight with scattered cloud over Berlin. I was to aim for a point slightly north-west of the former position; a provocative attack to bring up fire and further evidence. Terry requested to fly in Stirling W7431-'U' as five nights previously it had handled like a dream. 'Sorry,' replied the CO, 'a chunk of flak almost severed a wing spar and scored a deep line across a petrol tank. You were damned lucky.'

'Same crew?' Terry asked doggedly.

'Except for mid-upper gunner. You'll have a new chap to break in. He should be fine. He was dux of his gunnery school.'

Considering the weather and possible wasted time centring on the target, Terry requested more fuel and fewer bombs. 'Sorry,' was the reply. We were to carry eleven 500-pound armour piercing bombs, new-type incendiaries, photoflashes – and less fuel than before.

The briefing over, I suddenly experienced a spirit of discontent, of incipient failure, almost a scared nausea as I made my way to where Blondie worked in the parachute section, to defer our celebration date. I had never felt so edgy or disturbed but put on a cheerful front for her benefit. Odd that I should find her packing my 'chute, No. 88. Back in my barracks, I was supposed to snatch sleep but found it impossible. I lay watching drizzle skirmishing across the window panes. Sincerely I hoped the raid would be cancelled. Not so. Shortly before we were due to depart the crewroom for Alconbury, I left my fellow fliers joking about 'Berlin or bust' and managed to meet Blondie briefly. I took her memory into the sky. But I never saw her again. Three months later, during a visit to London seeking information about Richard Pape 'missing believed killed', she was killed in a German raid. The enemy did not leave me even a grave. I was in Stalag VIIIB in Ober Silesia when I learned of her death. It was a bleak winter morning in February 1942. I will never forget that day; the cold depression still haunts me. My sister Mary and her husband, Eric Hudson, went to see her at Chiswick House with Miss Standen after I had gone 'missing'. They would have done all they could for her. For me, her death changed everything. With Blondie and our child awaiting my return, I would never have taken such risks with my life as I did in the coming years.

Years later, after *Boldness Be My Friend* appeared, I received a letter from a Mrs Rita Wilkes, formerly a WAAF of 15 Squadron, who wrote:

Richard . . . I remember you more as Dick (to a mutual dear friend) and Ginger . . . I was extremely moved by your whole book. I know none of us had the slightest idea of what some of you boys would have to face in the future . . . we were all so young and even a war (in England) couldn't bring us to realize what was going on in enemy country . . . Now that perhaps brings me to a peacetime heartache of your own. I hope that time has softened it a little, and that I won't be opening a sore point too harshly in reminding you of our mutual friend. I believe the little blonde you referred to in your book was my friend Beatrice? I was overjoyed at first, but was dumbly shocked at the truth. I can well remember, Dick, how heartbroken she was (she lived in the same house as myself), we couldn't console her when we had no news of you at all. I know how surprised we were when you came together, she was such a quiet little thing and you had been such a gay lad. I took her home on a 48-hour pass, my mother always remembered what a nice girl she was . . .

Our squadron's contribution to the raid of 7–8 September 1941 was twelve Stirlings. Darkness was fast descending as ninety-six young airmen made final adjustments to their gear. Forty-eight 1,800-hp engines roared evenly. Our machine was N6045-'U'. The aircraft ahead of ours had just acknowledged the radio signal to taxi when there came blinding flashes over the field and the 'crump' of explosions. For a moment I thought one of our aircraft had exploded, but our engines had smothered the shriek of descending bombs. 'Christ Almighty,' cried out our wireless operator, 'this is supposed to be a top secret mission!' Somehow the enemy knew and nearly caught us. Sharply silhouetted against flickering greenish light from scores of gushing incendiaries, the Stirlings looked stricken and helpless. Seconds seemed an eternity before orders came for quick-succession take-off. Our throttles went forward, the earth slipped back and we slid upwards into the dusky night. Once in the air I felt cold and ruthless but passing over the English coast near Harwich, I said to myself, 'Farewell, England. I'll bless you again when I see you in eight hours' time.' Wishful thinking; for I did not return for three years.

# CHAPTER 4
# Hunted in Holland

I was setting out on the most significant and appalling years of my life. The events of those three years were fresh in my memory when I recounted many of them in the first edition of this book, but for various security reasons I was not permitted to reveal certain clandestine activities, crucial incidents or true identities of many persons. The time has arrived when I think they should be set down. While I do not seek simply to revive previous descriptions, certain episodes must be dragged back and briefly retold.

After leaving the English coast we entered an unbroken realm of ugly, cumulus clouds almost to the outer reaches of western Berlin. There, as predicted, gaps opened up and a watery moon allowed me to discern ground features and orientate our position. Zigzagging towards the northern forest zone, we were afforded a full welcome of ack-ack and searchlights of an intensity vastly expanded since our raid five nights before. Again I had little searching to do before pin-pointing the triangular forest. Standing off, we assessed the best approach to what was represented as a mere dot encircled on my target map; the Stirling's nose was lined up with infinite care. The run lasted only minutes. As it began, the noise of bursting shells abruptly ceased, but just before I released my bombs and photoflashes the Germans sent up a stream of shells. At 00.52 hours, our radio operator's message 'Task completed' was received in Britain. There was no failure of searchlights and anti-aircraft fire over Berlin this time. Running the gauntlet, skirting the torso of Berlin, we breathed more freely – but not for long. Searchlights stabbed on to us. 'I'm diving,'

yelled Terry, 'hold on!' But before he could push the
control column forward, there came a thunderous explosion
and a mighty greenish flash – a steely convulsion of
shuddering, bucketing bomber. Severed pipelines to a
smashed outer starboard engine gushed blazing petrol from
a 300-gallon tank. Dancing flames rose and spread over the
wing. For the second time, Terry plunged the machine into
a tremendous dive, shipping back the flames to the trailing
edge of the wing. Pulling out, the conflagration had been
extinguished but the port wing now listed alarmingly and
our state of flight was jerking and shuddering. To add to
our torment, the inner starboard engine, although still
functioning, was dangerously out of alignment and synchronization, running at ungovernable revolutions. I had a
piercing fear it would wrench itself from the wing
mountings; better it burn out altogether. The port motors
were functioning evenly.

We coursed westward. The inner starboard finally
petered out and the port engines were flogged to the limit,
but slowly, dismally, we lost height in the teeth of an
unpredicted fifty mph headwind. At 01.28 hours, we sent
our last message received in Britain: 'Hit by flak.' No
further contact was made that might alert night fighters,
for if attacked we had not a cat in hell's chance. Flying
wing-down on two port engines, with serious loss of petrol,
tail plane damaged, wind shrieking through gaps punctured
in the fuselage, we knew we were playing out our last act.
Height slipped away. As Terry gave the order, the three
gunners woefully unlocked their guns and, along with
ammunition and everything removable and expendable,
threw them into the night; anything to keep aloft. Our
fervent hope was to get as far across Germany as possible,
with luck to Occupied Holland. With strenuous efforts by
Terry and the second-pilot, and the wizardry of Flight
Engineer William (Jock) Moir, nursing engines, manipulat-

ing petrol cocks although the gauges said 'zero' fuel, we jerked along, rebuffed by the headwind gusting to over seventy mph, inching our way towards the frontier. Orders were given to check parachutes and open the escape hatch in my bombing well.

Navigators were not compelled to wear 'chutes in flight, as being too obstructive when required to move about. Taking my pack from its container on the side of the fuselage, I was horrified to find its elastic binders severed. Wind gusted through a hole the size of a football in the plane's side; a piece of metal had ripped into the folded layers of silk which fell listlessly about my feet. Blondie would never know; all her loving care had been cancelled out by a lousy chunk of bloody German steel. I stuffed the useless silk out of sight and resorted to angry blasphemy, my habitual antidote to fear. I had little time to brood over my fate, for the port motors started to splutter and gulp; like twins in mortal death throes, simultaneously they gave up the ghost. The wind howled in loud lament.

As the bomber began to fall, the skipper yelled over the whining, faltering intercom, 'Jump, bale out!' It was a 'Now' situation: individual action, no hesitation. No doubt the tail gunner swung his turret and was first away. In the general flurry, I glimpsed the second-pilot, the wireless operator, the front-gunner rush past and descend to the bombing well to vanish into the night. Terry was struggling desperately to get the machine into some gliding angle. I was shocked then to see the kid, the mid-upper gunner, lurching beside my navigational table. He seemed concussed; clearly he could not look after himself. And Jock Moir was still there. He had been frantically working, shutting off all petrol flow, a vital task with crash-landing inevitable. It was too late now to jump. I rapped Terry on the shoulder. He turned, gazing almost unbelievingly at three of us. It was then, as I flashed my torch, that I observed blood trickling from below his flying helmet; his face was ashen.

Adding my strength to Terry's, heaving desperately on the control column, we brought the machine to a more horizontal position for a few minutes before the nose fell with a vicious lurch to an acute angle. I recall a patch of water and hoping we might pancake . . . it went by. Then horrifyingly a church steeple. God! We're going to die in church with our boots on! Uncannily, an updraught lifted us lazily over the roof and we carried on, the earth terrifyingly close. Dark blotches on the ground raced up to meet us. I braced myself for the big 'dig-in'. Strangely I was no longer frightened. Thirty tons of bomber hit the ground at over 150 mph, bounced back into the air, then down, up and down again, ploughed deeply across a small field: a blinding white flash, vicious lurch, hideous grinding of metal . . . then silence.

I long believed we ended up facing towards home. Not so. We had done three complete turns; first about a small village, then around a farmhouse, just missing it as we began our bucking crashes; at the last, a wing struck an oak tree standing splendidly alone in a small open field – a stout anchor, it spun us about and settled us alongside its splintered trunk with a final grinding thud. That blessed oak may have been our salvation. We were down. Air Ministry cryptically records: 'Fl/Lt Terry in aircraft "4" failed to return.'

Seemingly coming out of a dream, mental fog lifted. I experienced ineffable thrill and excitement, finding myself alive. Jock was at my side with the first-aid box, bandaging my right hand; three fingers were floppy, severely gashed where they joined the palm. Apart from a goodly crack on the head and a painfully bruised, battered body, nothing else – no bones broken. Jock was also lucky; generally knocked about but nothing incapacitating. He showed remarkable courage and practical efficiency. Every ounce of our strength was challenged getting two unconscious men down the long, broken fuselage and into the open.

Heavy drops of rain were falling and the pale light of dawn lay pewter-like over the flat landscape. First sight of the skipper's face covered in blood was ghastly. I was seized by a feeling of despair at the sight of a fearsome wound on his forehead; a white mound of damaged bone a hellish size was exposed. The wound was pouring blood. I thought Terry dead until he gave low moans. A second wound, smaller with coagulated blood, had probably been inflicted by shrapnel. The young gunner was groaning, uttering meaningless words; his eyes looked enormous; he seemed transformed into an old man. He attempted to stand on the wet grass, only to fall to his knees with arms thrown wide in a gesture of hopelessness. We gave what aid we could.

Conscious of our desperate situation and of pressing needs requiring drastic action, we re-entered the fuselage and back in the cabin demonically set to work with the axe. All instruments were smashed and hacked. It almost broke my heart to see Jock drive the axe into the superb aerial camera. I heaped everything inflammable into a pile on the cockpit floor – film, maps, charts, air logs – even my useless parachute – and set them on fire. The cabin was a shambles. Flames eerily lit up the long interior; their glow outside would act as a beacon. Coughing and spluttering, we regained the open; we sucked in clean, cold air. It had been drilled into aircrew that the best chance of escape was immediately after being shot down – if not too badly injured – when moral and physical strength had not been sapped by prison conditions and while still in possession of practical aids, such as the non-rustling silk map sewn in the seat of my trousers and the minute compass under my navigator's insignia on my tunic. The thought of escape had to sit consciously and unconsciously in mind from the moment of starting operational flying. Its serious aim was to draw German soldiers away from combat, to thwart, upset and keep the enemy off balance by daring, intrigue and resourcefulness.

Jock lit two cigarettes, but scarcely had we drawn on them than we were riveted by the shock of two red rockets flaring into the sky and the sudden crackle of rifle fire not too far away. 'Come on, Dick,' he urged, 'it's now or never.' Nerves on edge, worn out from excess of experiences, nonetheless the impulse to escape was imperative. We knew from propaganda that infuriated Berliners would show no mercy to British 'luft gangsters'. In general, I expected a reception much as the Home Guard would mete out to a Luftwaffe flier 'downed' in Britain, but I did tauten at the thought of a German counterpart of a tough, maddened, Yorkshire farmer with a pitchfork, prodding my belly! Pausing briefly, I paid silent tribute to Wallace Terry. He was sitting, retching violently, bowing his head up and down. The kid gunner was stretched out, his staring eyes filled with fathomless misery. The once proud bomber was like a giant corpse, except for odd flickerings from the cockpit.

Came the next stunning surprise: Jock grabbed my arm. Two figures stood like statues not far beyond our companions . . . one a burly man in overalls, the other person shorter and standing slightly behind him. I expected to see a firearm. 'Bloody Huns,' I hissed, 'I'll tackle the first, you get the other.' My left hand tightened on a heavy brass torch salvaged from the Stirling. I called in German, 'What is the name of this place? How far is the Dutch frontier?' The big man moved forward. 'Halt,' I called, '*nicht so snell!*' (not so fast!). I raised the torch threateningly.

'Hold on,' Jock breathed urgently, 'I canna clobber a woman!'

The second person was a young woman, buxom, wearing skirt and jumper. The man spoke slowly in German. 'You are not in Germany. You are in Holland. This is the village of Hengelo in the Province of Gelderland. I am a true Hollander patriot.'

Utterly joyous, I fired questions and discovered we had sneaked some twenty kilometres out of Germany. Moir lost his Scottish dourness and jumped about, embraced Boer Enzerink and his daughter (their name I learned years later). We were on Enzerink's farm. I begged him to say nothing to the Germans of seeing us and asked the best route to start escape. He explained that the village was some three kilometres behind us but we should avoid it as every house and farm would be searched. He pointed another way and told us how to reach a small wood, where to hide until it was safe for friends to come to help. As I thanked him, I pushed the RAF torch into his hand to keep as a memento. His daughter tore the scarf from her neck and with shaking fingers wrapped it about the bloodied bandages on my hand. It was a poignant parting. (Thirteen years later, I was shown that torch by Enzerink. Again, thirty years after that fateful morning, when I returned with my wife, Helen, I found Enzerink had died but his daughter and her husband were living at the farm. Proudly the torch was placed on a table in the living-room where we were given warmest hospitality. The daughter had been only fourteen when she and her father had seen the Stirling – on fire, they had thought – pass the farm heading for the village, little dreaming it would return to miss their house by barely ten metres and buck across the field to be reined-in by the oak tree.)

Jock and I painfully pushed across the fields towards a dirt road. We had barely reached it when green rockets twittered about the position of the wreckage and rifle shots crackled, warning civilians to remain indoors. It was growing light; rain was falling fine, fast and cold as we plodded and slipped along the road, looking for a stone cottage . . . when it came in view we were to strike left across the fields. Sounds of motor cycles behind, stopping, starting, coming closer, warned of methodical searching near the road and stirred a frightful sense of danger; the fields were flat, the ditches shallow. I was just about all in and on the verge of telling Jock to leave me when he said, 'Wait here, Dick, I'll reconnoitre.' He hurried back. 'Come on, I've found a better hole.' German voices were shouting distantly, motor cycles revving and throttling back, and were less than 200 metres to our rear when we submerged like water rats in a deep, slimy ditch. When the machines receded, we emerged but scarcely had we set off than we heard others approaching ahead. Swiftly we retreated to the ditch and sank helpless, not daring to stir hand or foot. When all was silent, we went on. My head throbbed, my hand felt frozen in sodden, muddy bandages; my legs were stiff as iron bars, feet and ankles had swollen alarmingly inside flying boots. I was all for striking immediately to the left but Jock insisted we stick to the farmer's directions.

First came the barking of a dog then the cottage appeared, dismal, forbidding, among a few scraggy trees. Yet as I gazed it became, mirage-like, the most welcoming domicile. I was seized by an overpowering impulse to risk our luck. Uneasily, Jock acquiesced. I beat on the door and called in German that we were English fliers, injured, from a crashed aircraft. No answer. The dog snarled and barked as we moved to the rear, then returned to the front. I was sure someone was inside. We stood absolutely still and silent. The door creaked and moved a fraction. Enough to say we unceremoniously forced our way in. A wrinkled, dirty old woman flew towards me, screaming, trying to dash outside. I grabbed her and pushed her into a chair. She shrilled in German, 'English swine, murderous fliers, pig-dogs!' Memory is still ugly of threatening her to silence when vehicles rumbled past on the road. Our good luck, the cottage had already been checked by a German patrol. We learned later that the old woman was German and had lived for several years in the village of Hengelo but had never been accepted by the villagers. For the information which she later gave the Germans about Jock and myself, she received 250 guilders (about thirty pounds sterling in 1941). She died during the war.

Certainly her behaviour buoyed up our faith in Enzerink, for he had warned us to keep well clear of the cottage. We found food, ate ravenously and with all haste, knowing the Germans were at hand and might return. We boiled water and ripped up old petticoats for bandages. Jock went outside to assess the situation while I watched the old woman. He returned. 'Quick, the bastards are searching down the road again.' I threatened the crone – we would be hiding at the back of the cottage and if she screamed to alert the Germans, I would re-enter and kill her – a lie, as she undoubtedly guessed, for she sat in her corner, her neck strained forward, chuckling and grimacing as if enjoying some interminable joke.

We kept well down, reached a long meadow and from the lee of a few, low, stringy bushes, observed moving figures over a wide arc behind us. We fell in and out of dykes, crouched as we fled across open fields and rejoiced upon sighting grazing cows where Enzerink had said we would. We hid among the beasts for some time, staring at them and they stared back. Then on, mostly in the shelter of a long, straight dyke, slithering lopsidedly until, topping a rise, we saw the coppice. As we made a final dash, my heart almost stopped: a boy was standing half a field away, watching! Entering the wood, we fell flat on our faces, sobbing for breath. Our bodies steamed.

Woods are few in Holland, and certainly not large in the

border country where we crashed. This one covered about
two acres with spindly trees and small, thickish bushes . . .
some were blackberries; I recall eating the fruit. Realizing
that the wood's centre area was certain to attract closest
scrutiny, we searched the perimeter and found an ideally
shaped depression beneath dense bushes, four feet high.
We crawled in, covered ourselves with leaves, and slept for
a very long time.

While we forgot the world, it was not forgetting us.
When the old woman found her tongue with the Germans
– with little delay, no doubt – she reported our descriptions,
that we had forced our way into her cottage, stolen food
and clothes, and attempted to strangle her! Fortunately,
she was under an impression that we had headed for
Hengelo. The local Kommandant ordered the whole
populace of Hengelo, and of farms thereabouts, to be
brought in immediately and locked up in the village school.
Troops scoured the countryside, ferreted through farm
buildings and lay in wait in the village. In his efficiency,
unwittingly the Kommandant was facilitating conspiracy.
Locking up the community under one roof, he allowed
members of the local 'resistance' to meet in urgent
conference and without rousing suspicion. Leaders among
the resistance were a 33-year-old farmer, Bernard Besselink,
and 27-year-old schoolmaster, Jan Agterkamp. To them
came Boer Enzerink and his daughter with details of the
crash and of having set two of the British fliers on a route
to the wood; and the boy, who told of two men hiding
among his herd before floundering towards the wood, and
entering it; and Wilhelm Branderhorst, clog-maker, who
lived with his two brothers and sister in a humble house
adjoining the wood. Branderhorst offered the frightening
news that when the Germans had pounced and searched
their home and workshed, an officer had directed a dozen
or more soldiers to investigate the wood and, if necessary

to prevent violence or further escape, shoot to kill.

As the hours passed, there was nothing the resistance could do but discuss possibilities dependent on uncertain events. In the late afternoon, they learned that the fugitives were still at large. An officer arrived and addressed the restive citizens: their release was authorized; a curfew would come into effect before nightfall. Two escaping Britishers were in the neighbourhood and could be expected to seek food and assistance after dark. The penalty for aiding enemies of the Third Reich was the firing squad; on the other hand, the giving of information leading to apprehension of the escapees carried the reward of 1,000 guilders.

From the moment I had put my head on a pillow of leaves, I had slept like the dead. What roused me was Jock's hand clamping over my mouth. 'Don't move,' he breathed. 'Germans . . . ten paces!' I froze. In the minutes following, I had my first close, worm's-eye view of jackboots. The boots moved away; voices receded. Jock told me of two cursory searches earlier. More followed in the next hour: jackboots again, strolling close by; a bayonet thrust, so near I felt movement beside my leg. The tension was unbelievable. With the withdrawal of this last patrol, two sentries were left. It was dusk when they abandoned their vigil. Jock and I emerged after twelve hours, half-paralysed and caked with clotted mud and blood.

We had worked it out. The Germans would expect us to move under cover of dark. We decided to wait. With dawn on our side, we would be able to scan the landscape and dispose ourselves more shrewdly as we made our way westwards, deeper into Holland. Jock had a wife and two small daughters – willing to take risks out of the ordinary and face up to hardships in a desperate effort to get home, he was not prepared to gamble stupidly with his life; nor was I. We anticipated road blocks, cordons; certainly a drag-net about Hengelo – and bullets before questions in the dark! We were prepared to be content with cold and hunger, and master our impatience.

From an adjoining field, we dug potatoes; they and a few berries were our sustenance. As the autumn evening closed down on a dismal landscape, it was cold; very, very cold. Suddenly, alarmingly, the sound of wood-chopping disturbed the stillness – a rhythmic thud, thud, thud. We were not to know a clog-maker was deliberately making his presence known, hoping to entice us into the open, if we were still there. Decidedly cautious after the old woman episode, I watched from behind the bushes; the man chopped for perhaps ten minutes before disappearing indoors, leaving the axe embedded in a log. I also spotted a pair of trousers hanging on the door of the woodshed. Axe and pants would be precious escape acquisitions. The evening was not yet completely dark, but sufficiently so to merge my movements in the shadows. I slithered out, and back, dragging the axe and with the pair of corduroy trousers about my neck.

Stealing those articles set off a chain of consequences, some of which I recall joyfully and with deepest gratitude, others with lasting sadness. But perhaps the chain really began earlier, when inexplicable Fate ploughed a piece of steel into my parachute, cancelling any possibility of my floating to German soil and speedy captivity, like the four of our crew who had bailed out.

Little did we realize that the clog-maker, Wilhelm Branderhorst, had watched my filching from behind a darkened window. The knowledge that at least one escapee was alive and crawling enlivened him to carry out his next task. I had just pulled on the old corduroys over my own trousers when we heard the jangling of metal cans. The wood-chopper was advancing cautiously among the bushes.

Was it a trap? Unwilling to reveal myself immediately, I was curious and excited as he came nearer. He called softly in German, 'English flier [*Englischer Flieger*] I am true Hollander. We want to help Winston Churchill's airmen.' His back was to me when I quietly rose and coughed. I would have been utterly astonished had I known that, at that moment, one of his brothers had me within the sights of his rifle at the darkened window! And I would have been incredulous had I been able to foresee the impact our arrival was to have upon the lives of so many of that small village. (Thirty years later, the clog-maker's sister remembered: 'The day you came was the day of the Mother of God' (8 September, the day Roman Catholic churches celebrate the Nativity of Mary, Mother of Jesus). A simple woman with an attractive shyness and modesty of manner, while she knew the tragedies in Hengelo which had followed in our wake she was able to say to me without any bitterness that they were glad they had been able to help. She still lived in the same house by the same spindly wood, but with one surviving brother, our wood-chopping friend, Wilhelm.)

For Jock and myself in the clog-maker's company in the wood, life took on a new buoyant complexion, not just from the stimulus of hot coffee, schnapps and food, but with the excitement at our incredibly good luck in having made the linkage, from one courageous Dutchman to another; and it was not to stop there. Branderhorst gave us the route to follow to a rendezvous with other Dutch loyalists who would be out in the dark, defying the curfew, waiting for us; we would be challenged and the code word to give was '*Churchilldagen*' (Churchill days). He warned us that our greatest danger was in having to cross a closely guarded highway which formed part of the cordon around Hengelo. We thanked the clog-maker and handed back his axe, but not the trousers; I promised him a new pair, after the war. Years later when I went back, his eyes twinkled as he asked my 'interpreter', Gerard Nieuwland:* 'Has he come to return my trousers?' I made sure he received a brand new pair of corduroys.

Not unwillingly, Jock and I quit the sanctuary of that dismal wood. I kept the pole star in line with my shoulders as we dragged our stinking, sweaty, bruised bodies over rough fields and through the soothing sludge of dykes. Timely warning from a truck with its dimmed lights identified the highway and just saved us from blundering into danger. Twice we had to retreat from German sentries tramping 100-yard beats by the roadside, until we found a less well-patrolled spot, removed our flying boots and dashed like rabbits over and beyond. In all, we spent more than two hours working through compacted meadows and series of dykes. Four kilometres seemed ten! We were lying still after catching sounds like scraping boots, and peering at what seemed to be bushes. A 'bush' moved, then stopped and coughed slightly! I risked calling: '*Churchill-dagen.*'

We were met like long-lost brothers by three Dutchmen and assisted, arms linked, to the farmhouse of Bernard Besselink. Like his brothers and brother-in-law who had met us in the field, Besselink was a man of homely worth and value, long concerned with daily needs and narrow cares. They belonged in a devout Roman Catholic community; their contempt for the Nazis was limitless, their belief unquenchable that the hated invaders would eventually be driven out. Upon Jock and myself they focused their gratitude for a Britain refusing to be beaten, and their admiration for its leader, Winston Churchill. For days we were hidden by the Besselink family: at first in a

---

* *Gerard Nieuwland* married Betsie Besselink, second daughter of the farmer who was to help us, Bernard Besselink.

cornfield, then in more comfortable quarters in a cavity at the top of a haystack, finally in a barn alongside the house. We ventured out at night to join the family and trusted friends by the fire in the parlour and to listen to the BBC news. Good food and care soon undid the bad effects of the crash and the wretchedness at the start of the escape. My fingers, stitched by a patriotic local doctor, healed well and our bruises took on paler hues.

# CHAPTER 5
## The Dutch Underground

Early in the morning of our first day in the haystack, a visitor climbed the ladder; he was Jan Agterkamp, the schoolmaster, who spoke excellent English. For over a year now, Holland had been under the heel of Germany but in that time the Dutch resistance, in co-operation with British Intelligence, had successfully organized the escape of 'downed' RAF fliers. Some had been up-lifted by flying boats from remote stretches of the Zuider Zee or by RAF Lysanders from selected fields; others had escaped by sea. By late 1941, however, the Germans had plugged many loopholes and it was becoming increasingly difficult and dangerous to assist escapees because of the numbers of informers and stooges infiltrating the armed police, centres of administration and Government, and being planted even in isolated areas and villages. While some Dutch fell for the sops and doles dished out by their occupiers to infiltrate strongholds of patriotism, nevertheless there were true Dutch whom the Germans were never able to convert. To them, Queen Wilhelmina sheltering in Britain remained more than ever the symbol of the will of resistance; there could be no destruction of their beliefs. One such 'true Dutch' was Jan Agterkamp and, importantly for us, he was in touch with the resistance.

After subjecting us to stringent interrogation, Agterkamp took our identity discs and my navigator's wristwatch, an expensive Longines stamped with a number which could trace its issue to me. He wasted no time in contacting the fountainhead of Dutch resistance in Amsterdam. Three days later, a special agent arrived at the haystack. We were to know him as 'Tiny Peter', a somewhat inaccurate name for a man of large build and well over six feet tall. He spoke English and was adept at questioning. With an air of aloofness, he interrogated us about our flying careers, personal backgrounds, schools, families, pre-war occupations and even special features of our home towns. This data would be radioed to sources in Britain to establish if we were who we said we were and not infiltrators planted by German Intelligence. Secrecy was vital; the contacts in Britain would give no hint to our next-of-kin, our squadron, or anyone else that we were alive. We remained 'missing believed killed'. In the case of Wallace Terry and the kid gunner who had been captured, the Germans would inform the International Red Cross in Geneva that they were registered prisoners of war. Jock and I were warned that every minute without POW status and associating with a subversive organization in Occupied Holland would be fraught with danger. If captured, we must accept the possibility of death, or even worse – but never divulge anything we might learn of the underground movement.

They were anxious days: nerves kept taut with the Germans springing searches; lying deadly still atop the haystack beneath the pinnacle of its umbrella-like, corrugated iron roof, hearing German voices, the crack of rifle fire and the curious 'sizzling' of bullets ripping through the hay! As days passed, German visits and vigilance tailed off . . . completely. We learned of our bomber being expertly dismantled and carted away; and of a boy, shot at and wounded for daring to take a photograph. With great presence of mind the boy, I. Nieuwenhuis, threw his camera to a group of friends; the photograph survived and came to me after the war, showing the crippled Stirling and uniformed Germans like ants on a corpse.

Boredom was an incessant problem, alleviated a little by

watching the playful antics of the Besselinks' daughters, Annie aged four and Betsie aged two; the babe-in-arms, Minnie, we met in the evenings. The little girls and their playmates never knew the secret of the haystack. A swallow did: it plucked up courage and returned, accepting our intrusion; we nested together. Night after night we listened with odd, lonely feelings as British aircraft throbbed overhead, to and from Germany . . . the distinctive note of Stirlings, their pilots ever trying to get the engines into synchronization. Having tussled with them myself over Britain, I knew it demanded the sensitivity of a musician playing a violin to get them right; I never could – there was always an intermittent throb, as if one engine were jealous of the rest. Through long hours of dark atop the haystack, there was plenty of time for nostalgia and recollections. It was not helpful to peace of mind, and words did not come easily. The old life had gone. Now I was grounded, a new focus of philosophy and intellectual interest was demanded in a quest for freedom and hitting back at the Swastika.

Quick results followed Tiny Peter's visit. Our bona fides were verified, and when he reappeared he brought along a charming lady, Rene Nouvain, from Kampen by the Zuider Zee. She made the trip to dye my hair – a transformation I resisted until Tiny Peter explained that the Gestapo throughout Holland were roping in male civilians with red hair, not so much in the hope of catching me, but of recapturing a Dutch-speaking British agent who had red hair and was much my build. He was wanted for killing Germans; he *had* been caught, but the underground, with skill and daring, had freed him. So I hid humiliation and became the butt for merriment in Besselink's parlour as my bright locks were close-cropped and, along with my eyebrows, changed to a dirty brownish-black.

It was considered unwise for us to remain in the area any

longer. We would leave the next evening at dusk for concealment in a barn near the village – in fact, at Agterkamp's parents' farm – there collect suitable civilian attire and reliable cycles to depart the following morning for the ancient town of Zutphen, some twenty kilometres away. We would be exposed to danger as the Germans were swarming over the area, and the highway we would crank along had convoys of German transports moving over it packed with soldiers and military hardware from Deutschland, a mere forty kilometres away. If anything went wrong, we must lie to the Germans that we had stolen our clothes and cycles, survived by our own wits and not received any help from Dutch people.

It was not without emotion that we bade goodbye to Bernard Besselink, his kind sweet-natured wife and their brothers. We were painfully aware that the Nazis had subjected the Dutch to severe material sacrifices and impelled them to live under constant tensions and threats of deprivation of life, home and freedom. Mevrouw Besselink cried unashamedly. 'We can only pray for you,' she said. 'We are not permitted to know about you after you leave but you will be in loyal and clever hands.'

One of the brothers, a steadfast rural man with honest, friendly charm, handed me a small package. It contained teaspoons wrought in silver and bearing the coat of arms of the local Municipality of Steenderen. I was asked to give them to Churchill from the Besselinks, Agterkamps and people of Hengelo as a token of their faith in him. The spoons had been specially made by an elderly craftsman, given no idea of their intended destination. I promised what I felt could be kept: when the gift was delivered, the BBC would broadcast on its special European service something like: 'A gift of teaspoons and two books have been received by Mr Winston Churchill from admirers in Switzerland' (or maybe Sweden). This would confirm that

Jock and I, the 'two books', were safely home.

In Agterkamp's barn that evening, trying on our working-men's clothes and checking our bicycles, I was asked to hand over the teaspoons for safekeeping. Nothing must be in our possession to give the slightest clue to our past whereabouts. (I collected the spoons after the war and delivered them personally to Churchill.) In the morning, Jock and I cycled away vigorously, following a guide with blue trousers and with half the rear mudguard of his bicycle painted yellow. It was a hell of a trip, the worst cycle journey I had ever made, beset with a mood of nervous excitement. We pedalled in pursuit of 'blue pants', passed by lurching transports and truck following truck packed with stiff-sitting Germans, steel helmeted and rifles erect – and felt deadly scared when escorting motor cyclists stopped us at a crossroads and surveyed us disdainfully.

Despite our worries, we linked up with Tiny Peter in Zutphen and boarded a train *en route* for Amsterdam. Ironically the train was packed with young Luftwaffe fliers, fresh from a flying school and kicking up a hell of a din about 'Gegen England'. I felt the sweat rising and found myself thinking, 'Wait till the Spitfires get on your bloody tails!' Yet, if those young men had been dressed in RAF uniform, in appearance and spirit I could not have distinguished them from the young men I had known in RAF messes and English pubs. After one change of train, we climbed out at a bustling Amsterdam station. I had an overwhelming sense of relief and renewed confidence, with all the adventurous fascination of the unexpected ahead in a certainty of action. The episodes of Hengelo were behind us; we had set forth to make the best of a new chapter in our escape lives, win or lose.

It was late afternoon; every main thoroughfare was thronged with jackbooted military. We trailed Tiny Peter in what seemed endless tramping, making absolutely certain we were not being trailed ourselves. Suddenly it was all over as he slipped into a doorway and we followed with an air of peerless naturalness. The house was divided into apartments; Tiny Peter led the way to the second floor, called out something and signalled us to stay while he left. A door opened: a small, white-haired man with sharp eyes beckoned. He introduced himself as Mr X. After the war, I learned he was Edouard de Neve, chief of the Amsterdam resistance unit or 'ring'. Aged about fifty, before the war he had been a foreign correspondent for a British national newspaper and other foreign journals: now he was working for a German press and information section, the business of which was to cultivate good Dutch/German relations.

We spent several hours with de Neve and enjoyed a meal prepared by his 22-year-old daughter, and a bottle of Rhine wine, a gift to him from an often drunken German officer who lived in the apartment below; it was part of de Neve's job to fraternize. He related how the officer had let slip about a small German commuter seaplane moored on a waterway and immobilized, on his order, by draining the petrol tank and removing starter batteries. The plane was irresistible to a young Dutch nobleman and flier to steal from under the noses of the Germans. De Neve's daughter, a university student by day and resistance worker by night, swam time after time to the seaplane, pushing a rubber dinghy with petrol cans and batteries. It was an ambitious and courageous effort which proved successful, the nobleman reaching England to fly with the RAF.

I listened, even more fascinated – indeed, astonished and excited at our unbelievable good fortune – when de Neve disclosed a plan for returning Jock and myself to our homeland by British submarine. With no dramatics, he told of this escape channel having worked before and saw no reason to doubt its success again. But it might be days before we were taken to the coastal rendezvous, or weeks.

The deciding factor was awaiting the right occasion when everything coincided between British Intelligence and the Dutch underground to obtain the safest and maximum results in a two-way traffic with people, equipment or whatever else going to or fro. On the Dutch side, the man who engineered this 'sea-route' was Jo Huese, a former Dutch naval officer and flier, a prominent and brilliant member of the resistance.

De Neve explained that it was strict policy of the underground to keep fugitives moving, to switch conceal-ment from one loyalist home to another at short intervals, and it was not safe for us to remain in his apartment that night. There was no curfew. We left at about 10.30 P.M., following de Neve on a circuitous route to arrive at the fine home of Mr and Mrs Dirk Brouwer. It was rags to riches; our new quarters were luxurious and the clothes we changed into were top quality. Before the invasion of his country, Dirk Brouwer had been a successful private architect but, with the commandeering of factories for German armament production, he had been assigned to work on industrial installations. He had convinced the Nazis he was pro-German and his name was taken off the list of suspects, but in truth he was a master 'architect' of the resistance movement. His professional activities under German direction gave him access to sensitive manu-facturing plants and enabled him to keep British Intelligence posted about new processes and production developments.

Dirk Brouwer and his wife (who had British blood ties) spoke good English; but while Jock and I were treated with geniality and without any hint of patronage, living in that delightful home was an anxious time for us all. Dirk gave me some insight into the Dutch resistance which, like most underground movements, played for safety by operating in small groups, each with its sub-leader and headquarters. Naturally, a very few at the fountainhead knew the overall formation, but the sectional structure was designed so that the few comprising each 'cell' should know only what was essential to their own activities and morale. If anything went wrong and a member were caught, and cracked under interrogation and torture, that unfortunate person could involve only his own small compartment; the damage would be sealed off there. The Germans were training agents – including Dutch people, I was told bitterly – to work their way into resistance groups, affecting to be genuine Dutch loyalists. In my association with the Dutch resistance, I acquired a new strength in myself and philosophy about human beings which formed a better basis for trials and tribulations which lay ahead. These people were prepared to dedicate their lives, hearts and brains to the service of their country and, if caught by the Gestapo, never to squeal no matter how hopeless the situation, as long as they had a single faculty left inside them with which to give expression to their will. Holland, a flat, urban and densely populated country, criss-crossed by excellent roads, was not one where armed guerrilla-type fighting by tough partisans was possible. Instead, for the most part, qualities of courage, resilience and unwavering determination were aligned to scholarship and creative thinking in dealing with a brilliantly efficient and ruthless enemy.

We had been with Brouwer a few days when he was alerted that we must be switched without delay; the underground had information of an imminent, intensive search in the neighbourhood by counter-espionage experts with new orders that the only effective, lasting deterrent against resistance workers was the death penalty, or measures to leave families and the public uncertain or totally ignorant of the fate of persons arrested. We were collected by Willelm and Mona Leonhardt in a small car fuelled from a gas-filled container on its roof, and set out for Laren about thirty kilometres from Amsterdam. Our new home was a delight, in semi-country, its garden surrounded by high trees. The Leonhardts were charming and we lived royally. Willelm (Billy) was a wealthy Amsterdam businessman and his Canadian-born wife came from Nova Scotia. Her father, Lieutenant-Colonel N. H. Parsons, commanded the 85th Battalion in the First World War. Mona studied dramatic art in Boston but abandoned it for nursing and was working with a specialist on Park Avenue, New York, when she met Billy Leonhardt in 1937.

The day after our arrival, Edouard de Neve reappeared. He arranged for me to meet Billy's brother, 'Leo', realizing I could make some contribution against the magnitude of their needs in cipher work with so much leisure time on my hands; de Neve was aware of my craftsmanship in lettering and undoubtedly had checked my security rating with Britain. I represented a gift from heaven – skilled in penmanship, with some experience in undercover work, and intended for an underwater return to Britain in the near future. They had vital information to send with me – it could not be sent by secret radio, for their grave doubts about the security of that method of communication was a top priority part of the information I was to carry. Rapid and increasing arrests of Dutch patriots and British agents operating in Holland had become critical and beyond coincidence; there was good reason to suspect German Counter-Intelligence had broken the codes in use on radio between the Dutch resistance and Intelligence in Britain.

Given indulgent attention and guidance, I worked long hours through a large magnifying glass making minute scratch marks on the strong black type of an innocent-looking Dutch–German language book. It called for a steady hand and close eye, making varied-angled marks on certain letters, cast at irregular intervals through the pages. What I was enciphering was not revealed to me, beyond that I would be carrying materials for testing if the Gestapo arrests were with forewarning; years later I learned that Britain was being asked to transmit, in the existing code, information of fake planned acts of sabotage so devastating as virtually to compel the Germans to take preventive measures; monitoring the enemy's reactions would disclose if they were deciphering messages.

Alas, those suspicions of Dutch resistance operators in September 1941 were well founded. The chief of German military Counter-Intelligence in Holland, Colonel Giskes, was on the way to pulling off one of the wiliest and most brilliant coups in the secret radio war. His agents were infiltrating the resistance and acting out the parts of loyalist Dutch radio operators. German Counter-Intelligence radio contacts made with British Intelligence and Dutch resistance headquarters in Britain were sent and received in the proper code, resulting in the arrests of many Allied agents and the capture of valuable supplies landed or dropped into Holland for subversive activities in what was known as 'Operation Northpole'. Hard to believe but true, 'Operation Northpole' continued for over a year before it was appreciated in Britain that something was radically wrong in Holland. Colonel Giskes played the *England Spiel* (the English Game) brilliantly. By May 1942, only eight months after I was making my scratchings in the language book, German Counter-Intelligence would be in complete control of the Dutch resistance; for nearly twenty months there would be no really effective resistance at all until, by the end of 1943, a new organization rallied in Holland to develop slowly.

'Leo' Leonhardt's profession was in the field of radio and electronics. Before the war he was a key man with the Philips radio and communications manufacturing complex at Hilversum, near Laren. He was still a key man, having allowed the Germans who were now in command of

Philips, to 'win him over', along with the expertise he
controlled among Dutch technicians. With access to latest
developments in German technical and scientific fields,
which at that time were superior to our own, Leo was able
to radio coded information to Britain and even dispatch
stolen pieces of sophisticated equipment via the British
secret submarine service. Fearful that the Germans were
tapping-in on coded radio messages, Leo had me include in
my scratchings information of a sound-ranging apparatus
for German artillery and new radar techniques for air
operations.

He also took me to the Philips factory at Hilversum.
Dressed as a workman and given a Dutch name, work-
number and registration, I accompanied Leo and a foreman
who, although three parts German, was totally loyalist
Dutch. He worked with the Leonhardts on espionage, and
among fellow workers organized clever sabotage on the
assembly line, such as placing slow-eating acid on certain
connections in Luftwaffe equipment; in flight, vibration
caused the weakened wires to snap. In a curious and
complicated way of sympathetically looking back, I wonder
how many German wireless operators balefully twiddled
the knobs and touched ineffective morse keys with fingers
itching with nervousness, who lost direction and failed to
survive to tell the tale?

Leo and the foreman were influential in the factory and
beyond reproach as far as the Germans were concerned;
nonetheless, my heart was in my mouth as the guards
stopped us to examine our papers; they smiled and bowed
us on. I was shown production of radar screens for
bombers of the near future and other work for new radar
and radio guiding systems – a fascinating and frightening
eye-opener to me as a Britisher and a navigator. With a
tour of the grounds, I got a good fixation in my mind of
the whole set-up; compass bearings were worked out for

me later for possible low-level attack; for fear of destroying the whole of Hilversum and its populace, it had to be kept in mind that not far away the Germans had placed a massive bomb dump to deter the British from bombing the factory.

I was proud to play my part with those underground men of the like of Edouard de Neve, Dirk Brouwer, the Leonhardts and other loyalists who excited my admiration and imagination, who, unfussed and unshaken, compelled under extreme pressure of events, indulged in sabotage activities with no destruction of their beliefs and with an immensity of courage that was breathtaking. Their tutelage of me at Laren was to prove an invaluable stepping stone in my very near future.

At breakfast, sixteen days after we had crashed in Holland, Billy announced that a car would collect us within the hour. Edouard de Neve arrived, accompanied by a tall, muscular man of good-humoured face and easy smile. We met him under his resistance alias but his real name was Herman Van der Leek. Before the Occupation, he was a lecturer in German; now he was an adviser/interpreter to a Nazi labour organization for rounding up Dutch workers for compulsory allocation to factories and constructional projects, civil or military. Considered a 'cleared insider' by his German employers, he had a superb 'cover' occupation, with access to manpower movements and travel and zonal documentation of vital importance to the resistance and British Intelligence. When we were told we would be returning to Amsterdam to collect forged documents and identity papers, and attend a vital briefing before being hurried on to a coastal rendezvous point, the effect on my mind was startling, thrilling. I longed to know more, but appreciated earlier advice never to ask questions about plans or events among underground workers who represented our rock of refuge; equally to be warily alert to the unguarded moment if unexpectedly questioned by strangers.

In Amsterdam, we were at once shepherded to the large cellar of a house in a quiet suburb. Here we met a man in a wheelchair, whose name I eventually learned was Bossenkool, a talented artist with a subtle brain and deft hands for forging. Jo Huese was also present, the former Dutch naval officer and gifted operator who handled the nautical arrangements for the Amsterdam 'ring'. The coded language book on which I had laboured was handed to Bossenkool. His eyes were fixed on the pages for quite some time before he looked up. 'Congratulations,' he said, 'now I'll put the finishing touches.' He handed me a loose page of printed type saying, 'It's a test sheet. Make scratches on twenty or so letters, at random.' I may have looked puzzled, but obeyed. Bossenkool, with a swift and accurate pen, 'spotted' my vaguest scratchings with some solution; they were obliterated. Wafting the page before a heater for a few minutes, he proceeded to sweep across the lines of black type with another solution which made my white scratch marks again fully visible. I was instructed by de Neve that London was aware of this soft-covered language book and that as soon as the submarine's conning tower hatch was sealed, the captain would request me to hand over the book to him.

Jo Huese imparted the stupendous information that if the weather improved we might be lucky and put to sea that night, but everything depended on safety at the rendezvous point . . . and the weather, which could hamper operations for days. We were handed zonal movement papers, identity cards with photographs taken at Laren, and accommodation vouchers for a month's stay at a Workers' Registered Hostel in Leiden, near the coast. We were Dutch electrical apprentices, directed to work on wiring at a coastal radio beacon. Edouard de Neve and

Herman Van der Leek would accompany us with documents denoting them as Germans posted to Holland as officials of some standing in the Forced Labour Front. Jock and I were warned of dangers, particularly in taking a road which cut clear across Schiphol aerodrome. Normally, civilians could not get within sniffing distance of Schiphol, but I seem to recall that the alternative route had been blocked by the blowing up of a German ammunition train. Jo Huese tapped the language book saying, 'Getting *this*, and you, to the coast on time is an important risk.'

The Mercedes, driven by Van der Leek, had faked registration papers for Düsseldorf; a badge and petrol coupons had been supposedly issued by the German Technical Control Centre in Amsterdam. No detail was overlooked: in the boot was even the normal 'issue' to Jock and me of tool kits bearing the Deutsch *Arbeit* (work) insignia and, with typical German efficiency, each item was documented. We knew that if caught, our only chance of not being shot as British agents lay in convincing the Gestapo we were genuine RAF; we must never depart from the story of having wandered about Holland, scrounging and stealing, with absolutely no idea of names – places or people – until we arrived in Amsterdam and in the Americana Hotel, by sheer luck, met the two men who volunteered to get us to the coast. I experienced acute feelings of dread knowing we were trespassing on the lives of two valiant Dutchmen. 'If the worst should happen,' I ventured, 'what about you two?' Van der Leek flicked his fingers. 'We know what we are doing, and why,' he said and quickly changed the subject. 'Schiphol is swarming with Luftwaffe. You may feel acute anxiety at the sight of them, but you must not show it. Think of yourselves the whole time as Dutch technicians.'

As instructed, I was carrying the code book in my pocket as a young Dutchman anxious to learn German would do naturally, but once clear of Schiphol it had to be fastened to my thigh by sticking tape. If arrested, I swore to get rid of it in the best feasible way. 'Drop it down a drain,' said de Neve, 'burn it, rip it apart and flush it down a lavatory; even eat it!'

We approached Schiphol, the most modern European airport before the war, and halted at the first closely guarded check-point. We had to pass four check-points, a grave undertaking; of serious concern was that Jock spoke only a few phrases in Dutch and German. A Nazi officer of First World War vintage approached and was met by Van der Leek who gave the Nazi salute before handing over our papers. If we cleared this crucial point, a pass would permit us to proceed through the next three barriers, subject to checks of timing and that no one had left the car. Our Dutch protectors, masquerading as Germans, spoke in a cultured style which made ordinary German soldiers pull themselves together and show respect immediately. The enemy officer seemed to consider he had met his own kind; he chatted easily for a few moments while guards searched the car, examined the tool kits item by item, patted Jock and myself . . . the book was removed from my inner pocket and surveyed dully. I felt a cold fear but de Neve calmly leaned forward, feigning curiosity, then looked the guard in the eye, saying, 'At least he's one young Dutchman keen to learn our language.' The grim-looking guard returned the book with a hoarse '*Glückwunsche*' (Congratulations). With a sense of occasion, I replied woodenly, '*Ich bin Ihnen sehr verbunden*' (I am much obliged to you). Good old Jock didn't know what the hell was going on but smiled understandingly.

We were left, waiting. De Neve murmured, 'Richard, how many Spitfires will it take to shoot down a *luftflotte* [squadron] of Me110s?'

I whispered, 'One for three, over a period.'

'We may be able to make it one for thirty.'

'What do you mean?'

'If they're telephoning Amsterdam to check our papers, we're done. Any attempt to halt or delay us while they're waiting for confirmation, we're taking off!' He produced a duplicate ignition key; the other was with the Germans. I knew what he meant: we would drive headlong to get among the planes and dynamite the car which was fixed with detonator and explosive. It was die or bust. I certainly agreed we take as much as we could with us. If the aircraft were fuelled, we could depart this world with a spectacular send-off.

The German officer approached . . . and smilingly handed over authorization to proceed. Several bottles of Bols gin were in the car. 'Have one, with compliments,' de Neve said, passing a bottle to the officer. Van der Leek let in the clutch and my heart stopped palpitating. Before clearing the fourth check, I was in a sweat; not simply from fear of telephoning catching up. Never had I imagined seeing so many Luftwaffe men or such armadas of fighters, bombers and vehicles at such close range as on that journey at fifteen kilometres an hour across that enormous flying field. I had never fully appreciated how precious England was to me until I saw that massed force in blatant array using a Dutch airfield: to deliver horror and carnage to Britishers night after night or to intercept RAF aircraft, as I well knew. Fury and frustration had to be swallowed and instructions remembered: keep calm at all cost.

Clearing the last barrier, I congratulated the two magnificent Dutchmen on their superb actor-confidence. De Neve replied with quiet irony that many disasters resulted from an over-rigid approach when attempting to pull the wool over the eyes of a normally austere race; skilful, light-hearted side-play and patriotic baloney often wondrously slewed them from thinking twice and lured them from strict attention to pettifogging detail.

Leiden is about twenty miles from Amsterdam and five from the North Sea. Approaching its outskirts, de Neve left the car to telephone Tiny Peter who was already in Leiden to co-ordinate arrangements. The Leiden resistance group played an important part in Jo Huese's sea operations, including being in direct radio communication with London; this was vital where changing German naval, troop and armour disposals along the coast might necessitate urgent revision in British–Dutch tactics. As de Neve returned to the car, it was easy to read consternation on his white face. His news was a shock; desperately serious. Late the previous night, Jo Huese's chief coastal planner, the man with whom we were to stay and who had responsibility for seeing us safely off the coast, had been arrested along with three other important operators of the Leiden ring. Typical of the methods of the Nazi secret police, the men had just disappeared; nothing about them could be confirmed; it was all a tangle, but Tiny Peter was trying to pick up information and hammer out some reasonably correct picture. Over recent months there had been an alarming number of similar, sudden arrests in Leiden, which gave rise almost to a conviction that enemy infiltrators were within the ring.

Van der Leek drove us over various trying detours beyond the city until it was time for de Neve to make further contact with Tiny Peter. When he did, he was given an address where Jock and I were to be under the protection of a Mr and Mrs 'Drake'. I have never revealed their true name and will not now, but this youngish couple had proved themselves with the Leiden ring; while neither was known personally to de Neve, he was reliably assured of their trustworthiness. There was no alternative. De Neve was under considerable pressure, for the ring's radio operator was one of those arrested; it was imperative he return to Amsterdam to contact London urgently. Mercifully, the main core at Leiden had not been immobilized but its members were under great strain, apprehensive of what the Gestapo might wring from their captured colleagues. London had to be alerted, that nothing may be sacrificed; the present submarine plan would doubtless be cancelled.

It was lamentable. De Neve attempted to banish depression by promising to have us evacuated, next morning if possible, to a safer place outside Leiden. He was still optimistic; it was not the first time a marine operation had been reassessed at the eleventh hour; this one could still take place, even tonight. The unpredictable situation made me aware of a certain fear in having the coded book strapped to my thigh. I was prepared to hand it back, but the Dutchmen considered I should keep it, awaiting instructions from Britain; the book was tremendously important, even more so after this latest tightening of the enemy grip in Leiden. We could expect a visit from Tiny Peter next day to tell us of arrangements, and the matter of the code book would be given full consideration. 'Be cautious with the Drakes,' de Neve warned. 'If they try to elicit anything about your movements, past or future, be very firm.'

Taciturnly, we drove to a depressing suburb of tight little streets and rows of small, identical-looking terrace houses. I was sure our friends sensed our nervous unease at leaving their intelligent, courageous, resourceful company for an equivocal situation. Stopping at the end of a street, we shook hands firmly. De Neve spoke with conviction. 'Good luck and a safe return home. Remember, you are loyal and plucky RAF men; your courage and resolution must never flag.' Van der Leek added, 'Now, follow me to number 26 and go straight inside.' As we tagged along to one of the dowdy houses, de Neve's words jarred my mind and I seemed to envisage all too clearly the picture he was trying to draw, if the worst came to the worst.

Drake was small and pale-faced, with a saturnine expression belied by a hearty cheerfulness. His wife was short and fleshy in a tight dress; her unsmiling eyes, I recall, were a bleached blue. Both spoke good English, but over tea in their cluttered living-room it took little time to realize I would never like them; neither chimed in to my ideas and I had an intuition our presence was not desired. The phone rang and I overheard Mrs Drake speaking in fluent German; I did not listen intentionally and she spoke too quickly for me to understand.

The day was cold, we huddled before a fire. I kept glancing out at a build-up of fog which alone could suffice to delay any submarine action. It was depressing. I was taken aback by Drake saying he understood we had been shot down a week before near Haarlem in a Wellington after raiding the Ruhr. Lyingly, I confirmed this. He fancied hearing about it, and what we had been up to since. Jock took the cue. 'We parachuted and did a lot of wandering about and stealing before we were lucky to find friendly assistance near Leiden.' I was apprehensive and tired. As Drake produced a bottle of Bols gin and became not even cleverly persistent, I adopted de Neve's advice. We were sworn to secrecy, I said, and surely as members of the resistance they understood the importance of honouring an oath . . . just as we could never divulge having been assisted by themselves, neither could we discuss our previous whereabouts or other helpers. The Drakes offered profuse apologies, vowing their interest had been harmless, merely friendly curiosity.

When the front door bell shrilled, I tensed as Drake went out to the tiny hall. He returned smiling, to say it had been a messenger from Mr X – we were to stay the night and be ready to move soon after dawn. I breathed relief;

even if it meant no submarine that night, at least the stalwart de Neve was still looking after our well-being. Time dragged, conversation became awkward. Suddenly, and astonishingly, Drake insisted we all go to the local cinema. Looking back, I realize I should have seen it as the grossest of follies for a genuine underground operator to commit. As it was, we were in Drake's hands; he was totally confident of there being virtually no risk and, after all, the Drakes were in a far more precarious position than we; if we were captured in their company, they had no possibility of reprieve from the firing squad to become prisoners of war.

It gave me no sense of triumph to be among an audience far more liberally scattered with uniformed enemy personnel than I had anticipated; I would not have been there, had I known. It was interesting enough to observe the enemy's reaction to a German propaganda film on the invasion of the Ukraine, but I was overridingly disconcerted by Drake being prepared to bring us into a situation of such unnecessary risk. Unwisely too, he led us from the cinema before the singing of the anthem, 'Deutschland Über Alles'. Nearing his house, a heavily built man hurried around the corner and gruffly muttered, '*Goeden nacht.*' Drake made no reply.

I had had enough of the Drakes and I was relieved when after a light meal he suggested we get a good night's sleep. He led the way up a flight of stairs to the matrimonial bedroom and opened a flimsy pine door on to steep, wooden steps leading to the attic. Two mattresses, blankets and a bucket were on the attic floor. Bidding us good night, he closed the door and, disquietingly, I heard a bolt being shot home. 'Cosy,' Jock commented drily, 'like a bloody prison.' I said nothing, but a dreadful loneliness came over me. Throughout our experiences together, Jock, an unemotional man of few words and sound thinking, had grown very close; a subtle understanding had developed between us, needing no embroidery.

There was no globe in the ceiling light socket; the cramped attic smelt of mould and camphor. I raised the window, after breaking a lock which secured a rusted bar, and was met by fine, cold rain; closing it, I slumped – fully dressed like Jock – on to a mattress. Sleep had no attraction for me; I was too disturbed. There was something sinister hovering about this house. I had no feeling of trust – not even liking – for the Drakes. What a contrast in atmosphere to the lovely homes and homely farmstead where we had been concealed before, and the impalpable trust which had been part of our companionships, effortlessly, confidently binding us together! Perhaps I was angry at the sudden change of fortune. Or was it strangeness, dissatisfaction upon entering a different escape realm of plebeianism and insecurity? After a couple of hours, I had an intense desire to escape, a frightful premonition of danger. I put it to Jock: we try to get out the window and wait, one at each end of the street, for the promised assistance to arrive at dawn. 'No good can come of it, Dick. We must trust Mr X and not let him down. Try to sleep. If our goose is cooked, we'll fight on, as may be.'

Thank heaven Jock dissuaded me. At the first twitch of dawn, I reopened the window and looked out at the hazy rooftops, opposite. Suddenly, I distinctly heard a low buzz of voices. The street was not unpeopled. I called Jack from his mattress and we put ears to the window frame. The voices were there again, less subdued. I detected the German accent . . . soft shuffling of feet, a muffled cough. My heart faltered as Jock whispered, 'Look! Straight across the street!' At the sight of shadowy, steel-helmeted figures, hugging sub-machine guns, thrusts of fear deepened. 'The bastards have us trapped!' I breathed. Jock was whispering, 'Oh hell! Oh hell!'

Our whole world of escape to freedom slipped its sanity, distorted into dread, anger and disaster. A fierce desire to escape swept over me, like a wave of fire, 'Quick, Jock, out the back; even if we have to dodge the bastards' bullets, and run like hell! The light's bad for aiming.'

'What if we get separated?'

'Make for the town hall and mooch about.'

In our scamper to get down the narrow stairs to put our shoulders to the bolted door, I tripped over the bloody bucket and set up a din. We made a plunge at the door, but it was too late. In that early morning hour, all hell seemed to have awakened: guttural roars, yells, bangs and crashes, screams from Mrs Drake, the thudding of jackboots ascending. Jock and I threw ourselves back on our mattresses. A black-uniformed German burst into the attic, pistol in hand, and fired two shots into the wall between our heads. There was no argument. Our wonderful run in Holland ended in this lousy little attic.

# CHAPTER 6
## The Price of Treachery

Even today, I find it hardly possible to offer articulate expression to the devastating shock and helpless bewilderment of falling prey to a merciless enemy. In the living-room a middle-aged Gestapo officer, in black leather coat, was obviously in charge. Steel-helmeted guards with automatic weapons backed us roughly against a wall. A Luftwaffe officer, of about our ages, ordered us to remove shoes and coats, and outstretch our arms. I watched as he patted and pinched Jock, searching him from feet to shoulders. Every sense in me quivered with alertness: Christ Almighty, the coded book!

When one quivers with desperation, a flashing idea, a ruse which might work, seems to come from nowhere in the rush of emotions. The search came to my turn; the officer dropped on one knee and his hands advanced until fingers came very close to touching the edge of the book taped high in my crutch. I triggered off the greatest sneeze of my life, a wet, beastly explosion of raked-up saliva, straight at the brow and face of the half-crouched officer. He jack-knifed to his feet, savage with rage, spread a hand over my face and bounced my head against the wall. Looking as if he could murder me, he was pulling out a handkerchief as I spoke in German. 'I am sorry. I have a bad cold.' I was immediately conscious of a bristling; he stared at me. 'My God,' I continued in German, 'you do look like Rudolf Hess!' Across the room the Gestapo officer snapped, 'Finish searching him!' I breathed with relief, for when the search resumed, it was from the waistband of my trousers upwards. I was not fool enough to think that was the end of searching, wherever we might be taken from the house. Quite apart from any horrors I might be saving myself on the way to the firing squad, a duty lay on me to divest myself of that book. The lavatory, of course.

Somehow they already knew we were British; we were arrested as spies, in civilian clothes and known to be in league with the Dutch resistance. Clumping sounds came from overhead as soldiers searched the house. Drake and his wife were brought in at gun point, both looking admirably in control of themselves; he gave us a look, seeming to say, 'Sorry . . . bad luck.' Jock and I were ordered to sit, facing the two officers and their revolvers. The Gestapo officer studied us with what seemed to be a vague, pleasurable excitement. 'Now, you will tell the truth. I shall know if you are lying. Understand?'

'Of course we understand, but . . .' I grimaced, gripping my stomach, 'how the hell can I concentrate on answering questions when I need to go to the lavatory urgently?' I was given a look of suspicion. I added quickly, 'I always understood German officers to be gentlemen.' The Gestapo officer rose, wagged a finger and thrust his face close to mine. He had a brown fleck in the blue of his right eye. Unexpectedly the finger, like iron, flicked viciously beneath my nostrils. Through watering eyes I watched the bastard as he said, 'All right, a bargain; the truth, mind you!' A guard was sent to inspect the lavatory, and reported escape was impossible that way. 'Go, hurry,' I was ordered; the guard was told to keep me in sight and the door ajar.

Fortunately, the door was left half-ajar. Crouching, I suffered agonies as I tore the sticking plaster from my leg, and while making vulgar blowing noises with my lips to give effect of reality, I rapidly ripped the incriminating book to pieces. I thrust the pieces up the pipe to the bend and pulled the chain, but some swirled back to float in the pan. I scooped them up and stuffed them into my mouth, chewing and gulping. I almost choked: in fact I had sagged to the floor gasping and spluttering when the guard kicked the door open. The sight of me must have given him one hell of a shock; involuntarily or otherwise, he triggered off a shot which struck the lavatory bowl; splinters flew off. He drove his fist at my throat, and from rolling on the floor, I was dragged back to the living-room with my pants draping my ankles. 'So, you tried to commit suicide by choking yourself!' hissed the Gestapo officer. 'Don't worry, you will die soon enough, after we have finished with you.'

Poor, dear, loyal Jock was looking pale and startled. I managed to give him a reassuring wink. We were seated on chairs, hard against the wall with a heavy table jammed against our ribs; with hands wide apart on the surface, we remained for hours. To all the questions, we gave away nothing; through the grilling, the crude and degrading insults we responded with RAF name, rank and number, and packs of lies. If we lied with cold cunning to dizzy questioning, they knew we were lying and sneered with mocking disbelief. Where had we crashed? What routes had we taken? How had we come by such excellent clothes and appeared so well fed? What were the names of towns and villages we had visited; the names and addresses of Dutch 'traitors' who must have helped us? I said we had crashed somewhere near Nijmegen, wandered about for a time before breaking into a large store near Eindhoven where I had stolen clothes and taken quite a few thousand guilders from the office. My knowledge of German had proved of great value; we had posed as Nazi civilians; had travelled by train to Rotterdam, ate in cafés, managed to book a room for a night here and there, made our way to Delft and The Hague before coming to Leiden. It was farcical, tantalizing and embarrassing, and I felt like a fly in a cobweb. Why had we no papers or money in our possession? We had left our briefcase in the train. We stuck to the story we had been primed to give and had rehearsed.

The Gestapo maniac pranced and screamed and spat on us. 'You have no identification to prove you belong to a British military section!' he ranted. 'As far as we are concerned, you are espionage agents and not prisoners of war!'

To aid the Drakes who showed horror and fear when accused of being mixed up with underground traitors, I concocted a story of how we had wandered the streets, randomly picked on their house and intimidated them for food and shelter, promising to leave after a night's sleep. (How the Drakes must have laughed!)

Since our arrest at dawn we had been subjected to almost continuous nerve-racking interrogation over many hours, without food or drink, and we were feeling the strain. But Jock was as determined as I never to break faith with those magnificent people who had risked their lives for us. It was about eleven o'clock when the door bell rang . . . followed by a brief commotion in the hall before a young man, with bruised and bleeding face, was dragged into the room. We were not to know he was a solicitor, a resistance loyalist sent to warn the Drakes of a car arriving soon to collect Jock and myself. The Gestapo officer, with his speciality for spitting, and jabbing and slapping one's face, dealt out his treatment before the man was booted to the rear of the house.

Nor did we know that Drake, an infamous paid informer and infiltrator, then phoned the resistance in Leiden to say their colleague had called and departed, and it was safe for the car to be sent immediately. We heard a car arrive, the door bell ring and another scuffle in the hall, and a tall, handsome man was prodded into the room. He was searched, a revolver found, and again that Gestapo swine inflicted his viciousness on the captive. The Dutchman stood defiantly proud, scornfully silent as Jock and I watched, tense with despair and sickness. The car outside moved off. A German in plain clothes came in and spoke of another man arrested in the car, who also had carried a gun but who had been overpowered before he could use it. He was being taken to Gestapo headquarters. The man in the car was, in fact, Tiny Peter!

Not until after the dust of warfare had settled was I to learn that when the underground had contacted Drake to take us in, he had notified German Counter-Intelligence which had placed his house under armed surveillance from houses across the street and behind. Fortunately, de Neve had moved quicker than the Germans, getting us to the house and himself clear to Amsterdam to radio London. God knows what additional disasters may have ensued had his alert not gone out and had the submarine kept its rendezvous.

It was noon when military cars arrived with Gestapo and the cocksure interrogator stood rigidly to attention before a monocled superior. It was the first time I had ever stared a monocle in the eye! Weary and dejected, Jock and I were handcuffed and, under guard, pushed into the back of a car. Through a labyrinth of streets we reached a highway where motor cyclists took up escort with sirens wailing.

'Now what?' murmured Jock.

'*Halten sie den Mund!*' roared the guard.

'What's he say, Dick?'

'The bastard said, "Shut up".' I imagine Jock felt as I did. If the will to live and fight on was strongly within me, in 1941 the Third Reich was by no means on the way to destruction. The vision of ever enjoying a free life, a good life in the future, seemed pretty damned remote.

Until the war was over, I was completely in the dark as to the follow-on events in the lives of the valiant people who had aided us, or those who had betrayed us. In the early post-war period, while attempting to reorganize my life, I was persuaded to write an account of my wartime experiences. What became my first book contained the barest information about a few of the people with whom I had associated, for at the time of writing, research was difficult. It was not just my remoteness from sources – I was living in Johannesburg – but when things were still being rationalized in Europe, much information lay under official wraps. As time passed and information became more readily available, I returned to Holland on a number of occasions and sad if stirring facts came to light. The War Statistics Department at The Hague allowed me to examine German sentence promulgations and other documents which the Germans had not destroyed. But the most valuable information of the cause of so many arrests was disclosed by former resistance friends who survived the horrors of concentration camps. Also, dismal and disturbing news came to me from relatives of those who had died. It all added up to agonies, deaths, humiliations, lives spoilt after being torn and tormented by the Nazi oppressors.

I spoke at great length with that intrepid underground leader, Edouard de Neve, also the Leonhardts, Bossenkool, and others. I learned that the four Leiden loyalists who had been arrested the night before our arrival were never heard of again. Their capture had resulted from the radio operator remaining at his transmitter a fraction too long while sending to Britain. Mobile trackers of the German Abwehr* known as D/Fers, or D/Fing (direction finding), had monitored his signals and located the Leiden centre and its transmitter while information was being fed into it. The young solicitor and the driver of the car arrested in Drake's house were executed, as was the messenger who had come from de Neve the afternoon before. After the captures at

* Espionage, Counter-espionage and Sabotage Service of the German High Command.

Drake's house, and the 'arrests' of himself and his wife, Drake became suspected by the resistance and was liquidated; his wife hastened to Germany but eventually was tracked down and sent to prison in 1956. Two traitorous neighbours of the Drakes disappeared when also fearing liquidation, but returned to Leiden after the liberation: like so many Dutch/Germans who collaborated when the 'Master Race' was heil-heiling all over Holland, they imagined they could clean up and start afresh as loyal, law-abiding citizens. Not for long. They had to pay for their treacheries with long terms of imprisonment. Throughout the Netherlands, a great many true loyalists who had rejected their oppressors had been executed; thousands more had been banished to concentration camps. It was also true that in 1945 alone, over 90,000 persons were detained in Holland for investigation of collaboration charges, and on 12 December 1945 the leader of the National Socialists in Holland, a Dutch engineer, A. A. Mussert, was sentenced to death by a special court at The Hague.

Hard as I found it to grasp or imagine, I learned that Tiny Peter had succumbed to Gestapo treatment: whatever fiendish methods were worked on whatever weak spots, the Gestapo elicited from him information fatal to his resistance colleagues. With its undoubted ingenuity and relentlessness, the Gestapo penetrated the Amsterdam ring and backtracked to Hengelo. First knowledge of the tragedies which had lain in our wake came to Jock (I was in hospital undergoing plastic surgery at the time), in a letter dated 25 October 1945 from Mrs Besselink. She said:

At 7 o'clock on the morning of 26 September 1941, the Gestapo searched the house of the Agterkamp family and also our house, after which the Agterkamp brothers and my husband were arrested. For four days we heard nothing of them – all at once Gerrit Agterkamp came home for he had been found innocent. This gave us, and certainly me, the hope that everything would be all right for the other brother (Jan) Agterkamp and my husband. However, God decided differently.

On the night of 15–16 October, together with two other gentlemen, Mr Van der Leek, and Mr Brouwer of Amsterdam, they were condemned to death. What this decision meant to me and the Agterkamp relatives I cannot describe, but you can certainly imagine. On 16 October we were allowed to visit them in the prison at Scheveningen to say goodbye. This was something horrible, and yet we were so happy to see each other again, even though it was in the presence of a German. We were only allowed ten minutes to see and speak to each other. On 20 October we could visit them again, and after that there were two more visits. These visits gave us much hope and we thought that even though they were condemned to death, the Germans would be kind-hearted enough to let them live. But we did not realize yet the full hatred and tyranny of the Germans. Good heart and pity were ignored by them! When I visited my husband he was, like me, full of courage with the hope that he would be able to come back home soon. We prayed to the Lord and did everything humanly possible to get them safely back home. Then on 17 November 1941, my husband, Mr Van der Leek, Mr Agterkamp and Mr Brouwer were shot by the Germans. I am weeping as I am writing this letter to you, for it is still difficult for me to tell you about this without feeling distressed . . .

There are several families in Amsterdam who were in the same position as I, one of which was deported to Germany. I do not know them all, but I can tell you that Tiny Peter, to whom you both spoke in the haystack, was taken prisoner in Germany until the liberation. There was also Mr Bossenkool (lame in both legs); I believe you both took a cup of tea with him just before you were taken prisoners. But do you know that the two persons who were taken prisoners at the same time as you were actual traitors, and they told about you and us? The villains had told the Germans about you, but did not want you to know about it, so as a blind they were taken prisoners at the same time as you were, and for their traitorous work they were paid 1,000 *gulden* . . . It would not have been so bad had you been outnumbered and overpowered by the Germans, but to have been betrayed by people whom you trusted makes your internment much harder to bear. You will also be sorry to hear that Mr Huese of Amsterdam was deported to Germany, but he never returned – he died of starvation . .

When Bernard Besselink's widow wrote that letter in 1945, she believed the Drakes wholly to blame, even to Hengelo. In talks I had with de Neve who had returned from concentration camp a sick and broken man, I learned that Tiny Peter, waiting in the car outside Drake's house, had been approached and spoken to by Drake's traitorous neighbours and closely following them the Gestapo had pounced. Had Tiny Peter fired at his attackers and died, perhaps in a hail of sub-machine-gun bullets with the names of the Amsterdam ring and Hengelo locked in his heart, many destinies would have followed very different courses. What he revealed was certainly under abnormal pressures, savage physical violence and the cunning of psychological will-breaking. It would be unjust to reveal his true identity. His ideals of patriotism and resistance to tyranny, so precious to him before arrest and before meeting the intensity of Gestapo ruthlessness, were equally aflame in his brother who escaped to Britain, served with our Armed Forces, and returned to his homeland with a distinguished war record. Tiny Peter returned from German imprisonment too fearful to reappear immediately on the Amsterdam scene; for a considerable time after the war persons of uncertain loyalty were in great peril of meeting a sudden and nasty end. When I discovered the tragedies he had caused, I definitely had such an end in view for him myself. I had a sword-stick made by Wilkinsons, a beautiful, wicked weapon, a rapier sheathed in finest quality cane with a handle in the shape of the head of Lord Roberts which had been carved in ivory by a subaltern who later had been killed in the Boer War. It took me weeks and weeks of subterfuge, threatening and blackmail to find Tiny Peter. When I did, vengeance turned to pity: I realized the man's morale was broken, his self-confidence smashed; he was his own greatest torturer. At least I was able to tell him what he desperately needed to hear, that no one formerly associated with him to whom I had spoken, hated him. It was true. One after another they had expressed pity and forgiveness. Bossenkool had said, 'He sacrificed more than his life or his legs when he sacrificed his honour.' No one better expressed this cherished value than Jan Agterkamp when, only minutes before facing a firing squad, he had written in the margin of a prayer book: 'Faithfully and with honour.'

Nothing was revealed to incriminate Enzerink and his daughter, first on the scene of our crashed bomber; or the clog-maker, Branderhorst, or the doctor who stitched my hand, or Rene Nouvain who dyed my hair. Besides those executed, Edouard de Neve, Jo Huese, Bossenkool, Mona and Billy Leonhardt were sentenced to death but by some miracle of relenting Providence their sentences were commuted to life imprisonment. De Neve's courageous student–swimmer daughter spent a year in prison; the others, excepting Jo Huese who died, endured over three years of hunger, indignities and cruelties in German prisons. Like de Neve, Billy Leonhardt returned a permanent invalid.

Although I saw the Leonhardts several times after the war, I found it indelicate to probe into that grim, closed chapter of their lives. Later, I learned of Mona's story when I visited Canada and met Allan Kent, chief reporter of the *Toronto Telegram*. Kent was a war correspondent with the Canadian First Army advancing upon Germany through Holland when he encountered Mona on 15 April 1945. She had just walked barefooted, her feet badly blistered and bleeding, through a battlefield barrage of screaming missiles, bursting shells and bombs at Vlagtwedde and wept at finding the first Allied soldiers she met were Canadians.

Two days after Jock and I left the Leonhardts on 24 September 1941, frightening news reached them of arrests. Over two months passed before the Gestapo trail arrived at their door. Only Mona was home. She was taken to prison in

Amsterdam. Repeatedly questioned, she revealed nothing, nor did she whine about the foul conditions, the dirty straw bed, the humiliations and hunger. What gave her heart was the knowledge that Billy was still free. On 22 December 1941, she was taken before a German military court to face trial for her life. She spoke no German. Her counsel, a German soldier, spoke neither English nor Dutch. Five minutes before the trial began, an interpreter was found who spoke no English and, like Mona, inadequate Dutch. Unable to follow the proceedings, she spent hours gazing out of a window. Her demeanour throughout, her fine face calm with dignity, even when sentenced to death, so impressed the judge that she was allowed to appeal. For the month following, every time her cell door was unlocked, she expected to be taking her last walk to the firing squad. When her sentence was commuted to one of life imprisonment, on a bleak morning in March 1942 she was hustled to a railway station with another prisoner, a farmer's wife, also sentenced for sheltering two Allied airmen. While standing between guards, awaiting the train, three men prisoners under guard, approached and were halted a few yards away. One of the prisoners was Billy! In stark amazement, Mona cried, 'It's my husband!' She raced towards him and threw her arms about his neck. Their embrace was only for a moment. Angry guards parted them and dragged her away. When she turned, Billy had gone. Months later, she received a letter from him from another prison in Germany. It read: 'Until I saw you that day I hadn't much hope. But I know God brought us together that day to give me hope to live and go through with everything. Now I am all right. I am strong after seeing you and I can go through with it.'

Mona was taken to Andrath Prison, near Krefeld in the Rhineland. Her first month was spent in solitary confinement before she was moved to a small cell which accommodated four. Her cellmates varied, sometimes

German, French, Dutch, even an Englishwoman, formerly the head of a YWCA hostel in Paris. Most of the inmates were not political prisoners but criminals. Mona said, 'Some of them were noble people, women of great hearts and courage – like the French woman whose husband was the first French agent killed after France fell. She had stood for thirty-six hours with revolvers at each cheek, but still would not tell what she knew . . . Some, however, were unspeakable characters (thieves, murderers, prostitutes, perverts): some hardly acceptable, but at least amusing.' Hunger was perpetual, and while she refused to participate in the awful contest for food, she recalled fearfully waiting her opportunity to pounce like a rat on a piece of apple which had fallen from the lips of a woman gaoler.

For two and a half years at Andrath, Mona toiled twelve hours a day on deadly monotonous jobs, some of them backbreaking. In September 1944, when the German Army was being rolled back as the Allies advanced from Normandy, political prisoners were moved out of the Rhineland. Mona was taken northwards, finally to Bechta Prison near Oldenburg. On 24 March 1945, she escaped in the midst of an Allied air raid; with her went another prisoner, a lovely, 23-year-old Dutch countess from Arnhem. The countess spoke perfect German, and as she was twenty years Mona's junior they acted as niece and aunt, German fugitives from Stettin. To conceal her ignorance of German, Mona portrayed herself as a half-wit with a cleft palate. For three weeks the women walked and painfully, in bitter cold, made their way towards Holland, begging, pausing to labour on farms in return for food and shelter, sharing the suffering, the squalor, of the people with whom they sheltered, and always fearfully maintaining their masquerade. The Mona Parsons who long ago had abandoned a dramatic career in Boston would never have imagined the desperately serious role into which she would cast herself and in what a terrifying play. This was no better illustrated than at Ooserwalde, near Sogel, when she and the countess were taken by a Nazi police official to his home where they found other fugitives from Cologne. Mona related: 'The man seemed to accept our story, but his wife was sceptical. We suffered awful fears, believing we were lost; trapped in a Nazi official's house. All I could do was act not half-witted, but wholly out of my mind, and leave it to my friend to get us out of the hole. Finally the countess convinced them.' Mona must have played a brilliant supporting role, for the countess later commented: 'When I told them you were crazy I looked across the room at you, and I was almost convinced myself, the way you were creeping around, half-bent over, with a vacuous smirk on your face.'

Although the two were separated, sent to different farms near the final stage of their escape from Germany, like Mona the countess reached her home in Holland.

# CHAPTER 7

# Prisoner in Germany

When Jock and I were arrested and driven from the Drakes at Leiden with the siren-wailing escort, our destination was a handsome, white, four-storey building at The Hague. Inside its guarded entrance we were parted, not to see each other for some days. In a large room I again faced the fleck-eyed Gestapo officer; also another officer, and an interpreter in naval uniform. Over many hours, I stuck doggedly to our tale of wandering since crashing and denying knowledge of person or place: they projected photographs on a screen; did I know this man, that man? The faces were of villagers, farmers, people from up and down the coast; they even produced 'Papes' of Leiden. Had I been in this street, that street? They kept dashing off and bringing back more. It was all rather frightening for obviously the Germans were on to a big haul and we had been scooped up in the net.

The building we were in was Kleykamp, opposite the Peace Palace. It housed the Netherlands Inspectorate of the Population Registry where, in 1941, the Germans had begun collecting records invaluable to them, particularly in dealing with the Jewish population and in 'uncovering' persons operating under forged documents. Because of lack of understanding which was to exist for a long time between British Intelligence and the Dutch underground (stemming from German success with the *Englandspiel*), it was not until 31 December 1943 that a message reached London from a secret agent (P. L. Baron d'Aulnis de Bourouill) explaining the significance of Kleykamp and asking that it be bombed. It meant a very difficult attack. A full-scale model of the front of the building, and the surrounding area on reduced scale, were built on a showground in England; a handful of pilots in Mosquito light-bombers vigorously trained on mock attacks. On 11 April 1944 six Mosquitoes, two of them piloted by Dutchmen, flew at a height of fifty metres across the North Sea and on to the The Hague. It was three P.M. on a normal working day when they attacked. The time was chosen deliberately and with approval of the Dutch Government-in-exile in London: the staff was at work and as many as possible of the steel filing drawers open. The building was totally wrecked; fifty-nine people were killed including several underground workers but an important proportion of the records was destroyed.

Naturally, I speculate on the consequences had Jock and I been on the move through Leiden to the coast even two days earlier, and had I been able to hand over the ordinary-looking language book to a British submarine commander. There may have been no *Englandspiel* with its attendant tragic losses. But while I conjecture: what guarantee was there of the submarine making a safe passage home? I shudder at the thought of a watery grave . . . and events in Holland may have gone on, little changed.

It was evening when I was taken from Kleykamp and driven some few kilometres to the Gestapo headquarters prison, Scheveningen, commonly known as 'The Orange Hotel'. There I was slung into a rotten little cell; a bed was planks on the floor. I was damned hungry, having eaten nothing since the evening before at the Drakes', but only a mess tin of water came my way. Next day I faced a new interrogator, with interpreter and guard. He sat on the edge of a desk and opened up, icily calm, informing me I was a British saboteur; I had earned the death sentence. He boasted of being a specialist in dealing with my kind and of having broken down hundreds like me. I would be deprived of food and sleep until I made a full confession, for which my reward would be life imprisonment instead of a firing squad. I retold my story, striving to preserve its continuity and praying that my iron-willed Scottish companion would hold out too. I was reminded by my interrogator that liars had to remember everything and, in his dealings with liars, especially after they had been put through the 'organ grinding chamber', inevitably they forgot something.

Extraordinarily, every time I attempted to press home the fact that Jock and I were shot-down RAF aircrew, my questioner lost his temper, pranced, shouted and his large ears twitched! He was a small man with battered features and lustreless blue eyes. He warned that if I mentioned 'RAF' again, I would be taken away for softening up; as a foretaste, he slapped my face ferociously for at least half a minute. Sweat poured from my scalp and face as he tried to get me into a mental corner, coming back at me time and again from many angles, striving to get me to admit I had been dropped into Holland as an agent. My dyed hair was by now showing an honest undergrowth; sweat carried rivulets of stain down my face. The interrogator sprang, grabbed my hair and tugged me to my knees.

Back in my cell, a guard brought in a rough German civilian who carried a bucket of steaming water, a tin of soft soap, scrubbing brush and a bottle of what smelt like kerosene. Furious beyond measure, I cursed at being manhandled, but a kick in my middle quelled rebellion. Gleefully the bullet-headed civilian shoved my cranium into the bucket and scrubbed. Far from solving a problem, my emergent red hair with murky patches gave cause for new attack. Who had dyed it, when, where, etc., etc? There were hours of continuous examination with 'Twitching Ears' threatening to tear my brains out. The outlook was sombre indeed.

It was obvious from our appearances that we had not been on the run for weeks. But, of course, I had no inkling of just how much else 'Twitching Ears' knew with certainty. From the start, he knew from the Drakes that we had been aided by the resistance; and Tiny Peter must have cracked early, for Besselink and Agterkamp were arrested the day following his and our arrests. I would have been agonized to have known that Besselink and Agterkamp were actually sharing 'The Orange Hotel' with us. 'Twitching Ears' never mentioned names and I was certain he was lying when he claimed he had a number of others in the cells who were prepared to identify me as a British agent. What confounded me most was why he kept on about my being an agent parachuted into Holland and fanatically refused to sort out the members of my crew . . . unless the Gestapo suspected I was that escaped, red-haired British agent who had caused me to have my hair dyed! A grim prospect as *he* was wanted for murder.

Fortunately the various German Intelligence services and the secret police worked in tight liaison to sift, explore and exchange any fragments of information. Luftwaffe Intelligence was notified of our claiming to be RAF fliers. Later, I learned that while 'Twitching Ears' was shutting me up on the subject, Jock was being asked for details of being a flight-engineer, of our crew, our aircraft and mission. Members of our crew were then located and questioned; our bona fides confirmed. But the fundamental issue remained: we had been captured as civilians with the Dutch resistance which the secret police were determined to crush out of existence.

Several days elapsed before the Luftwaffe notified the Gestapo that Jock and I were genuine RAF – long enough for us to have had a hell of a basinful of Gestapo treatment: acute hunger, mental stress, physical brutality and, perhaps worst, loneliness. We had much for which to thank our skipper, Wallace Terry (so I learned after the war when the BBC brought the three of us together in London for the show *In Town Tonight*). When Terry was questioned about us, his interrogators disclosed that they knew we had operated on an independent bombing mission and that twice, in five days, a four-engined bomber had attacked over a forest region north-west of Berlin. They clearly disbelieved that in operating 500 miles from Britain we had pin-pointed a target by using dead-reckoning navigation and without the aid of some secret target-finding device. Terry had received the best of skilled medical treatment from the Germans. Serious as his head injuries had been, he had regained his wits and memory, although he was to suffer damnable head trouble for a long period as a POW before being repatriated.

He certainly gave the Luftwaffe interrogators an incredible shock. He gauged from their questions and inferences that if he talked freely the Luftwaffe would do all in its power to persuade the Gestapo to release us for interrogation at the Luftwaffe Intelligence centre near Frankfurt, Germany. That was our only hope. Terry searched the caves of his mind for a plausible story and, in so doing, invented a radar device which I supposedly had switched on when nearing Berlin. He professed to know much less about it than I did, but he asserted that it operated with the co-operation of persons on the ground in the target vicinity; they sent signals on a special frequency which provided me with a cross beam for a perfect target fix. When he was told that our Stirling had been dismantled and expert examination had revealed no secret apparatus, Terry was not at a loss: the thing was so valuable that after testing it as he said we had been, we had jettisoned it and a timed device had blown it to pieces in mid-air. What terribly alarming news for the Germans: a secret, deadly accurate navigational aid, and treachery on the ground! Terry could not have created a better fantasy.

I had undergone another desperate session of interrogation when, I can only assume, the Gestapo at The Hague received a request, or order, to 'lay off' and ensure I was well fed and watered for collection early next morning. 'Twitching Ears' suddenly assumed an almost benevolent air. He said he was aware that I had flown a four-engined bomber over Germany and I was to have parachuted into Holland on the way back but, unfortunately for me, the aircraft had been brought down! Perhaps a good dinner would encourage me to volunteer information as to where I was to have baled out to be collected by underground friends? 'Oh, Christ, what the hell are they up to now?' I asked myself.

I was back in my cell, bruised and dizzy with hunger, when the door was opened and the block-headed, civilian bastard who had tried to erase some of my scalp with the scrubbing brush came in carrying a large tray of steaming food. 'For you,' he said proudly, 'meat, potato, cabbage, bread, butter, cheese, coffee. More if you can eat it.' He grinned. I was possessed by violent anger, inflamed by a colossal hatred for the humiliation I had suffered at his hands. My shoes had been taken away but with bare feet I took a running kick at the underside of the tray and sent the steaming contents into his face. If the sender wanted an answer for the price of the food, he had it! I thought I had broken every toe of my foot. There was no reprisal, no invasion of my cell by screaming, kicking guards; no response. The food was still smeared over the floor when I was led away from the cell next morning and told I would be leaving in an hour for the Fatherland. The fear and anxiety this unexpected news aroused! I wondered if I was being taken away to be shot.

I was in a waiting car outside 'The Orange Hotel' when Jock was led swaying towards me. I was immensely glad to see him, but shocked by his appearance; he was a changed man. He clutched at the car door and spoke hoarsely, 'Thank God you're alive, Dick. They told me you'd kicked the bucket.' Anger rose in a great surge and putting my head out the window, I yelled at 'Twitching Ears' who was observing our departure, 'You filthy, low-livered bastard!'

'Silence!' roared a guard. 'You'll be shot if you give any trouble!'

The car pulled away with Jock and me wedged between two guards at the back. We had weathered many crises and although I had been told we were being sent away to a Luftwaffe Intelligence centre near Frankfurt-am-Main, I had a dread we were on our way to our last crisis: to face the wall. I was calm, but it was a horrible kind of calm. My whole body was sweaty. Jock was grey-faced and miserable-looking: I think we both admitted to ourselves, the sooner the better, now. All we could do was prepare to pass out of existence without cringing, accepting our fate with fortitude and composure.

I was dumbfounded when we arrived at Rotterdam railway station and were prodded into a train compartment. Were we really going to Germany? As we sped across Dutch terrain, I had a desperate desire for escape, before we severed all ties with Holland. The two guards had us well under their sharp eyes and any attempt to dash for it, at one of our stops, would end in a hail of bullets. Sensibly, too, I realized that my physical strength had been sapped, my health was shaky; I was experiencing bouts of acute giddiness. Jock was definitely sick and seemed to have a fever.

We changed trains a number of times, and from electric to steam. When we crossed into the Ruhr a strange mood of fatalism came over me. The journey along the Rhine Valley, which I had travelled in days when Germans had been pandering and bowing to their great English friends, was no longer a romantic or picturesque trip, but one of purgatory. Wretched with hunger and fatigue, at Cologne we endured a long wait for a connection. Akin to any main railway station in wartime Britain, the whole place was crowded with people in uniforms, including squads of Hitler Youth Movement teenagers strutting about, pushing trolleys, carrying bags and trays of paper cups with coffee. What affected my tattered nerves most and roused the terrible temper of a red-headed Yorkshireman were 'Heil Hitler' salutes, near and far, all over the bloody platforms. Up came arms in rigid alacrity from young and old, their faces flashing fervour. 'Stupid automaton bastards,' I muttered. Jock was very sensitive to my fiery reactions, and gripped my arm. 'Hold on, Dick!'

At the outset of our journey I had attempted to talk to our humourless guards in German, but had been snarlingly warned, 'Conversation is forbidden.' We were in civilian attire which drew little attention while we waited at Cologne, with our backs leaning against a wall . . . until our guards prodded us forward with their sub-machine-guns towards a train. Someone asked who we were and our guards' reply, 'English spies', quickly brought a small and hostile crowd about us. An ugly incident flared and was quelled by one of the guards smashing his gun-butt into a woman's face. For explosively giving tongue to my opinions, I collected a lip-splitting swipe from the other guard. My eyes watered but not so as to blind me to the sight of the twin towers of Cologne Cathedral as the train moved off. I sucked at my bleeding lip, silently scoffing at the irony of the situation as my mind's eye skimmed back to a moonlight night when I had made two precision bombing runs to get those towers perfectly positioned in my bombsights . . . and had lost a magnum of champagne. Now I was transfixed by the ground-level sight of the cathedral; I seemed to watch it for miles, and before it passed out of view the twin steeples looked like the horns of the devil. My thoughts were curdled. I was becoming enveloped in a cocoon of hatred for everything German, with a great swelling of emotions for revenge!

Towards evening, the train reached Frankfurt-am-Main.

Jock and I were dead tired and damnably hungry. Luftwaffe guards took over from the two repellent guardians, and in a large car we headed for 'Dulag Luft', some miles outside the city. Near our destination, searchlights began a rhythmic swing through the encroaching darkness. We passed a wall of barbed wire illuminated by probing beams coming from high guard boxes on stilt-like legs. Up a pine-clad slope a short distance beyond, we stopped before a solid timber building: Jock and I were hustled inside and again immediately separated.

I was staggered to find myself escorted to an airy room where soft music issued from a ceiling speaker. Here was no bed of planks on the floor as at 'The Orange Hotel' but an iron bedstead, white sheets and pillow, blankets, a chair and table, a carafe of water. A window, strongly barred, was masked by heavy curtains and, drawing them open, I realized why. The searchlights on the elevated guard boxes below cast glaring light into the room as they swept back and forth.

I really was puzzled as to why we had suddenly been moved to Germany and placed in the hands of the Luftwaffe after all my abortive attempts to convince that tyrannical swine, 'Twitching Ears', that I was an RAF flier. My first interrogator, who soon appeared, enlightened me; yet left me more bewildered. He was Oberst-Leutnant Lindermann, down from Luftwaffe Headquarters, Berlin. He was courteous of manner, fluent in English and purportedly a former Cambridge University undergraduate . . . certainly I was unable to trip him on his knowledge of Cambridge. But what he revealed of our missions over the forest north of Berlin came as a shock. Of course, I had no idea of what Wallace Terry had been fabricating; it certainly had rescued us from the Gestapo but now it was catching up and I had to cope, without knowing what the devil it was all about. I was astounded to be told by Lindermann that my pilot and I had undergone intensive training on a secret radar-electronic, navigational device, and a target-finding instrument working on signals and beams between ground and air; that we had used the equipment on two Berlin raids . . . and blown it up in mid-air. It was a rum story! I had no idea what the Luftwaffe, perhaps after all in sinister cohorts with the heinous Gestapo, was trying to inveigle me into. My heart was filled with off-beats. I stressed vehemently that I knew nothing about such equipment and the RAF had nothing like it, to my knowledge. It was all nonsense, a fairy-tale. I had found my way to Berlin by dead reckoning and had located the forest through assistance of moonlight, plus interpretation of topography.

He did not believe me. He said he appreciated that my duty was to deny, but honour had its limits when one's fate was in the balance. The Gestapo were angry and sorely reluctant to let me go; they reserved the right to have me returned and, airman or not, to hand me over to a firing squad if I was found to have engaged in sabotage or acted against interests and considerations of a nation at war. If I co-operated and relieved myself of a tormenting decision, he would use every influence to resist Gestapo demands and to have me removed to an accredited POW camp. He advised me to search my memory carefully before the arrival of a Luftwaffe technical expert who would be examining me. Lindermann remains in my mind as a decent man, sensitive that a measure of compensation was due to me after the Gestapo treatment. He promised I would have some solid meals and, as he rose to leave, he emptied his cigarette case on the table. I never saw him again.

Next to arrive was an amiable, fat little orderly wearing a white jacket; he brought a large, rose-patterned chamber pot filled with English magazines. He left and presently returned with a substantial hot meal, the like of which I had not eaten since arrest ten days before; also a jug of wine, a packet of Players cigarettes (captured at Dunkirk) and matches. He was now wearing the uniform of a *Feldwebel* (sergeant), and he said he and Oberst-Leutnant Lindermann were about to leave for Berlin. He bade me '*Auf wiedersehen*' in a manner I interpreted as sympathetic. But goodwill soon disappeared when a beak-nosed, rough diamond of a guard entered and ordered me to strip; he had no scruples about searching my person or carrying away my clothes, leaving me naked. He took my cigarettes and matches. 'They were given me by your officer,' I protested. 'Smoking is forbidden,' he replied.

So the party was over; this was the start of harsh Dulag Luft business. In the morning, the guard threw a bundle of clothing on the bed, ordering me to dress as I was to go before the Kommandant. My God! When I undid that bundle I was exchanging Leonhardt's quality clothing for the outfit of a buffoon: old French cavalry breeches with red-piped seams down the sides; they finished mid-calf and laced up, intended for riding boots. My footwear was over-sized Dutch clogs with leather bands to fit across my feet; no socks, but foot cloths like rag dusters. The shirt was my introduction to the rough, dirty grey material made mostly of wood pulp; on its front, stamped in large black letters, was 'KGF' for '*Kriegsgefangene*' (prisoner of war). A Polish infantryman's tunic, with two aluminium buttons embossed with eagles, completed my outfit. I looked a thorough clown. I never doubted it was done deliberately, mixing me up with our defeated Allies, to undermine my morale and make me feel a humiliated fool. When the guard returned and burst into raucous laughter, I felt like killing him.

I was regarded with almost malicious amusement by Kommandant Rumpel; also Sonderführer Eberhardt who wore a smart civilian suit, and another civilian who was plainly of the Gestapo. I was to combat many severe sessions of interrogation from this trio. The Kommandant seemed decidedly on the side of the Gestapo in wanting me returned to Holland; my association with the Dutch resistance and suspected alliance with the British SOE (Special Operations Executive) seemed the most important issues to them. It was bewildering; they made no reference to navigational devices and traitorous assistance from Germans, the matters of prime concern to Lindermann. Instead, they repeatedly took me over the ground on which I had been questioned exhaustively in Holland: places, people, my dyed hair; what had I flushed down the lavatory? A map? Did it mark the rendezvous with a British submarine? Again I was photographed and fingerprinted, and a blood sample taken, on Gestapo insistence. The Sonderführer questioned me minutely about home, schools, civilian work, where I had taken holidays, my parents, grandparents, great-grandparents. Did I have relatives in Germany? Why had I learned German? I nearly spun through the floor when asked if I was related to Claus von Pape, one of the twelve disciples to whom Hitler dedicated *Mein Kampf*. The Sonderführer hammered away about French and German Papes, perhaps to discover if I were in subversive league with them. Did I know my name was an old German one of some repute? There was a Berlin railway station named 'Pape Bahnhof' and in Königsberg, East Prussia, there was a 'General Pape Strasse'. Did he imagine the 'family' had signalled me from the floor of the forest near Berlin? He certainly had unearthed a great deal of personal data about me and knew more about the infrastructure of the RAF than I did. He knew of my pre-war flying and service with 609 Auxiliary Squadron, of my newspaper work and travel to Europe. I received shock after shock at just how much he did know of purely private family matters: my parents' divorce, how seldom I had seen my father, his war service, his living in France. It was extraordinary the facts revealed; for what purpose, I could not imagine. Why tell me my mother's house at Oakwood, Leeds, was seven miles from Harewood House? Or ask: did I know the young Lascelles, sons of the Earl of Harewood? 'Yes,' I replied, 'as a youth I rode a horse over the boundaries of the estate and often met young George Lascelles and his riding companions for a friendly chat.' (In truth, the meetings were also for the handing over of Wild Woodbine cigarettes, easy for me and apparently hard for them to obtain. I charged extortionately, one shilling for a packet of five which had cost me 2½d. This was the Lascelles who was to become a prisoner of war, 1944–5. Being King George VI's nephew, he was valuable property to the Germans and was imprisoned in Colditz Castle.)

Interrogation session followed session with the usual threats of dire consequences. It was exhausting and nerve-racking, keeping my wits unceasingly alert to protect friends in Holland, not to mention saving my own head. Then the Luftwaffe took over in the person of a Major Gerhardt, a good-looking, First World War flier; he spoke polished English and was an expert in electronics. I anticipated his questioning would be just another step in a series of misfortunes since arrest at Leiden, but on the contrary the Fates were spinning a fortuitous thread into my captive life. Major Gerhardt's understanding and goodwill proved a vital turning-point. With no one else present, he questioned me with courtesy and directness. At first I was coldly honest but tactful, stating I knew nothing about a ground–air, radio-beam device such as Lindermann had described; I told how I had navigated above a sea of cloud from England to near Berlin on luck, dead reckoning and taking astronomical 'fixes'. As his investigation proceeded, a subtle under-standing and regard developed between us. There were no threats, no violence, furious interruptions or twitching of ears! To my great relief, he believed me and realized that Luftwaffe Intelligence had been following a mare's nest.

Nonetheless, the story had not been such preposterous nonsense, especially with RAF Bomber Command stepping up its long-distance offensive. Research in Britain and Germany never flagged in the development of bombing and navigational aids; at the time, Britain had well in the pipeline 'Gee', a navigational aid specifically designed to help bombers to their targets. It came into use in March 1942: by long, fine radio beam, it lay an invisible grid over parts of Germany up to 400 miles from the transmitter and was superior to either 'Knickebein' or 'Gerat' devices which had been operated by the Germans and counteracted by the British. I was aware that in raids on Coventry and other British cities the enemy had used direction and target-finding devices, but I was ignorant of any details of the battles waging between scientists. Undoubtedly, Major Gerhardt would have been fully knowledgeable on the matter, and perhaps even aware that a new British invention ('Gee') was close to operational readiness. Small wonder Luftwaffe Intelligence was so alerted by Wallace Terry's revelations, for here perhaps was the new invention being tested!

Gerhardt confided that Jock had been cleared and sent to the main camp. From my window, I would see the moving figures of men inside the walls of barbed wire. Wing Commander Douglas Bader, I was told, was down there too; it was only three months but seemed an eternity since Bader and his 'beehive' had escorted us over France. Gerhardt was fully aware that my life was at stake unless I secured POW status and remained in Germany; but the Gestapo were an overriding power. From his manner rather than his words, I gathered that the major was at variance with Nazism, as were so many of his generation; indeed, there was a German Resistance Group which believed that Hitler and his government should be removed and peace negotiated with Britain before it was too late for Germany to avoid cataclysmic consequences. Gerhardt also held firm views about the pith and justice of what should not be denied to me. He was of the old school which cherished honour among fliers. Both of his sons were operational pilots at the Russian Front and he admitted to me that he would prefer them to die at the controls of their machines rather than fall prisoners to the Russians. He was a man of humane breeding who understood the character and mental make-up of flying men. The regard which developed between us was revived after the war when I met him in Paris; he had evaded the Russians and, as a scientist, had found employment outside Germany.

I told Gerhardt that despite my conspicuous clothing, I would have a crack at escape if the Gestapo tried to get me back. I recall clearly him beckoning me to the barred, open window. Standing with his back to the room – perhaps he thought or knew the room was bugged – he whispered towards the outside world what he planned to do: arrange our meeting with the Kommandant, the Sonderführer and the Gestapo agent; inform them I was suffering head pains and deafness in one ear, doubtless as a result of injuries received on crash-landing and the exceptional nervous tension I had undergone since. He would state that he was departing for Berlin to obtain maps and RAF navigational instruments; that it was of vital importance to the Luftwaffe that I prove on paper my alleged navigational ability. Before he returned from Berlin to subject me to a series of intricate mathematical and dead-reckoning tests, it was imperative I be admitted to the camp hospital for rest and treatment. Gerhardt advised that when I was under the surveillance of the trio, I should assume a sullen passivity; his attitude towards me would be stern. On one point he asked my word of honour: I would not attempt to escape from the hospital, no matter what the temptation or opportunity. I was not to make a fool of him; or myself, for if I were recaptured, still without POW status, he doubted if I would even see this Dulag Luft again, much less the inside of any other POW camp.

Fair blew the wind. The next day, 14 October 1941, nine days since Jock and I had arrived at Dulag Luft, I was admitted to its small hospital. It was not enclosed by barbed-wire walls and was indifferently guarded; food and medical attention were excellent. About a dozen RAF fliers were inmates, most with broken bones, a few with serious burns. In the bed next to mine was a Pole, Henryk Kowalski. His face and hands had been badly burned; he had been a bed patient for some time. Among the 38,000 soldiers and airmen who had made their way to France after Poland had been overrun by Hitler and Stalin, Kowalski had proved himself in France where Polish pilots had shot down sixty German planes; following the Battle of France, he had crossed to Britain where a Polish airforce was reconstituted as a number of RAF squadrons.

In honour to Major Gerhardt, I disclosed to no one that I was in hospital by any deception; in fact, some spinal dislocation was discovered for which I received manipulative treatment. To Henryk Kowalski, however, I did relate much about my adventuring with the Dutch underground, the crazy accusation that I had carried a secret target-finding device, and the threat hanging over me of being returned to the Gestapo in Holland.

'Make a break for it from here,' Henryk urged, 'you're about forty kilometres from the Swiss frontier; you'll never get closer to neutral territory than now.'

My absurd international uniform had been taken away when I was issued with Red Cross pyjamas. But clothing would have been no problem. Henryk and two other patients had a well-hidden collection of useful escape clothing. In the bath–toilet block, part of the floor boards had been worked upon and bricks on the outside wall had been loosened for easy removal. Escape would be a piece of cake. But I had given Gerhardt my word. The treatment I was receiving for my back had to be my excuse to Henryk for not bolting. But I learned a great deal from the Pole. A grapevine existed between hospital and main camp. He knew about Bader, warned me to beware of a certain RAF individual who had been kept there so long that he was suspect as a German plant; he told me where microphones were concealed in the four huts, and that a few weeks earlier, eighteen men had escaped from a tunnel dug from beneath one of the huts to pass under the wire. They had all been recaptured.

I asked Henryk where the hell I was likely to go if given POW status. He said that the last three batches of NCOs sent from Dulag Luft had gone to Stalag VIIIB, near Breslau, close to the German–Polish border. He knew a number of Polish fliers who had been sent there. He gave me their names; I could well draw upon them for advice and assistance if I went to Stalag VIIIB and decided to make a break for it into Poland. Despite his own problems, that Polish pilot was a stimulus and source of strength, deeper and stronger than I could foresee. Henryk stubbornly felt I would make it to Stalag VIIIB, escape and usefully employ myself in Poland's underground fight for freedom. He spent many hours teaching me useful Polish expressions. Although he had been out of his country for two years, he had some idea of the agonies suffered by the Polish people. During the alliance between Hitler and Stalin, September 1939 to June 1941, each dictator had set about methodically ingesting his newly acquired half of Poland – by murder or other diabolical means ridding himself of any possible alternative government, the same methods as each applied within his own country. Those Poles who were kept alive were to be ignorant slaves of their German and Russian masters; once and for all the Polish nation was to be destroyed. When the dictators' alliance erupted into war, the German iron heel ground down on the whole of Poland; enslavement, executions and wholesale deportations were gaining momentum in late 1941. No matter what the cruelties his people were suffering, or his own agonies, Henryk believed that every hour of every day was not one for despair, but for courage; belief in victory should rule our minds. He was possessed of the great fighting strength of the Polish character.

I feel to this day that in some peculiar, psychic way, Henryk Kowalski had taken the burden of my case upon himself; as if he might be preparing me for a darker, more hazardous future. In a strange sort of cheerfulness, he was demanding some of my intense energy and loyalty, sowing the suggestion that I might become in some way an indispensable factotum to their cause, if I could gain admittance to the Polish underground. He knew that with his disfigured face and scorched hands, he could never escape to cultivate his own garden of revenge.

When Poland was crushed militarily but not spiritually in September 1940, an underground army came into existence; its name was changed twice, and finally in February 1942 it became known as 'Armia Krajowa' (Home Army). This Army was under direct orders, communicated by radio and couriers, from the Polish Provisional Government in London. And in England a Polish section of the SOE was established to assist in maintaining and developing communications with the Home Army, in training of agents, couriers and parachutists, and in arranging the delivery of supplies and personnel to boost the efforts of the Polish underground movement.

I was called upon to leave the hospital without having acquired any great reverence for Henryk's philosophy and hardly exalted about ever crossing Germany to be interned in Stalag VIIIB, near the Polish border. I felt sympathetically immune upon a rational basis; his expositions and emotional fervour were of no consequence to me in the precise role I might be called upon to play as a British prisoner of war, if I ever became recognized as one. I had been flung into a captive trough and the only way out that I could visualize within the wartime ahead was certainly not eastwards across Poland to the Russian ally.

Early one morning my international garb was dumped on my bed. 'Get dressed,' a guard ordered, 'you are returning for interrogation.' I was brought before Kòmmandant Rumpel, Sonderführer Eberhardt and a Hauptmann (Flight Lieutenant) Müller. No Gestapo agent was present. A Red Cross form was handed to me, a genuine one. I filled in name, rank and number and it was accepted without comment. Rumpel told me to count my blessings; Berlin Intelligence was not ungrateful for my co-operation; it was recommended that I be removed to the main camp and given POW status.

I sensed Major Gerhardt's influence in this change of heart. Rumpel and Eberhardt were not pleased and I was warned that I was still liable to recall to Holland . . . possibly to give evidence at the trial of two underground civilians captured at Leiden. I assumed they meant the Drakes, but was told nothing definite. Nor was I released immediately to the main camp but taken to a small, cheerless room, not my former one, and left to reacclimatize to solitary; this time, with no white sheets or reading materials, and rations greatly reduced. After the friendly company at the hospital the hours crawled and monotony was fearful. Again and again, Gerhardt surfaced in my mind – that German scientist had come into my existence like a mysterious protector; all I could do was possess my soul in patience and stamp the belief into my mind that I would win through.

It was the close of the third day of solitary; hunger gnawed. Suddenly the peace of the night was broken by the

wailing of air-raid sirens, near and far. I pressed my face
against the window bars. The small searchlights on the
guard towers of the main camp went out. Then, blue-beam
searchlights came into action, criss-crossing, combing the
sky. I had an excited certainty the Stirlings were arriving. An
enormous barrage was put up by anti-aircraft guns. Down
came the bombs, dull crumps and loud crumps, explosion
followed explosion. It was a big strike and above the skyline
reddish glows spread, joined and deepened, indicating huge
fires.

Gone was the feeling of stark isolation. I experienced a
curious merriment, until two of the bombers passed
overhead after unleashing their loads to explode about a
quarter of a mile away. The building shuddered, an
experience none too pleasant. The raid was barely over when
armed guards banged open my door and ordered me to get
moving, to be taken to the main camp.

Our captors were not unaware that resolutely willed
individuals, steadfastly upholding the duty to escape, would
answer the urge to bolt whenever opportunity offered. With
the camp in darkness, the Germans were pretty sure that
some of the prisoners would be tackling the barbed wire: up,
over and away. But since the recent tunnel escape, Alsatian
dogs were released inside the wire. Two daring escapers
almost reached the wall of wire, but it was a clear night and
the well-trained dogs barked and bounded about them. At
such a time, unless the quarry stood stock still, hardly daring
to blink, the beasts would attack until called off by their
handlers.

The raid over, the camp was illuminated and roll-call
ordered. I lined up with the other prisoners who wore
British uniforms. I was stared at in amazement. 'Crikey,
what is it?' someone spluttered. 'It must have come down
with the bombs!' Eyes were popping at the sight of me in

clogs and fancy dress. 'Churchill sent me to cheer you bastards up!' I snapped.

A hundred or so Air Force prisoners were in the camp. I met Jock and was concerned by his worn appearance. Later in Germany his lungs played up, and badly so after the war. He was a great fellow, but he had had enough. As I have said, he had a wife and young children to think about and was not prepared to gamble with his life. Physical fitness, I was to discover, was vital for coping with the extraordinary hardships of the escape trail.

I was immensely relieved to be among Britishers again, but I was far from safe. Twice I was hauled to the Kommandant's office to face plain-clothes security officers and be asked if I had decided to talk about Dutch contacts and British naval landings on the coast of Holland. It was alarming to realize they had not let up. Had I known what was happening to friends in Holland, my sense of danger would have been so acute that it scarcely bears thinking about. So many whom I thought I was protecting were in fact doing the same for me but under far more fearsome stresses.

I met Wing Commander Bader who shared a room in one of the low, dreary huts with Lieutenant David Lubbock of the Fleet Air Arm. They were interested to meet me since various rumours and tales had drifted down the grapevine about a British agent who had drawn upon himself visits from the Gestapo and Luftwaffe Intelligence from Berlin. My admiration for Bader upon first acquaintance was immense, if some of his swashbuckling characteristics did not quite appeal to me. Such admiration was not of the gaping kind but for his mastery of physical disability, and the creed he ruthlessly preached and practised about escape. I played net-quoits with him on many occasions and soon realized his greatest gifts were a rare individualism and

courage. Despite the failure of the recent tunnel escape, and
the subsequent planting by the Germans of seismographs to
record the slightest earth tremors, a new tunnel was started
and I was one of those Bader set to work burrowing. It was a
strenuous, hazardous undertaking; digging and shifting the
black dirt demanded the greatest caution. The tunnel began
at a trapdoor below a bed in the centre of one of the huts
nearest the wire; Bader's job was to keep watch for
patrolling guards, and he spurred the tunnellers on with
intense energy; he wanted the tunnel completed before the
Germans whipped us off to some permanent camp deeper
inside Germany.

Our natural urge was to head west, or south to
Switzerland. Bader wanted my contacts in Holland. I
emphatically refused to give names and addresses, as I was
pledged. Some differences of temper between a wing
commander and a sergeant did occur, but I was not on a
Regular Air Force station now, with spit, polish, saluting and
bullshit. I was an independent operator and rank-pulling
was gone, as far as I was concerned. When the great time
arrived for the tunnel to pass beyond the wire, Bader wanted
me to piggy-back him up a pine-clad slope. I was none too
keen; my burning urge was to be up and away, fast, as a loner.
With the Gestapo all too eager to pounce, I knew I could
expect no gentlemanly treatment such as the famous and
admired Bader might have received if recaptured. As it
happened, Bader's own invincible nature spared me the
decision; he refused to salute Hauptmann Müller, his junior
in rank if claiming to be the Kommandant's representative.
Within the hour, Bader was on his way from Dulag Luft to
Oflag VIB at Lübeck, near the Baltic Sea. Then misfortune
struck at the tunnel; a German guard, stamping cold feet,
crashed through a section where it had risen close to the
surface to get over a large rock. Our only malicious joy was
in hearing howls from a guard with an injured leg. Our star

of hope hung very low as the Germans smashed our handiwork of long, tortuous hours.

Lieutenant David Lubbock had a remarkable ability for sleuthing and knew a great deal of what was going on behind the scenes at Dulag Luft. He alarmed me in revealing that a contingent of NCOs was listed to leave for Stalag VIIIB within a couple of weeks; my name was not included. Amazingly, Lubbock was also aware that Kommandant Rumpel was charitably inclined to getting me away from Gestapo pressures. This surprised me for Rumpel had never given me any impression of sympathy; but possibly, secretly, Rumpel's views of the Nazis and particularly the Gestapo were similar to those of his contemporaries, Lindermann and Gerhardt. Lubbock pointed out that the Kommandant had a peremptory right to remove obvious trouble-makers from his camp, and I should start kicking up hell to give a solid excuse for Rumpel to get me out early.

Forthwith, I became a proper bastard. I went around insulting the chaps, kicking them, throwing things, picking fights over trifles; even old Lubbock was at the receiving end, but he was able to explain to Rumpel that my moodiness and pugnacious behaviour were consistent with the head injuries and nervous condition for which I had been admitted to Dulag Luft hospital. I taunted the guards, made rude gestures and poked out my tongue; soon they were looking at me and saying '*Ganz verrückt*' (quite mad). As time was running out, I realized precious advantage might be lost. So I picked what was the most dishonourable fight of my life. I shared a ramshackle hut with various aircrew and a number of ground crew. The latter had been captured in Greece and imprisoned in the infamous 'Salonica' camp where conditions had been bad and sentries had treated them lower than animals. Most had suffered dysentery and were still in a deteriorated condition; clearly no match in a hell-for-leather fisticuffs which was what I decided was necessary to put me beyond the pale as a trouble-maker.

Then circumstances seemed to offer the right challenge. It arose over the touchy business of sharing out food and impulsively I made an accusation to an ex-Spitfire pilot; he flew at my challenge to come outside and settle the issue. I shall call him 'Hunt', in truth a man of ardent spirit, splendid physique and equal to the best in defence of honour and integrity. We were a match in weight. I thought I'd slay him; but I couldn't and he wouldn't give in. Rightly, he was as mad as hell. For almost an hour, on and off, we fought, bare-fisted in the open, close to one of the guard towers. Prisoners gathered; Germans watching thought it the greatest sport, a portent for disintegration of the British Empire with Englishman fighting Englishman. Rumpel demanded an immediate report and next thing I knew, I was on the list. Unknowingly, Hunt sped me on my way, his parting gift to me, two glorious black eyes, bruised face, split and swollen lips. I thought all my teeth would drop out.

We marched to a small railway station – about twenty captives, one barely able to see through eyes that were slits, and still in clogs, football socks with blue and red striped tops, damned pantaloons and Polish jacket, but at least a presentable RAF greatcoat. Herded into a foul-smelling cattle truck, for three days we jolted and clattered at the tail of a slow train. I lay on the straw on the floor. Each of us had a ration of sausage, a loaf of bread and flask of water, occasionally refilled. My mouth was so swollen I could hardly chew, but as we rolled ever eastwards, fears began to fall away. Nearness to Holland and home was receding but so too was the likelihood of being snatched back to the Gestapo. Some play of my senses touched upon the urgency to escape. I thought of my Dutch resistance friends who had schemed to the smallest detail. Like them, I would have to apply every atom of intelligence and energy; planning was my only road to possible freedom, never forgetting that in all undercover operations quick death was always a measurable distance away. I had to steel myself to such a prospect, erase thought of an alternative life and any self-sympathy; forget the past, or future dreams. I had to encapsulate myself in the hard reality of my present war.

# CHAPTER 8
## Plotting Escape

At Lamsdorf, Stalag VIIIB was despondently situated on a barren, far-reaching Silesian plain, an immense camp then holding about 17,000 various British and Dominion troops, captured in Greece and Crete, but the majority at Dunkirk. This 'Hell Camp', not lightly so-named, was boxed in by four high walls of barbed wire, each about a quarter of a mile long, and spaced apart on stilt legs were sentry boxes with menacing electric machine-guns. The RAF compound, a prison within a prison, was a wired-off section within the huge camp. This closely-guarded, inner enclave housed about 500 NCO fliers. Rated as top security risks, they were prevented from mixing even with the British soldiers. I entered the double cage with sinking spirits; prospects of getting out seemed very thin. The other newcomers were disillusioned, judging from their profanities, yet the spark of my determination somehow to plan a break-out refused to be snuffed. The alternative, for God knew how many years with the Germans winning the war hands down, was progressive malnutrition and helpless acquiescence to the moods of a cocksure and ruthless enemy.

The barrack blocks were overcrowded, each packed with three-tier bunks to accommodate about 180 men. Given a palliasse stuffed with wood shavings, I occupied a bottom bunk, my covering being one and a half miserable blankets manufactured with a high percentage of wood fibre; it was impossible to sleep snugly. How cold it was! The barracks were not heated, neither had we winter clothing. A piercing wind blew over the plain and before Christmas ice began to creep into our veins; beyond the wire there was nothing but long, white miles all around. Precious few Red Cross parcels were reaching the camp and when they did it was a case of one food parcel between two men. Basically, we subsisted on 350 grams of sawdusty black bread and a litre of watery cabbage soup daily.

I was escorted to face the camp security officers on a number of occasions, accused of being a trouble-maker and warned I would be kept under vigilant observation. Even yet, I had not Red Cross POW recognition and I was beginning to suspect a continuing tactic, with these security officers now anxious to knock nails in my coffin. But, presently, unexpected success came my way, the best Christmas present I ever received. I was summoned before the Kommandant, a man of calm demeanour who reminded me of my Uncle Jim of York. My fate was no longer in the balance; the unbearable suspense over, I was officially a British POW. It was a tremendous relief knowing that my family and friends would at last be informed by the Red Cross in Geneva that I was alive. My POW number was 24463, but the greatest shot in the arm was to shed my one-man-army uniform for British battle-dress, boots and socks, and acquire a Red Cross razor, toothbrush and paste. Funny, how one remembers little things: when I handed over the French pantaloons, Dutch clogs and Polish jacket, the storeman guffawed, 'Where the hell did you get this lot! I'll give them to the show group for its costume collection.'

Now, under Red Cross sanction entitled to escape, imagination was stimulated; day in, day out, my mind spun with ideas until slowly a feasible plan pushed itself forward. Innumerable problems had first to be overcome. The weather was atrocious but this was the time to begin preparation for a disappearing act with the arrival of spring. I was determined to follow my own conscience, instincts and reasoning; choose my own course, revealing nothing of my intentions to the 'X' (escape) committee. Confessedly and intentionally, during my war years in Europe, I avoided POW escape committees with their close-knit strength and co-ordinated planning. Such committees can certainly be credited with remarkably bold and efficient results but my nature impelled me to head on an essentially solitary course. At times, however, I was to be immensely indebted to 'X' committees for their support and, at other times, I was able to give them my assistance.

I decided to discuss my plans with a small coterie of Poles who had my regard. Henryk Kowalski at the Dulag Luft hospital had given me a letter of introduction to one of his colleagues; this brought me into the circle of Polish airmen, who numbered perhaps a dozen in the RAF compound of Stalag VIIIB. They rallied round and made me feel at home in their company. They were acutely alert individuals, candid, tough and dependable. I struck up a close acquaintance with Mieczyslaw Borodej, whom I call 'Mieteck'; he had been shot down after a raid on Hanover.

The German camp authorities had small respect for the Polish airmen who had cheated being roped in after the conquest of their country. But having found their way to Britain and enlisted in the British forces, much to the chagrin of the Germans, they were entitled to the same facilities and protection as the rest of us. It was agonizing for the Poles to be imprisoned on their own doorstep. The security officers realized that the yearning to escape must burn excruciatingly in the Polish hearts and sought to counter any escape ambitions by dire threats. The Poles were warned that if any one of them attempted escape, reprisals on the remainder would be swift and severe. Irrespective of any Red Cross nonsense or intervention, they would be deported to a military prison or concentration camp to undergo the process of prolonged misery, moving through stages of forced labour, slavery, malnutrition and starvation, concluding of course with annihilation. The Poles were left with no alternative but to stand as one in self-sacrifice, bound by a sacred agreement to which each pledged his oath not to embark on individual escape. Like Damocles, they existed under an awesome threat, lest any one of their number ceased to present himself for twice-daily *Appell*, a roll-call by count.

From within the massive soldier compound of VIIIB prisoners, the Germans organized working groups to be sent outside to labour on the land, in factories and coalmines. Under the Geneva Convention, officers and NCOs were immune from such labour – which was all very fine, but from where we were in the RAF compound the only way to the outside world was through two heavily guarded cages. I dreamed and cared only about escape, so I explained my plan to my Polish friends and my inflexible resolution to make eastwards for Poland to reach the Polish underground if I could make a break from a working party. The Poles agreed that the idea was bold and feasible but sensibly they pointed out that any private soldier prepared to be my stand-in had to be a man not likely to quit and leave me in the muck. It could impose a tremendous strain on him to leave his soldiering mates and adjust, for God knew how long, in the unfamiliar society of flying men. The Poles promised they would stand by any such man. But there were further very practical considerations. If I took a soldier's place in the Army compound, it might be some time before I was detailed for a work party outside. During that time, I would be sending letters in my handwriting to my people, but as a soldier with new name, rank and number. Similarly, my substitute would be sending letters in his hand to his people, but having suddenly become Sergeant Richard Pape of the RAF. We would be receiving each other's quarterly clothing and cigarette parcels from home. If either of us let something slip in his messages, or if next of kin queried or expressed alarm, keen-eyed German censors might pick it up and start probing. The subterfuges were unlikely to endure unless aided and controlled by British sources of Intelligence, completely in the know to be able to provide protective co-operation.

More unpalatable truths were forthcoming. I would hardly be likely to survive Poland's winter conditions; to escape before spring came around would be tantamount to suicide. I had to learn more Polish expressions if I expected to attract help from Polish civilians; even if they were able to comprehend appeals made in German or English, they could not be expected to believe tales about being a Britisher on the run. It was too tall a story; I would be considered a German stooge and my fate would be swift and sure. I learned that anyone not in uniform was at once suspect by German patrols on every road, curfews were enforced, and in open country wolf packs had grown and roamed at large, particularly at night. Further, my red hair would be taken as identifying me as Jewish and thousands of Jews were being confined to the Warsaw ghetto or transported to a recently opened camp at Auschwitz.

Proximity to the Polish underground outweighed, in my mind, the alternative of using my knowledge of German to escape perhaps to Sweden or Switzerland. Remembering Holland and, in particular, the vital protection afforded Jock and myself by de Neve and Van der Leek at Schiphol, it became clear that the only possibility of success lay in having a trustworthy Pole with me as mouthpiece, interpreter, guide and companion. I could not allow my plan to become a shattered dream.

The thought struck like a revelation one long winter's night when I writhed on my cold bunk in the squalor of the barrack block. Subject to finding a soldier to become me, supposing I could find another to replace Mieteck, so he might accompany me? I broached the idea to the Poles and

was surprised and stirred by their ready acceptance, their
assurances to act as a mouthpiece for a soldier in their midst
and protect him as one of their own. That fraternity of
Polish airmen was an unforgettable study for its recognition
of the obligation to get one of its number back on home soil,
free, and able to act against the enemy if he came under the
wing of the underground. It would more than compensate
for the others' enforced frustration if I could enable
Mieteck to continue the fight against their conquerors. No
loss, they told me, compared to the agony of losing one's
country. The Poles, all Roman Catholics, promised to apply
their prayers to the dangerous task ahead in a spirit of
patriotism and faith.

A raging snowstorm swept the camp late one evening;
wind was something of hurricane velocity, knocking askew
upright timbers supporting miles of barbed wire. Deep
snowdrifts built up at the base of the wire walls and the
Germans were quick to organize working parties to repair
the posts and sagging wire. The blizzard proved a blessing as
far as I was concerned. Next morning, a dozen British
soldiers and two guards entered the RAF compound to
repair the fence and clear the drifts which had buried even
the warning wires inside the main barricades. Anyone
touching or passing beyond the warning wire was liable to be
shot out of hand. At the sight of the soldiers, the idea
flashed into my mind to act quickly. It took little time to
persuade a soldier to slip away from the hard, cold work and
remain concealed in my barrack while I worked in his place,
shovelling snow, tugging and heaving to realign the posts.
Working alongside me was a New Zealand soldier, Private
Winston Mearil Yeatman.

After fighting in North Africa, Yeatman had been
captured in Crete and sent to Stalag VIIIB, soon to be put to
labouring on sugar beet in Poland. Sickness had brought him
back to the parent camp for a spell of lighter work. A man of

quiet disposition, a hardened soldier, Yeatman had a lively intelligence. I revealed to him my ideas for a foursome swap and my ultimate escape with a Pole. Yeatman doubted if anyone would take on a foreign identity – he wouldn't – but he showed interest in becoming an English airman NCO and not subject to hard labour. Obviously, nothing could be thrashed out under conditions of our present meeting but I was prepared to risk getting through the wire to visit his barrack at night, if swirling snow offered concealment.

Realizing I was determined, Yeatman introduced me to a wiry little English corporal who had been wounded at Dunkirk and walked with a limp. He belonged to a permanent work party on maintenance of the barbed-wire barricades throughout Stalag VIIIB, under a German overseer who had a mistaken trust in him. He came from Liverpool and was nicknamed 'Mickey Mouse'. He was a natural-born racketeer, but a good-humoured one, a wire-wriggler adept at robbing the German bread and potato stores. 'You can't waft through wire like a bloody phantom,' Mickey Mouse said. 'I'll show you what you do.' The guards were warming themselves at a brazier some distance away as I trailed Mickey Mouse to the most suitable spot nearest the road leading to Yeatman's barrack. Prising open staples on a post, he put his full weight on the two lower wire strands causing them to sag; the slackness gave a few inches spare. He snipped and restored the lengthened ends under the staples which he tapped back just sufficiently to make the wire look taut. I would be able to pull the wires free to provide a gap, enough to wriggle through: on the way back, I would reattach them.

The repair work was unfinished and was to resume next day, so I took up Yeatman's suggestion and remained one of the small squad of soldiers who tramped through the compound gate with airy flakes of snow falling over us. Mieteck looked after the soldier who took my place at roll-call and slept in my bunk. The majority of men in Yeatman's barrack were British Tommies, captives since Dunkirk and recently returned to VIIIB from outside working parties because of winter conditions; they were awaiting reallocation to factories or coal-mines. I played my cards badly when appealing to them for stand-ins for myself and a Pole, basing my argument on patriotism, duty to escape and honour to Poland as the first nation to stand up against the Germans. One man who had lost three fingers at Dunkirk was bitterly vociferous in condemnation of the RAF. 'Where were you Brylcreem boys when we were being blasted on the beaches?' My escape ideas were ridiculed and I was told to get back to my compound and not come begging for soldiers to make sacrifices. They were not prepared to trifle with their Red Cross recognition. Supposing the Pole and I were caught and shot? What would happen to the stand-ins who had disowned their true names, ranks and numbers, and particularly the one who had taken the identity of a foreigner? Could he not become irretrievably lost and forgotten?

That night out was a grim and unrewarding experience. I was glad to return to the RAF compound but I was determined to keep on trying. On the last day for the Army party to appear inside my compound, I again chose to work with Yeatman. There were other barracks beside Yeatman's which were the transit quarters for working parties and I was determined to visit them, even though wire-wriggling was necessary. Then Yeatman told me of two large work groups of New Zealanders due back; he would comb through them and, provided he could find one to swap with Mieteck, he was prepared to become me! He insisted the other fellow must be a Kiwi. To cut the risk of unnecessary wire-wriggling, he would get a message to me via a medical orderly when the Dunkirk diehards had gone outside again and the Kiwis were back. I was surprised and excited by

Yeatman's sincerity. I shook his hand firmly and watched as his party marched off, their boots crunching in the snow. My morale had revived.

In all, I made six trips to the soldiers' barrack. The weather was always frightful and Mieteck maintained vigil until I was safely back through the wire. My first wire-wriggle in darkness was carried out with camp searchlights vainly attempting to slash the whirling screen of falling snow. Confidence and adroitness grew with each visit; a human being can take only so much dosage of fear at certain times of life-and-death crisis, after which it's 'so what'. The in-between period of waiting for the right conditions proved the nightmare. Understandably, the men shied off when Yeatman tried to find a New Zealander prepared to become a Pole. I suppose they saw me as a study of obsessional behaviour. Only one man was wavering on the line of acceptance. He was an artilleryman, George Potter, a man of guts, strong of will and hard of sense, but Yeatman explained that incentives beyond immunity from labour were sorely needed; and he reminded me of my red hair if he swapped with me. My hair again!

Other events, tragic and ghastly, which struck the camp, were ironically to serve the escape plan. A British airman was murdered by an arch-fiend of a guard whom we called Ukraine Joe. The airman had moved beyond the warning wire to collect a piece of wood left by a working party . . . he sought it to brew his tea. His ruthless shooting sent a mass wave of emotion through the compound. German vigilance increased even to releasing dogs in the compound after dark. This, together with the cessation of snowstorms, made movement through the wire out of the question. To control disappointment, I set about constructing a code for communicating with Britain, knowing full well that if my coding activities were discovered by the Germans, I too would be shot without argument.

My first coded letters left Stalag VIIIB in January 1942. Initially, I adopted the racing codes which I had learned on my newspapers, sending my first messages off to my former chief, Alfred Willcox, head of the Publications and Publicity Department of *The Yorkshire Post*. He was to be my vital intermediary. My first coded information was masked in feeble humdrum accounts in which I nostalgically referred to our jolly racing days with that dear old friend, A. G. Thompson, who was real enough, our newspaper's renowned tipster known as 'The Duke' to a vast following of Yorkshire racegoers. I also acquired some two dozen, German-issue, letter forms from the Poles and other friends and had them write, in their hands, seemingly innocuous letters which I compiled. These letters would be tracked down from details I sent to Willcox. I felt it essential to outline past, present and possible future happenings in one complete introduction; also to advise of immediate steps to be taken if he received a letter in my handwriting but signed 'Winston' and the flap stating the sender as Sapper W. M. Yeatman, No. 32252, 5th Field Company, NZEF, POW No. 7490. Willcox latched on. It was a great thrill and relief to receive his letter which when decoded said the racing code was understood and to be careful.

That January also saw the arrival of big batches of Russian prisoners of war to occupy their own compounds adjacent to the British enclosure. They were a pitiful sight, shivering in rags, starved, filthy, dazed-looking, and many barefooted; the cold must have made every step a hideous agony. No Red Cross protection covered them, and no food other than German rations came their way. The arrival of this wretchedness from the Eastern Front brought with it body lice. A typhus epidemic struck the entire camp. Russians died off in large numbers; British and Allied prisoners also succumbed, and the German guards were not immune. When the epidemic went beyond the camp to strike at civilian communities for miles around, the authorities really panicked. Desperate measures were initiated to stamp out the pestilence by ordering all prisoners to remove the hair on their heads and bodies where lice laid eggs to hatch under the warmth of body temperature. There was no opposition; every man welcomed being sheared and shaved, for in every prisoner's mind was a persistent fear of being marked down . . . first the headache, then the eruption of purple spots, great prostration, delirium and death. My red hair fell to German electric shears, and a free issue of razor blades ensured craniums looked as bald as eggs. Yeatman's darkish hair also disappeared. For a time the entire Stalag was put in quarantine, portable delousers were brought in and each barrack fumigated; compounds were locked, no working parties left, and none on the outside was allowed to return.

When surging snowstorms again visited the vast plain, the working party compound being locked presented no problem, for Mickey Mouse had doctored the wire in various places. I made my way to Yeatman's barrack and could hardly believe my ears when he told me George Potter was prepared to become a Pole. There were conditions: a document must be lodged with the stalag camp leader, Sergeant-Major Sheriff of a Welsh regiment, a splendid character appointed leader by the prisoners and respected by the Germans. The document was to record full details of the four of us to enable the two Kiwis, through someone of authority, to re-establish their identities if, as Potter put it, 'the roof suddenly falls in'. I was in full accord, for I was all too conscious that Yeatman would be inheriting my German file. And the Gestapo, if infuriated by the trickery, were capable of retaliating in their own dehumanized way and, wilfully treating Potter as a Pole, dispatching him to a concentration camp. Potter also required that the Polish coterie confirm in writing unswerving commitment to stand by him in all circumstances. I promised that the documents would be delivered by Captain Spencer, an RAMC doctor who was regularly touring the varous compounds with a German doctor, Schmidt. I had come to know Captain Spencer reasonably well, revealing to him something of my plans, and he offered to act as courier whenever needed.

In turn, I required the two soldiers to set down their personal histories, as would Mieteck and I, for each of us in a new role would have a deal to commit to memory to be able to give a snap answer if put to the test by interrogators. Foolishly, I prolonged my stay that evening in Yeatman's barrack and committed a blunder in failing to keep track of the weather. When I left for my compound, I found the heavily falling snow had given way to light flakes and extended visibility. As usual, I kept low as I moved along a deep ditch at the roadside. I let myself through the barbed wire, reset the strands and was about to move towards the warning wire on the snow-swathed surface when a shapeless figure loomed through the thin veil of snowflakes. It was a guard, silently treading his round. I was spotted and to my dismay and horror, pistol in hand, he bounded towards me.

To this day, I have a vivid impression of the toe of a jackboot crunching into my face. I screamed, '*Lassen Sie mich vorbei!*' (Let me pass!). A group of RAF men, exercising not far away to get warm, unaware of my departure and re-entry, heard my scream. I yelled to them, 'For Christ's sake, stop him, I'm Pape!' They reacted like maddened hounds to attract attention to themselves while I continued to the guard, in German, 'Leave me alone, you have made a mistake!' In nervous indecision, he ceased hacking at my face, turning his attention to the frantic antics of the others. Mieteck assisted me to the barrack. It was a very narrow squeak, but no suspicion was roused about tampering with the wire.

It took some time for my face to heal but meanwhile the weather cleared and wire-wriggling was out. The required documents were exchanged through the medium of Captain Spencer and the explanatory document of the exchange of identities was with the camp leader, Sheriff. Suddenly and much to my delight, a blizzard swept across the plain and the searchlights rebounded like ghosts of another world off the swirling snow. One more wire-wriggle was essential to arrange the physical change-over. I went through the wire and returned like a phantom, with the switch-over settled for next morning.

Breakfast consisted of about 350 ml of atrocious liquid called mint tea but at least hot, useful for shaving and washing lice-ridden shirts. At 6.15 every morning, four airmen with a guard left our compound to collect two dustbins of the stuff from a central kitchen. The Germans never allowed too many carrying parties to assemble at the same time; the RAF went first and, with much scheming, it was arranged that Yeatman's party would arrive while we were having our bins filled. With scarves about our heads, and faces partially concealed in the below-freezing weather, Mieteck and I, with two Poles, moved off with our dustbins. One of the bins was filled and the second half-filled when I whispered to Mieteck, 'Where the hell are they? Tell Jozef to go ahead anyway.' Jozef, one of the Poles, unflinchingly passed his hand under the scalding, gushing liquid. Screaming madly, he lurched away from us as Yeatman's party, four New Zealanders, approached, marching up close to us despite a command to halt. Our guard was staring at the writhing Jozef; the guard with the soldiers' party, doing the decent thing, went across to Jozef. In a flash, Mieteck and I changed places with Yeatman and Potter. We marched away with the tea bins to the soldiers' compound, exhilarated by success.

In the battle of wits against the enemy, much had been accomplished in two months. Without delay, I wrote to Willcox identifying myself as Winston Yeatman, the signal for him to alert Intelligence authorities. In fact, MI9 was the appropriate authority, the British escape and Intelligence service founded by the War Office on the basis of belief that prisoners of war have considerable military potential, a belief which proved true.* Time was on my side, for the typhus epidemic still raged and no working parties were being sent out. When the moment arrived for Mieteck and me to leave the parent stalag, an unbridgeable gulf would open up. Upon Willcox's instigation, British and New Zealand Intelligence Departments acted quickly. The War Office assumed responsibility for all necessary to protect our interests. Intelligence experts called upon our closest next of kin and tutored them in procedures to be adopted. Adhering to secrecy, the kinsfolk had to be content with the barest information and assurances that in some specific way we were serving our countries. Frightening and frustrating as it was for them to be kept in the dark for some years, all involved obeyed instructions in the overriding desire to shield their sons. My mother received a letter from G. T. H. Rogers of the War Office:

In the interests of both individuals it is important that the enemy should not become aware of the exchange, and you are requested to write to Sgt R. B. Pape in the name of Pte Yeatman. No enquiries by letter or otherwise should be made.

Quarterly parcels should be addressed in the same way as letters and postcards. To facilitate this the British Red Cross Society, Prisoner of War Department, have been made aware of this exchange of identity and they will ensure that no confusion arises in the packing centre.

In matters of this kind the greatest discretion should be observed and it is suggested that the facts should not be discussed even among your friends . . .

* See *MI9 – Escape and Evasion 1939-1945*, by M. R. O. Foot and J. M. Langley, Bodley Head, London, 1979.

Another letter marked 'Most Secret' was received by my mother from Major L. Winterbottom of the War Office:

We quite understand, that in a matter such as this, you may wish to make sure you are dealing with the proper authority. If you are in any doubt as to the genuineness of the above address you can telephone the WAR OFFICE (Whitehall 9400) and ask for Major Winterbottom, Extension 1296, or get in touch with the local police. We ask you, however, on no account to disclose the nature of this letter to anyone with the exception of the police . . .

After the war it was revealed to me that letters which my mother and close kin had posted to me were intercepted by Intelligence, and the same procedure was applied to those closest to Yeatman and Potter in New Zealand. If our kin had unwittingly yawed from instructions, or spoken carelessly to outsiders, setback or disaster might have resulted for those playing their secret roles in far-away Germany. Not even my two sisters knew the mystery of my case and when I eventually met Yeatman's family in Christchurch, New Zealand, I learned that his mother had kept other members of his family in total ignorance about the reasons for his bewildering promotion to a sergeant navigator in the Royal Air Force.

I did not reveal to Yeatman or Potter that I was in secret communication with Britain. However, I felt compelled to reassure them; I told them a secret radio existed and full details of the swap-overs had been relayed to Britain, and their families had been briefed how to act. To give added scope for coding, I hit upon the idea of making Miss Lilian Rowe my 'wife'. Lilian, a capable and experienced newspaper woman, was responsible for planning *The Leeds Mercury* tours, especially those to various Continental countries; she must have had something of a shock when her former underling at the paper, some thirty years her junior, addressed her as 'My darling, beloved wife' followed by outpourings of sentiment and promises to let her have as many babies as she wanted in happy times when we could be reunited. I told her to rely on our friendship with Willcox, knowing she would recognize my handwriting and have the sense to confer with Alfred. I was thrilled when I received a letter from her as 'Mrs W. M. Yeatman'. She wrote as a pining wife and joyful at the prospects of lots of lovely babies after the nasty war. She must have wondered what sort of miracle she was expected to perform at her age. She and Willcox became charged with a trust upon which my life depended, and my secret was closely guarded. In a short time we devised a far more ingenious and secure code. Love-sick mush and gush lent scope; it may have disgusted hard-bitten German censors and crypt-analysts, but the concealed danger to them was never divined. Well in excess of a hundred messages were sent through Lilian and Willcox in a period of over two and a half years as information came to me from various sources throughout Germany, from different camps, and observant POWs sent out on working parties. Always, information from on the ground was vital to Britain, on enemy troop concentrations and movements, strategic targets and the effectiveness of Allied bombing. When, for instance, knowledge came to me of an oil pipeline being hurriedly constructed direct into Germany from Romanian oilfields, this information was sent through with advice where aircraft, flying from the Middle East, should bomb close to the construction base. In turn, too, I received requests from Britain to obtain particular information. When I reached home in 1944 and faced Willcox and Lilian, he jovially remarked that we had better get on with the baby-producing business! Lilian blushed, red as a beetroot. I was bloody embarrassed myself. Then we all had a hearty laugh.

For a time after the swap-over, my mail continued to arrive at the RAF compound and was smuggled to me by Captain Spencer on his medical rounds. A day in February sticks in my mind, a day of blizzard and hailstones hammering on the barrack. Spencer brought me a letter from an RAF padre. What I read left me dazed and mortified. Blondie had been killed in a bombing raid on London. My world might have collapsed, but I had to ride out this bitter blow, get myself in timing with immediate difficulties and try to look at them without wasteful tensions. Experience in Holland had opened my eyes to Nazi ruthlessness, creating an intense hatred, and now there was a new dimension to this hate. I was restless for vengeance and determined to take advantage of every dirty trick and cunning act in the trade of war. Mieteck did much to prevent grief turning to despair. A fervent Catholic, a fierce patriot and equally loyal ally, he had an absolute conviction – which he attributed to divine direction – that there were big things meant for us to do and, in his mind, our achievement to date was bearing this out. I didn't argue with him, not at this stage, but I determined that hereafter I would act according to my own lights, and to hell with God, man and the devil.

Before the typhus epidemic and the sealing off of the entire stalag, detachments of Russian prisoners had frequently been observed staggering towards the adjacent Soviet camp or wandering inside their enclosure. With the advent of the contagion, a puzzling silence clamped down and they were rarely seen. Shocking rumours began to circulate about their sub-human conditions – 'sub-human' was what the Germans considered them to be – and the many being carted away at night for burial in mass graves. Some were still breathing when flung into the pits and delirious brains energized strange, submerged sounds as lime was sprayed over the bodies and the holes filled in: bulldozers swept away all evidence of the burial grounds. Initially, the Russians buried their own, including the many who threw themselves into the pits. If we had not witnessed these horrors, we learned of them from a German guard, Knut, recently assigned to our compound. Knut (known as 'Nuts') was a simple type of soldier aged about thirty-five, wounded in the stomach after the capture of Kiev and, like many Germans seriously wounded, reclassified for guard duties. He told us that when the Russians became too broken-down to handle the burial task with the speed the authorities demanded, German guards had been forced to take over. They may have become hardened to burial procedures on the Eastern Front, but nevertheless had displayed spirited opposition to burying the lousy allies of the British and queried why some of the hundreds of British soldiers were not pitching their Russian comrades-in-arms into the pits; after all, the Russians had been doing the Britishers' fighting for them. For some reason best known to German military authorities, this was not a line they wished to take, not until almost the end of the epidemic.

Knut disclosed that some of the guards were charged with disobedience when cannibalism was discovered. Obnoxious but true, when a large, black covering over corpses was removed it was revealed that buttock regions of some of the dead had been carved off. Knut broke into a cold sweat as he described what he saw . . . and he had seen it before, in the Ukraine, in isolated villages where war and pillage had left an already destitute people with utter nothingness. I encouraged him to talk. He liked to, but never about Kiev; he would clam up and sweaty fear would smudge his face. I attributed this to bad memories of battle, but today I wonder if he had witnessed, or perforce had played some nauseating part in, the massacre of 70,000 Jews in September 1941 in the sand-quarry ravine, Babi Yar, outside Kiev. He would have been there at the time. Certainly something seemed to trouble his very soul; he was not a violent man, indeed his nature was kindly, and he was no ardent Nazi.

When we learned from Knut that his sister worked in a

film-producing laboratory, we quickly brought him under graft and blackmailed him for accepting gifts of Red Cross tea and soap, of which we held a reserve for just such purposes. Knut smuggled to us German newspapers and rolls of film for use in secret cameras. Many photos were shot of the Russians in their dreadful misery and of certain brutal guards such as Unteroffizier (corporal) Kussel, alias 'Ukraine Joe'. The negatives were smuggled back to the War Office in the boot-heel of a medically repatriated prisoner. After the war, Ukraine Joe was brought to trial at Nuremberg for the murder of several Britishers at Stalag VIIIB and, I understand, was executed.

One morning, three guards and a one-armed German officer tramped into our barrack. Everyone stood silently to attention as the officer gave, in fluent English, one of the frequent *Spiels* on such topics as our obligations as prisoners and how much the Germans were doing for us; the epidemic was coming under control and working parties would soon be going outside again. Then came the real purpose of the visit: six men were to volunteer to assist in burying the Russian dead. Understandably, no one stepped forward. Our barrack commander, looking insulted, shook his head when asked to nominate six. The German officer, slowly walking before us, stopped, jabbed a man with his pistol. 'You. Move!' Then a second, a third, I was fourth, and two others.

Our breaths white in the cold air, we climbed into a long, open lorry already holding a dozen Germans in overalls, a portable delouser and what proved to be two lime-spraying pumps. We rattled to the Russian compound and stopped at a barrack wired-off from the rest. Inside, bodies were accumulated, stripped and fumigated to kill off lurking lice; most were naked but sacking had been wrapped around the middles of a few. The hideous thought swept through my mind: 'This is where pieces of men have been eaten.' Along the gloomy, lonely length of the building, corpses lay on the concrete; the stench was frightening, a combination of gangrenous wounds, diseased flesh in decay, and fumigation. I seemed to be invisibly connected to these pathetic white remains, horribly ravaged by starvation. But there was little time for introspection; everything had to be taken almost at the run; all was action and noise, incessant German yelling, perhaps good for them to talk and yell to let loose their pent-up feelings.

Here we were seeing a result of the USSR's not recognizing the International Red Cross; it meant the USSR accepted no obligations in the treatment of prisoners of war, nor the giving of help to its own soldiers who had been captured. We obeyed mechanically; subjugated and quivering, we dragged corpses to the open where emaciated Russians loaded them into V-shaped, ox-drawn wagons. A squat *Feldwebel*, waggling a sub-machine-gun, repeatedly bawled, '*Schnell, wir haben es eilig.*' (Quickly, we are in a hurry.) On one of my sweating returns to the open air, after depositing a corpse full of scabs, I paused against the wagon. The fat *Feldwebel* screamed, '*Lauf, lauf!*' (Run, run!) and turning, I called him a filthy bastard. A Russian worker raked up a smile, said something to the German, and waved a withered hand almost in gratitude that someone in a lost world had compassionate anger. Whatever merest joy I brought to that forsaken Russian lasted only a moment, for the *Feldwebel* opened fire and killed him. A German soldier, almost a boy, ceased scratching in a notebook and looked up, calm as a tally clerk in an abattoir. Alongside me, a tough little Welsh coal-miner spat lustily and muttered, 'What a bleedin' luxury to die decently in bed one day.' Memory flashed to Britain. 'God,' I thought, 'if it could only be brought home to them what these Nazi bastards are capable of, these sights, these sounds . . . their determination to oppose any German invasion of our homeland would be a

hundred times more infused with desperate resolve and
energy . . . and to conquer these so-called unconquerable
inhumans!'

The death-barrack was sealed and fumigators set in
action. We moved to wash-houses at the ends of other
barracks and loaded a few more bodies. I was startled to
observe some showing twitching life and I shouted to the
*Feldwebel* whose only response was to tell me to mind my
own business – which I did, as there was no point in leaving
my bones in that terrible place, in a gesture for men past
saving anyway. The wagons traversed the snow for about
three miles and we tramped in their wake to a newly
excavated hole. The bodies were slung in; the pumping
machines swished an emulsion of lime. Not far away, on the
white plain, 'Tiger' tanks were carrying out training
manoeuvres. It suggested the beginning and the end.

On the three occasions when the six of us acted as
undertakers, the Germans fulfilled their promise to return
us to our barrack thoroughly deloused, clean as new pins
after hot showers and sprayed with disinfectant. In some
odd way it was macabre compensation, a most satisfying gift
from the Soviet dead.

Our barrack commander, a sergeant, was aware of the
foursome change of identity and, indeed, more than once
had to tell suspicious men to leave us alone. Mieteck could
never pass as a Kiwi and, naturally, the soldiers were
questioning, for it was well known that the Germans
habitually planted stooges among the prisoners. One of the
duties of the barrack commander was to select men for
working parties and he knew that Mieteck and I, being
prepared to forgo the relative comforts afforded fliers in
their special *Lagers*, were now looking to him for assistance
in getting us off German soil and into Poland as working
party soldiers.

# CHAPTER 9
## A Polish Coal-mine

Bad luck for others proved our incredibly swift, good fortune. When four British soldiers working in the Hohenzollern coal-mine were injured and removed to hospital, the Germans demanded immediate replacements. Our barrack commander was as excited as we, for the mine, over a hundred miles away to the south-east, was at Beuthen, Upper Silesia, just inside Poland. Normally he called for volunteers, but few offered for dangerous work in the coal-mines; his practice then was to nominate, knowing that otherwise, as with the burial party, the Germans would arbitrarily select. This time he had two enthusiastic volunteers, even though I felt a certain trepidation about coal-mining; the other two he chose deliberately as being unable to converse reliably in English and so not to worry us with conversation. One was a big Turk, known as 'Johnny', a soldier of fortune captured in Crete. He cared not a damn about coal-heaving or anything else. The other was a skinny, weasle-looking Greek, nicknamed 'Electricity', who threatened to commit suicide before he would die in the bowels of the earth; but the barrack commander brooked no nonsense.

Before we left next morning, I completed a number of letter-forms in code, advising Britain of my destination and purpose. It was mid-February 1942, and snowing, when the four of us, with one armed guard, marched through the big gate; probably we were first to leave since the typhus epidemic but of the 19,000 prisoners now in the stalag, within a few weeks more than 14,000 would be assigned to labour groups, playing their compulsory part, along with millions of other foreigners (forced and slave labourers), in keeping Germany's industrial war machine running.

At the local station, Annaberg, we entrained for nearby Breslau on the Oder, capital of Lower Silesia. Breslau's central station teemed with troops and while we awaited our connection to Katowice a series of trains arrived disgorging thousands of German uniformed men. A solitary thought dominated my mind, 'What a target for low-level attack!' I felt nothing for these soldiers as men, nothing but a loathsome presence against me; over and over my mind went back to VIIIB, the typhus, the dead and dying Russians; these German soldiers were bound for the Eastern Front to kill and capture and start that whole horrible cycle over again. An air raid such as I had in mind was impossible in 1942. Three years later, however, two-thirds of Breslau were to lie in ruins, and during a nine-week siege a thousand times more Germans than I beheld at that railway station were bombed out of existence.

For the present, however, to the smartly turned-out soldiers we must have looked an odd assortment. Johnny Turk was so tall, his head so overtopped everyone, that many turned to stare. 'Move on, please,' our elderly guard kept repeating. Johnny lived in a world of his own; one of perpetual merriment. He had thick lips, a grinning, granite-like face, the chest of a prize fighter, and an irritating habit of spitting into his outstretched hand. Electricity, the scrawny Greek, was jockey sized, reptilian-looking, with bulging eyes blinking incessantly. Mieteck and I were average enough, I suppose, but we all had bald heads. An army corporal, quite tipsy, stood and stared. What zoo did we come from, he asked? 'British prisoners of war,' growled the guard. The boozy one almost yelled, *'Wir müssen die Engländer schlagen!'* (We must beat the English!). I was livid. Giving the victory 'V' sign, I said, vehemently, *'Betrunken* (drunken) *Idiot!'* and followed up in English, 'Fuck off, you

square-headed Nazi bastard!' The guard prodded my middle
with his sub-machine-gun. A white-faced Mieteck cautioned
silence and control. He was right. I guessed his thinking:
now it was Poland and a new phase. Luck had brought us
this far in one leopard spring; I had to keep my temper no
matter what the taunting or humiliation.

Katowice on the Upper Silesian Plateau also owned a
central railway station filled with jostling, uniformed
Germans, and here I first witnessed Nazi brutality against
the Jewish race. Whistles shrilled, the crowd parted and a
straggling contingent of about a hundred Jews passed,
goaded by SS thugs, some cracking whips. I felt a rush of
swollen emotions, not only that the unshaven, ragged
individuals were herded like animals, but each was 'branded'
on back and front by a large Star of David made of yellow
material with 'Jew' in black across it. Brief though my
observation was of those grief-worn faces, they managed to
leave me with an impression of dignity. I was not aware, of
course, when I stood on that Polish station, that for over a
year the Germans had been transforming parts of western
Poland into collection centres for the wholesale murdering
of Jews under Hitler's 'final solution' policy and that
already the gas chambers were operating.

A short journey, perhaps twenty miles north-westerly,
brought us to Beuthen railway station. Dead beat, in a
violent snowstorm, we tramped to an old church hall close
to the Hohenzollern mine. It was one of the oldest, deepest
pits in Silesia, and its cobweb of tunnels stretched out from
the base of the mine shaft for scores of miles. For over sixty
years it had produced rich coal. Now in German hands, the
demand for its constant flow to be ever faster had brought
to the Silesian coal-fields thousands of slave labourers:
Russians, Czechs, Hungarians, Romanians, French and
other nationalities from over the face of Europe. Labour
camps had been rapidly constructed; some were barbarous

where foul conditions, coupled with hard labour in dangerous situations below ground, brought mortality figures high.

The church hall housed the British contingent, about fifty men; some were Dunkirk veterans who had slaved here for eighteen months. Many of the originals had gone, but over the long period the Britishers had been at Beuthen, they had become accepted differently from most of the other workers and had gained some popularity with the German and Polish professional overseers, as being reliable and capable of doing responsible jobs; indeed, many had secured favoured positions. Although very run-down, the church hall was hygienic and reasonable enough compared to other barracks.

Understandably there was always bias and suspicion towards newcomers. Mieteck and I were alert to our dubious positions among the well-integrated, old-lag regulars even without having arrived with Electricity and Johnny Turk, both of whom were notably lacking in English and equally short on intelligence. Mieteck passed muster as 'George Potter' when I put his accent and halting English down to the fact of his New Zealand father having remained in France after the First World War, only returning to his homeland with his French wife and their son 'George' in 1938. Fortunately, Mieteck spoke fluent French. Nonetheless, he and I kept much to ourselves, not that there was inclination to gossip, for our main interest upon returning to our barrack after twelve hours' absence each day was to eat and fling ourselves down, aching and dog tired, and sleep until six next morning.

Our barrack commander was a sergeant whom I call 'Simon'; alas, I do not recall his real name, but he was a fine man of a Dorsetshire regiment. Like many NCOs, he had volunteered for an administrative-type job with a working party as preferable to rotting at a parent stalag. Also, on the 'outside', these men found greater opportunity to help the

Allied cause, collecting Intelligence and being less hampered
in co-ordinating subversive activities connected with the
linkage system which operated secretly from camp to camp
among prisoners of war, over extraordinary distances of
German Occupied Europe. The energizing force behind this
system was graft, blackmail and, surprisingly, very often a
willing, if frightened, co-operation from anti-Nazi Germans.
Whenever Red Cross parcels arrived, as they did now at
reasonable intervals at VIIIB and no doubt at other stalags,
it was self-serving German policy to ensure that outlying
working parties received them first, even if inmates of the
parent stalags had to tighten their belts. The intention was
to raise morale and supplement the working-man's sparse
diet; in fact, items coveted by the Germans, such as soap,
tea, chocolate, cigarettes, tinned milk and meat, enabled the
Britishers to barter secretly, perhaps for a more favoured
work position, or to get a guard under graft to post letters
through civilian channels to another guard also under graft
at another camp; some reliable contacts were established
among Germans. Some of the tactics we adopted were
certainly not shining examples of British fair play, but in the
broad complex of war Germans who became our stooges
and those who aligned themselves to us were fair game. If, at
this later date, conscience compels me to state that I
subjugated, blackmailed and contrived to incriminate many
decent Germans, I also state that many Germans were
willingly prepared to become partners in opposition to their
military and Nazi masters. I never experienced difficulty in
finding an amenable German at the right time, and some of
them were wonderful helpers to me. One may tend to call
such German guards and civilians traitors, in helping to
build up British subversive activities and in offering, despite
the terrible risk, undercover assistance. Many had qualities
of courage and resilience that did not lie in their interests if
discovered. If seized by the Gestapo for 'fraternization'

with the enemy they faced imprisonment, or a firing squad or – what was regarded as equally fatal – immediate removal to the Russian Front. Looking back, many of those haters of Nazism have my greatest admiration. I dared not allow compassion or remorse to worry me at the time. All that mattered was preparedness and developing new plans; the unfortunate ends of German conspirators were lessons in carelessness and merely yardsticks to provoke better rules of caution. A callous, practical religion, no doubt.

Simon was aware of why Mieteck and I were at the mine and our concern to be placed among Polish workers. His role was to recommend soldiers for particular tasks below ground, and such was the integrity he had established that his recommendations were invariably approved by the German controllers. He decided it was wise for us to endure a couple of weeks of normal acclimatization to the atmosphere of the mine with its surprises and apprehensions, for our own sakes, and to avoid any suspicion if treated differently. My brief career as a miner began when I entered one of a number of large cages packed with emaciated, toilworn, foreign slave labourers for a one-mile descent of the vertical shaft. The memory of that first drop still leaves me breathless, for we seemed to fall like a stone until nearing a level of the workings when brakes promptly arrested our fall. I walked from that cage with a groan. Give me a flying take-off any day!

Mieteck and I became human pit ponies in Section Four (Abteilung Vier), about a mile from the shaft. Pre-war Polish management had sealed it off as too dangerous, but the Germans had reopened it. To reach Section Four, we travelled by small electric train through a high, wide, main passage, then to the coal-face on foot for a quarter of a mile along a tortuous, rising and falling tunnel of average height of not more than five feet. Our first assignment was pushing loaded trucks along this low, irregular tunnel to the main passage. All latent strength and dexterity were called upon, especially on gradients. If my body was less filled-out than when I had left England, my muscles became like steel springs.

Classed as heavy workers, our rations rose: 550 grams of black bread, extra sausage and turnip jam, and a substantial bowl of soup at the end of the day. Nine sweating hours were demanded at the coal-face and perhaps three more spent getting there and back, lining up for the cage, changing pit clothes at the mine block, showering away grit and grime before the tramp, in the dark, to the barrack. Poor little Electricity lasted four days. He collapsed and a truck ran over his foot, severing his toes. Johnny Turk was fated to be sentenced to fifteen years' civil imprisonment. When a Russian worker stole his 'bite', which consisted of two slices of bread, Johnny wielded his sharp-edged, heart-shaped shovel which contacted the Russian on the neck and lopped off his head; clean as a whistle. Ordered to clean up the mess, Johnny was taken away, carrying the Russian's head by the hair, dragging the corpse by the feet. He was completely unrattled. 'Fook 'itler!' he used to shout cheerily, an expression he had learned from us.

Before the war, I had never shown much interest in the mining area of Yorkshire. Indeed, it was the mark of the more prosperous to be contemptuous of those at the bottom of the pits. During the weeks I laboured with mixed humanity in abject bondage in that foul and dangerous labyrinthine, underground world, I quickly flung away snobbish memories. It was hideous the way German supervisors imposed their own form of Gestapo treatment on the Russians and Polish Jews; many, particularly of the latter, were infinitely their intellectual superiors. Screaming Nazi voices heavy with hate seemed a habit of mind, part of Hitler's conditioning to show no humanity or gratitude. Safer methods of 'coal-cutting' had been discarded for greater production with the use of explosives. Disaster was commonplace and German officials took vague notice of calamities and loss of life among foreign workers. A week before our arrival some sixty Russians had been crushed to death under a roof-fall. I heard frightening stories of tragedies. It was brought home to me in some march of human affection that many, forced at frenzied pace to the extremes of bodily fatigue, would never achieve freedom from the Swastika which completely overlaid their lives except by the kindness and release of death. Whenever I pushed a truck in that nightmare tunnel with its creaking pit props, especially after a shuddering explosion in another working, my nerves trembled on edge. Oozing sweat, naked except for boots, shorts and pit helmet, with my head constantly scraping the roof, I laughed loudly. I had come close to being killed on many occasions – had prepared myself for it in the sky. What a ponderous jest if I were to be crushed to death underground, closer to hell than heaven!

I sweated alongside a young Polish–Russian whom I liked. He was a bright fellow, Ivanov Kuznetski, a mathematician, captured at Minsk. I admired his alertness and stoic qualities. He spoke German and when we were utterly certain of his reliability, Micteck conversed with him secretly in Polish. Unlike most of the slave labourers who presented pictures of bewildered, 'shell-shocked' apathy, Ivanov was no subjugated animal doomed to die in a menagerie. Gradually, I became aware that his attention was focused on sabotage, on revenge for all the humiliation and agony he and his kindred were suffering. His fanatical ambition was to blow up the Hohenzollern mine.

The vicious, back-breaking stint in Section Four came to an abrupt end when Simon engineered our transfers to Section Seven, the most productive workings on the second level. Here the work was immeasurably less strenuous, the tunnels higher, wider, the pit props new and reassuringly

closer spaced. Mieteck was jubilant at being attached to a
Polish rail-laying and maintenance gang. I was a bit taken
aback to find myself with a German explosives team, and to
be told by Simon that I should be resourceful enough to
steal occasional sticks of dynamite, detonators and lengths
of wire for connecting back to Zimmer boxes. Simon was
well aware, and approving, of the major sabotaging of the
mine towards which Ivanov and other workers, in cohorts
with the Home Army, were relentlessly scheming. But apart
from this major operation planned for some time in the
future, there was an ever pressing demand for explosives to
be smuggled out for strategic sabotage at places other than
the mines.

It was stirring news when Mieteck met utterly reliable
Polish contacts, seasoned local miners in communication
with the resistance movement, the Home Army. This was
exactly what we had hoped for. Secretly and cautiously,
Mieteck disclosed the story of our false identities and
previous histories, knowing our bona fides would be
checked by the resistance leaders. As I have mentioned,
since 1940 the resistance in Poland had developed into a
complete underground nation, in direct radio contact with
London and the Polish Government-in-exile. I was thrilled
when Mieteck brought the news that our credentials were in
order, no doubt confirmed by London, and that underground operators would assist us to gain freedom and
advancement into their membership. Our driving ambition
was to escape but our minds were kept in blinkers, with no
inkling of how it would be achieved, or when. We were
warned on no account to attempt independent escape if we
hoped to come through alive. In any case, this was out of the
question while skies remained snow-laden and winds bitter.
Warm weather was weeks away.

Attention focused on the accumulation of explosive.
Werner, the German in charge of my team, was elderly, a

considerate man who never treated me roughly, never shouted, '*Raus, raus!*' but would say quietly, 'Come along.' He was prone to fits of depression. Secretly he was incensed at having been transferred from the Ruhr coal-fields, leaving home and family to give backbone to Polish miners in Silesia and keep slave-labourers operating at a frenzied pace. He was sorely troubled by bombings of the Ruhr and pessimistic that he would not see his home until the end of the war. I became fond of Werner. Sharp angles of acquaintance soon wore down. His confidence in me grew and I felt satisfaction as the fortress doors began opening. He increasingly parted with some of his rations and with patience I systematically increased my supply of Red Cross items – soap, chocolate – which he received with delight to send to his wife. I little cared about points of honour or that Werner was a decent German. In the event of any suspicion falling on me for missing explosive plugs, I was prepared to blackmail him to silence for accepting my gifts. Such was the way we worked. I was glad I never had to resort to extreme pressure tactics with Werner. After blasting, he filled in a required form stating the number of shots used. I learned the art of placing a dummy among a battery of shots. If at times I received an odd, searching scrutiny from him, he never probed for an explanation of why some plugs had not seemed to go off. In all, I stole sixteen plugs which I handed over to Simon. Werner's life was so empty that occasionally, when it was safe, we talked freely. He wept openly that the Fatherland had come to such a state of hate and confusion. I offered friendly advice that he play up sickness in the hope that the authorities might return him to his beloved wife. On more than one occasion, he mentioned a growing incidence of sabotage in Upper Silesia and, in a manner suggestive of wishful thinking, said that if ever the Hohenzollern mine were put out of action, it might facilitate his way home. Much later I learned that the mine was put out of action by an explosion and I wondered if what he had tentatively mooted did in some gratuitous way take him Ruhrwards? I rather hoped it had. Nevertheless, I took ruthless, remorseless advantage of him. As a Britisher I had to!

The Hohenzollern mine lay in the western half of Poland, the area annexed by Hitler in September 1939 and to become known as 'Generalgouvernement', a separate administrative entity under a German Governor-General, Hans Frank. Cracow was its seat of government although Warsaw fell just within the boundary to the north. The Gestapo were unusually alert in Generalgouvernement, but so too was the underground movement seething with activity. A week prior to my birthday in 1942 (17 March), urgent intelligence came to Mieteck via his doyen in the mine that Gestapo and military were about to sweep through Generalgouvernement, to stamp out sabotage, to hunt and destroy units of the Home Army; the coal-fields were a prime target. The Germans were well aware that the SOE in Britain and the Polish Sixth Bureau in London were parachuting agents and supplies to the Home Army. In just over a year since the inaugural mission of 15 February 1941, twelve flights had been made over Poland dropping forty-eight parachutists, two tons of arms, explosive, photographic and communications equipment, and large sums of paper currency and gold. Perhaps twenty-five per cent of the supplies and some money fell into enemy hands; one aircraft and crew were lost and two parachutists killed after landing.

News of the impending purge jolted us. Simon was forewarned from nervous sources under graft to ensure that our barrack was rid of forbidden items, such as schnapps and vodka, or anything to turn suspicion on Germans illicitly bartering with us. Pouncing searches on POW barracks by local Gestapo was accepted routine but rarely involved individual interrogation. What loomed now was something

massive, with ruthless interrogation and cross-checking by
the SS. Mieteck and I were in an extremely precarious
position. Anything unusual was bound to draw investigation. Why, for instance, had two New Zealanders, a Turk
and a Greek, replaced four British soldiers when the working
party had been wholly British from the start? Any probe
would certainly go back to Stalag VIIIB. If the SS
discovered that we were RAF fliers, one a Pole, the other the
man who had been under heavy suspicion of being a British
agent in Holland, we were doomed. Fliers did not volunteer
to slave in a coal-mine for the good of their health; escape
and subversion were obvious conclusions. Those who had
supported us, and particularly the Polish contingent in
Stalag VIIIB, were in deadly danger.

There was no alternative. Mieteck and I must be moved
out immediately. Travel by rail was out of the question;
always a hazard in wartime Poland, it had suddenly became a
nightmare with the SS clenching its grip. We would have to
make our way on foot to the underground centre in
Czestochowa, about forty miles to the north, but the
circuitous route proposed would take us about eighty miles.
Our loyalist helpers worked out everything. Money, maps
and civilian clothes were concealed for us behind lockers in
the bath-house. Simon supplied Red Cross chocolate,
raisins, tins of food, cocoa, Horlicks tablets and a little stove
with meta fuel to make hot drinks *en route*. Mieteck was
given names of trusted helpers in various villages and was
briefed on danger spots. We were confident and determined.
Our departure was fixed for my birthday (my twenty-sixth),
and underground leaders at Czestochowa were advised to
expect us four days later.

Mysteriously, two days before our planned break,
supervisors (*Wachmeisters*) were switched in a number of the
barracks. The amiable German who controlled the British
party was replaced by a *Feldwebel* we named 'John the

Bastard'. This short, pockmarked man, always with a savage Alsatian dog, was infamous for cruelty. I had encountered him when, for a time, I had been given light duty on the surface, following lacerations to my back caused by a roof-fall. I had been detailed to work with Russian women slave labourers in a coal briquette factory under the control of John the Bastard: a work experience unforgettable for the availability of free sex, if one was prepared to risk venereal disease, and I was not. On our last night at the coal-mine, we heard shots and were told an Australian escapee had been recaptured and killed by John the Bastard who ordered the body to be draped in crucifixion pose on the barbed wire. Then we learned it was not one man, nor an Australian whom he had killed, but two Czech Jews who had risked escape rather than face deportation, in all probability to a gas chamber. Frightening as these shootings were, we strove to remain emotionally unaffected. Whatever might befall us, nothing in the world would cause us to stop striving to keep our appointment in Czestochowa. Mieteck made the sign of the cross (as he did frequently) and murmured, 'As God wills. Amen.'

# CHAPTER 10
## Escape in Poland

Snow was falling, a heavenly birthday present, when we broke away from the party of Britishers on the way to the pit head. From that moment, timing and judgement were vital. The only way out was via a narrow steel bridge spanning a cutting with lines of coal trucks about forty feet below. Entrance to the bridge was blocked by a high steel door, always locked. Extending some distance from the door and above the parapets were lines of barbed wire, which meant clambering around the door and gripping the wire with leather-faced mittens, to heave ourselves over. We raced for the bridge. Mieteck was over the wire and on the footwalk when whistles shrilled and there were shouts. '*Halt!*' I joined my companion. We raced over the bridge and clanged down the steps on the far side. Our escape was discovered, not at the pit-head count as we had expected, but by a patrolling posse of guards. By the time they might have unlocked the steel door, we were zigzagging through lines of marshalled trucks on a width of tracks.

Our second real danger-point was a twelve-foot-high, finely woven, steel mesh fence. It allowed no grip and I had neglected to bring along our grappling hook and rope. Hearts pounding, we knifed out the hard earth and belly-wriggled beneath the wire. We raced to a nearby road, and a coffee stall lit by a kerosene lamp. Two waiting bicycles were propped against a low wall. Pedalling furiously through back streets of Beuthen, we struck the main highway outside the built-up area and made in the direction of a military hospital on a hill. Before reaching it, we abandoned the cycles in a hedge and struck out across the fields, towards the River

Oder. Here a quick assessment revealed a guarded bridge, and observation posts at intervals along the far bank. Crouching low in the fast increasing light and powdered with snow – effective cover against the pallid background – we found a semi-concealed spot. Sliding and splashing over big ice-floes, we made the crossing.

With renewed confidence, we set a compass course for the first 'safe' village about twenty miles away. We should reach it comfortably before dusk and curfew. Building up one muck sweat after another, we walked as never before. But woefully, within three hours, reasonable visibility and casual snowflakes vanished in a blizzard as we plodded over the plateau. It was atrociously cold. Spitefully, the weather changed again to soaking rain, then back to pitiless wind and sheets of white, flying murk.

Frozen to the marrow, we fought the length of each mile of unseen, unknown ground, floundering and slumping into deep drifts. The best I could do was stick to a rough direction, barely able to grip my compass. Speed and accurate traverse went to pot. When snow ceased at odd intervals, all we surveyed was a vast, white plain, as naked as in the days of creation. If I claimed to be a good navigator above the earth, I did not discourage Mieteck to trust my judgement, although I knew it was no longer valid in the blinding blizzard. After foot-slogging for sixteen hours, we were hopelessly lost, in the dark.

Our estimated time to the village had long since passed. Our spirits sagged. Exhausted, we sank on a bed of snow. My thinking took on a fatalistic, almost welcome mood, facing what seemed a bitter mockery: our first day on the trail would be our last. Morning would surely find us dead of exposure. What did it matter? Who cared about two struggling specks in a white wilderness? To hell with it all anyway! Yet I managed to light the stove, make a brew and we shared a can of beans. 'Our Last Supper,' I thought ironically, and lay on my back; it seemed that stiffened limbs would not permit me to rise again. But Mieteck was on his stomach, praying. As if answering his prayer, the wind lessened, the snowing tailed off. Moonlight shone over dazzling whiteness. Thousands of stars glittered around the pole star, once so vital to my navigation. Mieteck gripped my arm and shouted, 'Look, look!' He was pointing ahead to the right. Dumbfounded, I gazed at glimmering lights and was jolted back to the present. It was no ship with blurred lights sailing over the rim of the world. Uncanny for the snow and wind to have ceased and suddenly to glimpse homesteads, as if a frosted window had magically opened out. Had it been otherwise, we would never have seen the glow of oil lamps, and salvation, so close at hand.

Having failed to reach our safe destination, it was a case of knock on any door. Luckily, it was the door of a loyal Polish couple. We were given refuge in a warm and humble home. Mieteck explained who we were. They were thrilled to learn we were fliers from Britain, we had bombed Germany, had escaped from captivity: a Pole back in his homeland with a British comrade-in-arms. They seemed to draw immense satisfaction from being chosen to help us. We learned that our intended village was twelve miles westwards, but rather than waste effort getting back on our original course, we decided to push ahead. The next safest village, on a northerly path, was some eighteen miles away and it was essential we reach it before curfew at dusk. Curfew varied from village to village.

We set off next morning, warm and dry, and having regained much of our confidence. As if to compensate for the previous day, the wind was light, the cold less bitter. There were intermittent falls of easy snow and, at times, a weak sun peered from between cloud. Nevertheless, I distrusted the changeability of the weather and considered it a race against time. The largish village we were aiming for was not one of those recommended by our partisan mine advisers, but the couple had given the name of friends living almost next to the church. As the day wore on we passed hamlets and isolated farms and occasionally sighted people riding in horse-drawn sleighs. When we were alone on the plain, with all about nothing but a vast expanse of snow, I experienced a curious sensation of living where time was suspended. I was to sense this timelessness again years later, when in equally desolate places – in the Sahara, and Antarctica.

Hours passed inexorably and a smudge on the horizon indicated the village. None too soon, for dusk was dulling the sky and I disliked the look of thickening clouds. A well-frozen trail led to the main street and we found the church, but not a single person was about. The entire village might have been deserted except for oil lamps having been lit in some of the houses. The house we sought was silent, apparently unoccupied, though the sound of grunting pigs came from the rear. I had an uneasy feeling of being watched. We had been warned of Gestapo stooges planted in most sizeable villages, but that had to be risked. There was no turning back. Without much reasoning, we selected a house standing by itself and knocked on the door.

No lucky chance this time! A forbidding-looking man in a *Feldwebel*'s uniform confronted us, with one hand resting on his revolver holster. I stared, goggle-eyed and dumb, with an instinctive urge to act. Speaking Polish with a guttural accent, he asked what we wanted, why we were abroad at that hour, and demanded our papers. We were face to face with real danger. My adrenalin upsurged. Rapid, violent action followed. I delivered a lightning kick to his groin, followed by more in rapid succession. He bent double, gasping and groaning, reeling backwards from the doorway. We fled the way we had come.

Breathing in great gasps, we moved at the fastest possible

pace into the growing darkness and softly falling snow. Assuredly, a manhunt would be mounted for two straggling strangers who had attacked a German sergeant. The next village was ten miles on; fear drove us more vigorously than can be imagined. We were in a state of dizziness of mind and spirit when we slumped into the snow after covering about half the distance, our endurance worn to the limit. I got the stove working to brew cocoa. Assessing the situation, the only hope – despite the effort of movement being an agony – was to reach the village while still under cover of dark, and trust to falling among friends; then sum up the risks and determine how to act. I glimpsed Mieteck's drawn face as he leaned over to snuff the stove. I felt deeply for him, a fugitive in his own land among his own beloved people. How bitter the bread of exile must taste; as it would to me in similar circumstances in my country.

As we stood to move off again a faint, quivering, baying sound carried to us down the slight wind, as if from a long distance. Remaining motionless, straining our ears, for a time there was only the murmur of the wind, then again we picked up the lone baying. It was a dog. As we advanced, sometimes the sound increased, or decreased, or stopped but only to resume after a little while. Utterly weary, we slumped into the snow to rest. A dog could mean people, a house. What was making it so restless? It could not have caught our scent at such a long way off and upwind of us. But we soon discovered. There came from behind us plaintive moans and mournful howls. The realization awoke in our minds that wolves were lurking to our rear. The dog knew they were abroad; they must have gone about and picked up our trail. My heart beat madly. We had been warned of packs of wolves which roamed the vast plateau. No fictitious danger, the Germans allowed these predatory creatures to breed unchecked, as an aid to enforcing curfew. A voracious pack would tear a man to pieces in minutes. I shivered as all too close we heard a low, concerted growling, then suddenly a sharp howl.

The hair-raising sounds pursued us as we moved quickly in the direction of the dog, now kicking up a continuous and furious racket. A watery moon splashed the plain in a perfunctory way but sufficed to define the blur of a lonely farmhouse. As we staggered nearer, a yellow glow suddenly appeared at a window. It was a guiding light, but we avoided the house. Nearby stood two outbuildings, one a barn, its doors locked; Mieteck and I tore at two boards on its side wall, with a madness wrought of desperation, prising apart an opening to wriggle through. Prostrate with exhaustion, we flung ourselves into a pile of hay and within minutes were wrapped in profoundest sleep.

It was afternoon when I awoke with Mieteck's hand over my mouth. Through the hay I perceived a young woman holding in check by a leash a large, low-growling dog. She seemed not unduly frightened when Mieteck spoke first. Her father appeared, a hard-featured man who listened intently as Mieteck talked rapidly. We were taken indoors and met his wife, realizing we had struck honey. This was a Roman Catholic family of homely, simple, workaday Poles. The man, formerly a soldier in the Polish Army, now a small farmer, had a passionate devotion to his country and great faith in his fighting countrymen. They listened with proud joy, almost adulation, as Mieteck related our story.

Never was a kindly welcome more genuine. We were made comfortable and our savage hunger satisfied. The farmer disclosed that a German patrol had visited the farm mid-morning, enquiring if they had seen two men, strangers, known to be violent. They had replied they had seen no one. In truth, the farmer had detected our shadowy figures in the early hours, advancing from the plain and disappearing into his barn. Concluding we were fugitives, hunted by the Germans and no doubt in desperate straits, he had let us be.

Our gratitude to him was boundless, and also to the dog, 'Tandenz', some kind of great wolfhound. He was kept as a guard and for his speed over the snow, his strength and courage in attacking wolves; these marauding packs were such a scourge that all the farm animals had to be kept heavily fenced in. Tandenz lay now, like a lamb, in the kitchen. In all probability, he had saved our lives. Our errors in navigating the plain had turned, as errors can sometimes, to our great good fortune.

We had come far off course, to the north-east of our originally planned route, and we learned that the village we had been making for in the night was 'unsafe'. Our host took charge and we agreed to his suggestions. Our situation was ticklish; undoubtedly the Germans would revisit and it was out of the question for us to struggle on alone. Many Poles, though utterly loyal, would give strange travellers a wide berth for fear of German trickery and stooges. We must lie low in the barn and stay another night, sleeping in the house this time. He would make a quick trip to the village to alert true friends of our plight and arrange a safe place. He was right about the Germans being on the hunt for us, for that afternoon as we lay in the hay we listened apprehensively to the sound of three Storch light aircraft passing overhead, above low cloud, and circling for quite some time over a wide area of the plain.

As was the custom, fowls and geese were brought into the house that night. The air in the kitchen was pungent and the floor gave out certain emanations. I recall, with amusement, sinking into a deep feather bed and next morning a happy society of fowls coming clucking through my open doorway, in a carnival of unusual disorder. One big, flapping hen, making strumming sounds like a helicopter, seemed to challenge my right to occupancy by discharging her payload smack in my eye.

That afternoon, the farmer left by sleigh drawn by a pair

of lively horses, to travel some six miles to the village. The jingle of the bells faded. I sought to dispel anxiety and nervous hopes by singing:

> 'Jingle bells, jingle bells,
> All the fucking way;
> Hurrah for bloody good luck
> To last us all the way . . .'

'Shut up,' Mieteck growled, 'and stop swearing!'

I grinned. Swearing was my palliative. He could no more cure me of that than I could stop him praying, which I expected he was doing fervently.

As instructed, we gave the farmer an hour before we set out on foot in his tracks. His plan was to have us picked up, not at the house in case the Germans followed him home, but on the plain, and taken by sleigh to arrive at the village just on dark. But as we trod the miles, his overdue return gave rise to intense concern that something had gone wrong. It was with ineffable joy that we heard bells and saw sleighs emerge across the snowscape. The farmer arrived with two stalwart friends, each with a sleigh and brace of steaming horses. He told us that all was well, waved goodbye, and drove on alone. I climbed into one sleigh, Mieteck into the other. It was a new kind of thrill for me, speeding over the snow with its subtle, whispering sounds and the reassuring, jaunty insistence of bells, mocking the melancholy, silent expanse. A tolling church bell was signalling curfew as we passed through the village and went on, well clear, to a dwelling beyond. We spent the night with a man, his wife and two teenage sons; peasant people, poorer than those we had left, but equalling them in loyalty, devoutness and proud patriotism. We sat at their humble table and shared potato soup containing pieces of pig meat which had been received with joy from the good farmer who had arranged our shelter. As we handed over a few Red Cross items of food, they were looked upon as some marvellous gift from heaven.

We left at first light, facing a march of at least eight hours to reach a priest's house in a small township. Now on our fourth day of traversing the plateau, we were unshaven and tramp-like. The weather was favourable, but half-way to our destination a storm struck and windswept snow blotted out everything beyond a few paces. Again, inevitably, we veered off track. During a lull in the blinding storm, I was able to identify ground features from my large-scale survey map. We had entered an area where tracts of pine and spruce forest relieved the lifeless monotony of the plain. Little homesteads, though isolated, were more numerous, and the going was much easier as we followed worn tracks. Our host this morning had marked on my map the position of a friend's house and had given a letter of introduction. We found the house, a poor, wooden dwelling occupied by a man, seriously ill with tuberculosis, his wife and infant daughter. Here, as we sheltered until the blizzard abated, we saw the stark poverty suffered by so many of the Polish people, the abysmal misery and starvation inflicted by the German masters of Generalgouvernement.

In the final count of war, Poland was to occupy first place as the country whose losses were proportionately most severe, where the terror was greatest, as the nation most plundered and maimed. The Nazis robbed the Poles of thirty per cent of their personal property, destroyed thirty-eight per cent of the national property, and murdered 6,028,000 citizens. German retaliation fell on the starving and bleeding countryside for actions by the underground. Villages were burned, whole families murdered, and the hanging of hostages a regular practice.

And yet, in that poor dwelling, where sickness and malnutrition stared at us so distressingly, we witnessed the supreme fire of Catholic faith and reverence for country. I

admit at that period I was inclined to scoff at Roman
Catholicism; all religions for that matter, but my incredulity
received a rude shock in Poland when I perceived how faith
sustained spirit and hope. We left that tragic family with
more than we could sensibly spare of our meagre rations,
and plodded on dumbly. Our encounter with them was
unforgettable, heart-achingly depressing. Adding to misery,
the temperature dropped and snow began again, becoming
heavier with a steady hissing. Our nerves were overcharged;
a disturbing unrest obsessed me; Mieteck was brooding. We
lost our way, argued furiously and then, in some explosion
beyond containing, we lost our tempers, and fought. We
fought savagely in the snow. Strung beyond the limit, we
had snapped. It was a terrible folly, after all we had been
through. With precious strength wasted, we came to our
senses. Neither of us could have come this far alone. Our
trust in each other rekindled and became spiritually welded
as never before. As far as I was concerned, an everlasting
brotherly love was engendered.

We reached the township. Slipping our small packs from
our backs to draw less attention, we swung them casually, I
trailing some distance behind Mieteck. Fear stalked at my
heels and a number of passers-by regarded me curiously.
Mieteck eased off the main street and a few minutes later we
came to the priest's house, enclosed by a garden and fence.
As we made for the rear door, I breathed with immense
relief. We had achieved our goal. We had spent our last night
on the plain. Here we could expect shelter, necessary papers,
decent clothes, respectability of person and preparations for
our entry into Czestochowa, sixteen miles away.

Mieteck knocked. There was no response. We moved to
the front door, but unavailingly. There was only the vague
yapping of a dog from somewhere. We rapped, waited and
watched, our fate in suspension. We were hungry, fiercely
cold with muscles stiffening painfully. Rations were almost

gone, meta fuel used. Cover and rest were urgent, our wet clothes needed drying; we looked like derelict vagabonds. Somehow we had to clean up, now that we were to move among people. Our appearance would excite immediate suspicion if spotted by watchful Germans. Perhaps the priest was visiting late; then again, anything could befall him as a partisan operator. If he did not return, we resolved to force entry to the house after dark and do the best possible from then on.

Crouched on the back doorstep, I was thoroughly disheartened. Suddenly Mieteck started up. Alarmed, I looked at an elderly woman with a shawl draped over her head, standing at an open gateway in the side fence, staring at us. Mieteck spoke hurriedly, nervously, and the old lady's face brightened with excitement. He translated: 'Thank God you have arrived safely. We feared the worst had happened.' Despair vanished. It appeared that the priest expecting us had been urgently summoned to Czestochowa, but had left instructions with the housekeeper in the adjacent cottage. Obviously agitated, she said it was imperative we not hover about the priest's house, but leave the township immediately; it had many dangerous German elements. We had to direct our steps to a larger village ten miles farther on and we must cover the distance before dark. There we were to go to a church, enter and sit at the very back, on the left near the wall and wait until contacted. When approached, there was to be an exchange of passwords of which she appraised Mieteck. It was damnable enough to have to push on, more so when she added grim information. In the last couple of days – almost certainly because of us – the laxity of German patrols had been tautened to a high degree of vigilance, carrying out spot checks on people and papers. The only road to our objective passed through forest clearings. It was essential to keep away from the road and circumvent road blocks. We must use all our resourcefulness to make our way through the gloomy forests while remaining constantly alert for pill-boxes at intervals.

We thanked the old lady and hastened back to the open plain. Fringes of black forest came in sight and, following a wide arc, many times we dropped flat into the snow, waiting and watching before crawling on, even running on all fours with the alarm of the hunted. We came to a sudden halt. The distance between us and a patrolling guard was about 300 yards. In that dull forest, buried in the snow on a gloomy afternoon, we remained for what seemed two hours (we had no watches), our hands numb, bodies almost petrified, and the wind howling in gusts. If we lay much longer, frost-bite was a certainty. It was a case of imperative deeds. We secured a small pine tree apiece and, holding this camouflage in front, dragged ourselves yard by yard, closing on the guard's beat. It would need vigorous action and uncaring hearts to make a dash into the trees when the guard was as far away as possible, with his back to us. Fortune again played into our hands when voices were heard and the whole tempo of things quickened with the arrival of two other guards. The three entered a pill-box. We were up and running low. Fortune favoured the bold. No alarm was raised and we sped on until almost on our knees, our greatest concern to make up lost time.

Slogging on, we reached the village. The church was on a hill and making towards it in the twilight, we heard like some mysterious chant from heaven the sounds of voices mingled with organ music. Quietly, we entered and took up our positions at the back by the left wall. The mass over, the locals departed. Main lights were switched off and the golden roof disappeared into nothingness. What could we do but wait? It was agonizing until we heard a clip-clop of footsteps approaching from the altar. A man with a torch. We coughed when he was opposite our pew. It seemed a mad and mysterious moment. The light jerked our way. Mieteck quickly produced the right password.

The verger, or whatever official of the church he was, had been warned to expect us. We were quickly led to a private room where we talked, still under tremendous nervous strain, and the verger, it seemed, was semi-doubtful about our reliability. Somehow, whether by telephone or other means, it was confirmed that we were the right people: two airmen destined for Czestochowa and to be given every assistance. It was forthcoming, and we passed the night in the church. Early in the morning, when safe to travel, we were led to the cottage of an old lady, a retired nursing sister. Clothes had been arranged, we were given a solid breakfast, and feeling more like respectable human beings we were ready for the important move into Czestochowa. But still we had to keep our feet on the tightrope. We were facing the most dangerous leg, for without inviolable papers and identity cards we had to get out of Generalgouvernement. Czestochowa lay just beyond the administrative region's south-west boundary. Regarded by the Nazis as a formidable bastion of religious power and, in fact, inspiring Polish resistance beyond Teutonic belief, Czestochowa was guarded by the SS with intense rigour.

We had six miles to cover. Upon leaving the cottage, instructions were to make for an improvised wooden bridge, erected over a river for the use of workmen building a factory on the opposite bank. Mieteck had been told what to do. It was a bold performance; but sheer audacity was the greatest component of escape, probably next to luck. We walked straight up to a stack of timber at the near side, hoisted some lengths to our shoulders and headed across the bridge to the building site. A group of Polish workers idly surveyed us and, dumping the planks, Mieteck proclaimed authoritatively that a supply of scaffolding poles would be delivered next day. A single German guard was hovering about. Mieteck focused friendly attention on him, saying he didn't fancy *his* job in such cold weather, and would he make sure that a load of concrete, about to be delivered, was immediately put under cover.

I wondered if the Polish workmen had been primed to expect two civilian strangers and ask no questions. Our next hazard was at a wide railway cutting where two guards patrolled the embankment. We had to get past. For the act, we secured two pieces of wood, more or less shaped like rail-tapping hammers, and leisurely, as if inspecting the lines, made our way some distance along one track then back down the other, twice passing the not over-concerned Germans. With remarkable resilience, Mieteck forced some jokes with the guards who seemed to look upon him as a genial sort of railway worker. We then walked a distance away to link up with the highway. The worst was over. I congratulated Mieteck on his resourcefulness and applied psychology. He shrugged, saying we would not have pulled it off without the calculating support of the verger, which set me to wondering whether the guards at the cutting had not been 'treated' to turn a blind eye!

# CHAPTER 11
## Nunnery to Dungeon

Hans Frank, the German Governor-General of General-gouvernement, recorded in his diary: 'The greatest strength of Poland resides in the Church and in the Saint of Czestochowa.' Inside that city, standing on elevated ground, is the Pauline Monastery at Jasna Gora in which is enshrined an ikon, 'Our Lady of Czestochowa', sometimes called the Black Madonna. The picture was brought to the monastery in 1384 and a scientific examination, carried out between 1948 and 1952, concluded that it was painted in the Middle East in the sixth century. Attributed with miraculous power, it has long been the symbol of Poland's religious and political freedom. Czestochowa, or the Holy City as it is generally known, is the principal place of pilgrimage in the country and has played an extraordinary role in the lives of Polish people for centuries. During the war, the original ikon was removed and hidden, and a replica placed in its stead.

When Mieteck and I reached Czestochowa, we turned off the main highway as it rose towards the monastery, entering a small church, St Barbara's, in a narrow, crooked street. Mieteck found our contact, a tall distinguished-looking priest-prelate named Nasalski, and I recall our long conversation before he left us for some hours. When he returned, as instructed we tagged behind the organist, a priest named Andrzej Nowat who led us in the grim, grey cold of the evening to an old and large building which turned out to be the nunnery 'Szarytki' of the Sisters of Charity. This was a shock! The Mother Superior, a kind, compassionate person, informed us we would remain concealed in the building until underground chiefs finalized plans for our travel to the east, for attachment to permanently operating resistance units. The Mother Superior regarded it as her sacred and loyal duty, and that of her nuns, to protect us in the manner and spirit of opposing evil.

The accompanying priest made it clear to us that the city's populace was subjected to inflexible discipline and cruelty. The Gestapo had warned officials of the church that they would remain unmolested as long as they kept aloof from subversive activities and the harbouring of enemies of the Third Reich. They would be closely watched, and if treachery were discovered their doom was sealed. The possibility of a sudden pounce by the Gestapo could not be ruled out, a thought which provided little comfort to Mieteck and me. The benevolent nuns had learned to cope with their oppressors and to deceive them, putting themselves under the command of Our Lady of Czestochowa.

In a simply furnished room in the nunnery the Sisters of Charity treated us with noble magnanimity, but a feeling of unease crept over me when, a few days later, my whole body was seized with jerky shuddering. Pains developed in my lungs with high temperatures and extreme respiratory difficulty. Blood appeared in my sputum and severe pleurisy put me out of the running. I did not respond to treatment and for thirty-six hours I was in a delirious state. I hated the illness with a hatred one has for a stubborn enemy that threatens one's life. It came as a deadly blow. When Mieteck and I had escaped from Beuthen, we had been like whipcords; indeed, without our stint in the mines we could never have done that six-day journey of about a hundred devious miles across the plain. Now, my vaunted will of iron and boastful, savage strength had failed as a result of long, bitter, forced marches, sodden clothes, lack of sleep and food. I shall always remember one nun, Sister Maria, who spoke German and some English, a devoted nurse who remained by my bedside for innumerable hours. Despite my admitting to a rebelliousness against religion, she placed a photograph of Our Lady of Czestochowa by my bed, saying that if perhaps I offered a prayer it might result in some appreciable difference in choosing the right path in the dangerous world around me.

Plans went forward for our urgent departure by Trans-Polish express to Lvov in the Ukraine as soon as my health improved. At Lvov we would be met and taken under the wing of Polish underground operators. Various underground people visited me, and again my red hair would have to be close-cropped. Mieteck was absent for long periods, arranging forged passports and other papers for the journey. I was given the name of Henryk Kowalski, the same as the burnt Polish flier in the hospital at Dulag Luft who had put me in touch with his Polish friends in VIIIB. I took the name gladly, in honour to him, while my falsified documents described me as a concrete labourer, directed to the East by the German labour controllers for duties in road construction.

When an underground leader returned with Mieteck, I was jolted to be told we were leaving the nunnery at short notice and Czestochowa and Generalgouvernement for that matter. An Allied airdrop had taken place the night before, north-east of the city, and Gestapo reaction was expected, churches being under suspicion of concealing secret radio transmitters and receivers. Equally as efficient as in Holland, the German monitoring system was straining every effort to break down what was known as the 'Musical Cipher'. Secret radio signals, sent from Britain through the BBC to underground operators in Poland, contained many musical interludes, a few in cipher, giving information of the location, date and time for RAF 'drops' to be expected.

My health was mending, but still not too encouragingly.

In the urgency of the circumstances, it was considered I had sufficient stamina to stand up to a train journey to the Ukraine. My lungs would not be exposed to raw weather conditions, nor to harsh physical strain in a railway carriage. Surprisingly, it was announced that a Sister of Charity would accompany us as far as Cracow, seventy-six miles to the south-east, there to see us safely off on the Trans-Polish express for the second long leg of about two hundred miles east to Lvov. Despite our argument that we would be all right, that such escort might prove dangerous for the nun, with calm resignation the Mother Superior said the matter was settled. In the event of my being taken ill before arrival at Cracow, the nun would carry hot drinks, food and tablets; if I became too ill to go on, arrangements had been made for us to be taken to a safe address in Cracow, to bide our time until I was fit to continue. Before leaving the nunnery, my first time since entering it, a ceremony was conducted in a small room and an oath sworn before the Cross and a picture of Our Lady of Czestochowa that if captured, no matter what we might have to endure, no word would ever pass our lips about our place of sanctuary. If the Gestapo learned of help given, the Sisters of Charity could expect torture and possible execution.

For three hours at Czestochowa, we waited for the Cracow train, in bitter weather, and I found myself briefly but repeatedly catching my breath with accompanying chest pains. The platforms were crowded with ill-clad, half-starved men and women, *en route* to join forced labour camps in the East. I felt piercing sorrow for these poor creatures, and it was painful to conjure up a sensation of the black loneliness that must have been in their hearts. Another disquieting spectacle was huge war posters screaming a campaign of hate against Jews, with crude and revolting illustrations. One showed a beak-nosed Jew with a skull-cap, leeringly dropping dead rats into a mincing machine churning out sausages. The blatant caption read: 'No more Jewish foodshops for Poland. We must exterminate Jewish poison as we would exterminate rats.'

The train was not due in Cracow until the next morning. Within two hours of leaving Czestochowa my hands began to shake, I broke into sickly sweats and the rubbing pain in my lung worsened. As we chugged across a white-carpeted countryside, glowing maliciously in the moonlight, my thoughts wandered back to the endless hours of foot-slogging over this same inhospitable plain. If I had left the nunnery with a certain spirited euphoria, I was in for a rude awakening. As the journey progressed, I shook spasmodically and the lung pains invited waves of nausea. I was given fluid and tablets, but Mieteck had to assist me to the lavatory where I was violently sick. A frightening uneasiness crept over me, for it seemed that all our hopes were cancelling out. Mieteck and the nun pleaded for me to hang on until we cleared the barriers at Cracow when we could be led to a refuge for my rest and recovery.

I was moved by their encouragement and selfless concern. Aware of Mieteck's deep sense of purpose to get to the Eastern Polish Territories, to engage with the underground in attacks on bridges, roads and railways and the collection of military Intelligence for Britain, I made up my mind. If my staunch, courageous companion refused to leave me, then without any feelings of self-pity or heroism I would leave him, and the nun. It was madness to endanger their safety any longer. Mieteck had to go on, freer to manoeuvre in his own country without a sick Britisher in tow. The nun had to return to her place in Czestochowa. Her allegiance was unforgettable, but feeling as I did, wavering between living and dying, the sooner she was released of me the better. I really believed I was finished, and in my fevered muddled state of mind I told myself I would find some place where to sink down, privileged to die in the land of the Poles.

Cracow station was swarming and squads of uniformed Germans were moving among the crowds. After being cooped up for hours in the carriage, the chilled air outside revived me. The Trans-Polish train to the Ukraine was scheduled to depart a couple of hours after our arrival, but we had come in late. Time was pressing. I had been at a loss to know how to break away from Mieteck and the nun without fuss or argument, until I sighted a public convenience for men, beyond the ticket barrier.

Mieteck and I joined a single queue of waiting men, and the nun stood aside nearby to await our return. Moving up, my turn came first. Entering, I passed a long line of males standing at slate slabs. The vacant one, fortuitously, was near the exit at the far end. Soon after me Mieteck entered and, with no selection in public urinals, he took up a face-the-wall position at a compartment to my extreme right. Unobserved by him, I instantly moved from the lavatory block and outside made straight for the nun. Hastily, I conveyed to her that I was finished, too sick to go on, but Mieteck must. No fears must be entertained about my loyalty and honour. I stressed to that courageous woman that she must return to Czestochowa and run no more risks. She understood immediately and, not giving her time to reply, I stooped and kissed her brow before turning on my heels to lose myself in the stream of people. It was over!

I cleared the railway station and with desperate energy moved straight ahead along a wide thoroughfare. The sprinkling of German uniforms was terrifying. I swung away, following less congested streets, perspiring, steaming heat and fast losing clarity of thinking. Driven on by a mad desire to find some peaceful hide-away, I only wanted to sleep for ever. I was almost ready to drop, the exertion of prolonged walking having roused piercing pains in my lungs. Oh, joy of joys, ahead was a tree-dotted area, and closing with it, I found it to be a deserted park. I don't remember slumping on a bench, or how many hours elapsed before I was roused from slumber by two old ladies shaking my shoulders. I felt quivers of fear, my senses were whirling and I couldn't understand their gabbling. Inherent fear of the Germans and instinctive caution rang a warning bell in my mind not to place myself in jeopardy. I made off in the fading light; doubtless those two women in shawls imagined I was drunk.

I *felt* stupid-drunk. With no idea of where I was, I wandered towards the hazy lights of the city, blissfully unaware that I had failed to carry out a vital commitment at first opportunity after quitting the railway station – to destroy my forged papers. They were dangerous; even if found on my dead body, they would excite relentless questioning in Czestochowa where 'officially issued'. When I had put myself down on that park bench, I had been pleasurably sure I was going to die. Now I was confounded. Where was Mieteck? Oh yes, he would have caught the train. Why had we parted? Oh yes, I was dying. What the hell was I doing alive? I was stiff with cold. At least the throbbing in my lungs had subsided but, instead, I had a gnawing pain in my belly. 'Damn,' I thought, 'I'm not dead, and I'm hungry. I should have died; it was a matter of honour to have died.'

Perhaps this thinking was a reactive notion to an unconscious awareness that it was dangerous to be alive. Connections between life and death gambolled in my darkened mind. My muddled obsession was that I must not die like some starving animal. Whether on my way to greet St Peter or argue with the devil, either would be sporty enough to hang on until I was in a more comfortable position. As I walked, my legs took on an elastic springiness, and at times I was filled with wild bravado. I felt like a yacht scudding before the wind. I had no sensation of fear, no real concern for what might happen to me. A fat lot I cared about Germans. 'I've beaten them,' I thought, 'they can't get me now. I'm half a spirit and I'll bugger off for ever after a good supper.'

In fact, I was 'potty'. I have often reflected on the curious, hypnotic state I was in, with recollections of people and places swimming in my mind, then in a contradictory way a wave of conviction assuring me that I had died decently and would soon be on my way to the beyond.

My wayward legs halted before a building with gleaming, lighted windows; then moved to stop near a doorway. Soldiers were entering and leaving. It was strange they were dressed in German uniforms. The smell of food and coffee escaped in a flow of warmth to the chilling air about me. I was seized with a level-headed, cheerful remembrance of the Salvation Army canteen outside London's King's Cross Station. I entered a long hall, full of soldiers, smoke and clamour, and moved a distance inside finding a seat at a table shared by some Germans. They probably viewed me as an intruding, peasant nitwit as I stared at a huge picture of Hitler above a platform. It was laughable; the devil I had been conjuring up in my muddled imagining was oddly the same kind of bastard as was weighing me up from the wall.

Possibly the warmth, the smell of food, conviviality and visible contact with humanity increased realism and sensibility. Comprehension rediscovered itself; reason began to run, warning of the nearness of danger, imperiously urging me to get moving. I had asked a waiter for coffee and hot soup, such as the soldier in front of me was gulping down. The waiter had not moved. 'Show me your papers,' he snapped.

Misgiving struck, but mechanically I put a hand to my inner coat pocket. My fingers touched the forged papers. 'Oh, Christ!' my mind flicked over. I knew it was 'Farewell world' this time, but whether I died of natural causes or by German hands made very little difference now. The game was up. There was no time to bluff. A rush of emotions, of hate, rage and disgust, overwhelmed me. Thoughts had sharpened and in a flash I realized this was my last chance for vengeance, if only verbal.

I rose. A German laid hands on me and pushing him aside I told him in plain English, 'Fuck off!' Heading for the platform, I yelled, '*Achtung! Achtung!*' Silence, and I started. Hitler was called all the farmyard names I could muster, with a reminder that Churchill would rip his balls off and flush them down the sewer, and the British Army would do the same to the dim-witted German soldiers; as for the shithouse Gestapo . . .! The audience was dumbfounded, shocked silly: surely it wasn't true? I burst into rapid English using the choicest swear words in the language, and to cap the performance, I lapsed into Polish with wicked expressions I had committed to memory in Stalag VIIIB. It was polyglot vituperation. The stunned audience suddenly came alive. Berserk with anger, the enemy charged and kicked me senseless.

I recovered most of my senses as dawn was breaking, how many days later I do not know. I had been awakened by sounds of tramping feet, yells and dull screams, followed by a burst of rifle fire. There was a pause, then the sounds were repeated. 'Christ Almighty! What's going on? Where am I?' I rose wildly from a palliasse but a steel circlet, clamped about my ankle and connected to the wall by a length of chain, brought me to my knees like a lasso. That arresting chain represented with sudden alertness my entry into a Nazi spider's web. I was a battered and bruised mess, in an ugly, comfortless room with windows closed and barred. Harrowing screams, followed by concerted rifle fire, recurred at irregular intervals.

A dull-faced German in a dirty white jacket appeared and thrust some pills under my nose. 'Swallow,' he commanded, 'then I'll bring food.' He guarded me vigilantly for most of the days that followed, regularly administering pills and bringing four solid soups a day and potatoes and bread. He refused to answer most of my questions but I did learn I was in a hospital room of an SS political prison outside Cracow, a murder establishment for patriotic Poles and Jews. A

German doctor had drained pleural fluid from my left lung, but as soon as I was fit to stand, and in control of my faculties, interrogation officers would be more than pleased to see me. How long would I be able to stand up to them? I was clad in rough brown pyjamas; my clothes had been removed, together with my forged papers, and no doubt the SS had found two capsules of potassium cyanide concealed in buttons, the same as carried by parachutists into Poland. Mine had been given me in Holland, for myself or, if necessary, for the liquidation of false agents or traitors, and I had hung on to them as more treasured than a revolver for a quick exit, if the worst came to the worst. I cursed myself for not having destroyed the papers and taken poison, as I had genuinely promised myself to do when scheming my parting from Mieteck.

One morning, I was thrown trousers, shirt and my own boots. Dressing promptly I was taken under guard across an expansive cobbled courtyard to a medieval-looking fortress. It was sinister, and my new accommodation was a real, damned dungeon. The health cure was over. No more soft gloves, but mailed fists from now on. The dungeon was quite large, with stone-paved floor and thick walls of rough-hewn granite. In my chequered career I have sampled brief spells of imprisonment in various gaols in a number of countries, but none ever compared to the Polish dungeon for barbarous exclusivity. It was damp below ground, bitterly cold, with minute, crawling insects my only living company. A small grille, fully ten feet from the floor but at ground level outside, allowed a miserable ration of daylight to enter. Furnishings were three bare planks on low trestles for a bed, and a large metal bucket. A light bulb, high in the ceiling, was operated only from outside, by inspecting guards visiting morning, noon and night. On the middle visit, I received my food for the day, a can of swede soup, three slices of black bread and a pannikin of water.

# CHAPTER 12

## Gestapo Torture – and German Friends

Already introduced to Gestapo techniques after arrest in Holland, I never imagined I would experience another cataclysmic arrest in Poland. It was customary for the Gestapo to isolate one under cruel conditions for enforced contemplation and softening up before interrogation. I was also well aware that over a period, receiving only basic essentials to maintain life, with restricted diet, light, warmth, normal sounds, reading matter and exercise, and void of human society, acute disturbance of personality sets in. If prolonged enough, combined with fear-producing anxiety and harsh physical treatment, abnormalities increase to a state of despair and madness.

I dwelt on my pledge to honour the secrets of Czestochowa, and if 'death before dishonour' was to have real meaning, it was imperative I turn my mind to ideas of suicide. I could contemplate my future only with direst pessimism. The sole weapon I possessed to beat the Gestapo was lies and double words, until mentally and physically ripped to pieces when death would be the only withdrawal. I was not willing to await dying at the pleasure of the Nazis and planned to tear my shirt into strips and make a running noose. I could hang myself from the top of a bed plank; better still, use the boards for reaching the grille, to swing from an iron bar. The alternative for a quick departure would be to open a seam in the bucket and use jagged metal to rip open my windpipe or hack at my wrists. The shirt method was preferable for speed and silence; the bucket idea would involve noise-making and likely investigation. I would wait a little longer, but as soon as my mentality started to become confused and disregarding, and while I could still recognize this as happening, I would act decisively. There was at least a certain element of rebellious pride in my proposition.

After seventy-two hours of gloom, darkness and gnawing hunger, a couple of guards entered the dungeon to give me a few kicks, to dispel ennui before marching me along corridors to a higher floor to face interrogators. A firing squad was in action in the open courtyard but, oddly, the screams of the doomed and the crackle of rifle fire sounded less fearful above ground; though to tell the truth, the noise broke the monotony in the dungeon.

I have vivid recollections of interrogation in that prison and look upon it as the extreme crisis of my life. Three Gestapo officers were standing, grouped and smoking, when I was brought before them. Two were middle-aged: one squat, with doughy face and pig eyes; the other with a scarred face, almost chinless, a flattened nose and Hitler moustache. The third was younger, athletic-looking and very blond. Before seating themselves at a long table, they took their time scrutinizing me, while I attempted to stare back impassively.

The Blond One opened the questioning, asking my nationality. I said I was a New Zealander, born in Christchurch, a soldier of the New Zealand Expeditionary Force. He sat back, raising his eyebrows. '*Ach so!*' he exclaimed in surprise, then spoke in English, 'Incredibly interesting, but how is it you speak reasonable German and Polish?' Questions came quickly, unwaveringly, drawing out my life story, especially showing care in exploring my New Zealand background. His subtle examination required my having a stable knowledge of Yeatman's true history, also a lot of imagination and lying guesswork to fill unexpected gaps. The other officers made notes and I wondered nervously when they would attack on the crucial issues. I knew perfectly well what I had to say, a web of lies carefully rehearsed. It was clear to me that my abnormal story would be scorned, but it represented my only rock of refuge and I intended sticking to it.

I gave the truth as applying to Yeatman, about capture on Crete in June 1940 and transfer to Stalag VIIIB in Upper Silesia as a prisoner of war. I stated that a New Zealand companion, George Potter, was sent with me to work in a coal-mine at Beuthen; together we escaped and living from hand to mouth wandered the German–Polish border, heading north to the Baltic with ideas of gaining freedom in Sweden. Unfortunately, Potter fell sick and I was compelled to leave him almost dead in a barn in Neutitschein. Sick myself and in a state of desperation, I smuggled aboard the wrong train which carried me east instead of north. I left it at Posen where I chanced to meet a pro-British German–Pole who assisted me. He organized a generous supply of money, arranged for my photograph to be taken and forged papers to be completed in Posen for movement to the Ukraine. 'Why did you choose to go to such a dangerous area as the approach to the Eastern Front?' I was asked. Plying the lies, I said that I had been told it was possible to make my way to Russian allies, and of course, return to Britain and freedom.

The trio retired from the room for a brief interval while, under guard, I was permitted to take the weight off my legs. I sensed I was on the abyss of personal disaster. When they returned, obviously they had connived on a stratagem. I now faced men filled with hideous malice and hate. They were contemptuous of all I had told them and I was given a penetrating understanding of what I was to face. I betrayed nothing. I stuck to my rigmarole, shadowy as I knew it to be. The remainder of the session was a grotesque performance of mocking disbelief, threats, boasts and bouts of screaming rage. I was obviously an enigma and was protecting what, to them, were dangerous Poles. Scar Face screamed, 'You were dropped into Poland on a British parachute operation! Where? When? Your New Zealand knowledge is patchy, an obvious cover story. We want the truth and will get the truth!'

I have indicated earlier on that it is not my desire to redescribe certain episodes which I recounted in the first edition of this book. My sojourn in this vile prison is one such episode. It was a place of torture and murder, where moral decency and human treatment had dwindled into animal tooth-and-claw behaviour; a return to barbarism where the lowest, most filthy of creatures held limitless power over men and women whose only 'crimes' were giving proof of moral conscience and patriotism; or being simply members of what was falsely termed the 'Jewish Race'. What I recount here, I do because the whole experience had lasting impact in my life, and also I wish to put into context certain events not previously disclosed.

In interrogation, it was useless denying I had been arrested in civilian clothes, without military identification, with forged papers bearing the 'Arbeitskontrolle' stamps of Czestochowa, with a large sum of illegal currency and carrying two capsules of potassium cyanide. I was obviously not a Pole, Henryk Kowalski, nor it seemed a convincing New Zealander. Then what the devil was I? What subversive, dangerous purpose lay behind my presence in the all too rebellious Generalgouvernement?

While my denials were rigorous, I had to admit to myself that the convictions of my interrogators that I was a British parachutist in league with the Polish resistance were reasonable. A trial and, if found guilty, execution were the recognized procedures for subversion in the game of war. But as the Nazis played the game there was no clean, honourable line between arrest and execution. The only times when I sensed I made any score was in repeatedly insisting that it was my accepted duty to escape, as it was for any German prisoner of war: I would sense a faint hesitation on their parts.

I lost count of time, interminable hours of interrogation, black days of solitary, severe beatings, kicking jackboots. One day, I was starved; next day Pig Eyes and Scar Face had food brought to me. In their rage at my silence, the food was thrown at me and ground into the floor. For this filthy mess in the cell, I received further beatings and jackboots kicked at my kidneys. The time came when I determined to put an end to it. I wanted to die. Alone in the cell, I hurled my bucket about the stone walls, jumped on it in a blind fury, trying to open up a seam. I was cheated by noise and lack of speed. Guards took away the bucket and I was given another beating for the trouble. I tore my shirt to pieces but Pig Eyes found me still breathing after my running noose of lousy, ersatz fibres connected to the grille parted when subjected to my dead-weight jump from the bed boards; they wouldn't hang a cat. Twice I was taken to the courtyard and flogged, with other prisoners marched out to witness.

In their diabolical way, I was given strengthening food one day, and the next, taken to a room in the 'hospital' quarters where three of my fingers were slit open and a knife slowly pushed up under a nail. Intense anger and hatred were a barrier to pain. Then, early one morning, wearing only boots, trousers and improvised shirt bandages around my fingers, I was marched to the courtyard to watch as eight Polish women were led to a position facing a wall and shot. I thought of the same happening to Sister Maria and the other nuns of Czestochowa. My wrists were fastened to steel rings attached to the wall, my back to the firing squad. I was given a last chance. 'Where did you get those papers?'

My reply was a torrent of abuse. I heard a crashing burst of noise. Bullets slammed at the stone wall. I remained tremblingly alive. It was a well-known Gestapo technique to tip sanity and resistance over the brink, and all too often it succeeded. After that shattering burst of noise, something exploded within, deeply etching itself on my soul, something which is mysteriously difficult to explain. If I felt a miracle had happened, I also experienced a sinister nervousness that I had cheated Fate. For many years, on into post-war adventuring, I could not get rid of the feeling that a revengeful Fate was determined to catch up with me, sooner rather than later. The effect was to breed almost a bravado, a challenging attitude to Fate, to get on with it and call it a day.

After my mock execution, I was left alone and time passed excruciatingly. I was black and blue from all the football kicks Scar Face and the guards had practised on me, and my right lung was now playing up. The light was unexpectedly switched on one night, and three young German soldiers entered, carrying palliasses. It appeared that my cell-mates had run foul of the military police and were being lodged here, as the nearest detention centre, until collected to be taken to Cracow. They were surprisingly friendly, certainly not uncouth, but I was cautious and suspicious of Gestapo trickery. Obviously they had been given a clear picture about me and they revealed unusual interest, probing about my fighting activities in Greece and Crete, and asking a great deal about New Zealand. I parried and retold the story of escaping with a companion from a coal-mine, leaving him near dead, going on to Posen and getting papers from an old man to take me east, hopefully to freedom. Asked why I had made such a stupid mistake in reviling Hitler, I said I had been too tired and sick to be rational, and for that matter, I would have reviled Churchill for not heeding Rudolf Hess and concluding a hasty peace with Hitler! We would have been brothers in arms now, drinking schnapps and enjoying girls! This reference to Hess seemed to make a big difference to their attitude, but when they left in the morning, with an air of good-fellowship, I was puzzled and worried about their trying to win me over.

The next extraordinary event was a visit by Pig Eyes, no longer hostile or aggressive, and I nearly fell over with astonishment when told I would be returned to the sick bay where my lungs would be examined. I was completely taken aback when told my name and prisoner of war identity had been verified, and the authorities of Stalag VIIIB were anxious for my return. This was being considered, but I would have to be fit enough to make the journey back to Germany.

I was not removed immediately but passed another day alone in the dungeon, during which the silver lining to my cloud faded as I brooded over what might be going on. Was it another hoax? As things stood now, not a friend in the world would ever know if I were exterminated with thousands of Jews and Poles, lost for ever in an old fort. Or had the Gestapo learned I was a British flier? Perhaps the real Yeatman and Potter had been caught out? Were the Gestapo in Holland, with their counterparts in Poland, changing their tactics to get to the bottom of my duplicity? Had my secret code been broken down? If so, I would get short shrift, but at least I might be officially recorded as having been executed!

Then I was moved to a fair-sized room on a second floor of the so-called sick-bay, but close enough to the torture chamber where my fingers had been cut. It was heaven's own delight to have the full light of day pouring through wide, barred windows. I could hardly believe my good fortune, with a real bed, mattress and blankets and, this time, no circlet of steel about my ankle. Intense joy overwhelmed me to hear a kindly voice and find myself with human society, albeit a German, but one who greeted me cordially, if gravely. My room companion, a political prisoner, was confined to his bed with broken legs in plaster. He introduced himself as Professor Hans Burckhardt. (I am certain he was a professor and almost as certain his surname was 'Burckhardt'; I am less sure of his Christian name.)

A certitude that I was still sane and determinedly obstinate to resist pricked me keenly, immediately arousing my in-built sense of caution and mistrust. A Dr Ernst Wurm, old enough to have known the First World War, was responsible for our treatment. This quiet-spoken man had none of the characteristics of his SS masters, exhibiting no embittered feelings, crude anger or restless, cruel impulses. He informed me I would act as medical orderly for my crippled companion: bed pans and toilet needs were in a small bathroom–lavatory annexe; also an ultra-violet lamp which I was to use on my badly lacerated and bruised face and body. He visited us three times daily and invariably spoke in French to the professor in a low voice, and frequently strode to the window to stare out thoughtfully, as if seeking something which eluded him. He drained my right lung, bringing immediate relief, and together with sustaining soups, unlimited bread, jam and ersatz coffee, the sudden change to comfort greatly aided my mental and physical recovery. An elderly weary guard unlocked the door at intervals to inspect or bring food, but we remained unchallenged and he appeared to have no sharp eyes or interest in anything but popping things into his permanently chewing mouth.

The professor was of delicate build, with a fine-modelled but strong face, and was old enough to be my father. He spoke excellent English and his academic field was political philosophy. He had been arrested on two counts, one of which was for concealing a Jew, in fact his wife, who was part German, part Polish Jew. In their policy of Jewish extermination, the Nazis practised '*Sippenhaft*', the arrest of kith and kin. The professor had secured a hiding place for his wife and their two sons with German friends on a country estate.

The penalty for harbouring Jews was death. The Jewish partner of a so-called 'mixed marriage' would be sent to a death-camp, as a matter of course. The non-Jew who had tried to foil the Nazis was almost certain to go too, and so might their children. On a secret visit to his family, Hans Burckhardt had been tracked and pounced upon by the Gestapo who already had him under suspicion of being a member of a German group in opposition to the Hitler regime, a group which I have since learned was known as the 'Kreisau'. I am not sure whether Hans had jumped in trying to escape, or whether he had been hurled from an upper-floor window and so had broken his legs. Whichever it was, he was being restored to health to face far worse suffering.

He was a remarkable man and in that locked room we had endless discussions. He brought me to an abrupt realization that there existed an active opposition to the Nazis, Germans of intellect and consequence, with thoughts for the overthrow of Hitler and the reconstruction of a sane, decent Germany. He saw it as a terrible mistake that Hitler had been allowed to gain power; unless struck down in some *coup d'état*, the world and Germany faced unimaginable peril, moral and material. He adhered to a certainty that the German people would not allow Hitler to survive as the war became increasingly ruinous.

I came to realize that my sick companion was no clever Gestapo plant, but a certain type of man with an excellence of character and courage rare among any race, a Teuton who would never surrender his soul to a dictator or criminal oligarchy. In the situation in which we found ourselves, we drew together and a great deal was confided in almost mouth-to-ear conversations. Hans was obsessed by a strange, obdurate conviction that Hitler would be removed by some single-handed endeavour. If at first I stuck to my web of lies about being a New Zealand escaper, Hans listened quietly, never attempting to discredit my tale. But he was not fooled.

As the chords of trust became steadier between us, I finally unravelled my story. He too had concluded that I had been parachuted into Poland, possibly to join the FAN organization, a Polish Home Army unit whose members were forbidden to contact the Home Army network in any sector. FAN was kept extremely secret in view of the extent of its penetration into the German organization. This, he had surmized, accounted for my suicide attempt, to guarantee the safety of others after being captured by ill luck. What I really found bewildering to accept was that the top echelon of Polish resistance, at that period of the war, was liaising with German adherents of genuine opposition to Hitler and the Nazis.

My vigour was increasing – finger cuts healing, weals and body bruises vanishing – when unexpectedly the three Gestapo interrogators responsible for my disfigurements clattered into the room, accompanied by Dr Wurm. Scar Face acidly asked how much longer would it be before I could be removed to Germany? In stiff, official tones, the doctor replied that my lung trouble and certain heart disturbance were not entirely cured. 'If he's required in Germany alive,' he added firmly, 'anything less than fourteen days might not guarantee it.'

Pig Eyes focused on the professor. '*He's* required in Berlin. He can be transported on a hospital train from the Eastern Front.'

Dr Wurm pointed out the value of my nursing orderly services and suggested it would be sensible if we were dispatched at the same time.

'The limit is ten days from now,' was the parting ultimatum.

For all his display of Nazi rectitude, Dr Wurm had played for time on our behalf, but whatever his sympathy he could do no more when the time limit expired. He was one of many German medical practitioners forcibly recruited to serve the cause of Hitler's terror and 'Final Solution' in political prisons and extermination centres for Jews. Upon peril of his life, he dared not express opposition to the regime, but like many of his standing gave proof of conscience and professional ethics, where opportunity presented, to make things easier for the victims by acts of concealed assistance. Such certainly applied in our cases.

In our aloneness, the professor and I suffered torments of uncertainty. Days progressed and a stage was reached where friendship between two mortals of opposing nationalities had drifted into something deeper than could have been imagined. When one is helping a man empty his bowels, imprisoned with him, in equal peril from the same foe, inevitably each makes a penetrating analysis of the other's sheer edge of spirituality. With nothing found wanting, there is a strong drawing together, in trust, sympathy and support. I came to love that man, even as I tended his most fundamental needs.

The professor seemed to possess unwavering conviction that I was meant to survive and fight another day. It became unavoidably obvious that he held me, as I did him, in profoundest esteem. Aware that our association would be short-lived, his whispered talks to me revealed he was deeply moved and looked upon me in an entirely new and unforeseen way. He reminded me, time and again, that my nature, my outwitting the enemy from Holland onwards, my masquerade to gain scope of action on working parties, amounted to something he had a peculiar prescience about. To him it suggested that our coming together might have been planned by the more obliging gods of war. He had a feeling deep in his bones that I would escape execution, and if I continued to survive as a New Zealand soldier, with opportunity to get outside on working parties, I might be of further use in important schemes against the Nazi regime.

He became increasingly moved on this score, yet his thinking was particularly clear. His trust in me was unquestionable and it seemed he was conscious of clutching on to me as his last straw. He knew he was going to the gate. The idea dominated his mind that it would be honourable and totally appropriate for an Englishman to be part of the fulfilment of his hopes, as part of his destiny and mine, to effect the destruction of Hitler, or at least one or more of his co-tyrants.

Involvement in future top-level underground schemes seemed far-fetched and I was averse, understandably so, to adapting myself to extreme courses. I had no romantic or heroic ideas of getting involved in further mischief. I had had enough and preferred to sit on my backside until the war folded up, one way or the other. But he did not let up. In deadly earnest, he proposed a means for having me contacted in a prison camp, if opportunity permitted.

From my first encounter with the professor, my attention had been drawn to a heavy, gold signet ring on the third finger of his left hand. On closer examination, I was struck by the similarity of its crest to that of my former squadron; 15 Squadron's crest bore a hind's head between elevated wings and the motto 'Aim Sure'. His ring had a deeply engraved stag's head, with each antler bearing six points; its German motto was *'Festigkeit'*, meaning firmness, stability or solidity. I was asked to accept a replica of his ring as a token of esteem and appreciation of my efforts to care for him. If it so happened that we both went to the wall, at least it would be a kind of unifying satisfaction that the intrinsic brotherhood of man transcended all the evil of dictators, irrespective of whatever clan one belonged to. I said I would be honoured to wear a counterpart of his ring, and imagined that somehow he had a second one in his possession. At the same time, I tended to consider his gesture as stemming from the increasing anxiety of our going separate ways; something of a mental aberration of the professor's to give me a final keepsake.

I was thunderstruck when he said a slightly different version of his ring would be made without delay, and he asked for an English motto of fewer than ten letters. My squadron's motto immediately came to mind. Then he revealed that Dr Wurm, a silent supporter in opposition to the Hitler regime, a sympathetic friend, would be directed to a goldsmith in nearby Cracow, where the ring would be cast. The mysteries of the German resistance movement were unknown to me at the time, but four days later, after a routine visit by Dr Wurm, I came to own a heavy gold signet ring which I wear to this day. It had been made to look worn and bruised. The stag's head impression was perfect and, agape, I read the engraved motto, 'Aim Sure'. It had one other feature distinguishing it from his: one antler had six points, the other five.

Accepting the ring was not the last to be said about it. Should I be contacted, I was told, it would be by some special underground operator who would give infallible proof of his genuineness by producing a replica of the *professor's* ring. This ring idea was frequently employed for such clandestine purposes; Dr Wurm possessed a replica himself. It was impressed upon me that in wearing my ring I should keep it twisted with the engraved oval inside my palm; externally it would appear as a plain gold band, the symbol of married men in Continental countries.

I had told the professor of my marble-chiselling days, and in his almost obsessional discussing of Hitler he dreamed of the possibility of my getting into Berchtesgaden, perhaps as a stonemason labourer! He said his cadre knew backwards every detail of the construction of air-raid shelters and other building going on at Hitler's Berchtesgaden headquarters. I probably boasted, 'If ever I have a chance of getting into

*Above:* Debriefing after our exploratory raid on the night of 2–3 September 1941 to locate the triangular forest near Berlin, take night photographs and bomb Goering's master-brain complex as a prelude to large-scale onslaughts. I am second from left, our skipper Wallace Terry is second from right, our Group Captain is standing at the rear

*Right:* Prior to take-off on my last, ill-fated mission to Berlin. I'm holding my navigator-type parachute. Such chutes were not worn in flight since they obstructed movement. A piece of German anti-aircraft shell ripped through the folded layers of silk rendering it useless

*Below:* A photograph taken secretly by a member of the Dutch Resistance shows German soldiers milling around our wrecked Stirling

*Above:* Jock Moir. After his capture with me he was imprisoned in Stalag VIIIB, Luft III, Luft VI and Stalag 357 and was finally liberated in Lübeck and returned to England on VE Day

*Right:* Wilhelm Branderhorst, Dutch clogmaker of Hengelo (Gelderland). He came to our aid when Moir and I were hiding in a wood

*Below:* Bernard Besselink, the Dutch farmer who was shot by the Germans in November 1941 for the help he gave us

*Below Right:* Jan Agterkamp, schoolmaster of Hengelo, who contacted the Dutch Resistance Movement in Amsterdam on our behalf and was also shot

I returned to Holland in 1954 and renewed acquaintance with Willelm (Billy) Leonhardt and his Canadian wife, Mona (Parsons). Their wartime help had meant so much. Here they approve my Dutch award – *De Erkentelijkheidsmedaille* (Order of Merit)

*Left:* Winston Merrill Yeatman (photographed in 1953), the New Zealander with whom I exchanged identities

*Above:* Mieczyslaw Borodej (Mieteck), the heroic and noble Pole with whom I escaped. He operated with the Polish Underground against the Germans until the Russians advanced and began mass arrests of loyal Poles

*Right:* Mieteck after spending twelve years in a Soviet concentration camp in Siberia. He lost an eye and his feet were frost-bitten

*Below:* Unteroffizier Küssel taking the morning roll call at Stalag VIIIB. Küssel shot and killed an RAF airgunner near the wire. On my return to the UK I reported the murder and Küssel was subsequently arrested, tried and sentenced

Russian soldiers captured by the German Army during its initial advance into the Ukraine. Stalin had refused to sign the Geneva Convention so Russian troops did not have POW status. Hundreds died of typhus and hunger and I was required to help bury them

*Left:* Goering's Berchtesgaden house

*Right:* The house after the raid by RAF 617 Squadron. Goering himself survived the bombing

Prisoners evacuated from my last camp on the Baltic which was overrun by the Soviet Army soon after I had outwitted a medical commission and finally regained freedom

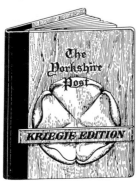

*Above:* The Kriegie Edition which we prepared in Luft VI and which contained coded information. It was smuggled back to London in less than three weeks

*Right:* Myself after Sir Archibald McIndoe had restored my badly injured face.

My host, Marshal of the RAF Lord Tedder (left) and Sir Archibald McIndoe, the famous plastic surgeon (right), at a reception given me at the RAF Club in London. This invention of mine is a hand-operated 'blower' for producing concentrated heat useful for cooking or melting certain metals

In spring 1954, not far from where our bomber had crashed, I unveiled a bronze plaque in memory of Agterkamp and Besselink. A translation of the wording on the plaque is: 'In grateful memory of Bernard Besselink and Jan Agterkamp. Greater love hath no man than this: that he lay down his life for his friends. Undying gratitude to two loyal Dutchmen. Richard Pape and William Moir of the Royal Air Force . . .'

With Group Captain Leonard Cheshire, VC, OM, DSO, DFC, on his arrival in Papua New Guinea, 1966, to visit the newly opened Cheshire Home for disabled children. In 1964 I volunteered to help establish the Home

Helen Prouting and I married in June 1966 in Port Moresby, Papua New Guinea. Helen became Deputy Public Solicitor for Papua New Guinea and I became Principal Publications Officer for the Department of Information and Extension Services

Berchtesgaden and meeting the bastard, and shooting him, I'd want to be dead before he's cold. I'm not taking a chance on being tortured for the sake of historical significance.'

'My friends will make sure of that,' the professor replied.

It all seemed impossibly far-fetched, but some things do arrest themselves in the mind. On the tenth day of the ultimatum, two guards burst into the room and tossed me my civilian clothes. They stood there as I dressed. I said, 'One last thing for my friend; a bed pan.' I went to the lavatory annexe, came back and stood by Burckhardt. We clasped hands. He pressed into my palm three capsules of potassium cyanide which he had kept concealed somewhere. He whispered, 'If you don't make it, good luck on the way out. I'll be going the same way.'

Looking back, it was Dr Wurm who no doubt had provided the capsules containing the same substance as was pressed into the mouths of Jews. Taking the pan to the flush in the annexe, swiftly I wrapped the sealed, metallic capsules in cotton wool, stuffed two inside a lower cheek and one in an ear.

Twenty minutes later, staggered and bewildered but no longer so fearful of the future, I was in a pounding truck *en route* to a railway station for a train back to Germany. Over hours of strained silence, wedged between two guards, I thought a lot about meeting the professor. It all seemed a melodrama, unbelievably fantastic. But gripping the signet ring inside my palm gave indisputable realization that every incident in that prison had been stark reality. What now? Contemplating arrival at Stalag VIIIB, I was aware that if the security officers were the same as those who had grilled me when I was the British airman from Dulag Luft, following my freedom run in Holland, my masquerade as a soldier would be over and I could expect little mercy. They would pounce on the real Yeatman and Potter in the RAF compound, but what would send the Germans into screaming fits would be to discover that a Polish airman had vanished into his native land. Remembering the threats to the Poles if any one of their number escaped, I scarcely dared think what retaliations might be inflicted upon Mieteck's compatriots in the air force compound.

# CHAPTER 13

## Postscript to Poland

Unknown to me on that journey, fortune had been stupendously kind during my absence in Poland. The entire swag of air force prisoners, including Yeatman and Potter, had been transferred on 21 May 1942 to Luft III at Sagan, near Berlin. Wonder of wonders, the security officers who could have picked me out as Richard Pape had gone with them!

It was late when I was escorted straight to a cell on arrival at VIIIB. Next morning when I was brought before interrogators, it was a great relief to find all new faces. I stuck to the story I had given in Poland and anger flamed when I gave the cock-and-bull account of leaving my New Zealand companion, George Potter, tucked in the straw on the verge of death. Charges against me were read out and I was threatened with a trial which could have led to civil imprisonment, or worse. After God knows how long, the chief security officer sententiously announced that it was considered I had been sufficiently punished, but for escaping from the coal-mine working party, I would spend thirty days in solitary confinement. Hardly able to believe my luck, I could have whooped for joy.

Solitary here was luxury compared to the not easily forgotten dungeon; three blankets, a palliasse on sleeping boards, a brand new bucket of featherweight metal – had I had one like this, instead of the galvanized boiler-type in Cracow, I would have been dead. Delicious daylight poured through a wide, barred window, so exciting that in a strange way, at first, I wished it would never end. I watched khaki-clad British Tommies wandering under guard on work parties and the greatest joy was to open the window to bawl at the top of my voice, 'What's the news?'

'The Yanks are in!' came the reply. I knew this already, but I thrilled to hear their voices. I no longer felt a forgotten exile in no man's land. In addition to bread and water, I received soup at midday, awaited with keenest gastronomic anticipation. On the third day, I was ravenously awaiting the soup when a British Army padre paid me a visit. Ashamed though I am to admit it, I am afraid I badly discouraged his confidence in returned escapees. I listened without sympathy to his fawning enunciations, that we kneel together by my bed boards and pray to lead back to a state of grace a misled and wavering German nation. 'Forgive them,' he said, 'for they know not what they do.'

'What?' I shouted. 'They know bloody well what they do! Pray for those bastards, after what I've seen? Never!' I really blew my top. I said first cut their fingers, flog them naked and get all the ecclesiastics to fire around them as the SS had done. Then screw barbed wire around Hitler's head and nail him and his whole gang, with their own bayonets, to swastikas on the Brandenburg Gate in Berlin! I told him to take a trip to a political prison and enjoy its hospitality before giving me a basinful of religious hogwash!

I had come in raw. Padres had no idea what was going on in political prisons and extermination camps. They never went outside the stalags. He kept tut-tutting as I raged on and must have thought I was a nut case. Next day, I gasped with delight when Captain Spencer came in, the RAMC doctor who had been such a splendid go-between and mentor at the time of negotiating the change of identities. He said, 'What are you doing here? I've heard you're going round the bend.'

He was astonished to see me back after months and was shocked at my condition, for despite the treatment at the prison hospital in Cracow the lash weals, bruises and cuts were still in evidence. I weighed eight stone as against my normal twelve. Spencer was a man who always seemed objective and even-tempered, but his anger was stirred. 'The sadists!' he exclaimed. 'I'm getting you examined by the German camp medical officer. You're half-starved and your lungs could qualify you for tuberculosis, unless you're built up.'

He listened avidly to the tale of my Polish adventure, while finding it hard to believe what was going on in the world outside. My information was valuable. Asked about Mieteck, I told of our parting at Cracow. Spencer was thrilled to learn that Mieteck had made his break to freedom.

Neither of us could have imagined what triumph, and tragedy, lay ahead for Mieteck. After the war, despite every effort by Air Ministry, Intelligence and Polish authorities in Britain, the only fragmentary information which came to me about Mieteck's fate was: 'After leaving Pape in Cracow, he managed to escape through Hungary and Bulgaria to Turkey, where he later died of tuberculosis.'

This was wholly incorrect. Early in 1956 I was in Canada when I received a letter from the Polish Air Force Association in Britain. I was astounded and overjoyed to learn that Mieteck was alive. Former Warrant Officer Mieczyslaw Boredej had gone to the British Air Attaché (Group Captain Ridgeway) in Warsaw seeking to establish his ex-RAF identity. The Air Ministry in London contacted me and agreed that I pose questions about our secret activities in 1942 which no one in the world but the real Mieteck could possibly answer correctly. He did.

Nothing I could write about Mieteck's years of agony and the greatness of his spirit and courage could reveal the same moving impressions as he portrayed in his own simple and

sincere words. He wrote to me from Poland in the first
months of 1956 after receiving a copy of the first edition of
*Boldness*:

After our parting in Cracow, I left for Lvov at 15.30 and I got there
at 7.30 next morning. I, of course, came head on to the terrible
German Occupation. I soon joined the Underground Movement
AK so that I could carry on our struggle against oppressors. I
became a leader of an Intelligence unit which collected information
about movements of the German Army to be sent to Britain and
Russia. It was a very difficult struggle and a lot of valuable lives
were lost on the battlegrounds and in the concentration camps. I
have lost a lot of friends who were worthy sons of their country.
Very often I found myself in difficult positions. Two of us once
freed about forty sick political prisoners in 1943. We were
successful in 1944 and used to take, or damage, tanks and annihilate
big units, etc.

Towards the end of July 1944, when Russia's armies were
nearing Lvov, we came out of hiding and again fought the Germans
openly. I took part in street battles against the Boche with our new
'friends' (Russians). The town took on a holiday look, our flags
with those of Allied countries were on nearly every house. But the
Russians of Stalin's regime refused to recognize Lvov as a Polish
town, and wanted to bring all our efforts to nothing. They started
mass arrests of people whose only crime was a great love of their
own country. I myself was arrested in the same circumstances,
although I fought as a soldier and had no political status, I was
sentenced to twenty years' hard labour, and the rights of
citizenship were taken from me.

I was deported to the north-east [of Siberia], the estuary of
Kolyma River, not very far from Kamchatka Peninsula [north of
the Arctic Circle, over the Arctic Ocean]; roughly 160°E, 70°N.
To be able to understand its meaning, one must experience it. The
life in northern Kolyma and severe climate (60° centigrade below
zero) were real hell, where we had to work and work like a machine.
Only a few of us came back to Port Magadan in 1955; the rest died
there in an unfriendly and cursed region.

I was truly shocked to learn where Mieteck had been, a
slave in Soviet gold-mines. He was released with the
rehabilitations which began in 1954, following Stalin's death

in February 1953. He returned minus one eye, his body partly paralysed and permanently injured by frost-bite. He was in a pitiful state, desperately in need of help. Kolyma is only one region of the vast penal empire in the Soviet east and north, named in its entirety by Alexander Solzhenitsyn as 'The Gulag Archipelago'. But Kolyma was also the deadliest region, to become likened to Auschwitz and labelled by Solzhenitsyn 'the pole of cold and cruelty'. The bones of some three million people lie in the permafrost of Kolyma, victims of murder on a horrible scale comparable to Hitler's Final Solution, Mieteck said, 'It is a miracle that I am still alive.'

He wrote in 1956:

We have kept our promises, you have found my friends and even made our sufferings immortal. I am studying your book and live through the pictures for a second time . . . often I go back in my mind to those days and the dangerous moments. I compare them to the very similar moments in the Far North-East, moments that were part of my life not so long ago. Now I come to the conclusion that our escape from Germany was nothing in comparison to those not so distant years. There I have tried it too, but I have failed. Failed because of a land absolutely bereft of human habitation, of food, of anything that could sustain any living person in my circumstances; because of 50° or 60°C of frost, because of climatic conditions. The result of this was a deterioration of my health and physical strength to wait for something, for God's grace. And I can only say He got me out of there. He and His pity. He enabled me to return to my Fatherland, my family, with the rest of my health and that something which we can still call human . . .

It is a pity that we were unable to continue our way to freedom together to the very end. There you would have found everything; excitement, thrill, risk, danger and the truth of life. But you have missed the bottom of human degradation and want. That's where I have been for almost twelve long years.

Where victory should have meant release and joy to millions throughout Europe, for so many, like Mieteck, it simply brought them to the threshold of a whole new battle for sheer survival in the most appalling conditions. Solzhenitsyn confirms, 'A certain number of Poles, members of the Home Army, followers of Mikolajczyk, arrived in Gulag in 1945 via our prisons. Honourable participation in an underground anti-German organization was no protection from arrest.' The years 1944–5 were to see an influx of prisoners to Kolyma from the newly liberated areas, the Baltic States, Poland and elsewhere under Soviet control. The next year, 1946, brought another influx to Kolyma, the 'homecomers', former Soviet prisoners of war in Germany, sentenced as 'deserters' on return to Russia, plus large numbers of slave labourers, including women and girls whom the Nazis had forcibly deported to work for the Third Reich, and now sentenced for 'collaboration'. To the enduring shame of Britain and America, to appease Stalin who wanted them all back, the Allies relentlessly returned hundreds of thousands of former Soviet citizens who had fled Bolshevism and had been fortunate enough to find shelter on Allied territory. All were sent to destruction on the Archipelago, for 'counter-revolutionary agitation' or other 'crimes'. By 1950–2, the numbers in the labour camp system of the Archipelago are believed to have reached twelve to fourteen million, nearly twice as many as in 1940. Only with the death of Stalin in 1953 was there an advancement of a policy of rehabilitation.

I never met Mieteck again. Regrettably, I was in distant Canada when he visited England in 1957 but I asked a good friend and neighbour in the village of Stratford St Mary, near Colchester, the writer Mrs Daphne Barclay, to meet him. She wrote:

He came to see us after the Battle of Britain ceremony in London, which meant so much to him. In it he had lost many of his friends . . . I watched the London train come in. How should I

know him? I saw a small dark man, pale and lame, very neat in grey
and a stiff collar. He looked at me and I saw that only one eye
moved. I smiled the sort of smile one could withdraw if it was
wrong. He came quickly up and kissed my hand. All was
well . . . We asked him nothing of his experiences, our early talk
naturally was of you. The physical signs of his sufferings were
evident; an emaciated and strained face which did smile, but
seemed as though it were unnatural to do so. One eye lost as you
know. One leg stiff (also resulting from being knocked out by a
roof fall). New shoes bought in London soon began to give
trouble, and we lent him slippers. It was then that we learned his
feet and toes were frost-bitten . . . His manner was extremely calm
and self-possessed. His only pressure seemed to be a fairly constant
need to smoke. Mentally, his 'un-bitterness' was remarkable (and
slightly shaming when I thought of the things most people feel
aggrieved over). He just shrugged his shoulders and said: 'It is an
incident of my life now over.'

# CHAPTER 14

# Flight from Czechoslovakia

All I knew of Mieteck up to our parting, I told Captain Spencer who promised to convey it to the right authorities in Britain. He also succeeded in having me examined by the German, Dr Schmidt, in charge of Stalag VIIIB's medical services; Spencer and the senior British doctor, Major McLeod, worked with responsibility to Schmidt. The German doctor viewed me not without pity, but still had to convince the security officers and Gestapo to release me. On the twenty-first day of my solitary, I was removed to the *Lazarett* (the camp hospital). Dr Schmidt was splendid, of the same school of thought as Dr Wurm, secretly co-operative in many ways.

The camp leader, Sergeant Major Sheriff, visited me, with others in command of the 'X' committee. It was a shot in the arm to them to hear of Mieteck's escape. I was handed mail addressed to me as Yeatman, some returned from the coal-mine after I disappeared. It was exciting to know my code was working splendidly and being handled by a department of Military Intelligence; today I know it as MI9 and derive satisfaction from learning it numbered me among early prisoners who initiated their own codes. Subsequently, MI9 developed its code and proceeded with intensive training in coding among selected men in the armed forces.

I also felt it something of a feather in my cap to discover that since my airman–soldier swap-over technique had been initiated, and before the air force contingent had been moved out of VIIIB a number of other escape-minded fliers had exchanged with soldiers to be able to join working parties on the outside. Among the fliers lying low in the soldiers' barracks was a 'Rifleman Godden', really Warrant Officer Reginald Barratt from Leicester; also three others, an Australian, Chisholm, and two Englishmen, Hickman and Rolfe. In time, just as I had recruited Mieteck as protector–interpreter, Chisholm and Hickman were to find a Palestinian, formerly a Polish Jew, to break loose with them from a working party to make their way east to partisan Poles. Of those three, Chisholm survived, so did Cyril Rolfe, who, after two abortive escapes, finally linked up with a Palestinian corporal who spoke perfect German and eventually, in 1944, reached the Russian lines.

After a halcyon spell in VIIIB's *Lazarett*, I returned to the main camp. My morale and strength had greatly revived. The lessons of Poland were still vivid in my mind, but something clamoured inside me to embark on a further escape attempt. It seemed that the sequel to my Polish odyssey was the implanting of a tremendous hate and grievance against the SS – an obsession for retaliation against the Gestapo. It was a strange and cherished insanity which had grooved my mind almost to the curves of my skull. I had somehow lost value for human life and seemingly had no fear of death after rifles had been levelled at me and I had heard them fire. Past strain on body and mind had peculiarly dispersed, and the whole edifice of my logic compelled me to try again. God knew how long the war would go on. Experience in Holland and Poland made it clear to me that the only way to have a chance of beating the enemy was as a masquerading soldier, able to rely on outside Intelligence sources. Otherwise, I might as well lie flat on my back. I could do nothing alone.

About this time, the 'X' committee found its resourcefulness tested in the monumental case of swinging a switch to get Wing Commander Douglas Bader out as a soldier, Private Fenton. Bader pitched up for treatment on troublesome leg stumps. Also, a Flight Lieutenant John

Palmer entered VIIIB's *Lazarett* for attention to a foot. I subscribed ideas to the 'X' committee, but trying to get Bader with his stomping gait out of the main gate with a working party while someone 'covered' for him for many days in a hospital bed was a pretty tall order. Palmer was to go with him, and a 'cover' also arranged for him. As against the almost insuperable problems, it would be the scoop of the war if Bader could be smuggled out, close to an enemy airfield, hopefully to pinch a German aircraft and escape with enough fuel to get him to Sweden, less than 400 miles away. What a boost for up-and-coming RAF aircrew, not to mention the morale of the British public, if it could be pulled off!

It was a coup in itself to find Fenton, a man of no mean courage and determination and roughly resembling an unshaven Bader. For an average private soldier to stand in for an internationally famous air ace and adapt to instructions on how to behave mentally and physically as Bader, was like asking for certain stars to come out of the galaxy. Holes were cut in the mattress and bed to allow the long-suffering Fenton to drop his legs with his toes nervously twitching on the floor boards whenever a German medical officer made his rounds and asked 'Bader' how he felt. The story is legend of how nearly the plan succeeded at the Luftwaffe satellite 'drome near the town of Gleiwitz, Poland. It failed with the discovery at the hospital of the 'covers'. The camp authorities were thrown into a state of fury. Phones buzzed. A senior camp officer and a posse of guards took off with all speed for Gleiwitz. The working party was paraded and ordered to drop slacks, the most expeditious way to discover a man with two tin legs. Bader stepped forward to avoid humiliation to the others. Gloating Germans rushed Bader and Palmer, who also had stepped forward, back to Lamsdorf to face solitary confinement.

By now, in late August 1942, the effects of the activities of Intelligence sources in Britain were really being felt in very many prisoner of war camps over their vast network within the Axis sphere. Among the many amazing activities, consignments of escape and subversive aids were being smuggled in, and secret escape or evasion lines were being set up, with partisan contacts, in enemy-held countries. It was suggested I should remain on the inside of the wire at Lamsdorf, concentrating on Intelligence work and helping others to escape. This was contrary to the demands of my make-up. Inside the cage, time dragged; outside it flew, in planning and preoccupation to regain freedom which tested fortitude, endurance, reckless *élan* and infinite control.

Aware of my determination to make a further attempt, loyal conspirators who lived and dreamed corrosive intrigue offered every possible assistance. This time, I would go to Czechoslovakia, with the hope of reaching Yugoslavia via Hungary. Time was needed for planning and, to avoid being rated fit by the German Arbeitskontrolle, the RAMC doctors played it up that my lungs were still likely to deteriorate if subjected to strain. I was given light duties in the camp. But as soon as I knew the direction of my escape attempt I sent off coded messages to Britain and anxiously awaited response.

Prisoners were allowed to receive from home one ten-pound clothing parcel every quarter, but an unrestricted number of cigarette packages. From my experience, I add confirmation to the assertions made by British Intelligence departments involved in smuggling to prisoners that the privileged position of the International Red Cross was never violated; its parcels were never tampered with. Certainly, I and others chose to tighten our belts and conserve Red Cross supplies for escape rations, or for blackmailing the enemy. Private parcels, however, were fair game for smuggling. Pre-warned by coded messages, we knew to look for certain markings or labels on parcels which might contain maps, forging materials, compasses, money, miniature cameras, photographic materials or other vital items. I received many pre-warnings from Willcox but parcels also came from fictitious friends and never-before-heard-of clubs or notional societies, all anxious to help the poor boys behind the wire pass away the tedious hours. Aids came concealed in sporting goods, musical instruments, study materials; money was stitched into the broad canvas hems of blankets; hacksaw blades were in cigarette packages and in all sorts of ways, many now forgotten, the contraband came in. Various moulds for making Arbeitskontrolle stamps arrived – and even a mould for an Iron Cross, together with the medal ribbon wrapped decoratively around a cigarette parcel.

The quarterly parcel I awaited duly appeared. It came from London, if purportedly it was sent by my 'mother' in Christchurch and bore New Zealand stamps and convincing postal marks. Additionally, I received a dozen cigarette packages from a Yorkshire prisoners' welfare club – in truth, Alfred Willcox in cohorts with Intelligence. I found all I had requested: foreign currencies, my most urgent requirement; clothing and heavy field shoes. I removed the heels; they were full of developing and printing chemicals and phials of copying ink. Pen nibs were between the soles and a bar of carbolic soap concealed a piece of powerful magnifying glass for forging work.

Meanwhile, Sheriff and other trusted friends were active on my behalf. It was essential that when I left for a working party in Czechoslovakia, it should be in the most suitable location for escape and where I could be contacted by resistance agents. Assistance from the underground was indispensable. Without it, I would have been a hibernating tortoise. I give all credit. I would be tackling Czechoslovakia at the worst possible time with dangers running exceptionally high. Disturbing news all round was being received in the camp via our various sources: secret radio, German newspapers smuggled to us by bribed guards, and by word of mouth. Throughout Czechoslovakia, terror of such ferocity had descended as to set us wondering if any assistance from the resistance would be out of the question. What happened was that two Czech agents, British trained, had been parachuted into Slovakia with the objective of assassinating the head of the dreaded secret police and Reich protector of the country, SS General Reinhard Heydrich, whose regime was notorious for cruelty and bestiality. In a street in Prague, one of the agents tossed a grenade into Heydrich's car; he died of wounds a few days later, on 6 June 1942. Hitler went berserk over this killing of one of his favourite and topmost men. On 10 June, the little mining village of Lidice, near Prague, took the full force of German reprisal. Alleging that the village had aided the agents, the entire 172 male inhabitants were shot; fifty-six women were shot and the rest, along with most of the children, were sent to concentration camps, where many died. The village was destroyed, the ground ploughed up and its name removed from official records. Ten days later the small village of Lezaky suffered a similar fate. Martial law overlay the small country whose people, since 1939, had remained bitterly and actively hostile throughout to the German oppressors. Considering the part played by the British in the assassination of Heydrich, it certainly did not augur well for any British soldier caught on the run in Czechoslovakia!

The other especially depressing news was of the Dieppe Raid. When we first got wind of this massive assault of 18 August 1942, we were thrilled and excited, believing that the Second Front had opened up. Such optimism was short-lived when the horrible defeat at Dieppe became known. The enemy's facetious ranting and rejoicing added to our depression. The prospect of endless incarceration, which in imagining had been gloriously foreshortened, reassumed dullest progression. It certainly revitalized my determination to get moving. Secret negotiations were in hand with Czechoslovakian loyalists to take me under their wing. It is still largely a mystery to me how it was being effected with the UVOD, the secret Czech army for internal sabotage and resistance, or the Czech Intelligence Organization known as Sparta I and Sparta II, other than that effective radio communication existed between these loyalists and their provisional government in London, which in turn was in liaison with British Intelligence.

All I could do was await instructions. Ingenious cog-wheels of planning revolved and an ideal working party was arranged for me to join in a village, Partschendorf, close to the town of Troppau (now Opava) in Sudetenland. Some fifty Britishers worked there. Sheriff paid them a routine visit, along with a German liaison officer, in accordance with Geneva Convention procedure to investigate conditions and any complaints. Four soldiers were returned to the parent camp at Lamsdorf – with real or invented complaints of ulcers, appendicitis, psychiatric disorders, or God knows what. Two more put on a disobedience performance of no-work and were brought back for punishment. The six returnees, of sturdy heart and anxious to co-operate with whatever the sergeant major had in mind, had to be replaced.

I was one of the replacements and so was 'Rifleman Godden' who, like myself, had been treading water until a suitable working party could be found for him. Sheriff told me that Godden knew I was masquerading as a New Zealand soldier, but I was instructed not to probe his background or let him know that I was alert to his identity, until a later date. Godden, as I have said, was one of the former fliers lying low in the soldiers' barracks. The less we talked the better, because of suspected German plants, 'funnies', we called them, posing as British soldiers in our midst. So

Godden and I acted as typical private soldiers, grumbling about leaving the security and known bedevilments of the parent stalag.

In fact, Godden (alias Reginald Barratt) and I would be virtual guinea-pigs testing prearranged escape lines. Our mentors at Lamsdorf made it clear that we would not escape together from Czechoslovakia when resistance people took over our individual destinies. Going singly would double the chances of either of us making it alone along prescribed lines. One would go first, allowing German reactions and other decisive factors to be assessed. It was absolutely essential for the Germans to believe our escapes were self-engineered, with no outside help, for the slightest suspicion of resistance implication could result in terrible civilian reprisals. There were many things we were not to know in advance, especially how we would be approached and identified at Partschendorf, but passwords would be provided and if changed, we would be notified by coded mail sent through a local contact. Everything was wrapped in secrecy and mystery.

Once more I stood with a group on the little station of Annaberg which served the vast complex of Stalag VIIIB. We were twenty soldiers with three guards. It was a late summer's day, bright, warm, comforting. Previously, I had scarcely bothered to invest a second glance at this Lilliputian station; now I saw it might have been a village station in Britain with carefully tended patches of flowers and shrubs. The sunlight struck a chord, with the reminder that: 'If you search, then the important thing is to carry the sun with you at every moment against darkness.' I was enveloped by the thought that I was again setting out for freedom and home. 'Third time lucky,' I told myself. 'First Holland, next Poland, now Czechoslovakia. In for a penny, in for a pound.'

*     *     *

The train chugged past German aerodromes and I attempted to draw Godden out on trumpery issues about flying, but he firmly stuck to his soldiering status. I was impressed by his behavioural pattern. He was the type to face challenges and interrogations unflinchingly. I certainly approved my escape companion chosen by VIIIB's escape selectors.

Tense and tired, we reached the town of Troppau and the party split up. Godden and I with four others, accompanied by a guard, continued by road for some miles, passing a Crucifixion shrine on high ground by the roadside just before reaching Partschendorf. It was an idyllic village of quaint, whitewashed, part-timbered cottages. Our quarters were at the bottom of the main street, a former school-hall of old but strong timber, elevated, with underground cellars. It stood alone in a fair-sized piece of ground bounded by a single wall of sagging barbed wire which any half-wit could easily have penetrated. Our arrival seemed an uncomfortable surprise to the *Feldwebel* in charge and to the forty-four long-term residents of the British working party. I soon discovered their reasons for concern. The middle-aged *Feldwebel* was obese and his six well-nourished guards were a weary, indifferent bunch, no more fit for battlefront service than a bevy of arthritic grandmothers. It became obvious that all were over-aged and under graft, and co-existence with the prisoners was on a relaxed friendly footing with a lot of surreptitious winks and nods exchanging.

Working party conditions varied widely. Coal-mines, factories and workshops were generally foul, with little movement, harsh discipline, meagre standard rations and filthy work. Agricultural assignments were most sought after, particularly in Czechoslovakia, and a few were known as 'cushy' and 'soft-skinned'. This German-controlled state farm at Partschendorf was considered the 'plum' and immune from seasonal roster, having a constant demand for labour. Most of the original volunteers were still there and few were willing to leave. Sheriff was well aware of what went on at this lax camp but the Germans were satisfied; it worked smoothly for them and no escape had ever taken place.

'What a bloody incredible state of affairs,' murmured Godden. We were working on our first job, not far from the village, and for two hours no guard had been in sight; he had entered the manor-house close by. This dignified building was occupied by a contingent of SS officers and men who were often passing us. Their primary purpose in the region was safe-guarding rail communications through the mountains. The underground had achieved notable sabotage in the passes, blowing up trains with men and supplies intended for the Eastern battlefront. If I looked upon these SS with loathing and anger, I felt nothing but affection for nature's surroundings; the green earth in wide, rolling valleys, the glorious air, the pine-clad slopes, a magnificent backdrop of blue mountains and unhampered waters of a wide, fast flowing river.

Our job, shared by the four other new arrivals, was knocking down six workmen's cottages, adjuncts to the manor-house. It was hard labour but just as formerly at the Polish coal-mine the toughest, lousiest work in Partschendorf went to the last to arrive. On the fourth day of navvying, I dislodged a beam and spotted a small leather wallet. I was staggered to find it contained three gold rings, set with large diamonds, rubies and sapphires. What a find! I told only Godden, but curious for information I enquired of a guard who was lazily sunning himself on the warm grass. He said the Jewish owner of the manor had been shot and his property confiscated.

In 1953, I wrote in the first edition of this book: 'I contemplated with amusement the consternation of the thief if he or she returned to Partschendorf to find the servants' quarters demolished . . .' Three years after publishing that, I received a surprise letter with a photograph of the manor-house. Dated 11 May 1956, the letter came from Mr A. Czeczowiczka, 68 Greencroft Gardens, London NW6. He said: 'You will be surprised from the enclosed photograph to be reminded of your enforced stay in Partschendorf after so many years. I was the former owner of the property on which you worked. I managed to escape and have lived in England since 1939. My possessions were nationalized. The former German population was driven away, and the German leader at that time was sentenced to twelve years' imprisonment . . .' I telephoned Mr Czeczowiczka and we met where I was living at the Pathfinders' Club in Mount Street, off Berkeley Square. In 1939, in the rush and confusion to get away with limited possessions, he had concealed the rings in the servants' cottage against the possibility of one day returning; they were a kind of insurance policy. By no means everyone of German descent in Sudetenland, particularly if Jewish or anti-Nazi, had welcomed the German occupiers. I certainly sympathized with my visitor in his loss and nostalgia. From all my wartime wanderings, Partschendorf remained the only place to stir in me a curious inclination that, had it been practicable, it was where I would most like to live for the rest of my days.

But all was not Elysian, particularly in the school-hall. Godden and I endeavoured to fall naturally in line with the atmosphere and practices, including the reckless thieving which was going on, and we ate as never before in captivity. Returning from work, men called at the nearby guard-house – formerly the schoolmaster's – and passed over to the *Feldwebel* a share of the day's booty, no doubt for favours in return. There was no concealment of the liberal supplies which came into our quarters: eggs, milk, cheese, vegetables, real butter, any number of plucked fowls, in addition to allotted German rations and Red Cross supplies. Racketeering was staggering! And that it had survived so long. General anxiety was lest someone blew the gaff, bringing Germans from VIIIB pouncing to investigate.

For my part, almost from the start an extremely disturbing problem cropped up. Four of the party were genuine New Zealanders. One was 'Riley', a tough, pre-war dock labourer who had lived in Christchurch, my pretended home town. He was a radical, aggressive type of man, a sometime boxer of the kind associated with fairgrounds, braggardly taking on any public challenger. He bore the marks – a cauliflower ear, bent nose, battered face, and I distinctly recall a twisted thumb. He cornered me, trying to draw me out on my supposed capture on Crete, imprisonment in the Salonika prison camp, and aftermath. I was acting under camouflage and he knew I was putting over a lying story. It was impossible for me to discuss intimate details of the Battle of Crete and certainly impossible to disclose that I was RAF. He jibed at my accent, my army career, my knowledge of Christchurch. Worst of all, he was loud-mouthed. 'He's no Kiwi,' he broadcast in the schoolhall. 'He doesn't know the North Island from the South. And he talked in German to the guards! What did you say to them?'

I blazed. 'I told them to fucking cut your fucking throat!'

Godden pulled me aside. 'For Christ's sake hold it, Yeatman. We'll have to resolve this by diplomacy.'

I make no apology for the swearing. Cursing and blinding in every camp or barrack was orchestrated. It went on from dawn to night. It did get monotonous and you didn't realize you were talking like that. It was a hymn of hate, of utter frustration, tension and a desperation which you veiled in front of your mates. Out of war, men alone and together still use it. In war, everyone did of whatever cut. There was no one to outrage, except padres. I recall a padre at one camp finding me kicking a tree and calling it 'a fucking tree'. I was trying to cut it, to get resin which we used as a substitute flux for soldering radio connections.

'Why call it that?' he asked reasonably. 'It's only a tree.'

'It's a fucking tree!' I replied heatedly.

He regarded me coolly. 'Very well then. I want all you fucking bastards to come to hear my fucking sermon on Sunday.'

I was shocked, and told him it was disgraceful for a padre to speak in such a way to a decent Christian! He wandered off shaking his head.

Riley was a damnable danger, arousing suspicion that I was a German 'funny' there to spy and squeal. The other Kiwis struck up the tune and the British boys were influenced to have suspicions. I was in a devil of a dilemma. Tension mounted and mistrust grew. In a matter of days, Riley and I became irreconcilable enemies and he remained intent upon stirring. I advised Godden to avoid any suggestion of close friendship with me; he was under no cloud, the others believing his story of being an English soldier rounded up in France. I told him, 'Look, I know you're masquerading, as I am, but whether you're aircrew or a parachuted agent, I'm not enquiring. I know we belong to the same side and I'm pretty certain I'll have to get out of here within the next week or two, if only to safeguard you.' At that stage we had not been contacted by the resistance. Soon to come about, it resolved the problem of being a phoney Kiwi.

After a week spent on knocking down the cottages, cleaning and stacking bricks and heavy oak timbers, a horse and landau halted on the driveway before us. Previously, on several occasions, it had passed by, driven by a civilian who merely stared at us disdainfully before proceeding to the rear of the manor-house. Now I observed he was in his mid-forties, with dark, wavy hair; beside him in the landau was a tall, vain-looking German Army officer of about fifty, wearing an Iron Cross. Our guard was ordered to show them the stacks of demolished building materials. We prisoners might not have existed. I moved as close as was prudent and gathered that a deal was under way. The civilian, whom the officer called 'Karel', wanted the materials. The officer replied that he was sure the SS Ober-Sturmbannführer would let Karel cart the lot away, for a few cases of schnapps.

A couple of days later, when the whole job was almost completed and it was close to knocking-off time, the landau drew up again. Karel's companion this time was a pleasant-looking woman, wearing a plum-coloured dress. He called to the dreary guard to 'stand by' until the Ober-Sturmbannführer arrived, as he did presently, driving from the manor-house in a Mercedes. While the SS officer and Karel walked off to inspect the stacks, the woman stood by the horse, holding its bridle.

Godden and I had grown beards and wore German workmen's leatherette peaked caps, given us by the 'X' committee at VIIIB. Also for identification purposes, I wore a red and brown check shirt tucked into khaki trousers; Godden had a green shirt. During the heat of day, we stripped to the waist, but now we had donned our shirts and as we waited, our faces sunburnt, eyes inflamed from the demolition dust, I little imagined we were on the brink of our great moment. Karel returned, called to the four others of our group, handed them sticks of chalk and led them off to mark the timbers he wanted from the stacks. While they were so engaged and Karel and the officer had their backs to us, the woman left the horse which stood quietly.

She came straight over to me with some sandwiches. A momentary hesitation, then she murmured, '*Erste Klasse hin und zurück*' (First class, return).

My heart beat wildly. These were the key passwords given me at VIIIB. I felt I could hardly breathe but I replied in a clear, low voice, '*Sokol*' (the name of a large physical-culture organization involved in underground activities).

With no trace of emotion, she spoke in English, 'How nice is the white rose.'

A kind of ferocious joy swept over me as I responded, '*Bringen Sie mir einen Kognak, bitte*' (Bring me brandy, please).

She gave a quick smile, saying softly, 'Friends are behind you. Things are being organized as quickly as possible.' She turned and went back to the horse.

As our party regrouped, I listened with taut attention as the officer told the guard he would be arranging with the camp *Feldwebel* to procure an ox-wagon next morning for the building materials to be carted to the property of Mr and Mrs Cech. Prisoners would do the handling work. On the way back to our quarters, Godden received my news with astonishment and delight. Our arrival at Partschendorf had not been unnoticed and what had happened was an indisputably skilled, round-about operation. Eagerly we awaited the next morning. But how quickly and confoundingly a seemingly certain situation can change. The *Feldwebel* announced that three were enough for the cartage work – Godden and two others. I and the other two would join a group trimming sugar beet. It was exasperating, but at least Godden had gone and would be able to bridge the gulf.

Karel Cech was obviously able to pull strings, for he kept the three soldiers working on his property for some time, assisting with the construction of a cow byre and boundary wall, using the old materials. Godden found ample scope for secretive talks with Karel and his wife Lida, both of whom spoke reasonable English. He brought me interesting information. Karel and Lida Cech lived in a two-storey house, set in a large meadow on the fringe of the village. Lida's sister shared the home; she was Gretel Karlstadt, married to the officer with the Iron Cross whom Karel had brought in the landau to the work-site; he had since rejoined his regiment and it appeared that his wife and the Cechs would have few regrets if he left his bones, and fervent Nazism, for ever at the Russian Front; it had been a pre-war marriage, now bitterly regretted by her.

Karel and the sisters were of Czech stock, passionately loyal to their country. He had served as an officer in the Czechoslovakian Army until diabetes caused him to resign, and for the last six years he had been employed as an executive with a large schnapps distillery at Troppau. He was a key member of the resistance. Before the war, anticipating what was coming, he had cultivated friendships with pro-German Sudetens and, professing like sympathies, had succeeded in placing his integrity with the enemy on a sound footing. Having a decorated German brother-in-law was of considerable value; locally it put the seal of acceptance on his relationship with the SS contingent at the manor-house. Mighty receivers of stolen goods as the SS were, Karel's regular contributions of schnapps, difficult to procure, certainly had them 'on side'.

While Godden worked for Karel, I laboured on various jobs until, inexplicably, I was 'promoted' by the *Feldwebel* to assist the Slovakian land girls in the milking sheds. That was just fine, except for Riley working nearby in the milk processing plant. Godden told Karel of my difficulties created by the genuine Kiwis, of my existing in an alien environment, shunned by most of the men in the school-hall. Karel viewed this with grave concern. So far I had taken pains to control my aggravation but a crisis was looming with deepened suspicion and resentment at my precipitate elevation to a favoured job. Soldiers working in the dairying sector guarded their positions jealously, not just for the cleanliness of the work and access to added rations, but because of illicit love affairs. If the most pressing urge in a prisoner's life centred on food, or for some fanatical few upon escape, nonetheless, everywhere that prisoners went the sex urge was sure to go. In a confidential briefing prior to our leaving VIIIB, Godden and I were told of the opportunities offered at Partschendorf: 'soft-skinned' was the term. But we were warned to resist amorous enticements, to avoid any possibility of traps or gossip which could jeopardize our missions, not to mention the safety of the resistance movement hovering behind us.

The Germans were implacable about prisoner fraternization with German women: the penalty for intercourse with a German woman was life imprisonment in a civilian gaol; for rape, it was summary execution. But with foreign female slave-labourers, usually Polish, Russian and Lithuanian, frequently found working in and around camps, liaisons were often easy to achieve. Prisoners were no paragons of virtue and starved, humiliated women were only too willing to exchange their favours for chocolate, soap, and occasionally simply for human affection. The Germans looked upon these sexual swaps with less harshness and, if proclaimed as forbidden, foreign women were relatively unimportant targets. Many guards turned a blind eye but if a prisoner were convicted, he usually paid with a stint in solitary on bread and water. It is true that at the end of the war there were marriages which had had their beginnings as dalliances in factory, field or farmyard; just as in Britain and other Allied countries many a German or Italian prisoner legitimized his wartime consorting with a local wench. Godden and I had not long been residents of the school-hall before we became aware that some nights, floor boards under a bed were being lifted; men dropping down to the cellar were going out through the wire for their rendezvous. With all the comforts so easily available to this working commando, it was no wonder none wished to leave and that all closed their ranks against a suspect who might wreck their idyllic prisoner existence.

Quick to gauge the temper of the situation, Karel realized its danger. The soldiers laboured in a heterogeneous community of foreigners and Czechoslovakians; among the latter were many true as steel, but also Sudeten Germans who could include informers. Stupid gossip among the milkmaids that Yeatman was a sham could be passed on to alert German Intelligence, hypersensitive after the Heydrich assassination, to look for a parachuted agent lying low and even hoodwinking his own side. There could ensue a merciless and brilliantly efficient comb-out of the entire region for resistance contacts with the British. Even if I returned to VIIIB, the danger would not necessarily vanish if Riley and his buddies mentioned a phoney Kiwi who had gone. It was absolutely essential to silence and discredit the trouble-maker. I hardly found amusing the solution Karel propounded. I had to fight *and beat* Riley!

As an urgent resolution, I reluctantly agreed I had to plough into him at the prick of any reasonable excuse. It came when I was working in a large milking shed, carrying filled pails for happy, chattering Slovakian girls. I was exchanging pleasantries in German when Riley, suddenly appearing, put an arm about a milkmaid and proclaimed, 'Don't trust that man, he's false . . .' I saw red and struck out, a straight blow to his mouth. Tottering rearwards, he slipped on a heap of wet dung. Recovering, he rushed at me like a lunatic; carefully, I delivered a fist hard at his left eye. He went down on one knee and blared, 'God help you, Yeatman, I'll slay you.'

'Organize a fair fight and I'll give you the chance,' I shouted. One of his colleagues, a spidery individual, made to cuff me on the ear; I lifted him bodily off his feet and dumped him in the green, steaming dung. Confusion reigned, females shrieked and the guard rushed in waving his rifle.

The men arranged the fight for six days hence, on our work-free Sunday. The projected fight seemed to arouse a quasi-unanimity; the atmosphere settled with less hostility, at least briefly, until the *Feldwebel* announced that Riley and some of his adherents involved in the milk-shed scrap were to join a gang of about twenty soldiers to work on agricultural machinery. My remaining with the milkmaids aroused immediate, jealous fury. It was unnerving to learn from Godden of whispers that I was to be 'fixed'; diplomacy was not equipped to deal with this situation and, upon Godden confiding in Karel, the latter insisted we act without delay; never mind waiting for Sunday. That evening, after the meal taken in an atmosphere of hostility, Godden and I drifted away towards our bunks. At a nod from me, Godden suddenly yelled as he gripped my shirt, 'All right, Yeatman, if the bloody cap fits, you wear it!' We scrimmaged between the two-tier beds and I bawled for all to hear, 'If you and the other suspicious idiots imagine I'm a Jerry stooge then the whole lot of you are nothing but traitorous, black-shirted bastards.'

Amidst cries and exclamations, I pushed Godden aside and strode to the middle of the room. 'Listen to me,' I yelled. 'I'm warning the whole bloody bunch of you. I intend getting you all back to VIIIB and out to work in the Polish coal-mines.' Voices started up, some jeering; some men looked at me in bewilderment. It gave me a strange satisfaction to go on, telling them I was no New Zealander, had never been near the country. I had never fought in Crete. 'If you want the truth, I'm a British evader from the Germans. I'm a sergeant in the Intelligence Corps. I served with a north country regiment in France. I've found it necessary to swing my identity under damned difficult circumstances and you bastards are putting my head in a noose.' A stupefied silence reigned and I went on swiftly. 'Cut it out, for God's sake. I'm as loyal to Britain as the best of you and the defeat of Germany means as much to me as it does to any one of you here.' I let it rip, that I was no plant or squealer but doing a worthwhile job, while they were sitting out the war with unbelievable comforts and gratifying their pleasures.

Riley challenged, 'If you're a Pommie sergeant, what the hell are you doing on this working party? And who are you to threaten to get us back to VIIIB?'

Murmurs ran through the ranks and someone called out, 'He's lying to patch things up so he won't get slaughtered on Sunday.'

I faced Riley, his left eye black and half-closed. 'The fight's on, believe me. Now, if you want it,' and raised my fists aggressively. I added that I was prepared to give Riley a second black eye to take to bed with him. I ventured to express quickly that if the guards rushed in at the din, I would demand an urgent telephone call be put through to Sergeant Major Sheriff for Riley's immediate removal. 'What's more,' I went on, 'Sheriff is due here soon. I'll return to VIIIB with him and make sure the whole lot of you are recalled.'

The men stared as though mesmerized. Godden threw in, 'So that's what you're here for – checking for Sheriff.'

I forced a fierce approach. 'Sheriff knows damn well about your rackets and doesn't condemn them. But maybe a new Partschendorf party will be interested in getting on with the war; with sabotage to dislocate German efforts at food production.' I made a point of stating that my being assigned to the milking shed was not of my doing but quite accidental. I would ask the *Feldwebel* to transfer me to work on the agricultural machinery. In short, a compromise came about. I would no longer be talked about and as for the Sunday fight, Riley and I would put on a match for entertainment, to smooth over any aggrieved feelings and to prove neither was a coward.

The fight did in fact take place, refereed by an Australian named Sunnley; even German guards, with beer mugs in hand, stood and watched what we told them was a traditional bout of fisticuffs. It was no shadow boxing but a deadly contest. For Riley, his blustering dominance of his coterie, his pride and prowess as a boxer, were on the line. I went in like a piece of raw steak. I knew I had to hammer him conclusively, to prevent any possible slipping back to the previous, dangerous situation. When I succeeded, the outcome was as Karel had predicted; no more trouble from Riley, and his former adherents were quick to disown him.

When Godden told Karel that he and the other two soldiers, having completed the work on his property, were to join the group assigned to the machinery sheds, Karel saw the opportunity for a bold, aggressive strike. Quickly, he contacted technical experts in the resistance who provided blueprints of the machines; precisely marked were vital parts whose removal would render the machines useless. Godden had a technical background, certainly in radio and what else I never discovered. He had to memorize the blueprints which were then destroyed. Sabotaging the machinery would mean that, when required next season, there would be inordinate delay and disruption of production; most had been manufactured by the International Harvester Company and unless replacement parts were somewhere in stock, each part would have to be specially machine-tooled. This state farm at Partschendorf was a major pool, supplying light and heavy agricultural equipment to many farms over an extensive surrounding locality.

All too often, British prisoners of war were stigmatized for doing nothing or too little to undermine the enemy, but to a great extent this was due to lack of organization and leadership. When I was sheltering with the underground in Holland, it was decreed that I should risk my neck with the same vigour as my loyalist helpers. Espionage and sabotage were the foundations upon which war was being waged in occupied countries; prisoners or evaders were not acceptable just as protected lodgers but were expected to share responsibilities in killing and undermining the enemy, and to stand up to meet an emergency. The same thinking had applied in Poland, and now in Czechoslovakia where Godden and I were called upon to play a part in one of the multifarious actions against the common foe. When we set about enthusing the soldiers of the working party, it was amazing how the real streaks of nationalism emerged, and their willingness to take risks. Carried away by zeal, the men became veritable daredevils, but the overriding consideration in efficient execution of the plan was unerring direction to get the best out of the men in loyalty and courage.

At the same time, Karel was cunning. Unwittingly, the men were being manipulated into involvement which could, if necessary, be used to enforce a frightening silence and to safeguard against slipshod methods among a working party of its kind, startlingly jolted out of its composure. It would ensure against slack-lipped pronouncements in a vicinity where there hovered a highly volatile, observant SS, ever searching for any clue. After all, Karel was living on a razor's edge and years of concentrated undercover work could be thrown to the wind by the faintest slip or inconsequential utterance.

Two engineers, elderly Sudeten Germans, came from Troppau to oversee maintenance and stowage of the equipment. For two days, along with the other men, Godden and I cleaned, oiled and greased machines, and helped with adjustments; when in perfect order, the machines were moved to large storage sheds. Karel had procured vodka, from a distillery in Poland according to the bottle labels, for dragooning the engineers into stupefied states of trusting indifference; he knew they were bedevilled by the serpent alcohol, as were our two guards, known as

'Toss' and 'Fling', who had long been under graft and invariably ignored the doings of the men on fatigue parties. Karel got the vodka in cleverly. An old man, looking like a tramp, appeared with a pony and cart, peddling what he said was Russian vodka smuggled in for Russian slave-labourers, but it had been 'diverted'. He asked to hide some of it in the watchman's nearby stone cottage. Probably only he, God and Karel Cech knew who the old man was, but the ruse worked. For inordinately long periods, the engineers and guards vanished into the cottage and raucous laughter came forth as we were left to get on with the job.

Godden and I stowed ourselves away in one shed after another – there were several – paying particular attention to the huge combine harvesters. Working furiously, we removed the vital parts – cog wheels, rods, pins and activating parts, some very heavy. Where possible, cover plates were bolted back into place. The dismantled pieces were carried outside and hidden behind a brick pile. Our eighteen other conspirators operated with fantastic vitality, while putting on an impression of carefree tomfoolery. A variety of small odds and ends was concealed in grubby overalls and taken back to the school-hall. There they were hidden in the toilets and wash-house, each item carefully listed to ensure none was overlooked at final disposal. In addition, Godden and I managed to funnel sand and powdered cement into the sumps and engines of a dozen tractors.

The tipsy engineers showed no interest in a final check of the machines before overseeing the watchman finally padlocking and sealing the doors to the sheds. Godden and I breathed enormous relief. A well-planned operation had been a resounding success and we revelled in the thought of the devastating end to the business, to come about months ahead when the machines were brought from hibernation for unremitting seasonal operations. The British party would be above suspicion for, apart from hauling the machines to the sheds, all their duties had been in the open maintenance bay, oiling, greasing and cleaning. To divert suspicion from local saboteurs, Godden left in one of the combine harvesters a knapsack containing German tools, some grubby drawings of missing parts, and an outsize shirt bearing the label of an outfitter in Prague. Careful not to leave my fingerprints, I tossed an old wallet under a machine; it contained a forged Nazi membership card and other oddments identifying a Sudeten German mechanic in Prague. He was a big man and the shirt would fit.

Next was to get rid of every ounce of the ironmongery swiftly. An ideal location by the river had been chosen by Karel. As usual, the school-hall was locked for the night and all but two of the guards clomped away to their drinking and amorous rendezvous. The two guards remaining, we observed through our barred windows, were Toss and Fling; knowing them as we did, they would sleep out their guard; none of our guardians ever bothered to patrol the pathetic barbed-wire fence. Before midnight, boozed guards returned to their quarters to sleep off exhaustion – from whatever causes – before roll-call at six A.M. All went quiet.

Five of us opened the secret hatch under a bunk and dropped to the cellar. The smaller items of machine parts were loaded into sacks and we set off for our riverside gambols. Spreading out along a quarter-mile stretch of bank, we flung the pieces into the swirling waters of the River Oder. Back to the stowage sheds, retrieving the heavy parts from behind the brick pile as noiselessly as possible, represented the worst bit of the act, for it was impossible to gauge if the watchman was about or his savage Alsatian dog left loose on the prowl. This part of the task gave no satisfaction to muscles, but it did provide solace knowing that getting rid of the damned metal was a guarantee of our immunity. We laboured for almost two hours and when the last big cog wheel sank to its muddy grave at a fast swirling bend in the river, we were filled with a sense of triumph and the joy of success.

Dog-tired, Godden and I separated from the others on the pretext that a few metal spindles were hidden in long grass near a shed and it was idiotic to risk more than two men. The countryside was solemn and peaceful as Godden and I moved off to Karel's house. It was a thrill to meet him for the first time. In the cosy parlour of his home his wife, Lida, had prepared a much-needed hot meal. I found him not prepossessing, but amiable, idealistic and analytically intelligent. Apparently he had exceptional qualifications for operating clandestine radio, not only a stationary long-range transmitter for direct communication with London but also, in conjunction with other operators, portable, British (SOE) short-wave sets which were moved to different locations with each transmission. We talked for almost two hours until I was suddenly contemplated with grave intensity and given the news that final arrangements were almost complete for me to embark on a prescribed escape trail within a fortnight.

It was necessary to make my way in darkness to Karel's house for further instructions, and the more I became acquainted with him the greater grew my respect and admiration. He was the soul of honour and I was happy to hand over the three valuable rings I had found; converted to cash, they would meet our escape requirements and relieve the underground of some financial pressure. I would make a break from Partschendorf, geared to the skill and control of the resistance, and Godden would follow soon afterwards; for some reason unknown to me, he was too valuable to be risked first. To account for my disappearance, I was to be presumed drowned; but the first thing to do was to get myself on to Farm Five. This meant putting my finger on the *Feldwebel* for an immediate transfer; it was easily arranged, especially after handing over 100 genuine Deutsch-marks and 200 Canadian Sweet Caporal cigarettes. We were on friendly terms and he suspected nothing peculiar in my request to work on Farm Five with my friend, Sunnley, and two others who were allowed to swim in a safe backwater of the Oder after a hard day's work.

I worked on Farm Five for about a week, assessing everything. I gladly chose to shift manure and in the process I encountered an elderly, dirty herdsman named Sudermann. He was strange to education but endowed with animal-like cunning. He often received a cigarette from my companions and I accepted him as repellent but insignificant in my escape plans. In the irony of human affairs, he was to prove an unimagined danger.

The little, bay-like, swirling backwater, gouged out of the bank where we took our dip after the day's work, was safe enough. Dangerously close, however, was the wide, deep and turbulent river. Leaving our work boots on the bank, my three companions and I immersed, wearing shorts, and washed away the perspiration and dirt of toil. The lone, dispirited guard usually drowsed nearby and although I was a strong swimmer, I deliberately gave the impression otherwise, splashing and ducking close to the shallow bank. Then we moved to a nearby barn to don decent boots and battle-dress for the march back to the school-hall.

The stage was set for my break, late afternoon. The scheme, if not exactly to Karel's liking, was devised by his superiors involved in psychological manoeuvring as much as in physical action, measure for counter measure. It was only two weeks since we had finished in the machine sheds. The British party had never given slightest cause for doubt about obedience but for one of its members to escape would certainly focus suspicion on the school-hall party as never before. Karel's superiors considered that nothing must be done which, even in remotest possibility, could lead to the unsealing and unlocking of the machinery sheds. On the other hand, the Germans, especially the guards, would feel natural sympathy towards the Britishers over the accidental death of a decent, hard-working New Zealander, even though resulting from his own wilful stupidity. I feel sure, had it not been for the dismantling of the machinery, the procedure worked out for my escape at the personal risk involved would not have been necessary. Nevertheless, before Karel would risk my entering a raging waterway, I had to convince him I was a strong swimmer. Also, using chunks of cork and bottles, he tested where the current was likely to assist me to reach the opposite bank; the point where I should emerge was about 500 yards downstream and in a wood just back from the bank Karel concealed clothing. Godden was aware of what was planned. It was not my scheme and the rushing, turbulent river with its fierce eddies and currents did stir nervous emotions.

The day was hot and humid. Smeared with cow dung and dripping perspiration, I slipped off alone for the river. I left my boots on the bank at our usual washing place and struck out for the main flow of the river. Swimming with the current, I discarded my shorts, hoping as they swept away that they would be found among the reeds in what surely would be a search for my corpse . . . for how could a naked man escape?

It was true, I had no papers, no money. I was going out naked and picking up whatever was planted for me in my path. It was a frightening and strenuous swim to keep on course against unsuspected cross currents, but once I rounded a bend, a high bank hid me from sight and the current aided me to the desolate landing place. I emerged thankfully and gasping, and rested a while, exhausted. Scaling the bank, it was with profound shock that I observed the idle, gaping Sudermann squatting close by with his sheep! He yelled as I bolted for the wood. With nerves badly shaken, I pulled on overalls, shoes, donned a cap and made off to a prearranged hiding place six miles away, in a coppice within shouting distance of the house of Cech. Time was my enemy. Why the devil did Sudermann have to be there at that moment? Filled with uneasy wrath I realized that had I been a trained underground operator, I would have immediately and forcibly drowned him and left him to be found in the reeds downstream – possibly interpreted as drowning while trying to save me. But I had been naked and not a trained operator; I had desperately needed cover!

It was pitch dark when I decamped from the coppice and crawled, metre by metre, to Karel's house with its signal illumination of a green-shaded lamp. He awaited me impatiently, already knowing about the abortive 'drowning'. It was imperative for me to remain secreted in his house for as long as the emergency lasted. It was agonizing; it had been meticulously organized that I depart from Partschendorf within two days with false papers, money and instructions for my escape from Czechoslovakia. Sudermann had invented stories that I had tried to murder him. My description was circulated with notices pasted on boards around the village, as they had been in Hengelo in Holland, and the populace reminded by the SS that any person harbouring a fugitive would be shot. Military and police were carrying out searches, local members of the Hitler Youth Movement were scouring the countryside; the alarm was spread. Illusions the resistance had entertained of foxing the Germans and offsetting suspicion on the British soldiers had failed; sharpest interest and security were directed to them on their work assignments and in their quarters. Godden managed to get clear of the school-hall and visit me a couple of times but doubted if he could again. A ten-foot-high wall of barbed wire was being erected around the school-hall grounds. Karel advised him, 'Get yourself out on a ditch-digging party where I can contact you.'

It was a week before security relaxed and it was generally assumed that a New Zealand soldier, Private Winston Yeatman, had fled the district and would be recaptured elsewhere. Karel's instructions were to get me away as early as possible, and also Godden. It was about ten days after the escape swim when I left Partschendorf as a comely female. Karel's sister-in-law, Gretel Karlstadt, had been a highly popular professional singer, but now she had virtually disappeared into obscurity with no toasts or loving sentiments from her own true Czechs. The wife of a Nazi conqueror, she was considered uppish among the local residents and subject to dark innuendoes. At intervals, she accompanied Karel in the landau, all in line with his astute undercover strategy. Invariably she was met with callous indifference or deliberately snubbed by the true local Czechs. All to the good!

I left Karel's home disguised as Gretel, with cheeks high-coloured, wearing a neat, black dress over my civilian clothes, a gem of a wig with blonde curls showing streaks of silver. I wore her favourite hat and supercilious rimless pince-nez. Karel's reasoning was cold. 'Gretel Karlstadt' had to be seen in Partschendorf that morning and a deliberate stop was made at the baker's shop and two other places in the main street. I was made aware that I might become conscious of stares and nudges, but to regard the locals archly. I digress to mention that in the first edition of this book I said I was dressed as an old lady, not an attractive female of about forty. After the war I tried, through British official approaches to Czechoslovakian authorities, to establish contact with my former friend, Karel Cech. I was only to learn there had been many round-ups of the resistance by the Gestapo in the Tatra Mountains area, resulting in massive deportations and executions. I could only surmise that Karel had met his end as a gallant Czech. But I was livid when through my publisher British Security insisted I become an old lady in my book; I had never been an old lady in my life! Obviously though, this was intended to protect identities of former resistance operators in Czechoslovakia where Soviet 'liberation' was of the kind which, in Poland, had swept my gallant friend Mieteck off to the Gulag Archipelago for twelve years.

Karel was too cautious to have attempted to pass me off as an old lady or as any stranger liable to stir comment among the villagers. I am not likely to forget trying to look like a sweet female and folding myself together to hide my shoulders, sinking low in the seat and covering my 42-inch chest with a shawl. A desultory wave here or there was necessary and a friendlier one as we passed the SS Standartenführer (Colonel) walking to his Mercedes as he waved to us amiably. I hoped like hell, at each stop in the village, that no one would come close to speak. Finally Karel livened up the mare, we cleared Partschendorf and proceeded at a brisk trot to an isolated house off the main road to Troppau.

There I met Milo Maurus, an elderly professional man holding a key position in the resistance corps in the eastern sector of Czechoslovakia. Time was limited and after I had thrown off my female attire Maurus took control. I listened avidly, excitedly, to incisive instructions in a carefully worked out plan. I received a beautiful set of forged papers; nor had I need to worry about money. I was handed a wallet with currency equivalent to over 200 pounds sterling, a handful of loose change and a ticket to Vienna. My bogus name was German, Willie Schmidt, and I looked appropriately anonymous in a well-worn, working-man's suit of loosely woven wool material which later was to prove calamitous. I would board the local train a stop or two

before Troppau where I would connect with the 10.05 A.M.
train to Vienna; this ran twice weekly, a mixed passenger
and goods train carrying farm produce destined for
Germany. On this occasion, two coaches would be filled
with French and Polish forced labour and I was to ensure
that I travelled with them; most foreign workers spoke poor
German and avoided conversation with Germans anyway.
Instructed on passwords and future contacts, I again, as in
Holland and Poland, had to swear never to divulge the
vaguest detail of Partschendorf contacts or others on the
escape channel ahead. From Vienna, I was destined for
Hungary and thence by stages to Yugoslavia. Once there,
safely in the hands of the partisans, I would either be
returned to England or instructed to remain and contribute
my quota to the war effort. A General Draza Mihailovic had
established a resistance headquarters in mountainous
Montenegro, and an army of full-time, well-trained guerrilla
fighters. By radio and secret emissaries, Mihailovic kept in
touch with the Yugoslav Government-in-exile in London.

I shook hands with Milo Maurus as he wished me good
luck. I drove on with Karel and he dropped me a quarter of a
mile from where I was to board the train, pulling off into a
lonely side road adjacent to a forest. In the rear, narrow
compartment of the landau, he transmitted on a British
SOE short-wave radio set – to whom I have no idea, but
when he finished he turned and kissed me on both cheeks.
'God bless you,' he said. Without more ado, he took the
driver's seat, flicked the reins, and as I watched the landau
move away he never looked back.

It was about 200 miles southwards to Vienna but the
journey went off uneventfully. It was late afternoon when I
left the train and made for the railway goods yard, looking
for a four-wheeled, yellow wagon drawn by two horses and
with an elderly driver wearing a green straw hat. There was
no yellow wagon or driver answering the descriptions given

me. I loafed around, watching motor lorries load up with the farm produce from Czechoslovakia until finally I approached a labourer and enquired laconically if he knew an old chap named Heinrich with a yellow horse-drawn wagon. He looked at me derisively, suspiciously, asking why I wanted to see him. I thought quickly and replied that I had met him at the local office of the Reich Ministry of Agriculture and he had promised me some loading work. I was surveyed with disapproval and informed brusquely, 'He's been laid off. Only motor vehicles are transporting goods for the Reich Ministry.' I experienced emotions of the blackest disappointment and, observing a station policeman approaching, made off quickly.

Now what? A hunch told me that something unfortunate had arisen. I had learned that my intuition was generally a very useful mentor; there was every reason for acute nervousness, even dread, if the old man had overrated his security and been arrested. We were to have delivered a wagon load for the Reich Ministry to a place on the outskirts of Vienna and then proceed to the home of Heinrich's employer on the Stockerau road, about fifteen miles away. His employer was Helmuth Zeitler who ran a printing house; while it was now controlled to turn out Nazi printed material, ways were still found for secretly operating its engraving department and other facilities of immense value for underground activities. Zeitler had already given a remarkably good account of himself in smuggling agents and couriers from Vienna to Graz, about 100 miles south in Austria, from thence to be passed on through Hungary to Yugoslavia. Obviously, I had to locate Zeitler. I found my way to the Stockerau road, north out of Vienna, and foot-slogged its attenuated course into the countryside; caution warned to avoid any form of transport and unnecessary danger. It was almost midnight when I located his home, as Milo Maurus had described it; a pale moon lighted the steep-roofed, long, two-storeyed house, the top half whitewashed; it was the right place . . . a sign on the gate said 'Katuana'. I had repeated over and over to myself the password, 'Reichenberg–Szekula', hopefully reminding myself that I would soon be indoors, secure among loyalist friends.

The place was unlighted, dead, weird and solemn in the moonlight and there was no sight or sound of life. I knocked softly, repeatedly, but to no avail. I explored the quite extensive garden with a number of sheds and a dilapidated sort of garage. Footsore and ravenous, I was in a dreadful quandary, mystified and powerless, so dazed and weary I could hardly think at all. I prised open a window in the largest outbuilding, climbed inside and spread myself out on a bed of old sacks. Despite hunger and disappointment, within minutes I was in a dead sleep, withdrawn from a world of bad experience, but not before I had been seized by an acute stab of remembrance to conceal my wallet and forged papers. All I could do was sleep and await the next day to think out my course of action.

It was daylight and I was awakened by the lamentable, non-stop miaowing of a cat; it was rasping to nerves already raw. All else was very still and as I continued to curse a strange cat I was suddenly brought to full alertness by the sound of footsteps . . . thunderclap to my ears. Leaping to my feet, I looked out at a short, corpulent old man wearing a green straw hat, its rim almost meeting a grotesquely hawk-like nose. He was fondling a cat. With his side whiskers and beard, there was no mistaking who he was. I forced a cheerful, commonplace tone. 'Good morning, Heinrich.' His astonishment was comical; his eyes fairly bulged and his mouth opened foolishly.

By a singular and happy chance, he had come to collect the cat belonging to his arrested master. The old Viennese gardener–wagon-driver was the instrument selected by Fate for continuing my journey to Yugoslavia alone. Had he not appeared to collect the cat, Lord only knows how I would have finished up. I gathered that the Security Police had swooped two days previously and arrested Mr and Mrs Zeitler and their two sons; Heinrich had no idea where they were. On at least six occasions after the arrests, the house had been searched and papers and various objects removed. With a quick grasp of the situation, Heinrich viewed the manner of my arrival and difficulties with complete sympathy. He regretted he had not been able to collect me at the goods yard; he was under surveillance himself.

My purpose remained unaltered. I could not go back but a good bicycle, maps and a supply of food were essential if I were to have any chance of reaching my objective. I gave Heinrich more than a generous sum of Reichmarks and he departed, appearing sincerely anxious and determined to help me, promising to return as soon as possible. When he had gone, I found a fresh hiding place in a large glasshouse in a small meadow adjoining the 'Katuana' property. Grapevines were growing in the glasshouse and I recall climbing them like a caterpillar to a place from which I could watch for Heinrich's return and, if necessary, make a swift retreat should he return with Germans, or should the Security Police take it into their heads to make another search. Remembrance of being cornered in the attic of the Dutch house in Leiden stirred warning signals. Constructive imagination was vital and I could not obscure the thought that Heinrich might be followed by the Gestapo, or even be in their pay. It was too shattering to contemplate the outcome of my recapture as Willie Schmidt and being traced back to Czechoslovakia. The Yeatman trick was just about played out. I could never do this again.

It was some hours before Heinrich returned, pushing a bicycle. It had been his brother's and was in first-class condition; a basket strapped to the handlebars was stocked with food. Maps and a compass were handed to me and with Heinrich's help I plotted a route, about 250 miles, to the mountain passes of northern Yugoslavia. I certainly had the physical capacity to make short work of this mileage and I clung to the idea that I could be in the mountain fastnesses with Yugoslav guerrilla fighters within a week.

Although forty years have passed, I still vividly recall saying farewell, with a deep sense of obligation, to the little Viennese gardener. Goaded by obsessional thoughts of freedom, I would have to apply all my faculties to solitary escape; fortunately I had acquired a deal of knowledge and training in Holland, Poland and Czechoslovakia. But Hungary was a very uncertain proposition, a very definite German satellite which had declared war on Russia in June 1941 and a few months later on Britain and the USA. Admittedly, as I had learned from Karel Cech, an escape channel was operating with friendly contacts and safe houses but the unexpected arrest of my Vienna helpers had put the subversive organization completely out of reach. I was also aware that considerable pro-British sentiment existed, particularly among Hungary's aristocratic classes; perhaps a kindly Providence or lucky coincidence might again put me in touch with secret aid.

By mid-afternoon the following day I had travelled some sixty miles and reached the Austro–Hungarian border control. By sheer good luck, I tagged on to the rear of a party of cycling youths who appeared to know the guards and were simply waved through. A feeling of intense relief descended upon me now I was inside Hungary. The border town of Sopron lay immediately ahead but luck did not hold out much longer. Soon after pedalling away from Sopron, I swept around a corner on a downhill run and twenty yards in front was a German road block, a horizontal red and white pole. Between one end of the pole and the sentry-box was a four-foot-wide gate. It was open. Without a second's hesitation I accelerated and shot through. Screams of rage followed me and a guard opened fire. He was no mean shot; two bullets struck the metal of my bike and sent me sprawling over the road.

Though I managed to get away uninjured, in dashing for the trees I lost my precious bicycle and food supplies. Maps and compass were in a pocket, but what a lousy, diabolical turn of fortune. I worked away from the frontier region in an easterly direction, struggling across rough terrain for two days and covering about forty miles. I had learned to accept hunger with abrupt hatred and defy it, as now, subsisting on berries, raw turnips and potatoes and gnawing at beetroot pulled from furrows. I walked with little rest by day and night, along dirt roads and interminable forest tracks, overcome by fatigue and my brain reeling. I was hungry, hungry like a hungry beast, and fear was sapping my strength.

On the third day I swung east-south-east, resolving to strike the railway line running south to Papa, and with a very clear idea of what I intended doing. The loose fabric of my lightweight suit was in tatters, little by little ripped to pieces as I had stumbled along, over mountain ranges, hills and through forests at times thick with prickly undergrowth. In my semi-naked state the clothes problem was nearest and most important if my escape bid was not to fizzle out. According to the justice of escape and with little thought to the injustices of violence or theft, I decided to find some isolated house, break in and steal some clothes, for if I emerged from cover improperly dressed I would soon be under lock and key. I desperately needed warm clothing and food; even a few crusts would have been a Ritz meal. I was still armed with bogus papers and money enough to get me on my way if I stole a bicycle.

Suddenly I was passing an old-fashioned, two-storey house on an isolated country lane. I watched a man and an elderly woman picking pears. I hid until darkness before breaking into the house by a rear window. Finding a well-stocked pantry, I ate and filled a bag before making for the upstairs in search of clothing. Unfortunately, when searching through a wardrobe, I disturbed the man and became involved in a fight. He was big and heavy; I was losing under his grip. Necessarily, I applied a commando move to snap his fingers at my throat and there was one hell of a to-do, savage, cruel and treacherous, before I slipped away into the night with food and clothes. 'Hell!' I consoled myself. 'There's no sportsmanship or decency in war or escape! What choice did Fate leave me?'

I cleared a nearby village by a wide circuit and forced a fast march climbing all through the night. 'Now you've really got to watch things,' I told myself, 'maybe, besides breaking his fingers, you killed that man.' At the first streaks of dawn, I looked about for a hiding place. The comfort and security a bush had provided in Holland – was it a million years ago? – prompted me to find something similar. It was broad daylight when I was awakened by the hum of an approaching light aircraft. I flattened beneath my protective screen as a Storch zoomed over at about 250 feet and did a search in ever-widening circles before the bloody thing buzzed off. I surveyed the bundle of clothes and ate some of the food. If my legs were stiff and swollen, I was less despondent; the clothes fitted reasonably and I was not uncheered by hope and resolve. To keep the Hungarian escape going, I had been compelled to act in a cold-blooded way, but in the world of escape and evasion, self-interest and camouflage are a reality that all men on the run must face. For two days, I dared not leave my protection. The whole area for miles around would be carefully watched. Hungarians and Germans would be suspicious of all strangers; police would be trigger-happy. After the feast comes the bill. I found myself remembering a saying, 'Believe that you have it, and you have it', and I started building up some basic belief that I was almost in possession of another bicycle.

On the third day, at dusk, I started out for the town of Veszprem where I imagined three-speed-gear bicycles were waiting to be pinched at every corner. After forty-eight hours I ran into tortuous mountain terrain; it was hellish going and, reaching the outskirts of the town, I was horrified to observe it was virtually a German military garrison. The few bikes I saw were mounted by bloody Huns. I was now closer to the northernmost end of Lake Balaton and, with food supplies almost exhausted despite disciplined rationing, I had to make up my mind whether to strike north-east to Budapest, or south-west to the Croatian border of Yugoslavia. I decided on the latter and, if I thought my will-power was in fine fettle, endeavours to maintain a superhuman caution lost their edge. Extreme bodily fatigue plays awful tricks with the mind; another memory of that long tramp was savage hunger, the kind I imagined had driven wolves to trail us for an attack on the Polish plain. Mental weariness and maddening hunger found a reaction in ridiculing and scorning all danger, when one is filled with a slow anger against mankind and Nature, loathing mountains, lakes and forests.

In brief, with involuntary phases of fear and hope, I started talking aloud. I had been two weeks on my own. With some resurgence of spirit, memory locked on to Mr Morley, my old school choir master, with his mop of snow-white hair. Through miles of forest, I sang to the pine trees at the top of my voice, all parts of the descant of the Seven-Fold Amen. I sang it for bloody hours; it's probably still echoing in those forests. Birds, foxes, beavers, wild pigs, more decent than Germans, never challenged but scuttled away. I was going nutty, without a doubt. The same as for men in any war, childhood memories came to mind:

Orpheus and his lute made trees,
And the mountain tops that freeze,
Bow themselves when he did sing . . .

I laughed, singing it as I had in the choir, 'Old Fuse and his
lute'. Morley would say, 'Dickie Pape, you'll either be
hanged as a highwayman or you'll end up Lord Mayor of
London, and I shall be pleased to dine with you.' Later,
when I had reached manhood, Morley once said to me,
'Dickie, I'm frightened for the future of you young men.'

In a state of dementia, I climbed steadily all night to at
least 2,000 feet. In the morning I was sitting on a mountain-
top, looking down at a string of railway lines and thinking of
riding the rods, when a plane came over. Then sense said,
'Look, Pape, you're not going to make it.' Deep inside, a
warning flame compelled me to realize that the long, strange
escape journey from Czechoslovakia was nearing its end. I
recalled Poland when, feeling all in, uncaring of dying,
believing I had conquered the world, I had neglected to
destroy forged papers. I still had sufficient control of my
senses to go through my pockets. Papers and passport were
stuffed into a rocky crevice and burned. Keeping only some
money, I went on.

I strode from a small wood to step on to a concrete
roadway. The relief from struggling was like arriving at the
end of a rainbow with a pot of gold somewhere at hand. I
heard a harsh, yelling Slavonic voice to my rear and knew it
was a command to halt. I was in such a state of utter
weariness and the shock of a human voice turned my legs to
useless slackness; my brain reeled. I still recall, however, a
heavy man in black uniform, wearing a peaked cap, covering
me with a sub-machine-gun. A few yards away was a green
hut, in the fringe of the wood. I had walked straight into a
road block. The Hungarian policeman was not running any
risks. I did not see him raise his gun and I did not feel
anything when it crashed down on my skull.

I came to my senses, my head pulsating and swathed in bandages, in a prison cell in Veszprem, guarded by a young German. The Germans had taken me from the Hungarian police for investigation, a tremendously lucky break for me. The Hungarians would have jailed and perhaps executed me for the attack on the householder. I possessed no incriminating papers and said I was an escaping New Zealand prisoner of war from Stalag VIIIB. I was treated with consideration, a startling change from my experiences in Cracow at the hands of the Gestapo! Two weeks after my capture, I was again returned to VIIIB as Yeatman, this time with a damned sore head.

# CHAPTER 15
## Rings of Conspiracy

Miserable, bemused and ravenously hungry, I was lodged in a solitary confinement cell. I knew to expect thirty days' solitary when hauled before the German security apparatus in the morning, but I was more apprehensive about remorseless interrogators winding in to the end of the reel every possible clue and hostile act right back to Partschendorf. Capturing me in Hungary, on a run from Czechoslovakia, would be of intense interest to them after the Polish escapade with its false papers and obvious linkage with a resistance movement. If any leakage occurred, Godden's escape could be jeopardized and heaven knew what might happen to Karel Cech, the Czechoslovakian resistance and innocent civilians in reprisals.

I had returned to VIIIB in a very poor state of health and was fretful about my capacity to hold the Gestapo at bay. Before the light of dawn, I experienced a boundless extension of physical pain and mental turmoil. I endured violent pains at the nape of my neck and when dawn did appear through the wide grille it burst upon my remaining field of reasoning that I was rapidly going blind. It was bewildering to find I could not get up: my legs had mysteriously stiffened and were drawing themselves upwards, as if my knees, with a will of their own, wanted to reach my chest. I raved and my moans and lamentations brought the guard, but before a transport arrived to convey me to the camp hospital, I was unconscious and remained oblivious to earthly existence for many days. I had fallen victim to meningitis and my injured brain had given birth to papillaoedema, a serious swelling of the eye nerves and tissues. I was given lumbar punctures, spinal fluid being drawn off to lessen pressure on the brain. When I did regain my senses and understanding, I faced the torturing reality of being deprived of most of my sight.

Whatever twisted satisfaction that Hungarian policeman found in clubbing me senseless, the elderly German, Dr Otto Müller, a grave and cordial man, more than repaid by his compassion and human decency. Now in charge of the hospital, he went to special trouble to obtain a supply of *Traubenzucker* for intravenous injections, to reduce blood-pressure, and for a period, every day or so, I received these injections. I fear to think what might have been the consequences to my sight had it not been obtained. Both Dr Müller and Captain Spencer were indulgent and endeavoured to assure me that all would be well.

But, 'ill blows the wind that profits nobody'. I cheated Gestapo interrogation and any endangering of Partschendorf subversive activities was wiped out. In due course, security officers visited me in hospital and I stuck to the story that foolishly I had embarked on a crazy escape jaunt, much to my regret as I had paid dearly. The understanding Dr Müller maintained that I was the type of prisoner of war always ripe for adventure in action and with a temperament always ready for a brush with authority. With no evidence to put them on the track of my Czechoslovakian helpers, no clues to touch them on the raw, nevertheless they laid down that on no consideration would I ever again be permitted to join an outside working party.

Anxious as I have always been to forget the disastrous end to my third escape, I revive it in order to lead in to certain events which, for reasons of post-war security, I was not permitted to publish in the first edition of this book. There, I said, 'It was eleven months after I entered the hospital before I was discharged from the sick bay and returned to the main barracks of the camp.' This was certainly not the whole truth.

It took three months for the inflammation and pressure affecting my eye nerves to downgrade and before I could again define objects with reasonable clarity, and about the same period before normal clearness came back. During those months of darkness and foreboding, my affliction imposed an unusual critical sense, a time to check up on my past life and high jinks and to draw on subconscious power and faith in my destiny. I recall clearly two medical orderlies who escorted me around the inside of the wire, constantly assuring me that I was on the mend and a good crack of the whip would be left in me when discharged. One was a big Australian ex-boxer named McNamara, with crinkly red hair, tough as nails but kindly, simply spoken. The other was an Irishman, Jim Bryant. While my eyes showed improvement, I went down with another bout of pleurisy and Bryant spent endless hours by my bedside in anything but flippant conversation. I owe a lot to those two men; each helped me enormously, in his own way. Blindness does not breed Quixotes and there is no pose in such an affliction for swashbuckling attitudes when one lives in a world of one's own. McNamara, the boxer, urged the spirit of never quitting, of resolute, unconquerable fighting spirit. Bryant stirred a power within me which I had not known before and gradually filled me with a quietude and humility, void of anger or resentment. He told me I was my own worst enemy. He was aware, at the start, of my consuming hatred of the Nazis and my overwhelming mania for blood revenge which was only retarding my recovery. In hating the Nazis, I was giving them power over my sleep, my appetite, blood-pressure and peace of mind. My anger was not hurting Hitler or the Gestapo at all but was turning my days and nights into hellish torment. Gradually, emotions of detestation for the German people and revenge at any price were conquered.

After about six months, I again ventured into the main stalag for varying periods to engage in clandestine tasks, but I was permitted to be something of a special come-and-go patient, as suited my purposes, ensuring protection when necessary. My association with the hospital and close assistance from its medical team remained a powerful factor in my life, both on the inside – and the outside.

Forbidden as I was to work on the outside but anxious to readjust myself to worthwhile undercover work, key men on the 'X' committee devised to place me in a number of camp jobs for assisting would-be escapers and collecting and sifting intelligence information. I was still firmly established as a New Zealand soldier and the real Yeatman was faithfully covering me in an RAF camp 1,000 kilometres away on the East Prussian–Lithuanian border. His stalwart friend, George Potter, continued to act as Mieteck who had vanished completely; the Polish escape had not been without reward. I threw myself wholeheartedly into coding activities and fortunately others had now been trained in the tasks. The volume of secret Intelligence coming to hand had increased enormously in 1943. The Allied air forces had gained the initiative and heavy blows were being delivered on German centres; at the same time, the tide of enemy conquests was continuing to ebb, in Russia and North Africa. An effective communications network linked many far-flung stalags, exchanging vital facts and warnings, and chosen men were transferring valuable information to British sources.

No airmen were brought into VIIIB. It was strictly an army camp and its captive population was constantly increasing. On 1 December 1942, three months before I had left for the Polish coal-mine, the stalag had held 2,627 French; 20,717 English; 220 Belgians; 1,402 Poles; 1,162

Southeastern-British; 22,975 Soviets; 60 Cretans; a total of 49,163 prisoners of whom 42,425 were on working parties. Just short of a year later, the period about which I am now writing, prisoner numbers in VIIIB had swollen to 121,384; Soviet numbers alone had trebled to 69,833, and other new arrivals included 2,648 Yugoslavs and 10,410 Italians. The total on working parties had more than doubled to 97,646.*

From this vast conglomerate of prisoners there was to be found every shade of intellect, education, skill, background and breeding. Meticulously sorted out for specific qualities and abilities, many were carefully briefed to collect information and sent out to work in Germany, Poland and Czechoslovakia. Valuable Intelligence was gleaned. With the right mentalities and allegiance, nationals other than Britishers also fulfilled information-gathering tasks. A remarkable flow of Intelligence was received and the coding boys were kept constantly busy on their extremely dangerous duties. Many of the voluntary Intelligence scouts made their way back to VIIIB at various times on various pretexts, or information came to hand over great distances by coded mail and through the posting and delivery services rendered by German guards under graft. A great deal was accomplished with assiduous skill and cunning.

Time has not blunted recollection of many worthwhile efforts. At this period of German retreat from Stalingrad, I came into contact with parties of Russians who had been working, nearly starved to death, constructing aircraft runways in western and central Germany. They had been rushed forward to VIIIB for onward transportation to their homeland to apply their airstrip-building skills on construction of emergency airfields in an effort to stem the Russian advance. Carefully interrogated, and given some assistance, they disclosed astonishingly valuable information about

* Figures provided by German 'Bundesarchiv' (Militärarchiv).

German night-fighter aerodromes, their locations and other relevant facts of extreme interest to the Allied air forces.

A Yugoslav soldier working on a major railway leading out of Germany to the Eastern Front conscientiously counted the number and size of troop trains passing and returned a vital piece of news of about 200 Tiger tanks, equipped with longer, larger gun barrels, passing his vantage point over a few hours, on flat wagons without even tarpaulin coverings. Able to speak German, he managed to discover their destination for unloading. Again, a British private labouring on a railway over the Polish border one morning counted three trainloads of military equipment, with fifty self-propelled artillery cannon, a new version, built to rumble over adverse, snow-covered or muddy terrain with tanks. Invaluable information about ammunition being manufactured at the Skoda works in Czechoslovakia found its way to VIIIB, as did a great deal about happenings in Poland, bomb damage in German territories and civilian morale.

I give these few illustrations of how prisoners continued to contribute to the Allied war effort as gatherers of military Intelligence. If all fighting men of the British forces were instructed to escape or take evasive action in discharging their duties to king and country, and even if the Geneva Convention laid down the legality of escape, it did not work out that way. Only a relatively small hard core of men in Stalag VIIIB, and no doubt in other camps, was prepared to risk life and future in a gamble to break free in attempts for the 'home run'. Those obsessed with escape, disregarding known cruelties of life on the run or the unpredictable mercy of Fate and the Germans, were afforded every assistance and encouragement by qualified escapers and escape committees, now well backed by Britain's MI9 (the American equivalent was MIS-X).

To be fair, the Germans did adhere to prescribed rules for

men who remained glued to prisoner of war camps, but not so to those who violated codes and disciplines. 'Back room' boys on the inside ran great risks in subversive activities and in equipping would-be escapers. So too did genuine escapers risk abominable fates with notional charges such as theft, assault and spying, resulting in summary execution or sentences of life imprisonment in civilian jails. One has but to remember the murder of fifty of the seventy-nine RAF officers who made the mass escape from Sagan, Luft III camp; on the direct orders of an infuriated Hitler, they were killed, each shot in the back, ostensibly while resisting arrest. Small wonder that prisoners in the main were not readily disposed to project themselves into the hazardous subterranean world of active escape. Only those with a will for prompt, audacious, creative action could take advantage of unexpected opportunities, or evolve opportunities of achieving objectives by weeks and months of meticulous planning.

Foxing the Germans, procuring clothing and manipulating issues involved lying, acting, bribery and blackmail. Some knowledge of German idiomatic language was of supreme importance. I shall never underestimate Jerry intelligence and brilliant theorizing, analysing what dirty business prisoners might be considering or actually engineering. If Jerry did latch on to something, he proved rationally and dispassionately efficient. The Gestapo and Counter-Intelligence were uncannily thorough and would not give up until they had pushed a camel through the eye of a needle. But they were up against men who were a good match in vibrant intelligence and acute common sense, intent upon inducing their opposition to draw the wrong conclusions.

Inside the barbed wire, I embarked on various activities which vitally allowed me to revive many of my pre-war interests in the graphic arts, carving, hand-lettering and fine penmanship in forging identity cards, travel permits and passes for our own men and even civilians. There was an excessive busyness in VIIIB; no deadly ennui. After an interval of subversive operations, I would return to my friends in the hospital, to lie low for a breathing space before the next assignment came along. Using my youthful training in carving, I went into action on toothbrush handles, manufacturing rings in the hollowed heads of which were concealed coded messages or poison capsules. These were carried far and wide. Perhaps in a foolhardy mood of confidence, I sent a ring to Ernest Osborn, director of *The Yorkshire Post*, containing a minute photograph of myself and a message of seventy words. It was delivered by 'Wingy' Woodhead, a Yorkshireman, medically repatriated having lost a hand while labouring in a Polish coal-mine. Wingy later told me his only anxious moment was during the final search by Germans. Stripped naked, his clothes and body were thoroughly searched, but all the time the ring on his finger lay in full view, yet the Germans ignored it.

My first allotted job was in the Red Cross clothing store, helping unload crates and checking supplies of British Army clothing. An elderly German, brought out of retirement, supervised the store on days of the week when not managing a German equipment centre servicing the needs of the large contingent of guards, the locally recruited militia equivalent to the British Home Guard, and members of the Hitler-jugend (Youth Movement) of the area. This elderly Fritz Shroeder reminded me strongly, in looks and personality, of Grandfather Pape, but I did not allow sentiment to affect my conscience or deter cold-blooded blackmail and *insouciant* acting. I pinched khaki trousers for dyeing to look like civilian duds; unfortunately, British battle-jackets were too distinctive, but the store held foreign military jackets, French, Polish and Italian, which lent themselves to tailoring for natty civilian suits. If Fritz turned a blind eye to the disappearance of various items, I hate to think what quantities of Red Cross supplies were passed over, for which I received some measure of return in home-made cookies and apple pies baked by his *Frau*.

Then I let the axe fall. One morning, I casually pulled from my pocket 200 Reichmarks. 'Take them, Fritz,' I invited, 'a crowd of our chaps has just come back from a working party with a stack of the stuff. No use to them on the inside. I'll swap them for some more sausage and apple pies from your good wife.' His eyes gleamed, little knowing each note had been marked. With confidence bred of experience, aware that he could not turn back, I thereafter put on the screw. That dear old Hun was on the brink of nervous disorder, but piece by piece, day by day, he smuggled into the British store jackboots ranging from sizes nine to eleven and two German uniforms complete with caps. Disguise played a great part in escapers' plans. Mission successfully accomplished, I put myself back into hospital, to submerge until the next job was worked out and I was manipulated into position.

I became a scrubber of floors in the Kartei (card) office where thousands of prisoner data cards, including finger-prints and photographs, were filed. In this, the Germans were observing provisions of the International Red Cross for protective custody of POWs. Unexpected opportunities arose for probing the records when a few old Jerry clerks left the rooms unattended for coffee or meal breaks. Records of exchanged men and false identities were considered best destroyed. Scores of cards were hopelessly mixed and muddled but, most importantly, a good selection of photographed faces, thin, fat, short- and long-nosed, dark-haired and fair, was required by the forging section. I carried out my bucket, with what was possibly useful covered by rags and scrubbing brushes. The job fulfilled, back I went with purported violent headaches to my sick bed in the hospital, to await the next round of jiggery-pokery.

Before Godden and I had left VIIIB for Partschendorf, the disastrous Dieppe Raid had occurred. Back in VIIIB, I now found a deterioration of morale with the arrival of Canadian survivors of that raid. Most declared the raid had been premature, a horrible mistake, if a joy-ride for the waiting enemy which inflicted 3,367 casualties on the 4,963 Canadians who had taken part. It was March 1943 when I met a splendid fellow from Toronto who had spent six months in a Paris hospital. Part of his lower jaw had been shot away and the Germans had roughly patched him up, but Merv – regrettably I forget his surname – experienced difficulty in chewing solid food and enunciating. His delay in arriving at Lamsdorf had at least saved him from being manacled, a fate which befell earlier Canadian arrivals who suffered the painful humiliation of wearing steel cuffs chained together; another of a maddened Hitler's orders, a reprisal for a number of Germans captured during the heat of the Dieppe battle having had their hands tied behind their backs to prevent escape. The 'X' committee experts entered swiftly into the locksmith business; keys were made whereby a wrist shackle could be unlocked, at least allowing a miserable man to visit the latrines decently. Even the regular German guards were disgusted and ready to look the other way when we quietly undid a manacle. Eventually, the Germans abandoned this barbarous practice when Canadian authorities threatened similar treatment of German prisoners.

The Canadians soon united in schemes to harass the enemy. Among them were some bright engineers and in conjunction with the 'X' committee a tunnel was conceived to start from a barrack and progress eighty feet to a point twelve feet beyond the wire. It was a most skilful, ingenious piece of planning with air ventilation fans and lighting provided by tapping the power lines, but German security guards suddenly pounced and located the tunnel's entrance.

Looking back and considering the Sagan murders, I feel that a mass break-out would have spelt doom for many Canadians who may be alive today. It was bad enough that the possibility of mass murdering of prisoners, if things went badly for the Nazis in the war, could not be ruled out and did not help our peace of mind.

It was at this time, in April 1943, that another grisly massacre was first made known to the world, ironically, reported by the Germans. They made a great scream about their infantry discovering mass graves containing the compacted bodies of thousands of former Polish Army officers. The site of the graves was on a hillside thickly covered by spruce trees in the Katyn Forest overlooking the Dnieper River, close to Smolensk. The Katyn story began when the Russians captured a large portion of the Polish Army in September 1939, when Russia carved up Poland with Germany. Some 15,000 Polish Army officers, NCOs and reservists were held as prisoners of war in camps at Kozielsk, Starovielsk and Ostashkov in the USSR. In 1940 these camps were 'wound up' but the fates of the 15,000 men were unknown; they disappeared. Now, at Katyn, the remains of 4,253 Polish officers were found, each with hands tied behind his back and shot at the base of the skull. In London, the news given by Radio Berlin was received with diffidence. Germany charged the Russians with the crime but a furious Kremlin accused the Germans. The latter invited an International Red Cross investigation which the Soviets so opposed that they broke off diplomatic relations with the Polish Government in London.

I came into this when it was proposed by the Germans to our camp leader, Sheriff, that three ordinary soldiers from Lamsdorf, a New Zealander, Australian and Britisher, might accompany a neutral delegation to the Katyn graves to draw their own conclusions and make their reports. When it was suggested I might be the New Zealander, I was prepared to go, but Major McLeod and Captain Spencer firmly vetoed the idea. Apart from any question of my health, too much and too many were at risk if the Germans subjected me to fine screening and discovered my true identity. What might I be up to, faking the visit, after my lurid exploits in Poland? As it happened, no one went from VIIIB – I understand instructions were received from London forbidding any prisoners taking part. The attitude adopted in Britain was to appease the Polish Provisional Government and not upset the Russian ally; the overriding fear of the British and American Governments was lest Russia sign a separate peace treaty with Germany and withdraw from the war. Time enough to go into the matter when the war was won. Today there is little doubt that the Katyn massacre was one monstrous crime which the Germans did not commit.

By mid-1943, Red Cross food parcels (each was barely the size of a shoe box) were arriving increasingly. Instead of one between two, it was now one apiece. 'Mucking-in' was popular with two men combining their parcels; honour bound, each disciplining the other to ignore tightening hunger pains and share one meal daily, in the evening. Merv, with the grievous jaw injury, became my mucker-in. The Germans provided no cooking facilities or eating utensils but ingenuity ran high among prisoners, fashioning mugs, cutlery, and plates from food tins and with the superior Canadian parcels now flowing in, 'Klim' powdered milk tins were a godsend for improvising saucepans. Although forbidden, Merv and I would light a small fire to impart some heat into a stewy mixture so that he could chew it more easily. Then we invented a 'blower', about two feet long and eighteen inches high; hand-cut, grooved wooden discs of various sizes to give gearing ratio were connected with cord pulleys to provide speed. When cranked, blades in a cylinder spun at up to 500 revolutions a minute, forcing a draught into the small firebox lined with clay or stolen cement. The heat produced was intense – a Klim tin of water boiled in a minute; anything inflammable was used as fuel and very little was needed. Soldiers on local daily working parties picked up or pinched bits of wood and often small pieces of coal. It was remarkable how a little heat induced into food on cold nights warmed prisoners' spirits. Blowers became a craze and many weird and wonderful contraptions appeared from our basic design. Eventually they were forbidden and confiscated if discovered, as severe scarcity of fuel saw the three-tier, wooden beds so carved down as to become unsafe, shaky skeletons.

After the war, at the insistence of my publisher, I remade Merv's and my blower. At a party thrown for me at the RAF Club in Piccadilly, among the guests intrigued by the invention were Sir Frank Whittle, the jet inventor; Neville Duke, holder of the world speed record; and Sir Edmund Hillary, famed for overcoming obstacles. A press report of the occasion said: 'At the RAF Club last Thursday evening, Marshal of the Royal Air Force, Lord Tedder, had a lesson in cooking under difficulties. Pape borrowed a pipeful of tobacco from Lord Tedder, and then led him to a "rotary blowing machine". This was a cooker made in prison from bully beef tins. Pape wound it briskly. There was a loud clanking. The machine started to glow. "Steady," cautioned Lord Tedder, "you'll burn the club down"' (*Natal Daily News*, 29 September 1953). Shortly afterwards at a public lecture in Edinburgh, chaired by the Duke of Hamilton, I again demonstrated the blower and a photograph appeared in the press. A furious parent wrote to the Duke that such an infernal machine should never have been exhibited or its function explained as his son had enthusiastically sought to construct a replica and had set the house on fire.

During this sojourn in VIIIB, I learned to my intense relief that my former companion, Godden, had got clean away, though it was not disclosed to me what escape line he had moved along. I could only hope and pray that all would be well for him and we would meet in Britain after the war, to sup heartily and gossip about the many risks mastered in Partschendorf. But I never saw him again and he never returned to Britain. The only information I could obtain was that Godden (Reginald Barratt) had either been killed or he might turn up out of the blue. After Mieteck's reappearance from Siberia in 1956, I visited Barratt's wife Kathleen in Leicester, holding to the hope that if Barratt had been sent to the loathsome Gulag Archipelago, he too might be released. Approaches had been made to the Russians by Prime Minister Attlee and the War Office. Results were negative. Over twenty years later, I learned more (from Foot and Langley's *M19 – Escape and Evasion*, referred to earlier):

[On the subject of what happened to escapers from German prisoner of war camps who got as far as Hungary] Details are only available in a single case, that of a quiet, well-spoken warrant officer Reginald Barratt, who was using at the time the name of Godden. He made his way to Budapest, where he was succoured by an English girl called Evelyn Gore-Symes who nobody had bothered to intern and by a young Hungarian lawyer called Dr Raphael Rupert. Rupert introduced him to Kristof Kallya, son of the Prime Minister, though it is no longer clear when.

Barratt stayed for some time in Rupert's flat, and was clearly engaged in some sort of Intelligence activity. In the last autumn of 1944 he had access to a clandestine transmitter . . . Rupert remembers taking Barratt for a pillion ride on a motor bicycle to investigate the results of RAF mining of the Danube, and of German efforts to demagnetize the mines by flying JU-52 trimotor transports over them equipped with anti-magnetic coils.

This was getting out to the edge of MI9's brief. Barratt met Weinstein [Sergeant Tibot Weinstein, a Jew who was spending the war in British uniform] and sent him through to the Russian lines early in December 1944 with some target information of which the Russians made use. On 8 December Rupert, Barratt and a Dutch officer, Lieutenant van der Valls, were overrun by the Russians; all disappeared. Barratt is known to have been held prisoner by the Russians in Bratislava at midsummer 1945; for many years there was no news of him at all. Rupert, who was eventually released, now lives in Ireland. Van der Valls's family were officially informed from Moscow in the middle 1950s that, by a regrettable breach of Socialist legality, he had been imprisoned in the Lubyanka [Secret Police headquarters and prison in central Moscow] and had died there of pneumonia. Barratt's widow discovered at about the same time that her husband had been shot by Communist police in Bratislava, 'while trying to escape', an all too familiar cover for the disposal of troublesome prisoners.

The span of the first half of 1943, so much of which I spent in VIIIB's hospital, saw the Casablanca Agreement between Churchill and Roosevelt decreeing 'unconditional surrender' by the Axis powers. It also saw the tables irrevocably turned against Hitler's delusions of world conquest. In central and southern Russia, German armies suffered appalling losses in the winter offensive of the Soviet forces. In May, Germany and Italy surrendered in North Africa and their power was broken in the Mediterranean. The first 1,000-bomber raid had taken place and formidable Allied strategic bombing was on the way to becoming without equal in history. On 10 July the Allies landed in Sicily, and on 24 July Mussolini was to resign.

Relegating my escape activities as memories of a useful and disastrous mixed past, I was prepared to sit out the war and work against the enemy in controlled captivity, aiding others to escape, giving propaganda talks to upgrade morale and carry on with code operations. I was disinclined to involve myself in further hard adventuring in the field. It was acknowledged that a Second Front was being prepared and it was only a matter of time before the blow fell. News received on our secret radio was deliberately delayed in release, to preserve this line of communication; then it was carefully and periodically circulated by padres and other reliable men. The best I could do was keep my nerve, act out my double game, and pray: 'Lord have mercy on me and get me home as Yeatman in one bloody piece.' I felt that my masquerade, surviving a year and a half, was now invincible.

Having settled myself into this groove, I was in for an extraordinary shaking. It was about June 1943 when, by chance I thought, I became acquainted with a Pole who had infiltrated into the stalag as a Czech. Devious underground means existed whereby Poles, Czechs and Yugoslavs seemed able to swap themselves about to suit their needs. My new Polish friend, Borguslaw – I called him 'Borge' – was about twenty-eight, of strong personality and decision, a courageous man of officer class, also a lucky one; he had narrowly escaped disaster when a large number of FAN* colleagues in Poland had been executed only months earlier. Admittedly, he had contact with the 'X' committee and the British doctors, but I was staggered at how much he knew of my Polish and Czechoslovakian activities. As I became convinced of his genuineness as a Polish Intelligence agent, we talked freely and frankly. I learned with interest that certain Polish strategists were secretly liaising with a small concentration of German conspirators, including certain intellectual forces and high-ranking officers of the German Armed Services, prepared to assassinate Hitler, then negotiate peace terms with the Allies. The Germans concerned knew that the days of Hitler's triumphant leadership were over and he would bring Germany down to final ruin. They also knew of the January 1943 Casablanca Agreement stipulating unconditional surrender. Any hope for earlier peace, on terms less than unconditional, the conspirators knew would depend first upon the irrevocable removal of Hitler and his cesspool of secret police.

* A diversionary organizaton of the Polish Home Army in the eastern territories.

As for the Poles, and indeed some Czechs and Yugoslavs, their motives in the conspiracy were certainly not the rescuing of Germany from total ruin but the restoration of their own countries to total freedom. They had neither affinity with the transcendental notions of the Nazis, nor sorrowing about the enemy's sufferings which it had brought upon its own head. As Borge explained, once the Soviets in pursuit of the now retreating Germans swept across Poland, the prospect for his country was the substitution of one oppressor for another. I was reminded of the Soviets' grab at the eastern half of Poland in 1939. Now, with the relentless ebbing of Germany's fortunes, Russia was looming again. The Poles saw as urgent the need for a speedy peace with Germany, to bring the Western Allies' troops pouring unhindered into Germany, Poland and the Balkans, to halt the Russian advance at its own pre-war borders. Irrespective of Churchill, Roosevelt or governments in exile, Poles and others on the spot resolved to follow their own decisive steps; the removal of Hitler and possibly an insurrection they saw as vital moves, even if Western leaders deprecated such actions. I listened to bitter reproaches about Western Allies being prepared to abandon Poland to Stalin.

Full well I knew the spirit and determination that rule the minds of Polish patriots and, indeed, I still say that next to being born a Britisher, I would plunge for being a Pole. I was deeply indebted to them, to the point of owing my life. I was idealistically attuned to the Polish cause, disappointed that Britain had let them down – had let *me* down in my face-to-face encounters with them. After my meeting with the German, Professor Burckhardt, at Cracow, I had no difficulty in believing Borge's assertion that the German resistance movement had never been more dynamic than now. I had no idea, of course, of attempts already made to kill Hitler; as recently as three months before, in March

1943, there had been two attempts: one by Baron Rudolf von Gersdorff, who had volunteered to blow himself up with the Führer but had been unable to get close enough; the other by German conspirators placing a captured British plastic bomb in Hitler's aircraft on a flight to his Army headquarters at Rastenburg, East Prussia – but again he escaped, this time because of a fault in the detonating mechanism.

Borge sought my assistance to aid the Polish cause; as he saw it, turning British spirit and purpose towards objectives for which Britain was also fighting. He questioned, 'Why should escaping prisoners of war expect the resources of the Polish underground to get them back to Britain? Why should they not stay and fight shoulder to shoulder with their Polish ally?' I had heard this argument before, in Partschendorf, from Karel Cech. Underground fighting men were contemptuous about assisting escapees to get home to their own comforts. Poles, like Czechs, were hazarding their lives and taking great risks, and it was reasonable enough they wanted a feed-back of fighting allegiance and a sharing of perils there and then.

It seemed incredible to me while remaining, if far from inactive, in VIIIB that attention had focused on me as a suitable recruit for more extended and dangerous action. I tentatively agreed to assist Borge on the 'outside', with no awareness of what was really in store. I appreciated that utter ruthlessness and self-dedication would be necessary to carry through to success the extermination of Hitler, but I was not getting mixed up in any death or glory operations, not in mid-1943, even if secretly I had the shadow of Burckhardt before my eyes. In the realm of risks and machinations against the enemy in three occupied countries, I concluded I had contributed my fair share.

Borge saw British connivance in a successful attempt on Hitler's life as having significance in German and Polish efforts to bring about a negotiated peace. I suppose I realized that Britain would, if necessary, disclaim as unauthorized any part I or any other Britisher might have in assassinating Hitler. What Borge wanted me to do was to go officially as a patient to a large German military hospital (Lazarett VI) at Breslau (now Opava), Poland. There it would be arranged for me to meet some German–Polish doctors who were willing to assist in returning underground agents to VIIIB, taking the places of sick prisoners removed to the military hospital. My experience of manipulating and safe-guarding changes of identities could be invaluable, and a reconnaissance of the workings of the hospital might reveal to me opportunities for future Intelligence exploitation.

I was already aware of the German procedure in VIIIB of sorting the scores of thousands of prisoners of various nationalities; classified for skills, groups were dispatched to many places under German control to work in all manner of enterprises. What I now learned from Borge was that some contingents, selected numbers with requisite skills, were being sent to Austria to work on the Obersalzberg – indeed, on the newly initiated tunnel complex in Hitler's territory above Berchtesgaden. Parties of Russian prisoners had also been sent north to work in East Prussia, some at Rastenburg, the Wolf's Lair. Borge disclosed that his Intelligence branch was ascertaining the strategic value of VIIIB for getting agents out to chosen sites as workers. It was true that, in certain extreme cases requiring surgery or specialist examination, the German medical authorities dutifully observed the Geneva Convention and did send prisoners to the military hospital in Breslau. Borge had already spent a few days in VIIIB's camp hospital and was well acquainted with Dr Otto Müller. It was obvious that some intrigue was going on with plans being developed for moving a few Poles or Yugoslavs to Breslau where swap-overs would be effected.

So began a new story, fantastic as it might seem but something of an intermittent nightmare to me ever since. I certainly let myself in for it and I was astutely taken over. The British RAMC doctors, Spencer and McLeod, would never have consented to my leaving to do a bit of scouting and undergo a minor operation on my sinuses had they known the true underlying purpose of getting me to Breslau.

It was impossible to gain admission to the military hospital without German medical recommendation. Dr Müller put me down as an urgent case for examination, with a suspected brain tumour – terrible headaches, bouts of dementia, optical fluctuations and God knows what. Sinus trouble was a second string, with a measure of truth, if a minor legacy from the crash in Holland and nothing which could not await return to Britain. Müller told me I might be away at most three weeks. I agreed to go, even if I was not at all keen for a sinus operation. Still, it was a pretty harmless commitment and a little action away from the pressures and masses of men in VIIIB would be a welcome change. I agreed also with Borge that top secrecy being so essential, I would not risk coding advice to Britain about my movement; in any case, I could be safely back in VIIIB before Britain would know.

Müller had me returned to the camp hospital while arrangements were made for my departure. Borge disappeared back into the Russian compound as mysteriously as he had arrived, saying he might see me in Breslau; what conjuring powers existed to work his remarkable comings and goings, I never knew. One evening, about three days before I was due to leave, I was summoned to Dr Müller's rooms for an eye check, a routine now familiar to me over the previous months. Observing a carved toothbrush ring I was wearing, a delicate innocuous specimen, Müller showed interest in my hobby. I little realized it was giving him the lead-in he wanted.

'I'd like you to make me one, when you return,' he said.

'Certainly; I'll be glad to.'

Following the eye examination, I sat facing the German doctor. He was a fine-looking man. There was nothing slack-lipped in his habitual geniality, but suddenly his expression firmed. 'Have a look at my ring.' He spoke in a level tone and, taking a gold ring from his pocket, pushed it across the desk. I picked it up and promptly stiffened as I observed the stag's head and motto *'Festigkeit'*. It was a replica of Professor Burckhardt's ring. My hand faltered as the heavy ring instantly evoked memories of the SS prison in Cracow, recalling the professor's supreme optimism about destruction of the Führer and his Nazi regime. I was scrutinized questioningly. I suddenly felt on a razor's edge, not exactly frightened, only curious and oddly excited.

'I'm proud to own that ring,' Müller said, and sprang the question. 'Do you still have yours?'

I knew something fateful awaited me. 'What ring? I don't understand.'

'You *do* understand. I have means of penetrating your medical records concerning your not very happy experiences in Poland.'

If I assumed to stare at him blankly, I realized this was a point of contact. 'You will recall Dr Wurm,' he went on, 'an old colleague of mine, and of course Professor . . .?' he clicked his fingers, inviting assistance.

'Burckhardt,' I said. 'Why ask me these questions?' Bewilderment, not unmingled with caution, bulked large in my mind.

I was studied speculatively; he stressed his next remarks. 'Our business is with the urgent present and future, not the past. You have heard from a Polish friend, Borge, the gravity of the situation and the desperate need for early peace.' He gestured to halt my interruption. 'I know,' he continued, 'that you received a ring almost like mine and with an English motto "Aim Sure". With your experiences and knowledge, we are satisfied you are the man to go to Breslau.'

In remembering the tragic plight of that splendid German professor, our resolute friendship and his faith that one day I might somehow be of value, I was prompted to say, 'What if I cannot produce the ring?'

'In that case,' was the swift reply, 'your services will not be required; the journey to Breslau cancelled.'

I think I underwent a rapid mental revolution founded on conscience and memory, and decided on the truth, to see where it led me. 'I have the ring. It's concealed in a cavity in a wooden post of my barrack bed.'

He tapped the table thoughtfully, then spoke in a manner cordial and composed. 'You'll return to the main camp for one night. I'll have Captain Spencer authorize a new battle-dress for you from the store.' He smiled. 'We want you to go to the military hospital as a smart British soldier. Also, I want to see the ring. Don't wear it; conceal it in your boot.'

'Will I be taking it to Breslau?'

'No. It is to remain in my care until you get back, but you will be given evidence of it to take with you.'

There the matter rested for that evening, but I had further private discussions with Dr Müller who took infinite pains in briefing me, and emphasizing the care and resourcefulness which the operation warranted. Dr Müller had obviously insinuated himself into the offices of the labour authorities responsible for prisoners of war and was in a position to elicit information. He was trusted and I could only conclude that they were unaware of his anti-Hitler outlook; his position of senior medical officer in charge of the camp hospital gave him excellent cover for secret work with Intelligence services. Three other prisoners were listed to visit Breslau with me; carefully chosen, they were already 'in place' in the camp hospital. One was a Yugoslav, Josif, a tough Chetnik who had fought in Greece and evaded capture for quite a time. I recall he was suspected of suffering from cancer. The other two were Poles, Stefan and Jerzy; I forget Stefan's complaint, but Jerzy was to have shrapnel removed. Our records, with photographs and fingerprints, had been forwarded to the security unit at the military hospital and clearance received back for us to undertake the journey.

As I understood it, the plan behind four sick prisoners going to Breslau was to have two of them replaced by trained agents for return to VIIIB. The agents were already 'planted' in Breslau awaiting our arrival and at an appropriate time they would assume the names of the men they were replacing and be given false identity papers bearing their own photographs and fingerprints. My qualifications in forgery and knowledge of the numbering and filing system of the Kartei in VIIIB would be put to use. Secret arranging would be directed to getting the agents, under the guise of common prisoners in VIIIB, out on working parties destined for Obersalzberg, there to gather all information they could: British prisoners were forbidden to work in the Hitler Territory above Berchtesgaden, but not so other nationalities. By then, I expected to be back in VIIIB as Yeatman, with perhaps a little more being divulged to me of the significance of my efforts, and of the signet ring, in the complexities.

# CHAPTER 16
## Breslau Intrigue

Towards 6.30 one morning, a Yugoslav, two Poles and a 'New Zealander' were assembled for transport to Annaberg, my sixth visit to the little railway station. During our pre-departure stay in hospital, we had been instructed to grow beards, always a useful precautionary advantage for camouflage and identity-card faking. I carried, well concealed in my clothing and boots, forging material and official blanks of record cards stolen from the Kartei; also a plentiful supply of German and Polish banknotes, although I had been assured by Borge that everything possibly required was on hand in Breslau. I must say, the camp authorities had shown some milk of human kindness in issuing each of us with two Red Cross food parcels and 100 cigarettes. I had also been told by Dr Müller, just before leaving, that the military hospital was to examine my head for any damage done by the sub-machine-gun blow in Hungary; it made my story about violent head pains more convincing. But once outside Stalag VIIIB, my brain had never seemed so wonderfully clear, or the spirit of adventure so alive again. I felt aggressively proud that this latest exploit might help in some way to bring about the destruction of a mad Hitler and his mob.

What sticks out vividly in memory *en route* to the station was the sight of about thirty senior Italian officers marching under German guard towards the stalag. I howled with sardonic delight at a scene that might have belonged to an operatic spectacular at La Scala. They were resplendent in plumed headgear, ornamental shoulder-pieces, sashes, plaited cords with dangling tassels, rows of medals and other colourful bits of uniform tutti-frutti . . . if I did envy their

magnificent knee-high riding boots. Subsequently, I learned
that the tramping officers, members of some illustrious
regiment, had been seized as nascent conspirators against
Mussolini and the Rome–Berlin Axis. On arrival at the
station, we witnessed a small army of Italian soldiers being
herded into columns by yelling guards, without any
humanitarian regard. Little did I guess it was only days away
to Mussolini's arrest on 25 July 1943, and just how close was
the Italian military collapse. Within two months, that first
bunch of Italian captives would enlarge to 10,000 in Stalag
VIIIB. The Germans were contemptuous of their former
comrades in arms, and all signs of past friendly allegiance had
gone out of fashion.

A solitary guard accompanying us to Breslau was a white-
haired old chap, plain, honest and friendly. He sorted out an
unoccupied compartment for his '*sehr krank*' (very sick)
party and as the train snorted and ground into motion the
old fellow started talking, and never stopped. He had
worked on a ferry most of his pre-war life and I discerned
that he was quite religious, a socialist and a pacifist at heart.
He spoke so frankly of the injustices of the distribution of
wealth and of it being against God's will that men should
butcher each other under the State's orders, that I was
concerned lest he be overheard; he certainly would not have
held forth in this manner in the presence of a second guard.
The only way I could stop his chatter was to complain of a
very bad headache. How different he was from other guards
on other train-rides who had sat stiffly with stick hand-
grenades tucked down their jackboots, and snapped,
'Talking is forbidden.'

The big military hospital at Breslau had a segregated
compound nearby for POW patients, despite the enormous
numbers of seriously wounded German soldiers arriving
direct from the Eastern Front demanding the greatest
exertions from the medical staff. The existence of this POW

adjunct may have been frowned upon by adherents of fierce Nazidom. But its functioning perhaps had something to do with the great numbers of Germans being taken prisoner by the Allies in various theatres of war, and the need for some reciprocal quality of mercy as defined under the Geneva Convention and the decent customs of war. There was, of course, no Samaritanism towards the hundreds of thousands of Russian prisoners, nor did I imagine Germans in the hands of the Soviets fared any better. The compound represented a small area of grassland with six large, clean, comfortable barracks. Two of the wooden structures, with clinics attached, catered for men awaiting surgery in the main hospital, and upon return for post-operative care. Occupants of the other barracks were escorted to the main building for examination, X-ray, pathological testing or whatever else was required.

After leaving the train at Breslau, we were provided with transport for the run to the compound and I well remember approaching it via a short, narrow lane named Kirsche Alley ('Wisniowa' after the war). One side of this cobbled lane was lined with old stone cottages; along the other was an embankment atop of which was a derelict graveyard with a number of leaning, time-worn headstones.* Little did I realize that one of the cottages in that alley was to have far-reaching meaning and repercussion in my life.

If I anticipated meeting strict security and tricky conditions, I was well off-beam. It seemed fantastic to pass through a rickety, unguarded gateway, although I later discovered that sometimes a veteran soldier did present himself for guard duty when a senior German doctor and medical orderlies arrived at the compound every second morning; a junior doctor, lodged in one of the small

---

* The military hospital and cemetery were destroyed. A new hospital has been constructed for railway workers.

cottages, was invariably on call for any emergency.

I have certainly no inclination to praise my enemy, but in all fairness one has to be seriously decent about 'good' Germans, and often I envied their philosophy of cheerfulness and the popularity of hard work. On arrival, a smart, agreeably rational officer interviewed us with the aid of a pinched-up little interpreter adept in various languages. Our bona fides were checked and we were rated as genuine patients. The little interpreter stiffened as he conveyed the final message from the officer: 'Captives brought to this hospital are on their honour and must not attempt to escape. They must show proper gallantry and politeness to German doctors and staff. If any man upsets this order of things, his sick comrades will suffer and will brand him with the mark of infamy. The authorities of the hospital will hound him out of the place and any prospect for medical treatment will be lost for ever.'

Shown to our barrack, one thing floats in memory – the different nationalities occupying the compound. My impression is of well over a hundred men, mixing amicably, moving freely from barrack to barrack, chatting in mongrel vernaculars, playing cards. However, it was not exactly amusing to find about a dozen Italian officers, bedecked in glamorous uniforms but segregated in a closed-off portion of a barrack; one had lost an arm, another an eye. This unhappy group sauntered aimlessly around the inside perimeter of the wire fence most of the daylight hours, generally 'sent to Coventry' by the rest, men who had suffered long captivity and privation, decimated remnants of true fighting corps, most in sombre, ill-assorted clothes and with little reason to praise Red Cross supplies. I felt more than a touch of embarrassment being admirably kitted-out in a brand new British battle-dress, even to wearing collar and tie. But nobody was deliberately rude, and in a short time I became an accepted friend, sharing some of my Red Cross food rations and cigarettes. I recall a dozen or so Poles, Czechs and Hungarians, a group of French officers and a number of Britishers whom I found a tremendous relief and comfort. About six of the Britishers were flying men, one with part of his neck and shoulder shot away; two were merchant seamen, one with a lower leg missing and the other with syphilis. Investigating the barracks, I was relieved to find no New Zealander to test my probity.

I did a reconnaissance of the compound. The encompassing barbed-wire fence was farcical, every bit as ineffective as at the school in Partschendorf. Patrolling guards or watch towers did not exist. Chatting with fellow prisoners, I exhibited my big silver pocket watch, a hunter, which I shook with annoyance, complaining that it kept stopping. I said it had been a poor bargain, bartered with a Stalag VIIIB guard for Red Cross supplies. In truth, Borge had given it to me. The inside of its metal cover over the dial was engraved in Polish to some long-time faithful servant of a legal firm and dated 1917. Inside the back cover were fine scratchings, watch repairers' identifications, so Borge had told me. Once a fine instrument and no doubt the pride of its first owner, it was now somewhat battered; it must have gone around the underground scores of times. At the moment it was a vital object for initial introduction to a Russian. I knew he resided permanently in the compound and had been advised to expect our arrival. The Russian, Feodor, was my intermediary, an agent for Polish Intelligence. As with the Poles, there can be no argument that a highly developed Russian Intelligence Organization had infiltrated its agents into camps and other German-controlled establishments where Soviet prisoners were held or laboured or were sent to apply their skills. Feodor was an instrument maker and electrical technician; working with two assistants, he had achieved a trusted standing with the German hospital staff, keeping X-ray and other essential equipment in good functioning order. In leisure hours, in their private hut in the compound, Feodor and his two assistants had acquired a repution as watch and clock repairers; a remarkable number of hospital employees, including uniformed men and women nurses, trod the path to the hut with defective time-pieces. He was obviously in a position to be very knowledgeable about the hospital working methods and key personnel.

I waited for Feodor's return to the compound from his day's work. He appeared wearing white overalls, with a satchel slung from his shoulder. When he was close to his hut, I approached and touched his arm. I confronted a slim, shortish man in his mid-forties, balding, with a thin lined face and keen brown eyes. 'Would you examine my watch?' I spoke slowly. 'It is giving trouble.'

His eyes immediately showed a sharpened awareness, but without a word he opened the watch-face cover. He scrutinized the engraving and, not giving the vaguest sign of surprise, requested me to step inside. I sat opposite him at a small table as he opened the back of the watch, put a jeweller's glass to his eye and studied the scratch markings. As he put the watch in a drawer, he said he would look at it in a day or so and added, 'Have you anything else to show me?'

'Are you interested in plaster of Paris moulds?' I asked.

'If they show a stag's head,' he replied.

'I can manage that,' and I took from a cigarette tin a plaster casting of my signet ring; I also had an impression in black wax, both supplied by Dr Müller. Again the glass went to Feodor's eye and he studied the casting intently. Laying the glass aside, his face creased into a smile. 'I trust your headaches are not too distressing,' he said.

We met on a number of occasions and invariably I was greeted with every mark of courtesy. I also met Dr Hermann Kafka, a Sudeten German and senior surgeon. He visited the prisoner compound with a younger doctor, the one who resided in the cottage in Kirsche Alley and was on call to the compound at night. Both doctors were involved in our deception and intrigue. Kafka was a close associate of Dr Wurm and Dr Müller and, like them, was prepared to co-operate with the German and Polish resistance movements in whatever secret ways his services could be utilized to save life, relieve suffering and see the war ended. I had several talks with Dr Kafka in the privacy of the little clinic attached to my barrack and I discerned that he had a sharp awareness of what was required to be done in respect of two Poles, a Yugoslav and myself.

Dr Kafka and Feodor were linked in secret communication. Besides his other qualifications, Feodor was a photographer. It was not unusual for him to take snapshots of prisoners, to give to them as souvenirs of their visits to this Reseve Lazarett VI; in return, Feodor received small gifts, perhaps something from Red Cross parcels from those lucky enough to have them. Dr Kafka indicated that Jerzy, Stefan, Josif and I were to be photographed, a planned act with double purpose. Souvenir snaps were taken and then, craftily, portraits suitable for use in passports or official record cards. Behind closed doors in the clinic, our fingerprints were also taken. It seemed there was no great problem in removing or substituting identity cards at the Kommandantur offices of the hospital. To this day, I retain my full-length picture taken by Feodor, and a slim, smartly dressed soldier I looked – if mysteriously part of one side of my face is blacked out, for what reason I have never known.

Suddenly, Jerzy and Stefan were removed to the main hospital. Josif and I were carefully briefed and transferred to a dark corner of one of the pre- and post-operative care huts. I had acted out many parts and put on phoney performances to suit occasions in outwitting the enemy, but in all honesty this latest piece of hoodwinking was rather a strain. My orders were to maintain perfect self-control while behaving in an acutely anti-social way towards the others in the hut, refusing to converse, pouring my soup on the floor and generally suggesting a rapid approach of lunacy, a state of morbid brooding. Poor old Josif obeyed instructions too, becoming uncommunicative with no desire for occupational interest, and generally moaning and groaning as if in pain. We received sedative injections, not for reasons our ward-mates might have thought, but as a tactic by Dr Kafka to alleviate the strain of acting. While the two Poles were in the hospital proper, I also visited it to have my nose X-rayed and tests carried out on my cranium for any injury or tumour. It was clear that Josif and I were being held back, awaiting the return of the Poles before the next advance in the plan.

The return of the two Poles awakens one of my strangest memories, when the two who appeared were perfect strangers. They were FAN agents assuming the identities of Jerzy and Stefan. I had been tipped off to exhibit no bewildered surprise, and while I was not stupid, and managed hushed conversations in snatches with the bearded substitutes alongside, I perhaps incontinently enquired what had happened to the 'real' two. 'Free men again; they'll be looked after.' The new Stefan growled, 'Keep quiet, bloody Yeatman. We're playing with dangerous gas! Act barmy until we get clear of this place.' The exchange of the men had been skilfully manoeuvred; both agents spoke good English and, I suspected, their pasts could reveal that they had been resident in Britain before parachuting into Poland.

That same evening, I was called to the clinic to see Dr Kafka and experienced a sudden shock finding I also faced Borge, grinning with his usual panache. He was wearing a white coat with the insignia of an ambulance man. At Lamsdorf he had been attached to a fumigating squad, a job which had presented him with opportunities to swing his identity and move about; it was far harder to get into VIIIB than here. He came immediately to the point. It was

confirmed that Josif had cancer. It was impossible to send
him back to Lamsdorf with the agents Stefan and Jerzy.
'We've decided,' said Borge, 'you'll go back in Josif's place;
there's no alternative.'

I was stunned. 'What do you mean, no alternative?'

'You've been at this game long enough to know about
espionage business, without asking for a lot of explanation,'
he rejoined.

'Bugger that,' I protested, 'it was no part of the bargain
when I came here.'

'We're well aware of that and totally sympathetic,' said
Borge, 'but in the urgency of the circumstances, we need you
to cover up for Josif in the Russian compound at VIIIB,
and to go out with Stefan and Jerzy on a special working
party to Bavaria . . . at least until they're established there
with key contacts. Then you can return to VIIIB as
Yeatman.'

The immediate question which gripped my mind was who
the hell would take my place as Yeatman? 'A ticklish
business,' Borge agreed, 'but don't worry; all preparations
have been made.'

It was inferred that Josif was an SOE agent; that what I
was being asked to do was in the interests of Polish and
British causes. I knew Josif was no Yugoslav, just as I had
known he was really sick, with a terrible grey pallor and
sunken cheeks. I first met him at VIIIB's hospital prior to
our departure, and I had ribbed him for speaking English
with a Scottish accent. He would talk of Scotland, but never
spoke much when anyone else was about; we also conversed
in German and hour after hour he had improved my
proficiency in that language. He would say, 'Winston, you'll
be picked up at once if you say that,' and he would instruct
me on what I should say. Once when I asked his background,
he told me he was Polish Regular Air Force.

It was Dr Kafka who said there were certain people who

were good at remembering my past services, resourcefulness and strength of resistance, and had trust in me to fight on. I realized in my heart that refusal was impossible. I had been manipulated into position with decisive steps taken to involve me in a specific undercover operation more deeply than I had imagined. This would be my fifth change of nationality – Dutch, New Zealander, Pole, German and now Yugoslav. Except for the visit as a Dutchman to the Philips works at Hilversum, each change had been for the purpose of escape and by luck, or someone's grace, I had hung on to POW status. This time, if caught, there would be no possibility of reprieve.

Quietly, I was told I would be leaving the barrack for the main hospital next morning and to take nothing with me, no Red Cross soap, towel, cigarettes; not even pyjamas. I would arrive in what I stood up in and would receive the same hospital clothing as German patients. Before leaving the clinic I was 'dressed-up' by Kafka; a broad band of sticking plaster was placed across my brow, another piece over my nose, which was plugged with cotton wool in the morning before I departed.

At the main hospital I entered a ward, dimly lit, about the size of a tennis court, and excessively crowded. Half the inmates had heads or faces swathed in bandages; blinded, mutilated. The section where I was placed was given over to amputees. On my immediate right, a blond young man had a heavily bandaged thigh stump and had lost the foot of his other leg. On my left, an older man had lost a lower leg, most of one arm and also had stomach wounds. This was no place for me to entertain private anxieties about myself. It was something of a nightmare, listening to the sobs and moans of that pocket of suffering and dying men. Dr Kafka had said I would be there for two days at most, but the arrivals of screaming ambulances on the first day with freshly wounded brought by hospital train from the Eastern Front seriously upset routine. On the second morning, I was taken to a room annexed to an operating theatre and placed in a chair, like a dentist's chair. For at least two hours I sat there watching a slow procession of trolleys with inert men being pushed to or from the theatre. Twice a young surgeon, his face taut with strain, came to me and apologized for the long wait, saying he would do his best to attend to me that day. But I was returned to the ward, and no one came to fetch me on the morrow.

For three days I lived in the ward among prostrate, sacrificial-suffering men while I pretended to have pains in the head and infrequently muttered to myself. I had already seen much of death and knew the savage indifference of bullets, shells and bombs. Existing among those grievously damaged or dying men, it all seemed pitiful, senseless and ridiculous. The blond fellow alongside asked where I was from and I answered vaguely that I was a prisoner of war, sent from a stalag because of worsening effects of head injuries received in fighting on Crete in 1940. It got around among the others capable of taking an interest. There was no trace of enmity, no disagreement or recriminations; we all seemed part of a brotherhood. I remember one young soldier – he had lost an arm – coming to my bedside and with trembling lips saying politely, 'You'd probably like to smoke?' and he offered a cigarette. The cigarette ration for the patients was three each a day, and those good-hearted fellows made sure I had two a day.

I learned that men were dying like animals at the Front, and if I wanted to express pity, I couldn't because pity in war has always made me sick. I preferred anger; that was my defence. Stuck with them there, inevitably I churned over the meaning of it all. The blond soldier in the next bed held a prayer book and read hour after hour. Surely he must have spurned all deification of Hitler and Fatherland worship, suffering the pain and torment he did? And I wondered how many of the others were suffering their pains with torments of vain regret. Those limbless, blind, disfigured men affected me in a peculiar way, for I seemed strangely interwoven with the living flesh and blood of the whole human race, with life stripped of all differences. It was a queer, impersonal, anonymous state of mind, assuming a twist of rudimentary understanding of humanity in a very simple way.

On the third morning, Dr Kafka made his round of the ward. He held the rank of major and was accompanied by a young doctor carrying a sheaf of papers. On arrival at my bed, Kafka scrutinized my record sheet; turning to his junior, he appeared riled as he said stiffly, 'Have this prisoner dealt with right away. I will not accept delay; this bed is wanted.' He moved on with set face giving no hint of recognition. Everything went with a rush then; back to the annexe off the operating theatre, my turn came ten minutes later when I was placed on a trolley and pushed into the theatre.

I came to my senses in the ward, and it seemed to me I had been too lavishly bandaged, but doubtless it was Kafka who influenced decisions. I remember my blond neighbour staring at me with sad luminous eyes and saying in a tone of absolute friendship, 'I am praying for your speedy recovery.' I thanked him, and if I pretended restrained lamentations of pain, I was telling myself the sooner I got to hell out of the place, the better. I felt like a condemned man in that ward of vast suffering, which now seemed full of menaces.

Early next morning, I was returned to the theatre annexe and the dentist-type chair where I held a large kidney bowl against my chest as lengths of bloodied dressing were removed from my nostrils. At the time, alarmingly, I thought it was part of me that was being dragged out! The surgeon was that exhausted young man who had apologized days before about the delay. He did slip up on the operation, a submucous resection, removing more of my nasal structure than precision required, but in the rushed emergencies of the hospital the treatment of a vastly overstrained German surgeon was forgivably inept. The mistake, which has allowed me to snore like a saw-mill ever since, is recorded among my pensionable war disabilities as 'injury nose with septal fenestrum'. (Just after the war, following plastic surgery repairs to my face by Sir Archibald McIndoe, I was passed over to a young specialist, Jerry Moore, to straighten up the bridge of my nose and then to restructure the perforated septum. I was booked in at East Grinstead hospital for this last operation when suddenly a rare opportunity arose to depart for the African continent – at that time it was next to impossible to get passage out of Britain. So the operation was left in abeyance; I couldn't hear my own snoring and had no intention at the time of sharing a bed with anyone over a long slumber period. The operation is in abeyance to this day; my tolerant wife gathers up her pillow and migrates to another room.)

Immediately after that overworked German surgeon examined and replugged my nose, I was returned to the prisoner compound. In the barrack clinic, the young doctor from the cottage in Kirsche Alley introduced me to a waiting person. This person had become me. His forehead was bandaged for camouflage and it was quite a dramatic experience meeting the new Winston Yeatman. Not unnaturally, I closely studied this man who was to safeguard my identity. He was a Pole, keen-eyed, alert, about my height and build, clean-shaven like myself, for I had been ordered to remove my beard before entering the hospital. He spoke excellent English, greeting me with, 'Well, well, my Yugoslav colleague, how are you feeling?'

He was led to my former bed in the barrack and I took Josif's – he had vanished. I was now alongside the Polish agents, Jerzy and Stefan, with a screen positioned between

us and the few others remaining in the barrack. The Poles
grinned and welcomed me back as I tried to think sensibly,
out of a maze of conjectures, what the hell I had let myself in
for. Later that day I saw Dr Kafka in the clinic; he said he
would be getting the four of us off to Stalag VIIIB as soon
as safely possible. I also learned that no more sick prisoners
of war would be admitted to Reserve Lazarett VI for some
time, owing to the growing burden on the hospital to
accommodate German wounded.

Borge reappeared a number of times; I made it clear that I
could hardly be immune from doubts about self-preservation
and the future. He assured me my new role would be
temporary and I recall him looking at me critically, saying,
'You are game, aren't you? You're not afraid?'

'Of course I'm not afraid,' I retorted; my nerves were
certainly on edge. But it was obvious there was no backing
out now.

All documents for the four new identities were forged to
perfection, with correct photographs and fingerprints. How
could Borge have moved agents into Lamsdorf except
through the hospital? It could not have been done at VIIIB
with our amateur forging facilities; carving out Reich
stamps and insignias from raw potato or damp wood, we
produced the best we could for escapees, and hopefully they
would pass cursory inspection. But Jerzy, Stefan and I were
intended for situations demanding infallible documents.
Now, as Josif Matos, I again had to commit much to
memory; facts about my birth in Zagreb, work as a builder in
Croatia, service in the army, and other basic details I could
fall back upon while relying on my knowledge of German for
any on-the-spot questioning. Jerzy and Stefan spoke Serbo-
Croat and would stand behind me.

Official British war records disclose that I was admitted
to the German military hospital in Breslau on 27 July 1943
and returned to Stalag VIIIB on 7 September 1943, an

inordinately long stay for a few preliminary examinations and a simple submucous resection, particularly in a hospital desperate for bed space for grievously wounded arriving straight from the battle zone. But somehow Dr Kafka played for time to manoeuvre seven men secretly into position. About a fortnight before we left Breslau, the disturbing news was imparted that Jerzy, Stefan and I were to undergo slight operations for identification capsules to be inserted in our abdomens. I was aghast at this cold resolve, unexpectedly announced. It was explained that grave realities had to be faced, and hazards which would obviously accompany the planned mission to Berchtesgaden necessitated availability of identification. I was rigidly informed that every resistance organization had its methods and reasons for identifying chosen operators; the Germans, for instance, used microscopic tattoo signs for identifying men in the SS. The Russians had their methods and, if I was not privy to the mysteries and complicated procedures of the inner Polish resistance corps to which Borge belonged, he did insist that men in the Polish resistance, willing to barter their souls in wartime subterfuge, must be prepared to carry a capsule inside them.

I agreed to undergo the operation. I had no option. I was already versed in a deal of secret information and negotiations. Apart from that, I was a rebel with no high-pitched dreams of a golden post-war era. I felt rootless, drifting, not even particularly wanting to go home. I was in some mental state of anarchy against Britain for its stumbling let-down of the Polish nation. I had already taken the oath to the Polish nation and its people for their freedom, and Britain's. I would conscientiously fulfil the duties of an Englishman in whatever direction required of me in the cause of victory, but at the same time I had become part of Polish solidarity against Hitler. That was all there was to it. I admired the Poles beyond any race on earth.

Dr Kafka eased the strain of my revulsion against being cut open. He assured me the incision in my side would be barely an inch long, such as a skilled surgeon would be proud to claim for an appendectomy; nor should I fear infection or painful reaction – as I was reminded, metal fragments still remained harmlessly in the soft tissues of many a First World War veteran. It was Borge who said, 'Suppose you manage to get a pot-shot at Hitler and you then die as a Yugoslav? What do you think would happen in reprisals against the Yugoslav people? But if you could be identified as an Englishman, you could not call down direct revenge upon an unconquered Britain.'

'There are thousands of British prisoners of war,' I proffered.

'So are thousands of Germans in the hands of the Allies,' Borge replied, 'but with Hitler out of the way, the best guarantee for the safety of prisoners will be with the German generals who would take control and sue for peace.'

Pressure was on Dr Kafka from the hospital administration to empty the prisoner barracks as soon as possible. Things had to move fast. Stefan was first to leave our barrack one night and head for the surgeon's house where a lamp shone from a window, a stone's throw away in Kirsche Alley. He walked slowly back to rejoin us next morning. Jerzy was next and returned languidly and stooped. Then I went to the small stone house. The kitchen was the surgery with sterilization cabinet and instruments, and the kitchen table was the operating table. I was nervous as a cat and determined that whatever was put inside me I'd have removed as soon as ever possible, if I didn't finish up a quixotic corpse. I have indelible memory of stripping to my pants before a woman whom I took to be the surgeon's housekeeper; she wore a white coat. Later I learned she was a Polish nurse. And I have never forgotten climbing on to the table, and awaking there. Some hours later, walking like something mechanical, I painfully and slowly made my way back to my barrack to rejoin a grinning Stefan and Jerzy. 'Bugger this,' I growled irritably, 'I'm giving up being patriotic.' When the stitches were taken out, we compared incisions, short, neat and clean, and we seemed to be far less strangers to one another; it was almost like a blood oath. A steady and frank attachment which exists among men in wartime had grown stronger among bogus identities about to operate as a team with a special project in hand; and like myself, they told me, their capsules identified them as English.

Dr Kafka was right about the capsule; for years it remained embedded, probably within muscle tissue, causing me no discomfort whatsoever. I never discovered its composition, whether of a metal such as aluminium, or possibly perspex as it eluded detection on radiography. When I got back to Britain in September 1944 I told British and Polish Intelligence authorities about it but received such un-interested reaction that I gave up. The end of the war in Europe was only eight months away; the Allies were going forward hell for leather and, understandably, what I had been up to in Poland and Germany a year before had become irrelevant. In my own interests, however, when I came into the surgical orbit of Sir Archibald McIndoe in 1945 before the end of the war in Europe, I asked him whether the capsule should be taken out.

'Is it hurting?' he asked.

'No.'

'Dick, I've a couple of hundred airmen to fix up, without going on a treasure hunt. You'll be in again for your nose. We can have a look then.'

So the capsule remained in abeyance. It caused one alarm

after a few years but quickly subsided again until 1958, when in New Zealand I suddenly experienced severe pains and was operated on by surgeon specialist Richard Orgias, at Calvary Hospital in Wellington. I warned him what he might find, and related its fifteen-year history. His strong interest in the matter stemmed largely, no doubt, from his having served during the last war with the Army Medical Corps in Italy and Japan; this former lieutenant-colonel probably knew far more than I imagined about capsules, Intelligence patterns and the extremes men face in the dangerous business of war. I was in hospital about three weeks and afterwards had a long talk with Orgias. He had left me with a ten-inch scar after removing a length of intestine on which, in a foreign body reaction, there had formed a benign, large, fatty tumour. Naturally I asked the fundamental questions. Had he found the capsule? Had he thrown it out with the tumour, or where had it gone? I considered myself entitled to know what it contained.

I still visualize him as he thought for a moment, then said, 'Please don't expect me to answer. I can't, much as I would like to.' He told me that as far as possible he had respected my confidences but, reasonably enough, he had had to make a report on his findings. His firm advice was to forget the entire incident and consider myself free of a long and burdensome worry which had obviously caused me considerable nervous strain, much as I had aimed at forgetfulness, maintaining secrecy about my past activities. After all, my activities were by no means exclusive in the Second World War. So I did not press the issue; indeed, if curiosity did linger, I had no difficulty in accepting his advice; I was only too glad to be rid of the pain. Also at that time I had not the vaguest intention of ever writing about this incident in my life, and as Orgias was aware I was intently preoccupied with plans for a new adventure which, in fact, began two months later in January 1959 when I sailed from Lyttelton, New

Zealand, on the USS *Arneb*, flagship for the US Navy on the American Operation Deepfreeze IV expedition to Antarctica (the follow-up operation to the International Geophysical Year of 1957).

Before leaving Breslau, I saw Feodor and asked for return of the silver hunter. He regretted this was not possible, but pressed into my hand a cheap, battered pocket watch which he said was unique; he had improvised a hairspring from a sliver of bamboo, and amazingly I found it a good timekeeper. Borge appeared in the early dawn of the day of our departure; along with the others, I swore an oath never to divulge the vaguest detail of the conspiracy, and each was given three potassium cyanide capsules to ensure that in direst necessity, none would lapse from his pledge.

The journey from Breslau was uneventful; our tracks had been successfully covered and three of us were 'readmitted' to the Slavonic area of Stalag VIIIB. I had not been in this section before; it had come into existence abutting the Russian compound, itself vastly enlarged since the winter of 1941–2 when I had so unwillingly worked at burying Soviet dead during the typhus epidemic. Now, more than two summers later, the number of Soviet prisoners of war and civilian slave-labourers based on this parent stalag had risen from fewer than 5,000 to over 69,000; now too there were about 2,000 Yugoslavs, of whom I was one, Josif Matos; and some 100 Poles including Jerzy and Stefan. Conditions were a change with a vengeance from the relatively civilized British section; I certainly missed the friendly sound of my English-speaking kind, not to mention blessed Red Cross parcels. It was a testing time, mastering acute hunger and harsh conditions and coping with my foreign identity which was far more hazardous than pretending to be a New Zealander at Partschendorf. From Jerzy and Stefan I learned basic terms in Serbo-Croat, and I had to act vigilantly, conforming to the taciturn mask I adopted and which my friends explained away as resulting from my head injuries and recent operation. I wondered how the fair-haired Pole was getting on as 'Winston Yeatman' in the camp hospital; he would be in good hands with Doctors Müller, Spencer and McLeod safeguarding my absence. As instructed I compiled, in my handwriting, a series of letters for him to send off at intervals, and in those to my cipher handlers in Britain I urged they risk no more coded communication until they heard from me again.

A week elapsed, then Borge – as the uniformed supervisor of a visiting fumigation team – miraculously reappeared, as he had promised, to take charge of our movements. Getting us into the heart of the enemy's country was a tall order but he had hooks into the German labour front in the stalag and, obviously, large sums of various currencies and gold came into his hands via the Polish resistance, doubtless from British air-drop sources. Within three days of his arrival Jerzy, Stefan and I were given jobs in the labour service office located in a large square hut within the Soviet area. The German in charge, the Arbeitsdienstführer, assisted by seven NCOs, was responsible for the mobilization of labour from among the massive component of prisoners under his control. All were weeded out for contributive value to Germany's urgent needs in its war productive drive. A chaotic state of affairs prevailed with hordes of ragged, starving new arrivals pouring into a stalag already bursting at the seams, with inadequate accommodation, food supplies and hygiene. Orders came from top authorities in Berlin that it was a waste of time, paper and effort attempting to record such debased, indifferent masses, particularly those too debilitated to work a twelve-hour day. With the steeply rising curve in enemy prisoners from the Eastern areas, it became policy to brand large numbers as 'unreliable elements', 'communists' and 'Jews'. Classified as superfluous and never registered, they were taken to the nearest concentration camps to be liquidated, and those responsible had no conscience or regrets about this quick method of disposal.

While we diligently worked in the labour office, filing documents, stamping papers and washing floors, there were opportunities for stealing maps and obtaining information wanted by Polish Intelligence. With the NCOs securely under blackmail, Borge arranged that we be placed on the next draft of skilled prisoners for the Obersalzberg region. He also procured accreditation documents for us as screened, safe prisoners with qualifications, certainly exaggerated in my case; my friends professed undergraduate status, Jerzy in civil engineering, Stefan in electrical engineering. I was a stonemason with specialized knowledge as a cutter and polisher of marble. According to Borge, who had an amazing ring of contacts, our qualifications would place us in a select labour group and afford considerable opportunity for observation and penetration of the target area and associated technical installations. It was heartening to know that reliable contacts were 'in place' on the Obersalzberg and that information was exchanged by secret radio transmission between them and resistance groups on the outside. It was also enormously reassuring to be told that if any critical issue occurred, necessitating my quick departure from that exclusively dangerous Hitler zone and a return to Stalag VIIIB, everything would be taken care of by dedicated helpers on the spot.

Anxious weeks of waiting passed before the Arbeitsdienst-führer was instructed from Berlin to organize the transportation of 100 craftsmen and 200 labourers to Stalag 317(C) located at Markt Pongau, a huge base camp just south of Berchtesgaden. Our way ahead had opened. At a final briefing, Borge issued us with flannel body belts; mine had flat layers of notes to the value of 1,500 Reichmarks. He bade us farewell and good luck, kissing Jerzy and Stefan on the cheeks, but firmly gripping my hand.

A special unit of SS guards had arrived to escort the contingent; a tough hard-core of Germans specially trained to handle large movements of slave-labourers or Jews to concentration camps. Borge warned that they were the worst kind of criminal bastards; we should act dumb and not glue together in the cattle trucks where almost certainly stooges would be planted. 'They're usually multilingual,' he said, 'and don't be deceived by their rags and unshaven faces; pick them out by their nourished looks and intentionally unhygienic practices.'

Six abreast, in squads separated by steel-helmeted SS with sub-machine-guns, we trod the five miles of dirt road to the railway. It was October, cold weather was approaching and a low mist enveloped the landscape. The brutal guards screamed, '*Schnell, schnell!*' Their tactics were to single out elderly individuals, jabbing them with the barrels of their guns, or making examples of some by lashing them across the face with the back of a hand. One had to harden one's heart to such treatment of half-starved, tottering prisoners whose faces reflected the torpor of their souls and weariness of life.

At Annaberg a steam engine snorted impatiently at the head of a long line of cattle trucks, many at the tail end already sealed and holding, so Stefan learned, about 500 Russians entrained from elsewhere. They were bound, as we were, first for Salzburg; but there our group would continue south while they were to head northwards to a large camp at Pupping, north-west of Linz. Jerzy, Stefan and I found ourselves locked in a truck with some seventy prisoners, deplorably uncomfortable, if considerably less overcrowded than others. The first stint of 900 kilometres lasted three deadly days, with endless stops, starts and shuntings for interminable hours of waiting on sidings. Just south of

Vienna we were released from the stinking, stifling trucks and, carrying overflowing latrine buckets, marched to a hutted compound for a wait of ten hours. It was sheer joy to exercise one's legs again. The compound also served as a transit camp for the large stalag at Kaisersteinbruch. Our stopping here was not so much for our respite, but to enable another contingent of about 500 Soviets from Kaisersteinbruch to join the train; they also were destined for Pupping.

The journey on to Salzburg, normally of three hours, took twenty-four hours before the train braked to a halt just short of a platform. I have no difficulty, all these years later, in recalling details associated with this train ride which made my other cattle-truck journeys seem like pleasure trips. This one nearly became a journey of no return. It was only by the strangest of flukes that I was not shunted off to a Russian death camp.

The VIIIB contingent scheduled for Markt Pongau was first to be released and marched across the tracks to be formed up and held as a waiting detachment. Then, in controlled releases, the Soviets emerged and as each group came from its truck it was held as a block. Rumour had spread that their destination at Pupping was a death camp, whether by starvation or quick extermination I'll never know. As the 1,000 Soviets in a column of blocks of men began to be moved towards the ramp leading to the platform, they started chanting, a low, slow swing of bass unison; it was ominous, spine-chilling. Jerzy, who knew the language, gripped my arm. 'Whatever happens,' he hissed, 'stand fast!' He must have got the whisper of what was about to take place.

'What the hell's happening?' I said. But before I finished the question, the answer came like a thunderbolt. The whole of one block of men at the tail end cut loose and flew apart in every direction; other groups burst, and others, all along the column. Soviet prisoners were running everywhere, gesticulating, screaming, ignoring weapon fire and men falling shot. It was vivid pandemonium, a suicidal mass escape attempt. Some surged across the tracks, hurling themselves into our detachment, seriously dislocating it and throwing us all over the place. Too weak to run, they may have thought to go along with us, clutching at a last desperate straw. Amidst the crackling of sub-machine-gun fire, furious guards acted with quick efficiency and ruthlessness as they stormed before and beyond us to bring order to the immediate surroundings; pursuit of those who had disappeared was impossible.

Separated from my Polish companions, I found myself carried outwards from my contingent and some distance across the tracks. I was in the grip of dread and overwhelming panic when, in the rounding-up process, I was forced by a frenzied guard with a threatening sub-machine-gun to the opposite side. Prisoners were being brought back, bleeding and smashed, to add to the ragged, emaciated horde to which I now belonged. A squad of railway police with rifles had raced to reinforce the scattered SS force and already groups which had been brought under control again were being marched towards the platform. Mute and terrified, escapees returned to join my waiting rabble, and any minute we would be ordered to move. I realized that within moments my fate would be sealed; marched away as a Soviet for Pupping camp, I would be lost for ever!

When moments counted between life or disaster, a steam engine pulling goods trucks and carriages groaned along the track and halted between my Soviet party on one side and the VIIIB contingent on the other. Whether the railway authorities had moved this barrier into position on purpose I shall never know, but suddenly fortified with immense resolve I charged the guard immediately in front of me and dived for it. It was a touch and go crisis. Ducking and weaving beneath stationary trucks, with bullets making resounding smacks and thuds on metal, I emerged and charged into my own mob on the other side. I ploughed into their midst, unrecognized by guards who were racing about like enraged animals. Jerzy had seen me, and as I welcomed his grip on my arm, I was still trembling; his white face creased into a grin which spoke volumes; together we found Stefan. Our contingent stood fast and order was restored. At least fifty Russian interlopers were dragged clear of our ranks and beaten back across the tracks; even then, some tried to run to us again, and were shot.

That episode at some substation approaching Salzburg remains among the most memorable, fortuitous and hard to grasp of my life. It was the most frightening experience I have ever had of massed humanity exploding, with opposing wills. There had been a curious, secret unison among the Russians, foreign even to German comprehension. Jerzy told me that similar flashpoints had been reached at stations in Poland, when men and women knew they were almost at 'the end of the line' and about to face an unknown world of uncertainty and death. Fervently, I thanked the high gods for the intervention of that train, a miraculous gift. Without it, I would have had to go along with no alternative except to try to escape, and I knew that I had never escaped without immense underground assistance; without it, the chances of success for individual escapers were pretty damned remote.

From start to finish of that sordid, protracted journey from Upper Silesia to Bavaria in crowded cattle trucks, I spent as much time as possible at the barred ventilation openings in the sides, avoiding the stench and watching silent telegraph posts slip by, and at night, glimmering lights like earth-bound stars. When we stepped out on to the platform at Berchtesgaden, the air was like champagne. Covered trucks, with two armed guards perched on the tail boards of each, took us by road to Markt Pongau.

# CHAPTER 17
## Obersalzberg – Berchtesgaden

Stalag 317(C) at Markt Pongau was the parent stalag for some 18,000 prisoners of whom, at the time, 16,000 were out on working parties; essentially, too, it was involved in providing quotas of workers for the Hitler Territory of Obersalzberg. The contingent from VIIIB was now split, with the 200 labourers being dispatched to I know not where. Our group of 100 with technical skills was confined in a hutted compound along with about 150 others of mixed nationalities. Three days later, officials and master workmen from the big civilian construction companies engaged on projects within the Hitler Territory, together with interpreters, entered the compound to check that we measured up as the skilled workers we purported to be. If the civilian interviewers were somewhat friendly, in a placid way, there was nothing agreeable about the uniformed SS scrutineers; it was their business to ensure that labour for the sensitive Hitler area was politically 'safe', free of assassination ideas, and not likely to put anything over. Jerzy, Stefan and I were cleared without complications; not so some of the others, mostly French and Italian whose claims to skills misfired, and they were marched away to become hewers of rock. The rest of us were to leave for the Obersalzberg in two days time.

Jammed in the back of an open industrial truck with Frenchmen and my two Polish friends, we drove past the town of Berchtesgaden and took the road to the Obersalzberg above. I gazed at the magnificent backdrop of Alps with a mulling hostility. The scene was not new to me; I could even name the high peaks thereabouts. Surging gusts of ironical memory drew my mind back to my newspaper office. In 1938, the German National Tourist Office had insistently invited Lilian Rowe (internationally known from her *Leeds Mercury* tours) to visit Upper Bavaria to carry out a feasibility study for *The Yorkshire Post* newspaper group to organize a conducted tour for 400 people in 1939. While remaining secretly opposed, Lilian, accompanied by my former travelling companions, Chapman and Cadwallader, was royally fêted as a special guest of the Tourist Office. She returned with maps, brilliant photographs and descriptive material. I recall her sitting opposite me at my desk, and with a humorous grimness requesting me to acquaint myself with the material and prepare a mock-up brochure that would please the German tourist authorities. With a twinkle in her eyes, she told me they had offered to pay all expenses for her publicity co-ordinator to visit Upper Bavaria. 'How would you like that, Richard?'

'Not damned likely,' I replied. I had recently returned from the bizarre experience of Koblenz, working out a bombing run on the exclusive SS nest at the Reisenfürstenhof Hotel. Although appeasement was at full tide, we knew war was coming. I was keeping clear of Germany. (So was Lilian; instead, she took 300 Yorkshire folk to the USA in 1939 and they reached home by the skin of their teeth before war was declared.) I almost laughed out loud in that truck with my French and Polish companions. Here I was, five years later with a gun pointed at me, in no Mercedes limousine and accorded none of the great courtesy and finesse the Germans could play up. 'Jerry is either at your feet or at your throat', the boys would say in prison camp.

The Obersalzberg descends in rolling upland meadows and forest formations from the base of the mountains Hohe Goll (8,323 feet) and Kelstein (5,674 feet); the picturesque town of Berchtesgaden lies 1,800 feet below and about four miles distant. Hitler's connection with the Obersalzberg

began when he sought refuge after his unsuccessful attempt
to seize power in 1923; there, in an alpine hut, he wrote part
of *Mein Kampf* and from its royalties he purchased in 1927 a
house, 'Wachenfeld'; the Obersalzberg, a peaceful farming
and alpine resort, became his new homeland. With his rise to
power in 1933, transformation of the Obersalzberg really
began. In the early years of his success, thousands of
supporters and visitors flocked daily to glimpse him or his
house which, considerably reconstructed, became known as
the 'Berghof'. Initially, he commissioned Rudolf Hess and,
succeeding him, Martin Bormann, to bring a new order to
the Obersalzberg.

Negotiations led to farmers selling their meadows and
others their properties, while those who were reluctant to
do so soon changed their minds under Nazi threats. In a
short time, ten square kilometres had been 'purchased' and
became known as the 'Führer Area'. It was surrounded by a
seven-foot-high fence, nine miles long, guarded by a State
Security Service (RSD); passes had to be shown by
everyone, of whatever rank or standing, seeking entry to the
Führer Area. Within the Area was an even more tightly
guarded small circle, the 'Hoheitsgebeit' (sovereign
territory) which contained the Berghof and Martin
Bormann's house. This inner sanctum, with a fence two
miles long, was guarded by SS men from stone sentry
buildings at the entrances.

The main Führer Area was generally referred to as the
Platterhof, deriving its name from a luxurious, modern,
150-room hotel where previously there had been a fairly
large guest house which Bormann had ordered to be torn
down; the new structure provided for top Nazis. Also in this
close-knit colony were the SS barracks, administrative
offices, housing accommodation for officials and men and
women civilian employees, a theatre hall, Bormann's
greenhouses, large garages, and the Führer's lavishly

appointed Bechstein Haus (Guest House), exclusively for prominent people such as Nazi propagandist Joseph Goebbels, foreign celebrities such as Mussolini and foreign diplomats. Importantly, here too were Goering's house, and the headquarters for the RSD with lodgings for the guards immediately behind.

Our destination was the largest labour camp, Antenberg, near the theatre hall, barely a mile on the Berchtesgaden side from the Berghof. The civilian construction companies were almost completely responsible for handling the labourers, ensuring their barracks were clean and lice-free, controlling their food rationing, canteen facilities, providing working clothes and equipment. Jerzy, Stefan and I were allocated to the firm of Polensky and Zoellner; our miserable-looking barrack was wooden, long and low in the vast hutted compound, Antenberg, which was enclosed by a two-metre-high wire fence. Each man had a single bed, pillow and blankets and every two shared a bedside locker.

Within an hour of drawing work clothes and boots, we were taken to the inner area, Hoheitsgebeit, as members of a gang loading rock being blasted out to form the Berghof tunnel. Only two months previously, Bormann had started construction on a bunker-tunnel system beneath the Obersalzberg, it finally having been realized that the war might come to the Berchtesgaden country after all. Our arrivals had coincided with a tremendous urgency of construction. I now saw the timing of Borge's initial approaches to me in Stalag VIIIB as no coincidence and I better appreciated the concern of Polish Intelligence to investigate through every possible probe what was obviously a vast new undertaking at the heart of the Hitler Territory; here were the beginnings of what could become a major control centre for conduct of the war, or even the final stronghold of Nazidom.

The first underground complex, upon which we were

working, was for Hitler, Eva Braun, his adjutants and staff. Cynically known as 'God of the Obersalzberg', Bormann as Hitler's deputy and director of the chancery of the Nazi Party had unchallenged power and command of unlimited funds. Some 6,000 men, of whom seventy per cent were foreigners, were engaged upon constructional projects on the Obersalzberg; the remaining thirty per cent were Germans, occupying key positions as architects, engineers and other specialists in building construction. With his power to terrorize and command, Bormann's overriding fanatical obsession was to have 400 feet of Berghof tunnel with adjacent rooms, luxuriously appointed, completed to present as a Christmas gift to his beloved leader and, with little more than eight weeks left, work was progressing at breakneck speed.

We worked the skin off our hands. Loading rock into trucks, we accompanied them up an ingeniously engineered road on the steep Kelstein Mountain which rose behind the Berghof. At various points we dumped the load over the side, into deep ravines. It seemed unreal being on Kelstein, although in a sense it was no stranger to me. Perched on its summit was Hitler's Tea House, or 'the Eagles' Nest' as it became known. Completed in the spring of 1939, it had been exploited by Goebbels, a mass of stories and photographs being printed worldwide about its engineering feat, symbolic of Germany's technological advances under National Socialism, and the eternal union of Germany and Austria. It was a show piece to impress foreign dignitaries and diplomats. Reading of it at my newspaper desk, curiosity and suspicion had gone hand in hand, if my imagination had been stirred: a 400-foot-long tunnel, reaching at the core of the mountain an elevator which rose 413 feet to arrive inside the Tea House at 6,020 feet. Viewing it now, I secretly enjoyed envisioning RAF heavies dropping stick after stick of 1,000-pounders, and the exhilarating thought of a time-delayed 'cookie' crashing through the building into the elevator shaft and blowing the Eagles' Nest clean off its mountain perch. Inevitably my navigator bomb-aimer's mind was stirred, as indeed was the intention. I told Jerzy a bombing attack should approach from the south, over Mount Hohe Goll which at 8,323 feet, immediately south of Kelstein, was a magnificent pin-point; ahead would lie the easily identifiable Eagles' Nest and the Obersalzberg below; the town of Berchtesgaden, to the left, would remain untouched and the attackers should swing around for home before Salzburg. I do not know if Jerzy passed on my assessment to Polish Intelligence, or if it was sent to Britain, but that was the approach made by RAF Lancaster bombers of 617 Squadron, the famous Dam Busters squadron, a year and a half later. On 25 April 1945 they saturated the Obersalzberg with 'tallboy' bombs but left Berchtesgaden and, indeed, the Eagles' Nest untouched.

After several days of rock removing, my two friends and I were unexpectedly taken to the central administration offices for the various construction firms. It was no chance attendance; Jerzy and Stefan had not gone to the Obersalzberg without contacts, if their identities were not confided to me. Two elderly German civilians examined our work credentials; one I recall seemed to regard Jerzy with a shade of personal interest. He expressed regret we had not been sent for earlier, but there were so many new arrivals; besides, it was routine for newcomers to be given gruelling labour for long enough to show up physical defects, or any oppositional tendencies. Jerzy was assigned to another firm, to join a team of quantity surveyors, visiting gravel pits, quarries and cement works and assessing requirements from stock-piles of building materials. Stefan was also transferred, to a concern specializing in electrical and diesel plant. I was to remain where I was except that I now became a stonemason, preparing granite blocks for foundations in the Berghof tunnel.

For the best part of a week, I laboured in an open workshop near the headquarters of the RSD which occupied the former Hotel Turken* close by the Berghof. Along with Italian and Czech stonemasons, wearing leather gauntlets I plied hammer and chisel shaping granite blocks to support steel arches for the Hitler tunnel; some blocks we drilled for interlocking steel ribs. As each of my blocks was chalked off as satisfactory, it took another slave artisan and myself all our strength to manhandle it in a canvas sling, down the long flight of steps to the first section of the tunnel, and to wherever it was required. On average, the tunnel was to go 100 feet below the surface. An incredible state of turmoil and confusion existed below ground with labourers and technicians falling over each other, pneumatic drills creating a fearsome din, walls dripping water, and continuous reverberations and waves of chill, tremulous air from the forward blasting teams. It took me back to my coal-mining days in the bowels of the earth in Poland. I experienced the same thrill of relief whenever I re-emerged to a world resplendent with sunlight and colour, vegetation, fresh air from heaven and not hellish underground stenches.

A high point of my stonemasonry expertise was on base blocks (each edge about eighteen inches long) for an armoured machine-gun post 'covering' the long, steep entry steps to the beginning of the tunnel. In 1973, I again descended those steps which I had known so well in 1943. My wife, Helen, was with me. I wanted to show her a granite block supporting armour-plated doors with their apertures for protruding gun nozzles. A base block, when last I had

---

* Damaged in the raid of 25 April 1945, it was repurchased from the Bavarian government by its pre-war family owners and reconstructed as the present Hotel-Gasthof Zum Turken.

seen it, had had deep, clean-cut carving at the left top: the letters 'P. E.' for 'Pape England'. I had carved the letters with some sense of patriotism, and perhaps for later identifying my presence thereabouts in the dusts of time. I had had it at the tip of my tongue, if I had been asked by any German overseer, that the letters stood for 'Persönlich Erfolg', the 'Personal Success' of Hitler. It was a foolish act no doubt, when I had had no wish whatsoever to be singled out for any attention. Thirty years later, I was disconcerted to find that since I had left my handiwork the foundation blocks had been covered with a veneer of cement. 'P. E.' should still be there, for anyone who cares to seek.

In the workshop, carpenters and masons were labouring feverishly when along with others I was put to inter-grooving sheets of the most beautiful, milky, off-white, carraric marble which, I seem to recollect, was for Eva Braun's bathroom. We carried the finished sheets in crates into the tunnel and left them; it was someone else's job attaching them to walls. I knew marble, but this was a quality I had never seen at Uncle Albert's;* its veining was created in heaven. Our rigid instructions were that nothing must be wasted and all unused sheets had to be returned for storage below the Berghof.

I sighted Bormann many times and twice while I was there he visited the workshop, and almost touched my elbow. Had I been armed, I would have had no trouble in dispatching him while his SS protectors stood well to the rear. He was a shouting, coarse, brutal man, broad and squat with a bull-neck. What particularly caught my eye were his hands – fatty with podgy fingers, bluish. He paused a yard from me to contemplate masons hammering away like speeded-up automatons, activated by a spitting, swearing

* My mother's brother. Engaged in the marble trade and skilled at hand-carved lettering in fine marbles, he had taught me as a young man the art at which I had become proficient.

German foreman obviously scared as hell of the arrogant Bormann. When he disappeared with his entourage of senior constructional officials to descend the steps to the tunnel, I hoped he'd slip and break his bloody neck. After every visit he left a wake of anger and hate as he pushed in ever greater haste men already driven to the limit. He was loathed by Germans and slave-labourers alike. The major constructional firms controlled by him were for the most part anti-Party and secretly opposed to the lavish embellishments transforming what had begun as simple air-raid shelters. In October 1943, German soldiers were starving and bleeding to death in their hundreds of thousands on the Eastern Front; millions of German citizens were destitute, bombed out of homes and cities. It made no difference to Bormann, or Hitler. Here was no austere necessity, no anxiety about the sufferings of the ordinary German masses, and it went on until the RAF put an end to it in April 1945; by then seventy-nine rooms and almost two miles of interconnecting tunnels had been constructed beneath the buildings of the Obersalzberg. On the day of the air-raid, 3,500 labourers were still on the site, but taking shelter in the bunkers, only six died and several were injured. With the tunnel entrances and buildings unguarded, the looting began; unbelieving eyes saw huge amounts of food, linen, clothes, china and soap and in Bormann's supply-tunnel people stood knee-deep in butter, sugar, flour and luxuries they had not sighted for years.

It was all at an acute, preliminary stage when I was there as a stonemason, involved in a feasibility study for exterminating Hitler on his home ground. The Poles were anxious to bomb him out of house and home, but it had to be precision, low level; *he* was the target, not the thousands of slave-labourers. Jerzy wanted information on anything technical about the tunnel: depth, thickness, gun positions, ventilation, electrical systems, canalization below floor level. Where for instance might plastic bombs be installed? Where were the labourers quartered? How long would it take to build them air-raid shelters? Some years after the war, in South Africa, I met Sir Arthur 'Bomber' Harris, former chief of Bomber Command, and I asked him why he had not bombed the Obersalzberg much earlier. He replied that he had wanted to, and I took it that he had been politically overruled.

My vision was fairly restricted to where I laboured in the workshop and where I lugged my finished work. But I did obtain a deal of constructional information, particularly from Czechs, chiselling stones with me. From them I learned also about prison quarters at the SS barracks. There were many defectors among the foreign workers; any misdemeanour, any murmur of disenchantment about food or work conditions brought the SS moving in quickly to arrest. The 'offender' was taken away to overcrowded prisons, never to reappear. Below the extensive SS barracks were rifle and revolver ranges and many workers met their deaths in the muffled target practice chambers. Corpses, it was rumoured, were disposed of in mountain caverns; when ready to be sealed, hundreds of tons of rock were detonated to block these burial places, their entrances hidden, to be forgotten for ever.

While I had acquired an interest in talking 'shop' among mixed foreigners, I had remained cautiously on guard, and had plunged without complaint into a dozen new kinds of work, dealing with hammer and chisel on granite, marble and concrete castings. My work had apparently proved satisfactory. Jerzy and Stefan, while moving about the Hitler colony and beyond, picked up information from their top civilian contacts. It seemed that the secret communications and Intelligence web had threads running in all directions. I was therefore not unduly surprised when, after about three weeks in the workshop, the German foreman

selected me as one of a party of six for certain tasks at
Hermann Goering's residence, 'Landhaus Goering'. My
work colleagues were two Italians, highly skilled with
marble and fine mosaic composition, and three Frenchmen.
As in POW camps, here on the Obersalzberg were to be
found German overseers and civilian advisers with an
appetite for money bribes, and men who so despised the
Nazi breed as to be amenable to risking involvement in
clandestine activities. Jerzy told me to glean as much
information as possible; surveyors and engineers were
already working above ground around Landhaus Goering,
planting markers, and he had learned that tunnels for
Goering and Bormann were next for construction. Also, I
was to keep my eyes open for passing military trucks, to a
site some distance away where anti-aircraft batteries were to
be established, and possibly a 'smoke unit' to produce
smoke clouds to cover the Obersalzberg with what would
seem like mountain mist.

Accompanied by three guards and two civilians from the
construction firm, our work party made for Landhaus
Goering sited on elevated ground, a short distance from the
Hitler–Bormann inner circle. Goering made regular visits
here, between official duties, while his wife Emma and
daughter Ebba stayed for months on end. It was a handsome
alpine villa in Bavarian-style architecture, standing freely,
not encompassed by wire fencing. Each of our work party
carried a coloured pass stamped valid for two hours; new
passes of differing colours were subsequently issued from
start to finish of the working day.

It seemed that Goering too was growing more nervous
about the war coming to the Obersalzberg. The three
Frenchmen and I were set to work building a short, bomb-
blast wall at the entrance to the small, private air-raid shelter
which Goering had had erected in 1941 adjacent to the
house. This shelter was to become the beginning of what

ended up as an underground complex, 150 feet deep, extending for 265 yards and with ten superbly equipped adjoining rooms. The two Italian craftsmen, under guard, were working inside the house on mosaics which featured flowers, leaves, butterflies and birds; ironic, for a man who commanded winged monsters raining down death and destruction.

The blast-wall completed, the Frenchmen and I began about four days' work on the large, outdoor swimming pool, at the front of the house. It had been drained for winter and our tasks were to clean, repoint and re-enamel its fine clinker base, and install a set of new steps. It was early afternoon when Goering, his wife and daughter suddenly arrived. Apart from two elderly civilians and a chauffeur in uniform, he had no protective escort. The two Italians, their guard and the two employees of the construction firm emerged from the house. All our passes were checked and new ones substituted.

I was working at the bottom of the swimming pool. It was almost finishing time for the day when a Frenchman gave me a quick nudge and, looking up, I saw a bulky Goering in a light suit approaching with the two elderly civilians. He was certainly a big man, but not huge as I had imagined from photographs. They stood on the outer rim of the pool, examining the metal ladder still to be fitted. From a few feet away, I stared at my most avowed, inveterate Nazi enemy, next to Hitler himself . . . or even ahead of Hitler, considering my personal losses, Blondie, Harry and his family in the East End . . . yet, looking at him, he stirred no hatred, unlike the very sight of Bormann. Goering seemed likeable, high-spirited, friendly. Again, had I been armed, it would have been all too damned easy. It would have meant the end of me, of course, with cyanide. The trio walked around the edge and Goering exclaimed in a voice quite clear as he pointed at some chipped surfacing, 'I think it needs a complete new outer strip.' I wondered what the devil he would be saying and thinking if he knew that the English RAF navigator bomb-aimer who had successfully attacked his headquarters north of Berlin, near his house 'Karinhall', was here at the bottom of his swimming pool masquerading as a Yugoslav slave-labourer.

I recounted the incident to Jerzy and Stefan that evening. 'If only I'd had a gun!' I said, only to be reminded that there must be no risk of tragedy and error, of attempts on the lives of top Nazis which could lead to disaster and unimaginable reprisals. I had to bear in mind also the back-tracking which *would* be done to discover how I had got here; it could threaten the survival of the entire resistance groups and bring all their plotting to nothing. The death of Hitler was not an end in itself but involved the total overthrow of the Nazi regime. Everything must be properly timed, and endless planning had been and was taking place, and involving top men of the German High Command. Since I had been manipulated and coerced into assuming my Yugoslav identity, I now learned that the resistance movements had changed their methods. Having met refusal from the Western Allies to negotiate a peace if Hitler were assassinated, the conspirators were now attempting to effect a peace with Stalin.

I was told little more. I was a mere pawn, if I full well appreciated the lengths the Poles would go to, to keep the Russians off their soil. I asked point blank: if the opportunity arose, would Stefan or Jerzy attempt individual action to kill Hitler? They replied that that was the reason for being there, and for my assistance to them. I put the question: supposing Hitler pitched up at Landhaus Goering next day, what in the name of hell was I supposed to do without a gun? Just spit in his eye? I was told a gun would come into my possession if necessary, but never for precipitate madness or angry idealism.

I saw Goering once more, towards noon the day we completed work on the pool. We had assembled under the watchful eye of the guard when Goering appeared to inspect the work, cutting a strange figure in plus-fours and a heavy sweater. He expressed approval and hurried back to the house looking somewhat inebriated. At the door he called, 'Wait there, guard,' and some minutes later Emma Goering appeared with a maid carrying a tray of meat sandwiches and chunks of cake. Frau Goering was rather plump but had a kindly, attractive face. Briefly she spoke with the guard; the Reich Marshal wanted the workers to have a gift of food in appreciation for their excellent work. She did not appear a heartless person, but staring at her I was involuntarily gripped by a feeling of fear and trembling.

Chewing hefty sandwiches from Goering's kitchen, I sensed a peculiar warning that if I did not get clear of Berchtesgaden neatly and quickly, I would slip into some kind of pit from which I would never emerge. I had been here nearly a month and while it may have represented an espionage triumph I was now getting nervous and anxious. I had never felt comfortable living on such unpromising terrain. I was a non-talkative, industrious stonemason, an agreeable buffoon, and perpetually on guard. I was not allowed to know any of Jerzy or Stefan's helpers who were the key to my getting out of the place. While I respected my Polish friends and their preparedness to remain on the Obersalzberg, I was also aware, after two years of escaping and subterfuge, that anything could blow up, even by sheerest bad luck, at any time. If they came to grief or if anything separated us, I could be lost and disregarded for ever. If anything fatal happened to me here, my stand-in 'Yeatman' in VIIIB would simply vanish, accounted for no doubt as escaping again, and the real Yeatman, acting Richard Pape, would sort himself out back in England after the war.

With such fearful thoughts, I resolved to force an issue with Jerzy and Stefan to get me back to Upper Silesia and Stalag VIIIB without delay. I could see nothing more of any particular consequence that I could achieve here; winter was breathing down the mountains, my lungs were beginning to play up, and I was tired. I had broached the question of my departure several times, but now I faced Jerzy and Stefan determinedly, saying I had done what was expected of me, for whatever purpose, and I now asked them to honour the promise to get me out.

While they replied that the Polish resistance did not forsake anyone whom it had accepted, I was nevertheless astonished when they could give me no tangible assurances as to when or how, and I detected something stilted, odd, in their demeanour. I was handed limp excuses about difficulties, delays and 'our employers' as they termed their contacts, doing everything possible. Disillusioned and probably bitter, I said I wished I could meet one of the 'employers' and find out what we were waiting for. Jerzy soft-pedalled again, advising patience.

A few days later, all was thrown into confusion and alarm as a contingent of SS and RSD swept through Antenberg camp. Purges and searches were routine enough but this had a distinguishable viciousness and vigour. Large groups of Russians and some Czechs, French and Italians were ruthlessly herded together with their paltry possessions and marched off to a second foreigner labour camp, Riemerfeld, and men from there brought back as replacements. This sudden reshuffling of manpower, breaking it up as it were, was rumoured to be a prelude to Hitler's return to the Berghof within a week or so; the SS was tightening security. What it did to me was bring home with fearful impact what I dreaded most, possible separation from my Polish friends; it really struck home to them too. But the SS was taking no chances with Hitler's life; it had had ample proof of the dangers. During 1942–3 Himmler's Gestapo had ferreted out and brought to ruthless account one German resistance group after another: the Rote Kapelle (Red Band) communist organization; the White Rose with members drawn from university and intellectual circles; the Solf group of intellectual and diplomatic dissidents. Currently it was penetrating what came to be known as the Canaris Conspiracy, rooted in the Abwehr under the leadership of Admiral Wilhelm Canaris. What Himmler as yet did not know was that an important newcomer to the German resistance, Colonel Count Claus von Stauffenberg, had just recently, in October 1943, joined its inner core, he who was to place the bomb under Hitler's conference table on 24 July 1944.

No doubt SS thinking was that on the Obersalzberg it was not inconceivable that among the thousands of Soviet and other prisoners were agents hoping for an opportunity to kill Hitler. When Jerzy told me that some of the prisoners taken from Antenberg had been interrogated and detained, my apprehensions were raised. I frankly spoke my mind, saying that if documents were not produced to assist me to get out, then I was going over the wire; I had plenty of Reichmarks, poison capsules to use if necessary, but I would make for Salzburg and hopefully 'ride the rods' eastwards.

Jerzy looked at me long and hard. He knew I meant it, and I knew his great fear was that I might be captured without being able to take a capsule; he believed that every man would crack eventually under full Gestapo treatment. I was staggered then when he told me he had a confession to make; a mishap had occurred with my identity photographs, copies of the one taken by Feodor; they had been on matt paper whereas photographs used on the Obersalzberg for identity passes were highly glazed and specially coated to prevent retouching alterations. Attempts had been made to glaze and coat my prints but extraordinarily, my image had peeled, rendering the pictures useless. 'God knows what kind of fixative Feodor used,' Stefan commented, 'but don't worry, contact has been made with him and new prints for the three of us, with the right glazed surface, are on their way.'

The news both disturbed and delighted me. I admit I had flutterings about what previously had been unquestioning trust in Jerzy and Stefan. I knew I was now a very considerable encumbrance, but I had kept my part of the bargain and they promised to keep theirs. No longer beguiled, plans for decisive action were put into operation without delay. The two Poles and those supporting them in the complexities for getting me away smoothly with genuinely produced documents saw as a vital preliminary my removal to a more favourable place of work. When the time came for me to move off, with a stand-in concealing my absence, it should be from a place where SS and RSD were considerably less in evidence, where only a moderate number of low-grade guards operated indifferently among trusted prisoners, Italian and others. The ideal place was an extensive housing estate, 'Buchenhoehle', under construction on the Obersalzberg about two miles east of the outer fence of the Führer Area. Apparently a few select prisoners had been spirited away from here with Italian connivance. Buchenhoehle, like the already completed splendid housing estate, 'Klaushohe', about a mile nearer the Führer Area, had been planned in 1941 for colonizing the Obersalzberg with Nazi faithful. Justification for going ahead with the even more elaborate Buchenhoehle as a 'war important construction programme' was that it should be used for bombed-out refugees. (In fact, it became allocated to chosen SS families and constructional officials, friends of Bormann.)

The foreman who had 'selected' me for the Goering estate party, a move which I now discovered had been to make me into a 'trusted' worker, was again bribed. I left the workshop with its degradations and cold, malicious granite, to cut and lay slate at the vastly more congenial Buchenhoehle, where lax guards scarcely bothered with checks or head counts. Here the construction firms employed a large number of Italians among whom certain skilled ones, well screened and with lengthy records as dutiful workers for their German masters, held positions of 'capos', or work bosses. On the whole, the capos were intellectually superior to the German foremen or guards and if greatly depended upon for supervising other prisoners and allocating labour gangs, these boss captives were cunning and clever. They practised graft and corruption, were notorious for favouritism and racketeering, could allocate men to good or harsh jobs or have them removed for punishment of wrongs, real or invented.

The capo into whose charge I was entrusted was a small, slightly round-shouldered, middle-aged man; his face had a yellowish consumptive look. This boss, by name Domincuo Severino, affected coldness, even hostility, towards me, but a flicker of knowing flashed in his eyes when he directed me to work on a slate floor in a passageway connecting the latest, partially finished houses, one of which he used as a sort of office for directing work gangs and issuing orders. Here on the Obersalzberg, Red Cross supplies were not the tools of graft for enlisting subversion or aid; only gold, pure gold, was acceptable to Domincuo. Aware of the inexorable pressure of events, the inevitable downfall of the Third Reich, and wishing to set himself up in business when he returned to Italy, he spurned Reichmarks. He knew of the uselessness of German paper money after the First World War. Jerzy and the inner coterie of conspirators on the Obersalzberg had supplies of gold to manipulate men like Domincuo. This capo was accomplished and clever. He spoke reasonable English and fluent German and French. From the limited amount I was allowed to know, before the war he had been gaoled in Italy, suspected of being a conduit, conveying Intelligence to foreign interests. He had bitter memories of Mussolini and his Fascist regime, and an outlook opposed to totalitarian suppression, except, it seemed, as practised by himself on a small scale in wartime.

He contrived for us to have brief talks, either where I worked or in his 'office' room in the empty house when German foremen were not present; the foremen respected him for his effective control of the prisoners and his apparent impartiality even though prisoners loathed him for what they viewed as his scandalous partiality. I also met Domincuo's fully-fledged colleague in racketeering and hoodwinking the Germans for the reward of gold. Through shifting veils of memory I recall him as a capo, or under-capo, middle-aged, a Sicilian named Ignazio; what sticks in mind were his dank, dark hair and strangely contrasting white eyebrows. He was a shifty-eyed one with a habit of silently smirking. If Domincuo was a downright opportunist, Ignazio was innately crooked at heart; but his standing was good with the Germans. He was in control of trucks which made continuous trips to the gravel pits and he was to prove of immense practical importance to me.

Jerzy came frequently to Buchenhoehle, assessing building supplies, and late one Monday afternoon he arrived with a truck-load of pipes. Domincuo had me brought to his office to hear from Jerzy the staggering news that I would be departing early on the Wednesday morning. I listened with appreciative fervour to plans for getting me clear. My identity card and travel papers were complete; I already knew of the arrival of the vital photographs from Feodor. A German civilian employee about my age had been singled out for me to impersonate; a heart ailment had exempted him from military service. He was Helmuth Heusinger, a carpenter engaged on a construction about thirty miles from Berchtesgaden and quartered near his work site. He was absolutely in the dark about what was being enacted in his name and the use being made of his file in the labour control centre, including the fact that he was months overdue for his home-leave entitlement of fourteen days. He was to be my cover back to Breslau, to visit my widowed mother who was employed in a German canteen in the region; lending special appeal to my background data, my father, Ernst, had been killed in action at the Eastern Front in 1942. The details were authentic, the papers genuine productions. Adding to credibility, correctly postmarked letters from my not over-educated Mum would be in my battered wallet, along with a grubby snapshot of my poor, dead, infantryman Dad.

Every fortnight or so, a group of Germans, civilian and military, departed on leave and I was to go with the next group of about forty. A spasm of relief swept over me. The sudden urgency to get me away was explained: secret information from an underground contact in the railway administration at Berchtesgaden indicated Hitler's impending arrival; his private train, complete with flak wagon, was expected within a week and would be parked with Goering's splendidly appointed train already there in an exclusive shed. While knowing Hitler's erratic schedules and sudden changes of plans, deliberately making himself a difficult target to pin down, the information had to be acted upon as if true. From other sources had come advice that top Gestapo were also scheduled to arrive, and an impossible state of affairs for the prisoners, with swoops and purges, was surely imminent. My friends and I knew all too well that I would not last two minutes under questioning as a Yugoslav and, if I were exposed, attention would focus minutely on every one of the VIIIB contingent, including Jerzy and Stefan; it was of very real importance to them, as top agents, that I be out of the way, dead or alive!

Jerzy visited Buchenhoehle twice next day and Domincuo organized long delays in the unloading of his truck, providing time for Jerzy to pore over my false documents with me and concentrate upon what to do, where to go and what to expect on arrival at Breslau. I was enormously heartened to learn that radio contact had been made with the underground in Breslau, and a scheme devised to protect and pilot me through; as soon as I safely departed Berchtesgaden Station, further radio contact would alert my helpers ahead. In addition to my personal papers, I was given a street map, unmarked, of Breslau, a telephone number and two addresses. I was somewhat amused when my Polish friend passed over a packet of different coloured chalks, but I was deadly serious about their significance when he explained how I was to use them. Above all else, I was gravely instructed, my primary duty was to destroy my false papers immediately after reaching Breslau. I had to die out instantly as Helmuth Heusinger.

They were taking a big risk with me, but thank heaven I was deeply trusted. To my surprise, I was handed a small .22 Browning automatic with an underarm holster. Jerzy explained that I would have to use the sharpest practical and intuitive judgement, all my ingenuity and resolve on the long train journey, but if something went wrong and I knew arrest was inevitable, the gun might hold it off long enough for my papers to be torn to pieces and scattered to the winds or flushed down a toilet. While I was well aware that posing as a non-combatant and found carrying arms meant execution, I knew Jerzy was right and willingly accepted the gun. I was prepared to fight it out to the bitter end; as he said, cyanide was the *very* last resort, and I would carry it, not sewn in a button but loose in a matchbox, ready for immediate swallowing. In a few words, I was reminded of my oath.

Domincuo was in a better position to provide certain instructions, which he did with unqualified directness. He produced a medium-sized suitcase, new, with clothes purchased from the shop on the Platterhof which operated for German civilians and military. There were new socks, shirts, underwear, big green handkerchiefs and the usual toiletries. In a small box with an Obersalzberg inscription reposed a little bottle of perfume for my phoney mother, a bonus ration of cigarettes, confectionery and other special oddments available to workers on the Führer Territory who had earned leave; this was the one good thing about Bormann. Also, I had a new blanket, of a quality superior to POW issue and invariably bought by those going on leave, knowing the crippling shortage of this item on the home front. From a sack, Domincuo withdrew partially worn shoes and a suit which fitted well; neat, modest, working-man's clothing. In addition to looking the part, I would have to live it convincingly from beginning to end. My unknown handlers were certainly security conscious and privy to exact methods and points affecting leave-takers when passing through the SS movement control centre. Much thought had gone into preparations for my departure, even to an official receipt for the purchases in the suitcase and a list, issued by the civilian construction firms, of special items at reduced prices available to leave-takers. By what stratagems all this material had been acquired was a mystery, but I was deeply grateful and relieved for such indispensable guardianship. My stalwart Polish friends had stuck to me loyally and courageously. It was a memorable final briefing.

That evening, after finishing work, I did not return to Antenberg barracks but slipped into a half-completed house adjacent to the one where Domincuo had his office. A trap-door in the floor linked with wooden steps to an unusually deep, spacious cellar used for storing tools. Here I would pass the night. Heavily barred windows had been covered with cloth, bearing in mind that a lone guard or so did patrol during the night; in fact, on occasions when Ignazio remained on the site, it was usual for them to take coffee with him.

It had all been well worked out. For a 'consideration', a stand-in would use my bed at Antenberg and another would take my place as a layer of slate. Tonight, Ignazio would bed down in a room next to Domincuo's office, as his German masters allowed when he was required to set off at an early hour to collect a detachment of prisoners from a nearby camp for transportation to an outside working party, an *Aussenkommando*. Timing had been meticulously calculated. He would take the work party to a stone quarry beyond Berchtesgaden and return to Buchenhoehle around eight A.M. with a load of stone. I would be waiting for him to run me to a point near the Turken in the Führer Area where I would slip from the truck and join the others going on leave; the assembly place was a hall adjacent to the movement control centre and the absolute deadline for assembling was nine A.M.

In the cellar I found a straw mattress, pillow, two blankets, a latrine bucket and a jug of drinking water. A candle, matches and, thoughtfully on someone's part, six small cigars had been placed under the pillow. About three hours passed before Ignazio brought hot food and drink. There was something alarming as he left and I heard the trap-door being noisily locked above my head. What a night! Memory still illumines it as a dark, eerie experience with no comfort after reflecting upon what had followed being locked in an attic in Leiden, Holland, in 1941. The dread was there! I strove to feel security and confidence in the Italian capos, while knowing that the serpent of temptation to acquire gold had got the better of them. I could only pray that no higher bidder was enticing them to double-cross. Had the trap-door remained unlocked, my mind would have been far easier. I awaited the start of the next day with taut nerves and feverish intensity; sleep eluded me and time hung heavily, yet passing silently by as recollections pulsed through my mind. Even with a couple of worn blankets, the cold was penetrating. I lit and snuffed the candle a number of times. Had I but known! Away in an unimaginable future in a post-war life, there lay in store for me, in dangerous and isolated places – at the top of the world, at the bottom of the world, and in many countries between – episodes far more threatening of death and disaster than this sojourn in Hitler's Territory.

I was thoroughly awake when Ignazio tapped on the trap-door. It was a silent pre-dawn as I followed him to Domincuo's office where a pot of coffee was simmering on a portable stove. Picking up a kerosene lantern, I preceded Ignazio to the floor above which was bare and uncompleted, but a water pipe protruded from the wall where the bathroom was eventually intended. Cold water had been laid on, improvising a shower for foremen and capos. I breathed relief at the sight of my civilian clothes laid out on a wooden bench against the wall, together with shaving gear and a towel.

'Hurry,' said Ignazio, jerking his thumb in the direction of the water pipe. There was no screening or privacy and he was giving me no option but to undress and shower in his presence. The distracting thought leapt through my mind that I carried a revolver under my armpit and a body belt stuffed with paper money.

'Would you bring me some hot water for shaving?' I asked.

'Shave back in the office,' he replied curtly. 'Hurry.'

Standing in the doorless entrance with the lamp's glow casting flickering shadows, the rough, ruthless and apparently unbending capo remained with his eyes fastened on me. It was a predicament. Intuition, which had always served me well, was alive and warning. Turning my back, I raised a foot with a working boot and placed it on the end of

the bench. While bending low and cursing the difficult knot
I had tied in the leather lace, I released the holster and
stuffed it with the gun into the boot as my foot came out.
Off came the other boot and I pushed both into a dark
corner. Preserving a gloomy silence, the Italian watched me
remove my work overalls. I released the money belt and
slipped it off under cover of removing my shirt and, folding
the shirt, placed it on the bench. I was satisfied my artifice
had worked.

With my back to the scowling onlooker, I turned on the
tap and cold, stinging water gushed over my naked body. I
was inwardly furious; being watched inspired no respect for
a fellow slave-labourer, albeit a boss. The icy water was
invigorating and revived morale, but was cold comfort as I
moved to snatch at the towel. Ignazio was seated on the
bench fingering my money belt in his dirty, knuckly hands.
He had turned the tables, and despite a sinking feeling I had
to think and act quickly. My best ploy was indifference,
commanding myself to calmness. Humming casually, I
donned underwear, trousers, socks and shoes. Drawing a
deep breath, I confronted the capo whose face held a
mocking grin. Extending an arm, I exclaimed stiffly, 'That
belongs to me. Pass it over, please.'

'*Fülle Geld* (plenty of money), how did you get it?' he
rasped.

'It is needed for my journey east,' I responded, 'give it to
me!'

I could have wept when he said slyly, 'You will give me
some of it. I have helped for your safe departure and you still
have to rely on me, eh?'

'What you are saying is, you want some of that money?' I
managed to speak unaggressively while thinking, 'You foul,
felonious bastard!' With a show of unconcern, I put on my
new shirt.

'I have an old mother to think about,' he whined, 'and if

you won't show generosity, I need not be back here on time to get you to the movement centre. Anything might delay me.'

He had the whip-hand. Dressed except for tie and jacket, I said I would be happy to reward him, but first let us move to the office and I would shave. He fell for my ruse. Walking over to my discarded work boots, I grabbed the gun, moved towards him and jabbed it in his ribs. He was holding the lamp in one hand and my money belt in the other. I wrenched the belt from his grasp. 'Put that lamp down and get down those stairs. Quick,' I hissed, 'or I'll kill you, if Domincuo doesn't have you murdered.' An inner certainty had told me that Domincuo would have no part of this blackmail. I was right. Uttering some strangled words, Ignazio appeared paralysed with fear.

In the office, I sat him against the wall while I shaved. He had his face in his hands, murmuring and moaning that he had been a crazy fool and it would be the end of him if Domincuo learned the truth. He began to cry. I realized the urgent need for compromise as streaks of dawn were appearing and he begged me not to expose him to the master capo. I vitally needed Ignazio, and no disturbance of plans at the last minute. 'I won't breathe a word,' I consoled him. No longer fierce or threatening, I peeled off a hundred Reichmarks and in an almost brotherly tone told him that if he kept his side of the bargain, I would double the money and keep my promise of silence.

He grasped my hand and his tearful, small eyes glinted with a look of almost affection. Tucking the Reichmarks in his pocket, his voice quavered, 'God be your aid, and mine too.'

I was worried about the time and impatiently told him to get moving, collect his outside work party and return quickly. He paused, speaking hesitantly. 'Domincuo ordered me to lock you back in the cellar.'

'Fine,' I replied, pocketing the automatic, 'take me back, but leave the trap-door unfastened.' I returned to the cellar, shaven, clean and a respectable-looking civilian, my hand in my pocket gripping the Browning as if it was my last mate in life. Heaven only knew what I would have done without it.

# CHAPTER 18
## Crisis to Crisis

The time was 8.30 A.M. and Domincuo scowled worriedly. 'Why the hell hasn't he turned up?' he breathed through clenched teeth. If he was filled with fears about Ignazio's non-return, I was almost on the verge of panic. The Italian boss-capo looked at me comprehendingly, knowing the importance of what was involved as the minutes slipped by. 'You'll have to take my bicycle,' he said decisively. 'You must be at the document clearing centre before nine.'

I knew that failure to do so would result in back-checking and escape from the Obersalzberg would be irretrievably lost, and with what consequences? 'Carry your suitcase on the handlebars,' he said, 'now you must get moving . . .' He opened the outer door, stopped abruptly and raised his hand. We listened to the throb of an approaching engine. 'That's Ignazio's truck,' Domincuo breathed, 'he must have been held up. I know his reliability; he would do everything possible to get here on time.'

Out of my maze of thinking, I wondered what Domincuo's reaction would have been had he known of the money belt business. At the moment, I could only feel a surge of thankful relief that I had kept my head and said nothing.

The heavily laden truck jerked to a halt before the office-house, and briefly gripping my hand Domincuo said urgently, 'Good fortune, now get going.' He thrust my suitcase into the driver's cabin and I followed, keeping my head down and lying low.

As we drove on the main road in the direction of the SS check-out centre, Ignazio spoke in a rather broken voice, 'You said nothing to Domincuo?'

'I said nothing at all, Ignazio, rest secure.' I gave him the other promised Reichmarks.

The journey was about three miles. It had started to drizzle and with time short, he decided to drop me off at a point closer to the control centre than planned. 'When I stop to change gear and rev the engine, drop clear at once,' he instructed.

Pausing fractionally, I followed my suitcase on to the road-side and barely had time to straighten up before the truck was gone. Nobody was about that Wednesday morning; the drizzle ceased and, sucking in cool mountain air, I arrived at the large assembly room with about five minutes to spare. I had cleared a nerve-racking phase and was through the first green light. Moving towards a corner window, I stared casually at the silver snows on the mountains, awaiting developments with a fast beating heart. The sun was striving with the day. I was now alone, my own goal, my own meaning, and safety lay in the technical evidence of my papers, my ability to avoid blunders by keeping my nerve, while everything involved the play of luck and chance.

The assembled party numbered close to fifty including about a dozen women, a handful of military, and the remainder a mixed lot of civilian males. Those around me in groups conversed good-humouredly; an obvious, expectant excitement reigned, just as when a body of RAF trainee aircrew finished a course and assembled for distribution of travel warrants and ration cards before breaking up for leave; such memory was singularly vivid of a close-knit group of qualified navigators, having newly received their brevets, to follow various postings to operational training units.

A sharp, shrill whistle commanded immediate silence and a down-to-earth realization of Nazi discipline as a body of SS officers and a party of RSD entered. The entrance door was locked. A squat, pompous SS major with a Hitler moustache called almost cordially, 'Heil Hitler! Good morning everybody.' Then began a roll-call of name, occupation, employer and leave entitlement. The responses came out in all manner of tones and the neatly dressed females were the first to pass into the next room for identity pass and documentation checking; next the men in uniform, and last the civilian males. I waited tensely.

'Helmuth Heusinger, craftsman carpenter, employed by ARGE, fourteen days' leave.'

'*Hier*,' I called out and raised my arm.

About six at a time were shepherded into the room beyond. The flow was quick and continuous. My turn came and I faced an elderly florid-faced examiner who was standing. Mechanically he took the papers I presented, scrutinized my identity pass, and me; he gave a brisk nod and handed back the pass. He took more time with my information document issued by my employer and already stamped by SS security as satisfactory; it listed dates, such as my arrival on the Obersalzberg, a medical report and various other data. I assumed a humble demeanour; my tongue was dry. Cold blue eyes looked at me. 'Your father was killed on the Eastern Front,' he spoke, as a matter of fact.

I nodded, meeting his eyes unflinchingly. 'Any knowledge of how he sacrificed his life in the service of his country?' he asked.

'All we know,' I responded sombrely, 'is that he was killed on active service.'

He nodded and his countenance was less severe. Something prompted me to add meekly, 'My mother and I dare to hope he is a prisoner of war and will come back one day . . .'

He looked at me closely, almost agreeably, but his reply was rather hesitant. 'Perhaps . . . you keep on hoping. Look after your mother.' Unexpectedly he reached out and lightly patted my shoulder a couple of times. I was handed my papers with the comment, most civilly expressed, 'Now away with you, and have a good leave.'

'Thank you,' I murmured, feeling more appreciative than he could possibly have imagined, and moved on to the next room.

I joined a short queue to have my suitcase checked. It seemed a random inspection; not everyone was ordered to open his case on the low bench. The man in front of me had to, and an RSD officer casually fumbled among the contents. He was passed and I lifted my suitcase to the bench. For a few seconds I was looked at in silent speculation, and then curtly instructed, 'Go ahead; join the bus.' I obeyed in silence and walked out of the control centre, scarcely believing my luck. I boarded the bus, which was waiting with its engine running, and taking a seat I felt a ferocious joy. As the transport travelled towards Berchtesgaden, my mind sang in RAF jargon, 'A piece of piss. I went through the bloody lot like a hunting dog!' I might have offered a few words of decent acknowledgement to Helmuth Heusinger, to his brave, deceased Dad and poor, sorrowing Mama, slaving in some smelly canteen to make ends meet, and hoping for the dead to come alive. I wished Helmuth well, and hoped the poor sod would get his fourteen days' overdue leave.

At the railway station my nerves steadied. As far as waning memory can be reasonably accurate, most of the departees boarding a train to pick up a connection for Munich left about eleven A.M., and mine to Salzburg left half an hour later. I walked up the platform and, near the engine, selected an undivided coach where I took a window seat. I wanted no snug, intimate compartments. An ear-splitting hoot blew from the engine. The train slowly rattled into movement. I had set off for Upper Silesia, hundreds of miles away to the north-east. I was suddenly dead tired and unconcernedly watched several women on Berchtesgaden platform waving handkerchiefs. I was clear.

To telescope the journey, on arrival at Salzburg I changed to a regular passenger train for Vienna and proceeded at a satisfactory pace. God, what superior comfort after the disgusting cattle truck trip in the opposite direction. At an early stage, I sat near a batch of soldiers who were no more interested in conversation than I was; they seemed exhausted. From Vienna, I crossed Czechoslovakia, via Brunn, to continue on to Breslau in Poland. Rolling back the years, memory fails on points, but dominant aspects have stuck in the mind. From start to finish of that long, hazardous journey, fatigue – both physical and mental – was never absent and it was a constant struggle to keep my wits about me as I rattled over seemingly endless railway tracks through enemy territory. What I had hoped would be, at most, a thirty-hour journey, dragged on for over forty-eight hours. I travelled on at least half a dozen trains and spent long hours awaiting connections in cold, inhuman waiting-rooms. At least there was no problem with money or in passing over some of my issue of ration cards for refreshments; I have no memory of hunger as a distracting worry.

My papers were examined at least a dozen times by train inspectors accompanied by a member of the State Security Police. There were no scares, no suggestions of further investigation, of being ordered to the guard's wagon where there was always a lock-up installed. I distinctly recall that the inspectors and police combing through passenger trains had identical attitudes, cold and precise; papers were invariably subjected to quick but minute examination; they were no fools. While the Browning tucked under my arm was a moral support, I was always in the grip of suspense until my papers were handed back, then relief and cold sweats temporarily manifested themselves. I was compelled to note during these febrile checks how indispensable were genuinely produced papers and I had little reason to wonder why so many POW escape attempts foundered on trains. Whatever the artistic skill in hand-drawn lettering in Indian ink, it was virtually impossible to reproduce printed forms and hope to escape the eagle eyes of the examiners placed on all main line trains. Even if the lettering was damned good, the Germans were forever changing official stamps and identification symbols.

It was not just documents that counted. Jerzy had tutored me on performance and intonation; he had told me my tone was wrong, that I spoke too high on the palate, and I should pull my lower lip down and deepen my resonance. At first, through the strain of the situation, I imagined my voice was false, but somehow I always managed to rise to the occasion and as the distance to Breslau lessened I acquired more confidence. My mind slid back to the train journey in Holland, from Zutphen to Amsterdam, when seated in a coach full of young German fliers. Acting as briefed, I had picked my nose; it turned the decent, clean, young fliers away from me, but not without one slapping my face in disgust. For this present journey, I had been instructed by my underground handlers to appear odd, gazing blankly into vacancy, with noticeably impatient, restless hands; to behave as a rough, semi-civilized labourer with an apparent obsession for repeating 'Heil Hitler'. At no time was I to be in a receptive mood for conversation. People had to be surveyed with annoyance and, if compelled to talk, it had to be abbreviated and my voice shuddery. It was important I be viewed as a somewhat unstable individual with a hypertensive nervous system.

The one really pleasant memory, after so long in the male, militant world, was being in the presence of women. Whether German, Austrian, Czech or Pole, just ordinary women, peasant or refined, they seemed to be the only people who smiled. I was forcibly struck. They reflected serenity, a refuge of sanity and normality. Instead of uniforms and lacklustre faces, they wore dresses and expressions clear of hatred. There was something about them, even as they walked, that was lovable and sympathetic.

The nerve-racking journey ended around noon on the Friday when I alighted at the large, sombre station at Breslau and with a fast-beating heart passed through the barrier. The weather was now very cold and I was grateful for a blue gabardine coat, also serving for identification along with a green scarf and a rather loud, chequered cloth cap; a 'Berchtesgadener Land' souvenir sticker showed on the outer side of my suitcase. As usual with a main junction station, it swarmed with uniformed Germans, and a few immaculate officers peacocking about, greatly out-numbering the civilians who for the most part were poorly clad, carrying battered cases or just tied-up bundles. I made straight for the main waiting-room, my mind running hastily over lessons memorized.

Before entering the waiting-room, I had placed two sticks of chalk (brown and green) in my left pocket, and two (grey and red) in my right one. The room was not overcrowded but groups of soldiers were standing and quite a few civilians, men and women, all elderly it seemed, were seated on the long benches. Just inside the entrance, I casually backed up against the wall, put my case on the floor and, slipping a hand behind me, with fingers gripping the brown chalk, I inscribed on the wall a rough circle, about the size of a saucer. After a couple of minutes, I drifted across to the other entrance just as a white-haired old man in overalls shuffled in with a long-handled broom and began sweeping the littered floor. Again I backed against the wall while indifferently observing some women with shawls over their heads busily knitting with a kind of heroic tenacity. This time, I moved my hand rearwards and with green chalk, drew three small ticks; when I bent to pick up my case, I glimpsed they were inconspicuous enough.

Now I headed for the men's lavatory. I took a position facing front between two slabs of slate and, using grey chalk, outlined unobtrusively at hip level on my right, three ticked crosses, and on my left, but higher up, two crooked swastikas. Behind me was a long line of toilet cubicles and I was on the point of entering one when I spotted the old, white-haired floor-sweeper moving into a space between two slabs. His face was impenetrable and not a whisper of the password was uttered.

In the toilet compartment, behind the closed door, I acted quickly. Every scrap of documentary evidence went down the closet; all I kept was money, and ration coupons which were of a general German issue. I scraped the sticker off my suitcase, then opening the case tore up and flushed away the small cardboard carton with the Obersalzberg inscription; I scratched the label off the special gift bottle of perfume intended for my phoney mother, poured the contents down the closet and slipped the empty bôttle into the cistern overhead. None of the other items in the suitcase offered any trace of Upper Bavarian history. I took the piece of red chalk then, and drew another symbol in the imaginative plan to establish I was not a 'snare' and ensure underground recognition and approach. This time it was a simple, snowman-type face, such as a youngster might draw, just behind his right shoulder, while sitting bored or constipated. As I left the cubicle, the jolly, sketched face and the stink of perfume were the obituary of Helmuth Heusinger. He had ceased to exist. The underground was notified and could rest in peace if I were captured.

The white-haired man had left the lavatory block, but I was surprised to see him outside, talking to another man who was holding a bucket; each had the yellow letter 'P' for Pole on the chest of his overalls. I experienced a surge of expectation as I passed them but there was not even a glance or quiver of a smile although intuition told me I had been identified. Explicitly carrying on with Jerzy's instructions, I made for a coffee stall and about fifteen minutes later headed back to the waiting-room. I had been briefed that allowing for wartime transport disruptions, underground scouts would be on the lookout for me for several days, and once I had gone through the identification ritual, the most likely place of contact would be the waiting-room. It had also been impressed on me that if a contact failed to materialize within an hour of my leaving the coffee stall, I had to launch out on my own. I was running a great risk now with no identity papers and I was well aware that among the crowds were plain-clothed secret police as well as uniformed police and railway scrutineers watching for anything suspicious or untoward. Shirkers, deserters and criminals existed in Germany as anywhere else and random checks were frequent. Men of working age did not loiter around stations unless with watertight reasons.

At the waiting-room, I was abruptly taken aback. Railway police were barking at the civilians to get out and snooze elsewhere. About fifty grimy, terribly weary but nice-looking girls in school tunics were being shepherded into the room, and at the entrance two women in some sort of charitable-volunteer uniform were handing out cartons of food. The girls were still voluble, and some were already stretching out on the vacated benches. Now I felt something of real anxiety. Where was the old man with his magical broom? I drifted around outside for a time, as if waiting for someone. My heart was twitching. One of the last of the old ladies to be removed from the benches, still clutching her knitting, hesitantly paused before me. Much to my surprise she said in halting English, 'Are you well?' I replied in English, 'Thank you, yes.' 'Good luck to you,' she said slowly, 'get on your way.'

In great perplexity, I did not utter a word but moved

without delay. Railway police were approaching, gripping
two outraged civilians. Fears racing, I felt like screaming but
walked off nonchalantly, quitting the station and its
distressing scenario. On a main thoroughfare, with relief I
spotted a green telephone booth. I dialled and redialled the
number Jerzy had given me, but it was a dead line. I took out
my matchbox and selected a used match; on one of its
slender sides was the telephone number, except for the last
two digits, '24'. No, I had made no mistake. Two patrolling
policemen strolled past the booth. I decided to get moving; I
dared not push things too far. Some curious misunder-
standing must have occurred, and the thought assailed me,
'Oh Christ, I hope the underground cell handling my case
has not been suddenly broken up . . .'

The two contact addresses I knew by heart and, taking
out the Breslau map, I found the nearer was about three
miles away, but time was wasted in dodging around side
streets, pausing in doorways and concealed places to ensure I
was not being shadowed. Oddly, the address was not far
from the German military hospital and Kirsche Alley. It was
a long tramp; the sky was angry, the wind came in short,
blustering gusts. I came to the flat-roofed church which, I
had been told, was about 300 yards before my destination.
The small, two-storey, semi-detached house, painted grey,
was exactly as described behind green, iron railings. Not so
the signs that it was safe to knock! There was no lady's
bicycle minus a front wheel chained to the inside of the
railings; no bucket and mop were on the front doorstep; no
pink curtains partly drawn over an upstairs window above
the front door; nor a white vase with red artificial flowers.
With the safety signs not in evidence, I knew I should not
stand and gape, or wander indecisively back and forth. It was
a shock of bewildering disappointment, but I kept moving,
after perhaps the most imperceptible hesitation, for I had
bitter memories of a house in Leiden having been under
observation from across the street.

It began to drizzle. The second address was some miles away but it was getting late and if it too proved to lack indications for safe approach I would be in great danger if not off the streets by curfew. With darkness little more than an hour away, I decided to retrace and locate a small park not far from the railway centre. Jerzy had told me of it, in case my train had arrived at night. This city oasis boasted a bandstand, unused in wartime, but below its elevated floor was a changing room for bandsmen. The door was heavily padlocked, but a key was concealed under a flagstone. I was profoundly worried, dog tired and hungry. Passing a general store, I turned in some of my ration coupons for provisions which I stuffed into my suitcase. Past lessons had taught that exhaustion and hunger were chief causes of carelessness, impairing motives and control of actions.

I strode out smartly, aware that soon the streets would start emptying. Sighting the green telephone booth where I had made the fruitless call, I was jabbed by a burning desire to try again. I had been warned not to attempt to phone after curfew with the risk of German Counter-Intelligence monitoring calls, but darkness had not yet descended. I dialled. This time a bell burred at the other end and I could have yelled with sheer, ecstatic joy when I recognized a man's answering voice. It was Borge! I was stirred with powerful emotions as I gave the password, and the matching reply was returned. Conversation was short, to the point and twisted about, but sufficient to give essentials as to what had happened. 'Time enough to talk later. You must get on with the music, quickly,' I was told, knowing he meant the bandstand, and his concealed, crisp instructions were to await his arrival there next morning in a white ambulance with Red Cross markings.

I reached the park in deepening twilight, but veered away from the bandstand which was about 500 yards from the highway; at the same distance from the highway and some 200 yards from the bandstand, I came upon bushes adjacent to what seemed a botanic gardens. I was still ruled by the caution which had made me vacate a toolshed in Vienna when an old Austrian gardener had gone off to find me a bicycle. I had no intention of getting close to the hiding place until complete darkness, but found adequate cover under a thick screen of the bushes, remaining there until the last traces of daylight melted away. I was horrified when soon after darkness two soldiers and their girls, joking and giggling, approached the bandstand and, climbing the steps, settled down under its roof. They must have been blissfully unaware that it was a damned cold night as they remained for at least a couple of hours. When they did depart, I had already determined not to swap the bushes for the bandstand. While I did not doubt that no one outside my helpers knew of the key to the padlock under the flagstone, if roaming police or Gestapo took it into their heads to check the edifice and chanced to find the underneath door unlocked (as I would have to leave it), then I would be caged!

I resigned myself to a lonely night in the open. For some time I had the unwanted company of a heavy drizzle which, strangely, seemed to arouse a vague smell of disinfectant, whether from the bushes, the ground, or perhaps my blanket, I do not know, but the memory remains. More than two years had slipped away since I had crashed in Holland and had burrowed below a clump of bushes, with slim hope of salvation. Now I was in a much more fortunate situation, able to get up and stomp around, swing my arms to restore circulation. I was not devitalized with emotions half-paralysed; I had food in my suitcase and sound hopes of salvation by the underground next morning. Real sleep was out of the question. I heard a few odd sounds coming from frogs and small creatures and, throughout the night, the rumble of trains arriving and departing; easy enough in the imaginative clarity of night to visualize the fresh young soldiers off to the east and hospital trains returning, full of

German wounded, festering with lice and reeking with front-line odours.

At long last, dawn's fingers probed the heavens. The Berchtesgaden blanket was sodden, but it had more than served its purpose in the freezing hours. I pushed it out of sight below the bush. Some birds gave a few chirps, and a welcoming sight in the broadening light was a number of venerable trees between me and the highway; they had hardly interested me the previous evening. Factory whistles and sirens were heard in the near and distant vicinity, and slowly the city came to life; a subdued hum of activity seemed to hang in the air. People appeared on their way to work, some on cycles but most walking as I strained my eyes for a white ambulance with Red Cross markings to come into view. Never had a post-daybreak seemed so protracted or brittle and I began to experience flutterings of fear. 'What if Borge . . .?'

Then it happened! Over a slight rise on the highway, the ambulance came out of a misty drizzle. I quivered with excitement as the vehicle pulled in to the roadside. Borge and a companion, both in white overalls, strolled around the ambulance as if trying to make some complicated calculation. There was a lull in the flow of passing pedestrians; the signal came, three blasts on the ambulance klaxon. I moved forward, from cover of tree to aged tree. The rear doors had been opened and with a final dash, I followed my suitcase into the interior of the ambulance. We were on the move before the doors were closed by Borge, there with me on the inside.

We changed conveyances, into an official fumigation truck, and drove to a four-storey block of flats. The one we entered was on the ground floor near the entrance. After a hot shower and wearing clean, dry clothes, I felt I had found an important missing piece of myself. Borge's housekeeper was an elderly widow, Julina, who worked from 8.30 A.M. to

3.30 P.M. in a paper factory and was also one of a group of elderly women in the resistance (their male counterparts were known as 'Greybeards'), who carried out scouting and liaison missions. When I met Julina late that afternoon, I was flabbergasted to discover she was the woman with the knitting who had approached me at Breslau station and had whispered in halting English what I had thought to be a warning, '. . . get on your way.'

I now discovered what she had said was 'he's on his way', meaning the white-haired broom sweeper, the 'Greybeard' contact. But I had turned and fled instead of hovering a little longer for a hand to be placed on my arm and the passwords exchanged. Apparently I had put my underground handlers under strain until I had telephoned and Borge had answered. The unsuccessful phone call was accounted for; installed by the ambulance administration for official use, the phone was left unplugged whenever no one was home to answer. Julina had 'gone sick' from work to be 'on duty' in the station waiting-room in the hours when I had been expected to arrive and she had not returned from the station when I had first phoned. Regarding the grey house which had revealed none of the safety signs, events had moved fast since my being briefed and there had been no opportunity to warn me to give it a wide berth. The Polish couple who had rented it had been obliged to flee and find other shelter for themselves and two Jewish refugees on the run. The house had been surrounded by Security Police but loyal friends had been able to warn the quarry of the impending peril and they had not returned home.

I shared a room with Borge for a little over a week and was provided with ample reading material, a pipe and tobacco to help pass the hours. Whenever Julina or Borge returned from work, they tapped a signal on the outside door and called a watchword before the bedroom door. Somewhere Borge had access to the latest British and American broadcasts and in the evenings I was kept abreast of the war news. I admit, I nightly hoped to hear of the Obersalzberg being pulverized but it was not yet to be. Came the unexpected and cheerful tidings that I would leave Breslau as a member of an official German delousing team. Also there came the tragic news of Jerzy's death on the Obersalzberg. Borge returned to the flat, pale-faced, and it was obvious he was very upset indeed. I certainly found my feelings hard to express. I listened in some kind of waking-dream state as Borge revealed that my indomitable Polish colleague had supposedly been accidentally killed when a load of rock from a big tipping truck had crashed upon him while he was inspecting deep foundations. Borge resisted entering into more details. 'And what of Stefan?' I asked.

'He arrived in Warsaw last night. He's too good an agent to be left alone in Berchtesgaden with so many risks and uncertainties. Besides, he's a man who needs to be actively supported by a strong-willed person, such as Jerzy. Stefan will be placed somewhere else.'

Along with five others in the fumigating team, with Borge as supervisor, we left Breslau early one morning in two lorries carrying equipment and chemicals. Each of us wore white overalls with a badge of accreditation and carried appropriate identity passes. It was extraordinary how Borge had the others, all second-class German citizens of mixed Polish ancestry, not simply under control of graft, but interested and keen on this trip as apparently they had been on previous visits. It was a journey of several hours from Breslau to Lamsdorf and re-entering Stalag VIIIB proved no nerve-wrenching event, but a smoothly conducted operation. It was not revealed to me if Borge had manipulated the visit; all I knew was that the camp authorities had made a request for a vermin control party some weeks ahead of schedule. True it was that many outside working parties were returning to the parent stalag for the winter months and there were bitter, dreaded memories of the 1942 typhus epidemic which had spread from the Soviet compound to the civilian population. In addition, the British compound had a plague of fleas and there was growing infestation of rats in and about the long, open-trench latrines; the rats had always existed there but some now were apparently as big as cats, and more than one prisoner when seated on the rough wooden support had experienced a rodent driving its teeth into testicles. Visiting the trench latrines had become a monstrously frightening business.

No fuss was encountered when we reported to the administrative headquarters and guard blocks; indeed our arrival seemed to have a mesmeric effect of welcome. Our first call was to the British section of the camp where Borge made certain the first phase of activity was fumigation at the segregated hospital block. There was something thrilling about being safely back in VIIIB. For the first half hour, I stuffed clothes and blankets into a large fumigation cylinder, then Borge suddenly gripped my arm. 'Get into the medical orderlies' room and change clothes with your stand-in. You'll go back to the psychiatric ward and our man will take your place and carry on with us.' I ceased to be a German fumigator, whose name I now forget, and once more slipped into my basic false cover of Private Winston Yeatman which, after two years, seemed as authentic as Richard Pape. The fair-haired Pole, safely removed from the hospital, remained working with the delousing team in the vast camp for over a week before it returned to Breslau.

I lay low in the psychiatric barrack for a couple of days and was visited by one of the RAMC doctors – I think it was Captain Spencer. The German, Dr Müller, had recently left the hospital and his replacement had small interest in mentally disturbed prisoners and had acquired no real idea of their facial identification. Then I was discharged for return to the main camp where I submerged myself among

the hundreds of men in the working party barracks where
the British NCO in charge had been pre-warned to extend
me brotherly support. The German labour supervisors were
made aware that I was back in the working party compound,
but I was still under restriction imposed after my recapture
in Hungary and confined to the camp.

Before I had left Borge's flat in Breslau, I had given him
the .22 Browning and ammunition which would have spelt
certain disaster if found in my possession in the prison camp.
We had also discussed the signet ring which I had left with
Dr Müller. Before his fumigating team finally left for return
to Breslau, Borge visited my barrack, inspecting it in his
professional capacity, and he signalled me to follow him
outside. 'Here's your ring,' he said quietly. 'It's been in safe
custody here all the time. Keep it as truth of our allegiance
and it may still have a binding effect on your destiny . . .
especially if we can get you to Yugoslavia.' He grinned
slowly. 'Or we may find work for you in one of our
Intelligence centres in Poland.' Borge and I shook hands and
that was the last I ever saw of him. I strode back to the
crowded, noisy barrack pressing the ring into the palm of my
hand. It now represented far more than anything I had
imagined, and I would carry it with me as a kind of sacred
symbol. It had involved me in an almost unbelievable
sequence of events.

# CHAPTER 19
# The Bleak Baltic

The British camp of Lamsdorf was miserably much the same as when I had left it months ago for the nose operation in the military hospital at Breslau. The bulk of the toil-worn prisoners, many veterans of Dunkirk, Greece and Crete, had endured up to three years of captivity but they no longer suffered the pessimism of former times, knowing that Germany's fortunes were waning and being convinced that the coming spring of 1944 would see an Allied landing in the west. I did detect a change; no doubt bitter winter again and general debility contributed greatly, but the growing line of reasoning among prisoners was to forget individual escapes as the call of duty, and personal breaks had lost much of their glamour. True, there was always a number of enterprising, even foolhardy individuals prepared to take all risks and such escape-minded men were provided with every possible advice and assistance by back-up colleagues on the escape committees.

Personally, I entertained no further ideas for escape or needless adventuring with the likelihood of being swept out of existence, unless backed to the hilt by underground planning and assistance. Even then, I doubt if I could have stood up to the stresses; my health and strength were far from satisfactory. On the face of things, I had to stick it out and endure. The lung trouble had started up again on the Obersalzberg with the cold and working in stone dust. The hard labour and constant hunger had reduced me to almost two stones lighter than when I had departed for the military hospital. Fluctuating fevers and profuse sweating at night were an increasing anxiety. I was far from dead, however, but intended seeking readmittance to the camp hospital as soon as my loyal confidant, Captain Spencer, returned from a short tour of outside working parties.

It was during this period that I was approached by the chief of the security committee (a prisoner organization like the escape committee), and asked if I would employ my blackmailing techniques on a German carpenter to get parts of his six-valve radio set back to camp. I agreed, being all too vividly aware of the crucial importance of accurate radio information from Britain at this particular period of the war, and being told that the security committee's secret radio was almost on its last legs. Somehow it was 'worked' and the embargo on my movements was eased to allow me to join a working party which went out daily for light duties to the carpenter's shop a few miles away.

Three days before I first went out with the work party, Captain Spencer returned. He examined me and was decidedly unhappy about my health. The new German doctor-in-charge also carefully checked me over and I was taken aback when he proposed listing me among those to be examined for medical repatriation by the next International Red Cross Medical Commission to visit the camp. I did not like the sound of it one bit and was naturally worried and apprehensive; it seemed damnably ironic that sicknesses incurred on past escapes might betray ambitions for future survival. Spencer was adamant I return to the hospital for rest and treatment as soon as I had pulled off mission 'Contact', the obtaining of the radio set parts. Truth to tell, I welcomed the thought of returning to the hospital, to the British doctors and one or two medical orderlies who knew something of my past activities. I found the impersonal, overcrowded working compound a strain, with idleness a leaden weight after the exciting life I had led. The succession of soldiers coming and going, virtual strangers, was monotonous and I realized that living here indefinitely would have a stultifying effect upon my mentality. It was out of the question to take any of them into my confidence. I dared not give an inkling of past exploits or even reveal I was living under an assumed name. All I could offer was that I was simply a slave soldier who had worked in a coal-mine, then on the land, fallen sick and had had long spells in hospital.

Letters were handed to me that had arrived after I had left for Breslau hospital, and before my advice had reached Britain to cease correspondence. I immediately now got off coded letters stating that the long break in communication had resulted from my taking an extended holiday in the mountains. I deciphered information that the two New Zealanders living as Pape and Mieteck were preserving their covers; they were in Luft VI, a supposedly escape-proof stalag solely for NCOs of the RAF and the US Air Force. It was on the Memel Peninsula, at Heyderkrug on the East Prussian–Lithuanian border (today part of Soviet Russia), and only a few miles from the Baltic Sea.

To tide me over health-wise during mission 'Contact' I was given sulpha drugs and sleeping tablets, also thick Red Cross pyjamas. Like the other inmates of the barrack, I normally slept in my clothes, but all too frequently I had been crawling from the lower bunk of the three-tier bed with my clothes sodden in stinking sweat. Spencer considered I should not set out with the working party in the bitterly cold mornings in damp clothes.

The radio-pinching coup was a complete success. The elderly German's six-valve receiver was dismantled and various parts were carried back into the camp concealed on the persons of trusted colleagues. It was the fourth evening after all the bits and pieces had been handed over that I learned the technical boys of the security committee had the secret radio functioning perfectly. They were jubilant and so was I; the next day I would be on my way to a respectable bed in the camp hospital. Taking my pills and donning pyjamas, I was soon wrapped in sleep. If the methods employed in ensnaring the old carpenter had not been exactly sporting, I was not at all bothered by any sense of shame.

All was in darkness in the barrack with its occupants in slumber when suddenly there was a roar of voices and the crashing of boots. Imagination fails to record the workings of my mind when the thunderbolt struck around midnight. A German voice yelled, '*Achtung, achtung!*' Then came the order for the barrack commander to step forward. 'Take us to Winston Yeatman, prisoner of war number 7490. He's under arrest.' Lights were switched on from the control centre and I was certainly not going through some kind of nightmare when I observed half a dozen guards with sub-machine-guns standing behind two black-leather-coated figures, Gestapo agents. More guards were on the outside and patrol dogs were barking with excitement. The immediate thought which tore at my bewildered brain was that something had gone wrong with the radio stealing . . . perhaps a Fifth Columnist in the working party, or had the old carpenter decided to come clean? I felt I was standing on quicksand. The barrack commander had no choice but to point me out. I was grabbed, my straw palliasse ripped apart and my bunk searched, then wearing pyjamas and with a blanket around my shoulders, I was taken away by two guards, with a Gestapo officer clutching my working clothes. Luckily my signet ring was not in my battle-dress but concealed within me, as some prophetic foresight had advised.

I was not lodged in the block of cells for prisoners inside the wire but taken to the Vorlager on the outside, an area used by the Germans and where the administrative office and stores were located; there was also a small gaol, used for Germans under arrest. Thrust into a cell, I thought,

'They're really going to bump you this time, boy!' To my astonishment, it all had nothing to do with the radio. For several days I was grilled with merciless precision by two Gestapo officers who exhibited exultant relish in acquainting me that the real Winston Yeatman and George Potter were also under arrest. Typical of Gestapo methods, I was told they had revealed everything. I was completely in the dark about what had occurred in the Baltic Sea camp to occasion this abrupt arrest. Fencing almost blindfolded, what undercut my morale and jeopardized the security of the situation was ignorance of what information had been extracted under brutal interrogation from Yeatman and Potter.

What had really happened at Luft VI was that the two New Zealanders had complicated themselves by making second changes of identities. George Potter, who had faithfully represented the missing Pole, Mieczyslaw Borodej (Mieteck), suddenly had every reason to be dreadfully alarmed when the RAF Polish fliers in Luft VI, now numbering about 200, were facing removal by the Germans to a special Slav concentration camp. The Germans detested the Poles as much as they loathed the Russians and plans were to remove them from Luft VI to some place where they would be deprived of the influence and protection of the Geneva Convention. The threat was very real, possibly enforced by the rapid Soviet advance and the probability that the camp would be overrun, allowing the Poles to scatter to wreak vengeance for all the violence and suffering their nation had received at the hands of the Nazis. Not unnaturally, Potter concluded that if he were moved out as a member of the Polish contingent, his chances of ever seeing his beloved New Zealand again were bloody remote.

An Australian flier, Foxley, not long a prisoner of war, was so fired with a craving to escape that he considered the Polish move a glorious opportunity to make a break. He

cared little about acquiring a Polish name, and apparently
had blinded himself to the inextricable situation he could
get himself into if he failed and finished up in a Polish camp.
An urgent three-cornered swap took place. Yeatman (alias
Pape) became Foxley; Potter (alias Mieteck) became Pape;
Foxley became Mieteck. A party of Poles left a short time
later and as the train moved up the Baltic coast, Foxley
jumped and got away. Unfortunately, he was recaptured,
taken to the Gestapo and any claim to being Mieczyslaw
Borodej was quickly exploded; he knew scarcely a word of
Polish. It was discovered that he had swapped with the Pole
who was still in Luft VI.

The Gestapo pounced on Yeatman, believing they had
collared the evader, but to their anger and consternation,
after grilling him severely, they were compelled to acknowledge that he was no Pole either. The Gestapo were not to be
fooled and all hell was let loose. Two prisoners were hiding a
Pole. Where was the real Mieczylaw Borodej? It was
Yeatman's turn to find himself in a desperate plight. The
Gestapo were hopping mad, and to them physical violence
was the basis of authority. Threatened with all sorts of
reprisals, Yeatman had to talk to save his neck. He told the
Germans that his real name was George Potter and that he
had engineered a change of identity with Mieteck in Stalag
VIIIB two years before. Down to Stalag VIIIB came the
Gestapo to grab the real Pole living as George Potter.
Apparently they threw every kind of fit when they learned
that a prisoner named George Potter had escaped with
Winston Yeatman and had never been recaptured; indeed
Potter was supposed to have died in a barn in Poland! By
now the Gestapo, the Kriminalpolizei and Counter-
Intelligence were all involved, believing they were on to
something special. Nothing was said to me at the time.

Back to Luft VI raced the frantic inquisitors again to
tackle the man they knew as George Potter. The genuine

Potter, living as Dick Pape, was keeping dead quiet. The
Germans, cleverly and misleadingly, informed the man
claiming to be George Potter that a man of that name had
been shot dead while escaping with another New Zealander,
Winston Yeatman, in Stalag VIIIB and that I had confessed
to being Mieteck. They also told him that I was to be
executed and that only he could save me by confessing all he
knew. Yeatman was in a devil of a dilemma, and in pretty bad
shape by this time. He told the Gestapo, to their utter
amazement, that he was not George Potter at all, that
Potter was masquerading as Dick Pape and his own name
was Winston Mearil Yeatman. The German investigators
were now spitting blood and raving as they endeavoured to
sort out the thickets of mixed-up identities. When I met
Yeatman after the war, he grinned and said, 'Oh boy! In
spite of the gravity, it was bloody marvellous witnessing
Gestapo brain-storms and almost floods of frenzied tears.'

Here was a man first claiming to be an Australian, then a
New Zealander, and now a totally different New Zealander;
his admission had also brought in another man, RAF flier
Dick Pape. The Germans were not to be thwarted and
resolved to dish out punishment with interest. So 'Dick
Pape', the real George Potter, was roped in. At the same
time, I was grasped and gaoled at Lamsdorf. German pride
was seriously offended; mongrel prisoners, not even officers,
had made monkeys of their captors for two years. Gestapo
wrath fell on Yeatman who was to be dispatched to the Slav
camp for punishment, and to make up the numbers of Polish
fliers sent there! It was pitiful, terrible and ridiculous.

But I was their main target, the originator of the whole
business that had got a Pole to freedom. With the love and
habit of the Gestapo to rake up every incriminating item, I
was told that because of my treacherous record, I had lost
my status as a prisoner of war, that I should have been
summarily shot as a spy at the outset in Holland or later in

Poland, and I certainly would have been had the Komman-
dobefehl* of October 1942 been in force as it now was. In
addition, there were criminal offences committed in
Hungary where I had broken into a private house and
attacked its owner. My reward for all my villainy was to be a
court-martial, charged with espionage, collaboration with
Dutch and Polish enemies, and a host of felonies. While it
was all damned distressing, with little doubt which way
things would go, had my background in all its truth been
known I would have been summarily executed at dawn.

The senior British officer was notified of my arrest and
the involvement of two New Zealand soldiers who were
brought back from the Baltic camp and placed in VIIIB cells.
To my relief I was removed from the Vorlager gaol and
returned to the camp enclosure, albeit to a solitary cell. The
game was clearly up when Yeatman and I were brought face
to face during an interrogation session. But we were still
deep in the woods with the Gestapo maliciously adamant
about treating Yeatman as the Pole he had purported to be,
and determined to have me brought to trial. We were
refused visits by any British officers, even the medical
officer, and all I recall now after so many years is a brief visit
by a camp padre when I was coughing my head off and
sweating with the recurrent fever.

What happened soon after seemed something of a
miracle. The camp was visited by representatives of the
International Red Cross from Switzerland. I have often
speculated if the senior British officer or the security
committee somehow got through an urgent request to the
Protecting Power; it was almost too extraordinary for the
representatives to drop in by chance at the eleventh and a
half hour for Yeatman and myself. Details of our cases were

---

* Hitler's 'commando order' refusing protection of the Geneva Convention
to commandos, saboteurs and parachutists on legitimate operations of war.

placed before them with the immediate outcome that the Gestapo were checked from removing us until charges had been fully investigated. It cannot be denied that unlike the Gestapo and SS, the German organization responsible for handling prisoners of war (Kriegsgefangenewesen), did respect the Geneva Convention. The rules proclaimed that it was not dishonourable for prisoners to escape, though we had somewhat overstepped this by the manipulation of aliases.

The Gestapo punishment designed for Yeatman was dropped. Issues bubbled for some time about the pattern of my hostile wickedness on the outside but, despite high-flown protestations of the Gestapo, efforts to remove me from the camp to be put on trial were postponed. My incredible luck held fast, seeming to have had a strange quality of watchfulness all along the line. Official punishment was meted out to the three of us, but solitary confinement on bread and water was paltry now we were no longer under the threat of disappearance under the '*Nacht und Nebel*' (night and fog) system. With joy and relief, we complied with the Kommandant's order to be re-photographed, re-fingerprinted and re-registered, each tagged with his correct identification disc. Yeatman and Potter were to remain at Stalag VIIIB, while I, as RAF again, was to be transported to Luft VI by the Baltic Sea. After facing death on innumerable occasions, it seemed hard to believe, and I had a strong, instinctive eagerness to hold on to life, wherever it might lead.

Fairly soon it led me, with two guards, to the little station at Annaberg which I left almost affectionately for the last time. With frequent delays, the journey to the north-east lasted four days and throughout I was handcuffed and chained to one or other of the guards, except during periods when I was lodged in various gaols. The guards were elderly, ordinary, low-grade soldiers; we were soon conversing on friendly terms and they were decently concerned that I receive my due rations. One for some reason I nicknamed Wilbur, which tickled him immensely; the other was Karl Stieber who wrote to me after the war asking for food parcels as things were tough in West Germany. (Gladly I sent them; he and Wilbur had saved my life.) It was tiresome and ambiguous to be publicly chained to another man, but my guards had been given a hell of a warning that if I escaped, they would be shot for neglect of duty. I too had been given a severe dressing down before being handed into their charge. I was warned that if I gave any trouble or attempted to escape, I would be on my way to hell in double quick time.

Additionally, in my new camp, I would be under constant surveillance for any acts of subversion. This particular warning certainly stirred deep concern, for I had only shortly before been handed a number of coded letters from Britain. I should have received them long before but they had been allowed to lie in the office of the camp hospital, no doubt awaiting my re-entry as a patient. Decoded, the letters advised me to discontinue cipher activities imme-. diately as such operations were under investigation by German counter-espionage experts and alerted censors. The news came as a shock, but what really gave me chills and fears was knowing that I had a few coded letters out in the pipeline to my UK contacts. Coding was a precarious business, punishable by death, and while I had operated safely for two years, as had others for long periods, it seemed that as the war had progressed and MI9 had developed, selected officers of the three Services had been taught coding for use in the event of being taken prisoners; too many, it seemed, had been trained and in time slip-ups and blunders were bound to occur.

One way and another, my trip to the Baltic was far from carefree. At a small town preceding Königsberg in East Prussia, Wilbur, my big, burly guard, was obviously ill at ease, and before he and Karl led me from the train to be locked up overnight in the local gaol, he said in a resolute voice, 'For God's sake, don't move across the threshold of your cell by one centimetre. The Gestapo plan to trick you.' How Wilbur and Karl had come by the information I will never know, but it was a heaven-sent tip-off. Frightened thoughts passed thought my mind, and I tried to put reasons together for bumping me off. I wondered if my code work had become suspect and I cursed the medical orderly who had hung on to the warning mail from Britain. Or was it a typical Gestapo ploy, a pay-back for being defeated in their plan to have me put on trial? The cell door would be intentionally left open, and if I ventured into the corridor, if only for a leg stretch, I would be shot. The Protecting Power would have to accept the German explanation, 'shot while trying to escape'.

In the prison house, I was yanked into a cell chained to Wilbur who put on a convincing act of being a tough guard. He released my manacle and handed me over to a police sergeant; the cell door was slammed and locked. A couple of hours later, the sergeant, all smiles, returned with a bowl of soup, bread and coffee. He said, 'If you give me your word not to try to escape, I'll leave the door open so you can exercise in the corridor.'

I affected sternness and anger. 'I insist you lock the cell door! I have no intention of escaping and if the door is not sealed you will be failing in your duty . . .' I asked to speak to the superintendent of the station, whereupon the obsequious sergeant departed, slamming and locking the cell door. It was a demoralizing night with not a wink of sleep. When Wilbur and Karl appeared next morning to snap on the handcuff, I stared at them as if in a trance; they might have been saints.

As 1943 turned into 1944 I began the new year on the bleak, monotonous Memel Peninsula. Here for the first

time I met the prisoners' elected camp leader, Warrant
Officer James Deans, generally known as 'Dixie' Deans. He
said, 'I wondered when you'd turn up.' He had long been
aware of my close involvement in the hotchpotch of
espionage risks. In liaison with British authorities he had
done his utmost to protect vital false identities. Luft VI was
a camp of exceptional unity with a vigorous escape
committee known as 'Tally Ho', and a security committee
which was able to keep morale high by providing, from a
secret radio, verbatim reports of BBC and American news.
The man who took down the bulletins in shorthand was
none other than the radio operator who had sent the last call
from our Stirling bomber after being 'hit by flak' over
Berlin. He was Cyril Aynsley, later to become chief reporter
of London's *Daily Express*.

During the two years when I had lived more or less on the
'outside' as a private soldier, I had experienced a great deal
of scope for imagination, independent activity for freedom
and subversive operations. Now I struck a very different
situation, sealed in a camp where no work parties left. Most
of the inmates had stagnated for years with escape
opportunities few and far between. I found myself under the
strict discipline of the escape committee which had a limited
list of men waiting to make a break; guts alone were not
enough for selection, but total qualification for success,
which included good workable knowledge of German. I was
no longer a law unto myself. The committee was aware of
my brash runs for freedom from working parties and
subsequent captures, but I remained tight as an oyster about
co-operation from underground movements in Holland,
Poland, Czechoslovakia and Upper Bavaria. I had sworn
certain oaths and nothing on God's earth would persuade
me to violate them.

I had arrived at the Baltic camp when the stage of the war
was of extreme consequence. The siege of Leningrad ended

in January, the Red Armies were forging ahead and the tiny Baltic States stood to be overrun and, indeed, by the end of March, the tremendous south-westward Soviet drive reached Estonia about 250 miles to our east. It was anyone's guess whether the Germans would evacuate the 4,000 or so men in the stalag before it became embroiled in the battle front. 'Tally Ho' with urgent foresight had initiated a brilliant escape line to the Baltic ports. Civilian Poles and Germans had been bribed or manoeuvred into the scheme, with 'safe houses' found to enable escapees from the camp to lie low until able to stow away on neutral Swedish ships. In January 1944, Warrant Officer George Grimson escaped from the camp with the dedicated concern to set up this escape line.

I was too 'hot' to be considered as a candidate for the run. I was frequently being hauled before German security officers to have my fingerprints and photographs checked, to make sure I had not turned into someone else. Knowing it was impossible for anyone to cover for me if I vanished up the line, I began to feel I was doomed to control my restless spirit, to face the irremedial idleness and stick it out until, it seemed, the Russians and Germans determined our fate.

It had been no capricious decision when the senior German doctor at my former camp, Stalag VIIIB, had decided to recommend me for examination by the International Red Cross Medical Commission when next it should visit Lamsdorf. In moving to the Baltic, however, I had forgotten the issue, and had never considered it of consequence anyway. To my astonishment, I was now summoned to attend for medical examination. Two British doctors, one I recall as Forrest-Hay, worked in Luft VI camp hospital under a German chief medical officer. I had a chance for a chat with Forrest-Hay, a fine, friendly type, and enquired what the devil it was all about. He said, 'With typical Germanic efficiency, a wad of your medical records has followed you from VIIIB with the recommendation that you go before the next Medical Commission which is due here in May.'

I was dumbfounded and baulked at the idea. 'Look,' I said, 'my lungs are not giving much trouble, and I never asked to be put on any repatriation list. I'm no shirker. I'm not trying to work my ticket. Get me off the list, can you?'

'Sorry,' I was told, 'it's out of our hands; it's a German matter. Your name was put forward by a medical officer senior to our Jerry medico here and he has to accede to higher authority.'

Wearing only shorts, I faced the German camp doctor; he was short, elderly, wore pince-nez and had slightly protruding eyes. He examined me disdainfully, as if I were something of a repellent snake, studied my X-rays and said icily there was no evidence of tuberculosis; I had recovered well from meningitis with only slight residual optical oedema. With a dry laugh of derision, he said I should never have been recommended to go before the Medical Commission and I was an idiot for imagining I could get myself repatriated when there were hundreds of gravely ill and injured men to be considered . . . I almost choked with indignation and yelled at him, 'Shut up! I shall report you to the Kommandant! Your remarks are insupportable. The sooner you're sent to the Russian Front to certify dead horses for *Wurst*, the better.' He was thunderstruck and I carried on, telling him I had never nominated myself for repatriation and I would request the Kommandant to inform the Red Cross in Geneva that I declined examination. Before Forrest-Hay took my arm and led me away I had one last crack. 'We'll all be repatriated soon anyway. But you'll be stuck here . . . with the Russians!'

Red-faced and eyebrows bristling, all the German could mutter was, 'Go, go, and no more disrespectful remarks.'

Outside the room, Forrest-Hay chuckled. 'Nice fighting words. He's been needing someone to pitch into him.'

It had been a prickly interview and with my mind whirling, I collided with a bearded stranger at the outside door. My shoulder was gripped and I was stared at in disbelief. 'Richard Pape! You are, aren't you? You're not dead!'

I studied the man askance. 'I'm Pape, but who the hell are you?'

'Laszek,' he replied excitedly, 'you remember, one of the Poles with Mieczyslaw Borodej at Lamsdorf two years ago when you changed places with the soldiers.'

I gripped his hand. 'Good God, man! I didn't recognize you. Where are the others of your group?'

'All here, still clinging together. Which barrack are you in?' I told him, the one for newest arrivals. 'You're not staying there,' he was emphatic, 'you're coming with us.' I went with him immediately to meet my former colleagues and soon obtained permission to move to their quarters. Still an exclusive coterie among the almost 200 Polish–RAF fliers, they were thrilled to meet me again, just as I found it exhilarating to be back among them. Through their secret grapevine, they had long known of Mieteck getting clean away after our coal-mining adventure at Katowice; but they had heard I had been captured by the Gestapo at Cracow and executed. They were also relieved to learn that Yeatman and Potter were alive, for when they had been suddenly dragged from Luft VI it had been rumoured they were being taken away to be shot.

These Poles trusted and admired me for my imagination and the risks I had taken in getting one of their original number to freedom. As for the Germans' awesome threat which had hung over their heads at Stalag VIIIB if any of their number attempted escape, Mieteck's disappearance had remained undiscovered for so long that now no reprisals were taken. My bumping into Laszek that day was to prove one of those curious quirks which changes the course of one's life. When I told the Poles of my altercation with the German doctor, the fact that I had been nominated to go before the Red Cross Medical Commission in May really excited their imaginations. They saw me as half-way home already.

I shook my head. 'I haven't a chance in hell of passing the Commission.' I still hear their protestations, their excited eloquence. They would fix it! They had a pre-envisaged plan which now seemed tailor-made for me!

Their plan involved an artificial penis filled with urine supplied by a prisoner dying of nephritis. I called him 'Jimmy', the unfortunate donor of the urine full of flotation specks; he was a gallant Polish flier. In furtherance of the plan, skilful Polish colleagues manufactured a penis (uncircumcised) on a basis of rubber hose-pipe configured with a hard rubberized substance. Realistically moulded, if enviably oversized, it was painted flesh colour, with a Michelangelo genius even to revealing vein formations. A stopper sealed the top and the outlet duct held a tiny wooden plug which was craftily withdrawn to release, with a squeeze, the germ-laden fluid from the hollow inside. Taped securely into position, it lay concealed below my pants until it was necessary to produce part of it when I had to pass water into a beaker. I learned symptoms of nephritis – swollen ankles, dizziness, a yellowing complexion – before I visited the hospital to complain initially to the British doctor. Creating puffy ankles without bruising was expertly done by one of my Polish friends, a former physiotherapist, gently flicking with damp towels, and my skin was tinged with light yellow dye from crepe paper. I had a breathing space before May, for a period of sustained practice and strain, visiting the sick bay regularly for testing. I was nervous when required to confront the German doctor, expecting him to be awkward after our first dismal encounter, but he evinced no resentment.

Duly, I was told I had advanced disease of the kidneys and my deteriorating condition was being entered on my medical records to be presented to the Medical Commission. My Polish fighting brotherhood beamed at my success. I was certainly alive again and back in focus in their company. They had persuaded me to take a chance, not just to pull off a last quick one against the Germans but, as a matter of duty, to get back to Britain with my panoramic knowledge of resistance operations. Also, it was conceivable that Polish Intelligence might make use of me as a courier to Britain with the latest V-2 information. Behind the barbed wire, at varied periods we watched mysterious missiles streaking into the blue, creating sinister vapour trails before hurtling out of the stratosphere faster than the speed of sound. They were being launched from the experimental base at Peenemunde, on a lonely little island, not far off shore, to our west. Only a few months were to pass before the first of the 'V' weapons – 'V' for *Vergeltung* or vengeance – were to fall on Britain, on 13 June 1944. Disguised as slave-labourers, Polish Home Army Intelligence operators were working in the factory at Peenemunde; indeed, it was they who had supplied the Intelligence reconnaissance for the RAF raid of 17 August 1943. Unfortunately, the raid and Polish sabotage had only delayed production and the new 'secret weapons' which Goebbels boasted would win the war for Hitler were awesomely in evidence to us, looking skywards from our camp.

From arriving at the Baltic camp at the beginning of 1944 and over the next few months, a series of disastrous and strange happenings occurred. The Grimson escape route was discovered and snuffed out by the Gestapo and Kriminalpolizei after a number of fliers had made clever escapes. Two of them, Flockhart and Gilbert, had smuggled aboard Swedish ships, crossed the Baltic and returned from neutral territory to Britain. Others were less lucky. One, named Callender, reached Danzig (Gdansk) and nothing was heard of him again. Another, Townsend-Coles, was arrested on the gangway of a Swedish vessel. Wearing civilian clothes, he was lodged in a civilian gaol charged with espionage and collaboration with the Polish underground, and shot. George Grimson, the remarkable escape route organizer, vanished in April 1944 and what finally happened to him was never discovered.

The Great Escape from the air force officers' camp of Luft III at Sagan, near Berlin, took place on 24 March 1944, and of the seventy-nine men who got clear through a secret tunnel, three made it right back to Britain; seventy-six were recaptured of whom fifty were shot 'while attempting to escape'. This was announced to us by our camp Kommandant one morning at roll-call, and a torrent of abusive, infuriated cries was hurled at him, his surrounding guards and officers, until they stalked off clearly shaken. It was a horrifying revelation, but closer at home the Gestapo continued investigations into the Grimson escape route and brought more agonizing revelations to light. A high degree of corruptibility among the guards and Polish and German civilians drove the investigators into fits of frenzied fury. Fifteen German guards of the Armed Forces had been bribed and blackmailed into co-operating with 'Tally Ho', and I understand all were executed. Additionally, Polish and German civilian helpers associated with the Grimson line were arrested and never seen again.

Escape was now a desperate risk with trigger-happy Germans. 'Tally Ho' was virtually closed down; escapes and certainly mass escapes after the Sagan murders were sternly discouraged to avoid unnecessary casualties at this stage of the war. Unfortunately, among those of the German Armed Forces arrested was one named Sommers, in truth a Pole and a member of the Polish resistance; when he asked 'Tally Ho' to provide him with means for a swift death, he died in the

night in his cell before the Gestapo had a chance to begin
their agony of interrogation. But he died not before he had
given me crucial assistance for which I was to be deeply
indebted. When instructions had reached the camp authorities well in advance of the due date for the Medical
Commission, all examinees listed with lung troubles were to
have up-to-date X-rays taken at a hospital in Königsberg.
Sommers had a first-rate knowledge of the photographic
identification markings vital to an X-ray plate. A pro-British
guard named Adolph Munkert, also to be executed in the
Grimson line purges, accompanied about a dozen of us to
the hospital. There he personally handed me over to a
radiologist, a special friend of Sommers, and for a cash
reward my X-rays showed galloping consumption had
overtaken my fairly quiescent pleural troubles.

The deaths of Sommers and Munkert were a grim
setback, not only to 'Tally Ho' but to my Polish
companions who had no intention of staying put in the
camp knowing Russian forces were looming to overwhelm
us from the east. They had no fallacious views of Soviet
humanity and saw their futures as full of traps and pitfalls;
they were not going to stay to face Soviet slavery – or
disappearance or death, like the 15,000 of the Polish Army at
Katyn and elsewhere in the USSR. By some means unknown
to me they still had contact with the outside. They were well
aware, as was I, that if I failed the Medical Commission the
Gestapo would resume its cat and mouse tactics with me or
even have me removed and slung into a civilian prison, to
face a similar fate as Townsend-Coles; being nominated to
await the arrival of the Medical Commission was, for the
moment, my safeguard – much as it chafed the Gestapo, the
Protecting Power had to be respected.

If I failed the Commission, my Polish friends confided
that they would take me with them when they broke out,
that they had assistance organized with Lithuanian and

Polish loyalists on the Baltic. By some of the British prisoners, often with derogatory overtones, I was called 'Polenski Pape' which worried me not at all, knowing what Polish loyalty had meant to me. I was one of ten in the Polish group which schemed to the last detail our clearing of the camp to connect with Lithuanian underground operators. It would be no casual arrangement but meticulously planned, with properly produced, official documents; adequate clothing was already prepared. We would separate into groups, I with two Poles would move to a reliable destination at Hamburg, and there, sheltered in a 'safe house', would lie low until, hopefully, rescued by Western Allied troops; surely, the offensive in the west *must* open within a matter of weeks.

Fastened up in our Baltic camp were almost 300 Yorkshire airmen who could only await the course of events in a misery of debility and boredom, like the rest of the captives. The Yorkshiremen had previously formed themselves into a society, 'The White Rose Club,' and now an idea suddenly occurred to me, with a secret motive, to compile a magazine-type book; it would absorb leisure time and, as far as I was concerned, it represented one last shot in my locker. 'Dixie' Deans, the camp leader, was enthusiastic that I had thought of a way to arouse action and pride among the Yorkshiremen and motivate them into creative enterprise. Unaware of what was at the back of my mind, he secured from the Germans, paper, Indian inks, brushes and water colours, all Red Cross supplies. Pen nibs, especially small mapping ones, were forbidden, the Germans now being well aware of the skilful forgery that had taken place, but this problem was overcome by a former instrument maker who manufactured superb and flexible nibs from steel tape which bound Red Cross crates. In championing the effort, 'Dixie' agreed the book had to be rushed through before the arrival of the Medical Commission in May and he confided he had undercover handlers who could get it over to Sweden and back to Britain. But it must be a worthwhile and impressive achievement.

As mentioned, I had been strictly forbidden to use coded letters. Whether from defiance or conceit, the whole point of the book, to me, was to get back to my code handlers in Britain some idea of my likely hideaway in Hamburg. In two articles which I contributed to the literary endeavour, I resorted to code, indicating where I might be found, or meet my end. I disclosed to no one in the camp that I was coding.

Members of 'The White Rose Club' rose magnificently to the occasion, believing the book was all for a memento and an exhibition of their morale under privations. Most of the contents were innocuous enough and the book (nine inches by eleven, and ninety-three pages) was a combined effort of literary and artistic talent. It contained 30,000 words, carefully hand-drawn in lettering slightly larger than 10-point newspaper type; interspaced among the various articles and poems were drawings – some in water-colour, some humorous – of camp existence, and a few caricatures. Although a Yorkshire 'foreigner', there was included a fine frontispiece drawing of J. A. G. Deans, camp leader. If my imagination was at first excited, at times the effort to continue seemed too demoralizing and senseless to carry on at breakneck speed. But it became an obsession and I persisted with careful editing and miles of hand-drawn letters. Too many men had put their very best into the articles and illustrations to let them down.

I admit, it did give me a satisfaction to put my best into the book. After 6.30 A.M. roll-call, shivering in the outside bleakness, I would return to the barrack and stretch out on the floor below a three-tier bed, hard at work. When darkness fell and the lights were switched off, I dropped into bed with my boots on. When I closed my eyes, mirages of tiny Indian ink characters marshalled themselves like slovenly soldiers on parade. During the day, trusted men maintained vigil and when I heard the cry 'Goons up', I rapidly removed three floorboards under which I concealed manuscripts and materials; then I would put on a star act, lying on my bed, groaning and complaining of chest pains. At the cry, 'Goons gone', I was back at work as editor, layout artist and printing machine. It was all finished in just over five weeks, and dated May 1944.

I would certainly not have entitled the production 'The Yorkshire Post Kriegie Edition', had I known that my old newspaper figured in the Gestapo list of thirty-five British publications whose offices would be seized, their records confiscated and their executives arrested in the event of German invasion of Britain. Had the book fallen into German hands, its very title would have excited curiosity and analysis. In the officially issued letter forms and postcards, I devised coded information to give Lilian Rowe and Alfred Willcox sufficient clues to be on the lookout and know where to find my coded messages should the 'Kriegie Edition' ever turn up.

For reasons best known to him, 'Dixie' wanted the manuscript bound between two sheets of Red Cross plywood with a spine of green linen. I carved the front cover with the name in the familiar, old English lettering of *The Yorkshire Post* and with a large rose, symbolic of the county. This work I did quite openly while sitting close to the barbed wire to get the sun on my back. With a dribbling nose and an inane look in my eyes I scratched away hour after hour with glass pieces, and carved deeply with old razor and penknife blades. Meandering guards asked what I was doing. I held up the partially carved rose and replied with a stupid grin, 'I used to grow roses. When I go home, I'm going to grow a new one and call it "Yorkshire Kriegie".' They looked at each other, one tapped his head and muttered with amusement, '*Er ist schwer verrücken.*' If they thought me quite mad, that suited me.

I was appreciably relieved when I finished the whole work. It looked magnificent from the outside. I had used brown shoe polish and a lot of elbow grease to give the plywood the appearance of seasoned oak. 'Dixie' had added a list of 272 members of 'The White Rose Club' and of twelve non-member contributors, and all concerned with the production were filled with considerable pride and mutual respect for producing it with inconceivable rapidity. I remained silent about its main, inglorious reasons, for as far as I was concerned it was my last fling before the gates shut behind me for ever on that Baltic camp. If the book got back, all well and good; if it didn't, so what? When I finally handed it over to 'Dixie', he gave me a smile of confidence. 'I'll do my very best to get it home,' he said, 'or those White Rose Club Yorkshiremen will skin me alive.' James Deans was an unusual character with remarkable undercover contacts. He had all the qualities of a born leader – fearlessness, decision and temperamental mastery over the toughest Germans; he was without conscience or a sense of righteousness about clobbering the bastards in every direction in defence of freedom, justice and democracy.

With the 'Kriegie Edition' finished, I could now pursue the pattern of misery and boredom, sauntering aimlessly around the barbed wire. My nerves were flickering cheerlessly in a moody mistrustfulness of myself, a dull reaction that I had let the others down, that I should stick it out with the rest of the camp's inmates. But such thoughts were quickly repelled. I had a duty to get back, to disclose what I knew of my underground helpers, and other matters. Misunderstandings and ambiguities were to be expected in the first months of peace, or even earlier, and I could surely contribute important information.

A New Zealand colleague, Wallace Crighton-Brown, from Nelson, was also on the repatriation list. Pale with suppressed excitement, he slapped me on the back and said starkly, 'The Commission's arrived! We front up tomorrow morning.'

Mastering my feelings, I said, 'Good luck, Wallace, and thanks. I've got to get myself into pukka dying condition.'

No time was wasted. My physiotherapist went to work on my ankles until they looked like water-filled tubes. Roman, the leader of the Polish coterie, had me smoking dried sunflower seeds hour after hour until my bronchial tubes emitted sounds that might have emerged from the wrecked chest of an octogenarian. I was fed pieces of soap and instructed not to wince or complain as I had to look a heart-rending spectacle with a greenish-yellow complexion. The nephritis victim ('Jan' was his real name) was made to urinate into several bottles to get the best possible sample which was kept at blood temperature near the stove before the artificial penis was finally filled and plugged.

In the morning, with a thudding heart and churning with indefinite hope, I faced three doctors, a Swiss, a big Swede, and a German whom I had never seen before. As best I remember, all wore uniforms of their respective countries. The Swiss examined my ankles and wrists, and looked me over with despairing eyes. The big Swede, obviously the one in command, called an orderly to have a sample of my urine taken and tested immediately. A foreign orderly, apparently one of the medical team, beckoned me to a nearby screen. He handed me a beaker and with distressing chilliness, told me to fill it. I indifferently took out only as much as necessary of my artificial 'John Thomas', withdrew the hardly discernible plug and let it flow, giving the rubber tube a modest squeeze for realistic squirts and not just dribbles. The orderly carried away the result for testing, having instructed me to strip naked. I thought, 'You stupid bastard, leaving me unsupervised,' and quickly undressed, stuffing the 'John Thomas' into my trouser pocket.

I returned to the trio of doctors. One was holding up my faked X-ray plates; the corners of his mouth dropped. My urine when tested proved beyond doubt that my kidneys were almost ready to collapse into my boots. The German went over my spindly, starved frame and applied a stethoscope all about my chest and back. I sadly surveyed him and with almost swooning diligence obediently took gasping breaths. I was told to spit into a vessel and what was produced looked like some substance in which I imagined sunflowers were about to sprout. The Swedish doctor then examined my chest and to disgust him into wanting to get me out quickly, I started making repellent noises, raking up and spitting sunflower residue into a grubby-looking rag. My wheezing lungs ran the whole gamut of asthma and bronchitis, and the noises that went into the stethoscopes ranged from profoundest intermittent bass to shrill animal squeaks, or the hoarse crow of a young cock.

'Why is there no mention of fluctuating heart condition on this man's records?' the big Swedish doctor asked of no one in particular. I could have told him. The temporary heart jerks and jumps, the high temperature, had been occasioned by my Polish advisers; with pharmaceutical precision, the bloody scented soap I had swallowed had been mixed with bits of cordite slivers taken from a German rifle bullet.

'Get dressed,' said the orderly, 'be quick, please.'

When I re-emerged from behind the screen, with the artificial 'weapon' safely tucked in my pocket, I faced the trio. It was the big Swede who announced with gravity, 'You are sick enough to go home. Good luck.'

# CHAPTER 20
## Breaking Covert

I passed the Medical Commission on 4 May 1944. The rest of the month ran out with no further information being revealed to the men classified for repatriation. On 6 June, the Second Front opened up in northern Normandy and this exhilarating news came over our secret radio. Seven days later, it was sickening to hear German broadcasts proclaiming that hundreds of V-1 missiles were crossing the Channel to fall on Britain. June passed, and we were still without the vaguest idea when, or if, we would be moved; everything had fallen flat. I decided to throw the whole thing over and make an early escape with the Poles while reasonable opportunities remained. The Soviet Army had advanced into Poland and Romania and liberated the Ukraine; in our northerly remoteness, the months since March had seen no great Soviet thrust into the Baltic States, but it could not be far off. 'Dixie' Deans and the security team were vigorously making plans for a necessary forced march in the near future; already the sound of gunfire was carrying to us on the winds from the East.

By some mercy of Providence, about a week before I was due to break out with the Poles, the repatriation men were hurriedly rounded up and driven to the railway station at Königsberg. It was only then, when given rations, we were told we were travelling to a transit stalag 1VD/Z near Leipzig, 500 miles or more away from the Russian advance. I found myself huddled into an old railway compartment with nine others, including my Kiwi friend, Wallace Crighton-Brown, and one German guard who was quite a decent chap. My artificial penis now served another purpose; it was filled with rolled notes to the value of some 5,000 Reichmarks for unexpected contingencies. Wearing the contraption constantly was not exactly comfortable.

I was acting as interpreter and our guards surprised me by their frankness. They were genuinely pleased the Allies had landed in the West, that Hitler's regime would soon be vanquished and, fearful of facing the Russians, they were every bit as relieved as we were to be on the move. Our guard explained we would change trains at Potsdamer Station in Berlin where we would pick up other sick and injured prisoners from various camps and continue immediately to Leipzig. After two monotonous days, we chugged into the outer suburbs of Berlin. I gazed in shocked bewilderment at fearful devastation. Whole districts had been bombed into small mountains of rubble, houses and buildings had fallen in heaps, and stark silhouettes of burned-out buildings cut the skyline. When I had bombed this capital almost three years before, it had hardly been scathed, but now it was the most bombed city in Germany. We passed through districts reminiscent of London's poorer East End, long, straight, characterless streets with great yawning gaps and pyramids of piled-up debris. I was filled with rushing, disquieting thoughts of a cockney family that had perished beneath its burning home when the Luftwaffe had bombed the London dockland. I also experienced a wave of anger at the terrible stupidity of it all.

Unexpectedly, we shunted into a siding near the Pape Bahnhoff. We waited and waited as the last of a rosy sun touched Berlin. Suddenly we heard the doleful howl of sirens and the sound of distant aircraft. RAF Mosquitoes unloaded their 4,000-pound blockbusters, and the boom of exploding bombs at intervals was too damned close. 'What a bloody sense of humour,' I thought, 'if Fate has brought me all this way to get me bumped off by my own Air Force near a railway station of my own name.'

We were on the move again before dawn and, arriving at Leipzig, were transported to our new stalag, an old German castle named Annaberg Schloss. It was wired around and guarded only loosely, for repatriation prisoners were not expected to escape. The medieval castle with its thick, rough walls was not particularly large but the hundred or so of us shared rooms off its long, stone corridors. We had no idea when we would be moved on but as days turned into weeks, we grew restive, bored and disillusioned. At first we had to rely on German sources for news until an antiquated radio was somehow acquired by our officer in charge, who, as best as I am able to establish now, was Major Charles N. Barton of the Australian Army. Crighton-Brown, a radio expert,* managed to get the instrument working. Receiving the BBC news again certainly boosted morale, though it became obvious that the advance of the Second Front had been slowed down and it was doubtful if the war would be over before 1944 faded out.

Living with men of all sorts, many with amputations and most in a pretty poor state of health, was depressing, particularly as the majority had suffered years in prison camps and were generally pessimistic and dulled of mind. Personally, I was overjoyed when news came of Stauffenberg's assassination attempt on Hitler at his headquarters at Rastenburg, East Prussia. It brought back vivid memories of Berchtesgaden and it was later revealed that this bomb attempt had been intended to take place at a staff conference in the Berghof on 11 July; with his unpredictability, or his phenomenal psychic warnings, Hitler had suddenly transferred himself and his staff to Rastenburg where the abortive attempt took place nine days later. On the other hand the news of the Warsaw Rising, which began on 1

---

* Since the war he has been a radio ham in Nelson, New Zealand; call sign ZL2ADT (20-metre band).

August and has its own disastrous history, came as a depressing blow.

August dragged almost to its end, with our existence at Annaberg Schloss becoming a nightmare; food was not plentiful. I was terribly restless and craving a loophole for challenge. If it is true that Satan finds some mischief for idle hands to do, he certainly found a plenteous measure for mine. With a home ticket in my pocket, thanks to the wonderful stroke of fortune in having been accepted by the Poles as a brother, instead of now just sitting quietly I became involved in actions with devastating consequences; all my other good fortune might have become so much dust in the balance.

A rear section of the castle, sealed off from us by a seven-foot-high, wire-mesh fence, was used exclusively by a small contingent of Luftwaffe concerned with handling carrier-pigeons. Leaning against a tree, I used to watch the white, quivering bodies of large pigeons take off through a wide, open window at the top of the castle. They invariably flew around the castle a couple of times before setting off like white darts on a westerly course. Sometimes six, sometimes more, were released at intervals. I also watched them homing, flying high, circling overhead and descending in curved lines, their dark, darting silhouettes clear against the sky, especially pre-twilight. As they wheeled towards the open window, they made a shrill, twofold note, and whirred inside from sight, one or two at a time.

Among our contingent was 'Taffy', an ageing, coal-grained Welshman. His legs had been badly crushed in a fall in a Polish coal-mine and when he balanced on crutches, his head seemed to be sunken between two hills. Taffy spent many hours at my side, bitterly cursing those German pigeons, yet at heart he was a pigeon-lover. Not only had he handled them in the First World War when such birds had been used by both sides extensively as messengers, but in peacetime his hobby had been pigeon racing. He explained that the type of birds flying from the top of the castle was capable of covering 1,000 miles, which meant they could easily reach German Western Front areas facing the advancing British and Americans.

We had no idea, at first, what was going on when suddenly all our younger guards were removed and we were astonished when they were replaced by old guards, some approaching their seventies, some with artificial limbs. Every able-bodied German was being roped in to defend the Fatherland at the Front. It was almost six weeks since we had left the Baltic and daily, impatiently, we waited in vain for removal to Sweden and freedom. To crown our misfortune, some extremely heavy air raids were being directed against Leipzig, particularly the Beuna synthetic rubber works, and accidentally some bombs had dropped dangerously close to Annaberg Schloss. Both Crighton-Brown and I still recall, vividly, our taking a stroll in an adjacent wood late one afternoon after an 'all clear' had sounded. Suddenly he screamed, 'Down!' and dragged me to the ground. I had not seen or heard a Flying Fortress with silenced engines, tearing straight towards us. It swept past, so low and close I could almost see faces at its windows. It kept up its shallow glide, then came a great crash beyond a screen of trees. We looked at each other, shocked and trembling. German motor cyclists and screaming hooters headed towards the downed plane. 'Hell, living's dicey,' complained my companion as we headed back to the castle. 'Almost blown up by the RAF at the railway siding in Berlin, and now the Yanks having a go.'

One of the aged guards, with a slow, dragging walk, we called 'Doodlebug'. He had been a Luftwaffe pigeon expert of the First World War and was on friendly terms with the six Luftwaffe pigeon operators who occupied a miserable barrack on the forbidden side of the castle. With much in common, he and Taffy also struck up an easy companionship, but it was some time before I realized what was going on. Doodlebug loathed the war, detested Nazism and resented being dragged out of retirement to this miserable life. He was not averse to telling Taffy how the pigeons roosting in the castle were being used. With Panzer divisions on the retreat and the Western Allies in pursuit, groups of German armour lay concealed in ambush or reserve and, rather than risk breaking radio silence, pigeons were being used where communication was essential.

For Taffy, the castle pigeons became the enemy and he seemed injected with an almost ridiculous resurgence of youth and spirit. He was a bit mad, I suppose, but he didn't seem to care if he lived or died, and he became obsessed that it was his responsibility to support the oncoming Allies by obliterating those Annaberg Schloss pigeons. He was a wicked old bastard really, the way he worked on me. He needed Reichmarks, of which I had a good supply other than those concealed in my private contraption, and he needed a man with a sound pair of legs and game to take a risk. I did not warm easily to becoming a murderer of pigeons, but when I learned how Doodlebug was involved in the scheme, the old Welshman wore down my opposition.

Crafty, crusty old Taffy had promised Doodlebug reward and protection from the British, with the war nearly ended. Before the war, Doodlebug had worked in a large chemical factory near Berlin and still had valuable contacts there. I parted with a sum of Reichmarks for him to exploit his colleagues and obtain various mixtures to produce giddiness in homing pigeons, disturbance of sight and paralysis of their muscular flight systems. Almost every evening, when the last of the birds had returned to roost, the six Luftwaffe handlers made off to their loves and pubs in Leipzig. One man often remained and always two hungry Alsatian guard dogs were left chained close to the bottom of wooden steps which rose to the pigeon chamber. While internal access to the lofts did exist, it was tortuous and the way securely barred and bolted. For ease and speed of access, steps had been affixed to the outside castle wall, zigzagging upwards in a series of sections, with outer handrails and arriving at a small platform facing a wooden door to the pigeon chamber.

The night arrived, dark and noisily windy. In the interests of security, Doodlebug had departed two days earlier for Dresden on a four-day leave pass. Taffy and I had told the other prisoners nothing of what was afoot so as not to jeopardize their repatriation. Crouched in shadows by the wire-mesh fence, Taffy counted six Luftwaffe men climb into a truck and take off. Doped meat was tossed over to the dogs and within minutes they were unconscious. I used a prepared rope contraption to get over the wire without noise or scrambling. I carried a knapsack, a heavy old table leg which I had raked out of a cellar, and in my pocket a small masked torch. In a short time I was up the steps to the platform and facing the door.

As so often, here was the contradiction of German efficiency and meticulous methods. As I had been warned, the door was held closed by a padlock and short chain, but by lifting it a few inches, the whole door came off two pivot hinges. I trod softly, and used the masked torch; soothing, concerted cooing greeted me as if my arrival was welcome, but as soon as I closed the large, sloping window unexpected trouble threatened. Two large birds suddenly fluttered around me, issuing peculiar gurgling noises. Careful throughout about fingerprints, I emptied the feeding pots and refilled them with the poisonous but obviously delicious seed preparation from my haversack. The pigeons started pecking away. I partly emptied the water containers and topped them up with a fluid from a metal flask taken from my pack. When the birds drank, as the seed preparation would make them want to very soon, they would be overcome by a sense of suffocation and their instinct would be to head outside to the fresh air. There they would drop down dead in flight and hopefully their bodies would never be found.

The two big birds ceased their mad weaving and diving to plod along the edge of the bench as if brooding suspiciously on my generosity. In a kind of reflex action, I made a sweeping lash at them with the heavy table leg, felling them both. Swiftly putting an end to their flapping and squawking, I stuffed the two plump specimens into my pack, threw the wide window open, reseated the door on its hinges and descended the zigzag steps. The dogs were recumbently silent as I reclimbed the wire fence where Taffy was waiting.

Back in a cellar, the old Welshman was elated, examining the dead birds, while I found myself breaking into a sweat. We went into immediate action, plucking the birds and having them in the cooking pot in next to no time. It was a tasty and memorable supper; all feathers and remains of the meal we burned and carefully disposed of. Taffy examined me minutely to make sure my clothing carried no fluff or little feathers.

The next day, Major Barton was ordered to parade all prisoners for investigation. All quarters in the castle were searched but nothing was discovered. Certain mobile individuals, including myself, were taken into the Luftwaffe enclosure for the fully awake watchdogs to sniff and try to pick up a scent; they treated me with as much indifference as the others.

Doodlebug returned and triumphantly informed us that when the handlers had visited the loft the morning after my visit, they had been shocked to find the cotes abandoned, and so to remain. The open window and the locked door were the same as they had left them and there was a general air of unreality and mystery about the whole business.

Within a week, after investigations by the Gestapo, the Luftwaffe group vanished, the outside stairs were torn from the wall, and the Annaberg Castle pigeon Intelligence unit closed down. A little later Major Barton called me aside and said, 'Did you have anything to do with that pigeon business?'

'Why do you ask?'

'The Security Police have not dropped the matter and this morning checked through each prisoner's records pretty thoroughly. The bastards have their eye on you, Dick. You have a stinking past as far as they're concerned. They can't get at you at present so for Christ's sake, don't put a foot out of place.'

It was now the third day of September. We were bored, having given up any idea of getting clear of Germany. With about five others I sat in the open by a large wooden tub, peeling potatoes. An argument developed about cricket, triggered off by the news that Hedley Verity, Yorkshire's greatest fast-bowler, had died in a POW hospital from wounds received in the Sicilian campaign. Who could replace a man who had once taken ten Nottinghamshire wickets for ten runs? My boasting of being a fast-bowler developed a wager for fifty cigarettes between a Nottingham soldier and myself. It involved hitting a bucket on top of another at fifteen yards. We each chose five large potatoes and with Wallace Crighton-Brown's help I set to work rounding my spuds like cricket balls and rolling them in the sand to give weight.

Then something astonishing happened. Great waves of cheering broke out behind us, yells and singing 'Rule Britannia' and 'God Save the King'. Crippled men had hurled their crutches into the air and were rolling and crawling about like demented centipedes. Others were linked together, jigging and dancing in circles in an outburst of ecstasy. Wallace looked at me with bewilderment. 'The bloody war must be over. The bastards have thrown in the sponge.'

Major Barton was approaching; grinning broadly and calmly knocking out his pipe, he imparted the mind-boggling news that orders had arrived that we were to leave on 7 September for the Baltic port of Sassnitz. There we would immediately embark for Trelleborg in Sweden.

With whoops of joy, the potato peelers started slinging Jerry potatoes in all directions. In the commotion I had not observed a nice old guard named Fritz, a thin, pitiful member of the German Armed Forces, approaching the target buckets. In the throes of elation, I grabbed a big, sanded potato, took a short run-up and giving a hearty howl, pitched it with considerable force. If I had promised the Major not to put a foot out of place, I had charged out with both feet. My aim proved indifferent, and one could almost hear the thud as the spud struck Fritz below the eye. He gave a wild scream, dropped his rifle and staggered about like a drunk. A second guard and a *Feldwebel* were quickly on the scene, my arms were grabbed and I was jerked to the Kommandant's office. Major Barton trailed behind, anxious, solid and tangible.

The Kommandant listened calmly and politely. A First World War officer, his rank was equivalent to a British Lieutenant-Colonel. He had spiked eyebrows giving him a saturnine expression which belied his character. He was popular with the prisoners, showing them honourable respect as wounded fighting men. Major Barton supported me splendidly, saying I was a very sick man and it had been an unfortunate accident in a moment of exhilaration at the overwhelming news. I would not have been so stupid as to assault a guard deliberately when on the verge of going home. He begged the Kommandant not to pursue the matter.

The German studied me intently with my file open before him. My heart sank as he said he had to observe strict discipline and obey superior orders. He had no alternative but to submit a report to the Polizeipräsidium (the regular police in Leipzig) which was subordinate to the SS and Gestapo. He was genuinely upset. 'A great pity this happened,' he said, 'particularly with the pigeon matter still under investigation.' He smiled thinly. 'Some prisoners' names were noted; the special police were interested in your escape activities and references to your being as resourceful as the devil.'

What it boiled down to was the practical certainty of facing a German criminal court on charges of attacking a guard, a highly punishable offence. There was a gleam of light on the Stygian horizon when the Kommandant made it known that his report would have to go a-begging for a few days. Intensive American air raids on Leipzig had so considerably damaged the police and Gestapo headquarters that only the most imperative charges or threats to German security were being handled immediately. More heavy raids were expected, a pressing reason why the prisoners in Annaberg Schloss were being moved without delay. The Kommandant, like so many of his kind fully aware the war was almost over and lost for the Nazis, was looking to the future with increasing agitation. But he was still an officer of the Wehrmacht and compelled to hunt with the hounds. Major Barton was a tower of strength. I do not know the unspoken faith he and the Kommandant had in each other, or the *quid pro quo* for not submitting the report until quite late on 7 September, or even the 8th, by which time I should be safely across the Baltic to Sweden.

I was supposedly under arrest and kept in one of the cellars. A statement had been taken from the injured Fritz and he had been sent on leave. The only foreseeable danger was if the wily *Feldwebel* who had arrested me and also made his statement decided to report independently to the Polizeipräsidium to stop my departing with the others. I recall Major Barton and an RAF officer sitting with me in the cellar. Barton assured me the Kommandant was reasoning things out in his own way but I found it very distressing that the *Feldwebel* was listed to escort the repatriation party to Sassnitz. I recall, too, the major saying to me, 'Dick, we're bloody delighted with those pigeons vanishing, but I'm asking you again?'

'All right, sir. I did bugger up the pigeon nest but there's only one of our men who knows how it happened.'

'Who's he?'

'Old Taffy.' I gave further details and filled him in on Doodlebug's involvement whereupon Barton asked the RAF officer to get hold of Taffy.

When the officer came back he said he had Taffy waiting upstairs and added, 'I found him with Doodlebug and when I asked him what he was talking about, the silly old bastard pointed to the top of the castle and said, "Whatever happened to all them lovely pigeons?"'

'For Christ's sake, shut him up and keep him away from Doodlebug,' I said.

The major assured me, 'We'll have him in bed soon enough without his crutches.' Thereafter, to his great puzzlement, Taffy became a very drowsy cot case; even on the ship and when carried aboard on a stretcher, he was still half asleep.

I have recollection of the *Feldwebel* being rushed to hospital with suspected appendicitis shortly before we left Annaberg Schloss but, taking no chances, I went out on crutches, wearing spectacles and balaclava, and keeping in the midst of the group. It was still an early hour when the train pulled out of Leipzig on our journey north some 350 miles to Sassnitz, a German Baltic naval base on the island of Rugen. About twenty-five miles short of Sassnitz, the train halted in a siding a dozen miles west of Peenemunde on the 'V' weapon island of Usedom. It was over a year since the RAF had carried out a massive attack on Peenemunde's V-1 and V-2 rocket base. Later I learned 570 heavy bombers had taken part and 41 had been lost.

The halt in the siding provided plenty of time to take in the scene. Viewing that virile atmosphere I clenched my teeth. I was staggered at the immense activity in the area with military personnel everywhere, armoured vehicles, screaming motor cycles and convoys of long trucks lumbering southwards. I wondered if that supposedly massive RAF attack had been anything like the *coup de grâce* it had been made out to be. In truth, it had set back Hitler's V-weapon programme by several months. It ever remained beyond my comprehension why that scientific flying-bomb and rocket base had not been blasted off the face of the map, along with everything in the vicinity. Surely it was a priority target in the strategic air offensive which merited raid after raid? The date I was there was 7 September 1944, only one day before the first V-2 rocket fell on London. More than 1,000 were to be launched in the next six months on London, and over 2,000 were to fall on the Allies' supply port of Antwerp and bases at Liège and Brussels.

At Sassnitz we boarded a waiting German ship, *Deutschland*, and sailed with little delay. It was three years to the day since I had left England. I stood at the stern gazing at the receding German mainland. Many of the men on deck were plainly overwrought. One sick soldier fell on his knees with tears streaming down his face, praying aloud. I was certainly aware I had a great deal to be thankful for. Ruthless terrorism and butchery were behind me and thanks to my Polish friends I was no longer teetering on the verge of disaster. I kept apart from the others, thinking over innumerable and vexatious drifts of the war I had survived. My eyes were riveted on the high-flying clouds, remote from the evil of squalor and misrule of humanity, when suddenly the vapour trail of a V-2 heading north-east streaked across an opening in the clouds. The observation repelled and chilled me; it might have been mocking, suggesting the play was not yet over, as if a sign in the sky was signalling 'Look out'. That brief glimpse brought the acid rising to my throat.

Some hours later, as the Swedish coast emerged dark and impalpable out of the sea, I felt a weird and glorious sensation of flying wide and free, spectre-like above the vessel. We stepped ashore at Trelleborg to freedom and wonderful Swedish hospitality. From there, we travelled by rail to Göteborg and embarked on the *Gripsholm*, a Red Cross hospital ship with Red Cross representatives aboard. Our route from the west coast of Sweden was to take us out to the North Sea and around the north of Britain to Liverpool.

We were in the Skagerrak, abreast of Kristiansand at the southern tip of German-controlled Norway, when the *Gripsholm* was stopped. Two German patrol boats raced towards us and several German naval officers came aboard and remained there; the patrol boats left as we got under way again. It is difficult to explain, but certain instincts sure and true had guided my life, and on this occasion I had a positive feeling of apprehension, an anticipatory suspicion that the visit had something to do with me. The instinct was right.

The German naval officers, the captain and Red Cross representatives disappeared together, presumably to the captain's quarters. I was standing with a small group on the top deck when a junior officer of the *Gripsholm* strode quickly towards us and spoke hurriedly in good English. 'It is very urgent, please, which is Richard Pape?'

'I am,' I replied nervously, 'what's the trouble?'

'Naval police and Gestapo will board the ship at Stavangar or before, to arrest you on some charge and take you back with them. The Red Cross people are resisting . . .'

I was trembling as I asked, 'What charge?'

'They say you are not a genuine repatriation case and you assaulted a guard.' Rapidly addressing my companions, he said the captain had sent him and he outlined a plan to convince the Germans that I was not on board. 'You will be questioned,' he stressed, 'and if you want to save your colleague you must be very alert.'

He explained that I would be hidden while the ship was searched. Reliable witnesses had to vow that I had boarded the ship at Göteborg, 'signed in' so to speak, and then slipped back along the gangway to merge with the public. One soldier was prepared to swear blind I had confessed to him I preferred the sweet, Swedish air and a freedom already won, rather than risk a watery grave if the ship struck a mine or was mistakenly torpedoed. Various of the others would swear they had not sighted me on the ship, that I had tried to borrow money, that an old, gold, kronor coin presented to one soldier by an admirer in Trelleborg was mysteriously missing. Crighton-Brown, having witnessed the potato incident, would vouch for my terrible anxiety that I might be stopped from leaving Germany. In all, the young Swede thought the story of choosing to remain in Sweden was more than likely to be believed.

I hurried below decks with him to an office with a panelled window overlooking the engine room. 'My name is Siegfried,' he said, 'I am a loyal Swede and anti-Nazi. So is my captain and we have assisted others to freedom.'

I assured him I was extremely pleased to meet him. Swiftly he pushed aside a stack of files which were on the deck beneath a corner bench. He crawled under. I watched intently as some 'rivets' were unscrewed from a bulkhead and a steel plate about two feet square was lifted away to reveal an aperture leading to a high, narrow space between the bulkhead and the outer plates of the ship. He re-emerged. 'Do you have any money?' he asked and explained, 'the German naval commander who will bring the secret police aboard can be bought. You see, he wants to be taken with his family to Götgeborg just before the war ends. Money does help him decide to exercise his authority to call of a search and allow a ship to proceed . . .'

It was Siegfried's turn to observe intently. He was

speechless as I dropped my slacks, unstrapped the artificial penis and with my index finger screwed from the hollow 3,000 Reichmarks tightly rolled. The engine room bell suddenly clanged and the ship slowed down. Siegfried recovered himself. 'Quickly, I am instructed to hand you this Mauser pistol and a clip of eight rounds. Should you be discovered, which is not likely, you will shoot yourself without hesitation. Your body will be taken ashore, of course, but the other prisoners will be allowed to continue. The captain asks me to say, if you don't shoot yourself, he will!'

'I'll spare him that,' I said, thinking of the certainty of cyanide before I would risk botching the job with a pistol. In the narrow space I heard the rivets being screwed back, and locked away in the darkness I experienced vehement anger and aggravation. What the devil had aroused suspicion that I had hoodwinked the Medical Commission? To this day, I do not know. Standing cramped with swishes, roars and thunderous crashes of ocean on the outer plates I thought, 'Oh shit, I hope they're better riveted than those plates inside!' Breathing rank engine oil with a sense of suffocation, time seemed to stop. At last I stiffened expectantly as I listened into the void and voices came muffled but unmistakably German. A short, stark interval followed before I heard the scream of the high-pitched motors of German patrol boats moving away. Then the *Gripsholm*'s engines took up the strain and noisily revved into rhythmic business-like action.

There followed the steady pace to sea. It was all over. The captain was a jocular man but of shrewd sagacity and action. I struck a bargain with him for the Mauser. He never told me how much, if any, of my money had been given the naval commander, but he offered no argument when I said 3,000 Reichmarks was a fair price for the pistol. I was not overlooking even remotest possibilities; a U-boat might surface and investigate. I signed him a paper stating I had taken over the Mauser and I undertook to declare it to

British authorities. It was a German Secret Service pistol with special markings and in due course I registered it with the London Metropolitan Police, at West East Central Station. In view of the circumstances, I was permitted to retain it. While I still have the London receipt No. B.871176, I no longer have the pistol. I kept it for twenty years until 1964 when I carried it to Port Moresby in Papua New Guinea and decided to lodge it in the custody of the police through the medium of a big Irish inspector of police. When I sought to retrieve it some years later, it was 'missing'. If it has a present-day possessor, he might be interested to know something of its unusual history . . . and even consider returning it to me! For his part, the captain of the *Gripsholm* wanted my artificial 'John Thomas' but was not interested in my price when I said, 'I'll sell it to you for your ship.'

The captain of the *Gripsholm* was not the last to covet the 'John Thomas'. Nine years later, after the publication of *Boldness Be My Friend*, the BBC arranged for my former skipper, Flt Lt Wallace Terry, and Sgt Jock Moir, the one-time flight-engineer of the Stirling bomber, to appear with me on *In Town Tonight*. The date set to go on the air was 26 September 1953. A get-together briefing was held a short time before at Broadcasting House, London. Here we met the producer of the programme, Peter Duncan. Seated at his desk after our talks had been mapped out, he laughingly brought up the subject of the manufactured organ, 'Surely,' he said, 'it was the *pièce de résistance* of all escaper aids! I certainly would have liked to have seen it.'

I shrugged and said nothing. When the three of us left the office and went off for a drink, Jock questioned me. 'What have you done with it?'

'It's in my security box at the bank.'

'Well now . . . bring it along next time and let's have a joke with Duncan.'

Nothing recalls the past so potently in respect of the 'John Thomas' as when, after the final broadcast interview, I inconspicuously drew the phoney male organ from my pocket and casually tossed it on Duncan's blotting pad. Duncan recoiled! I still see the genuine look of horror on his face. Rising, he sucked in some air, and went through certain odd motions of prodding the naked-looking 'John Thomas' at various points with a pencil. Terry, Moir and I could contain ourselves no longer and burst into laughter. 'You did express a wish to see my secret weapon,' I remarked.

No longer unnerved, Duncan joined in the fun. For all that, he picked it up gingerly as he asked, 'Could I borrow it for the weekend?'

'Not on your life,' I responded, 'it's going back in my bank.'

I don't know the final history of 'John Thomas'. While I went adventuring about the world, it resided secretly in the loft of my sister Mary's house. When she and family moved home, I rather suspect my 'faithful friend' was despatched to an ignominious end in the fireplace or dustbin. But then, the last time I had seen 'John Thomas' it had been showing incipient signs of pallor and weariness of life. No family mention was ever made of its existence in the loft or of its demise. Alas, it deserved restoration and an honoured place on exhibition in the Imperial War Museum, London. Herein must rest the obituary to the brilliance of its Polish invention and former glory.

# CHAPTER 21

# Swing of Destiny

After leaving the ship at Liverpool and placing my feet on British soil, I recall my encounters with officialdom. Taken directly to the RAF hospital at Weeton near Blackpool, the doctors were astounded to discover my urine was as clear as champagne and new X-rays of my lungs suggested a Lourdes miracle. The reports of nephritis and tuberculosis baffled them. I left them baffled, but to visiting officials of War Office departments I revealed the truth of my repatriation deception. Their orders were it was not to become general knowledge, and similarly I was not to disclose names of my underground helpers or facts of my clandestine activities. While I was interrogated about coding, changes of identity and some of my activities, and requested to submit confidential written reports, the official attitude was one of polite indifference and casual thanks. I was told events of the past would be sifted and sorted out in good time. At that juncture everything was subordinated to the Allied advancement into Europe.

As soon as possible I took myself off to London where I called upon Polish Intelligence of the Polish Provisional Government. There I was received with far greater enthusiasm. They already knew about me through their secret channels in Poland, but they questioned me closely about my activities in their country and in association with Polish patriots in underground exploits. I reaffirmed that I would honour my Polish oath never to divulge names or highly secret operations, not even to certain British War Office officials. The Polish community in Britain and the leaders of the Provisional Government were bitterly disappointed and disillusioned at the disastrous way things had evolved affecting the future freedom of their country. It was a foregone conclusion that after the Allied victory Poland would fall under ruthless communist domination. It was with pride and pleasure that I received the Polish Air Force Eagle with permission to wear it.

I was surprised and thrilled to know that the 'Kriegie Edition' book under *The Yorkshire Post* name, secretly compiled on the Baltic coast in Stalag Luft VI, had reached England in a little over five weeks, via Sweden and undisclosed means. After vetting by military authorities it had been passed over to the management of *The Yorkshire Post* and had aroused wide publicity in government and newspaper circles. The Ministers for Air and Information publicly acclaimed it and the Prime Minister, Winston Churchill, wrote: 'It is an interesting and moving record of the talent shown by these prisoners during the years of their captivity, and I am glad *The Yorkshire Post* had decided to preserve their achievement by printing a reproduction of the work.' Indeed, my old newspaper had rushed to reproduce souvenir copies for the next-of-kin of the 300 Yorkshire fliers of 'The White Rose Club' who had contributed towards its creation. Hand-printing 30,000 words had been a prodigious effort but now I had no regrets. It all seemed ludicrous and fantastic when handling the book in England, especially when I knew that only a trusted few were aware of the coded messages hidden in its contents, the real reason for its invention and completion behind barbed wire in Lithuania with the advancing Russian Army so close at hand.

With the war in its last phase, Air Ministry proposed I settle down to a safe, easy job in its publications section, but I strongly opposed anything so humdrum. I was looked upon tolerantly, as if a little unhinged, when I said I wished to fly again, if not permitted operationally then in attachment to some training station. I was firmly reminded I had deceived an international medical commission to win freedom, that it must remain secret lest embarrassment be caused to certain international organizations and disadvantage to prisoners still in captivity; medical repatriation was always a touch-and-go business with the Germans who would have liked to abandon the reciprocal system at the slightest excuse. Perhaps I would prefer – with a commission of course – to lecture aircrew on techniques of escape and evasion? I had no wish for a commission at this late stage and my warrant officer's pay was far higher than a pilot officer's. I persisted that I possessed an intense craving to fly again, if only on safe training flights. If I couldn't 'tootle' about the skies, filling in whatever monotonous gap remained before the damned war closed down, then I preferred to be discharged from the Service altogether. Air Ministry was not keen to allow me to make my own way from its jurisdiction – knowing so much of what had gone on behind the scenes in Hitler's enslaved Europe – and agreed to give consideration to my request subject to my passing the strict medical tests for aircrew.

My future did not hang in the balance for long, and on 22 November 1944, a little over two months after reuniting with Britain, I was posted for flying duties and made my way to No. 5 Air Navigation and Bombing School on the Isle of Man. But I had no idea what was in store for me. A cohesive plan of action might have been framed for my destiny for long into the future. I was now aged twenty-nine and felt a greybeard among aircrew trainees a decade my junior. I might have been a Rip Van Winkle expecting to reacquaint myself with the scenes of my last gambols with 15 Squadron, 1941, before having had my wings clipped. It was hard to accept a totally different atmosphere; everything had changed – I had changed more than I realized. In earlier times, on every flying station where I had served, I had found the spirit of aircrew, their honour and that of their flying unit, alive and glowingly expressed in the mess. It was the central point of indomitable comradeship from which we drew invisible strength and courage to face a thousand dangers. But here the mess was embarrassingly deserted most of the time, the young fliers seemed to want to lead solitary lives and if not noticeably shaky, harboured fears of the calls soon to be made on them if the war did not fizzle out quickly. They had a fair idea of the rate of losses which were still very high in Bomber Command, and they had every reason to fear the Luftwaffe's new twin-engined jet fighter, the Me262, superior to any fighter plane in the world. In the final phase of the air war enthusiasm for action was obviously diminished.

It was only after the war that figures were released of the long and bloody offensive of Bomber Command showing that 55,000 young RAF aircrew had been killed, 20,000 wounded, and 12,000 taken prisoner.

Even though I flew on safe training flights I was soon to find out that my nerves were far from what I had believed and all too often my mind was filled with memories of the drama of operations over enemy territory. A certain nervousness began to creep in and a restless feeling began to stir in me on approaching the ground to land. I began to doubt my calculations and former navigational skill, and flying became increasingly irksome and worrying. On the ground and in the air, I experienced unpredictable jitters, secretly wishing I had never been such a damned fool as to persuade the authorities to let me fly again. I became more disspirited and lonely, and missed the companionship of my comrades still on enemy soil. I felt as if some peculiar occult force was calling me back to share their vicissitudes. Information came to me from a War Office source that within a month of my leaving the Baltic Luft VI prison camp, the Germans had evacuated it before it was engulfed by the Soviets. I was lucky to have got clear, but now I was back in the world of freedom I experienced some of the most wretched and miserable periods of my life. The Isle of Man posting proved a testing time and I had enough sense to recognize that most of my unsettled state stemmed from past reactions and hazards experienced. A second crash abruptly ended my flying career. My next move was to the RAF Queen Victoria Hospital, East Grinstead, Sussex, for repairs to a disfigured face. I came under the care of the renowned plastic surgeon, Sir Archibald McIndoe, and also a member of the oddest club in the world. It was 'The Guinea-Pig Club', started as a joke after the Battle of Britain. In that hospital I lived and mixed for almost a year with fliers who had received ghastly burns, injuries and facial disfigurements. German cannon shell, blazing petrol and crashed aircraft had wrought havoc with skin, flesh and bone. I was more fortunate than most, having incurred a faceful of gashes and the loss of part of my upper lip, luckily having narrowly missed parting with an eye. Sir Archibald gave me a lip graft and did some brilliant sculpture on the rest of my face.

I distinctly recall a badly burned and disfigured patient cheerfully approaching me one day. 'Hello, Richard.' I gazed at him, perplexed. 'Who are you?' 'I'm Henry Standen,' he said. I hope I did not betray my shock as he revealed he was the nephew of the two ladies of Chiswick House, Huntingdon, who showed such kindness to fliers of 15 Squadron. In 1941 when I gratefully knew their hospitality, their handsome nephew was still a schoolboy, listening avidly to our tales of flying and living for the day when he might join the RAF. He achieved his ambition but, alas, he crashed in a Hampden bomber while preparing to take off for a raid over France. Henry was the only survivor and, badly burned, he was to undergo over fifty operations to have his nose, forehead, lips, eyelids and hands rebuilt. It was said of Sir Archibald McIndoe that he had the gift in his hands which could smooth out the handiwork of God and repair the ravages of the devil. He certainly possessed a rich understanding of humanity and a firm friendship developed between us. He was to become a milestone in my life, a premise, a single known factor for mysteriously solving many equations of the years ahead. He took an extraordinary interest in my wartime exploits and urged me to give myself purpose and relate as far as possible the histories and fates of the courageous people who had helped me in Holland and elsewhere, insisting I tell my personal tale of war behind the swastika.

After discharge from the plastic surgery hospital and the RAF, I returned to *The Yorkshire Post* and its honourable calling, but I was far from being in harmony with myself. Returning to a decorous civilian role seemed a savage irony, after a six-year interruption in my life because of the evil catastrophe of war. When I retrod the newspaper's corridors I had loved and known so well, I might have been nervously stepping on mines. Staff members who had known me as an ambitious young man attuned to the excitement and adventurousness of newspaper life were the warmest, most understanding people one could wish to find. I could not settle down and pity was something that seriously jarred whatever composure was left in me. I felt warped and changed in the maze of immediate post-war thinking, and there seemed nothing left but regret. Regrets for all the murdering and killings I had known personally, the loss of so many fine friends, and regrets for my pre-war life. I seemed to have been robbed of something valuable which could never be relived or replaced. Ambitions and aspirations meant nothing; I felt beaten and dejected.

A deep gnawing was developing to escape from everything – newspaper attachments, family, friends, home town and country. I had to find some sense somewhere, away from war-torn Europe, for my meaningless existence, and I was stirred to follow the route taken by the former Commander-in-Chief of Bomber Command, Sir Arthur Harris. After the end of hostilities, 'Bomber' Harris was denied the public honour which his achievements in helping to bring Nazi Germany to its knees would normally have merited. He left

Britain to settle in South Africa. It was far from light-heartedly that I resigned from *The Yorkshire Post* only months after rejoining it.

In 1947 there was an enormous shortage of sea berths available, and air travel was out of the question. It came to my attention in a roundabout way that a small, 2,000-ton ship, forty years old, Greek-owned and flying the Panamanian flag, was anchored in Marseilles and preparing to sail for South Africa. This cockroach-infested vessel had been stopped by the British Navy from running Jewish refugees across the Mediterranean to Palestine, at exorbitant prices. I crossed France and obtained a berth on the SS *Cairo*, still a racket ship as it turned out, cramming aboard Indians at Aden and Mombasa for smuggling into South Africa. It was a memorably uncomfortable trip, but at least it carried me to Beira on the Mozambique coast. From there I made my way to Southern Rhodesia (Zimbabwe) and then to Johannesburg. Strangely, timed exactly with my arrival, the Argus South African newspapers carried the stop press announcement that I had been awarded the Military Medal for wartime services. It was the first I knew of it. I secured a position on the staff of the Argus group's *Johannesburg Star* newspaper and a few months later I was honoured to receive the British decoration from the Governor-General of South Africa at an investiture in Cape Town. The venerable states-man General Smuts was present, as also was 'Bomber' Harris.

I was wholly in tune with modern, sun-drenched South Africa with its dramatic scenery and incredible variety of living things. My new land and creative newspaper work did not lack compulsion and I soon became alive again, imbued with an inspired sense of liberation and visions of the future, remote from the hideous apparatus of warfare I had so intimately known, and a Europe full of confusions, restrictions and the perils of change. A year passed quickly after joining the *Johannesburg Star* and my new way of life was immensely full, absorbing and pleasant. I was again a keen golfer and spent a great deal of leisure time in the saddle, horse-riding and training for show-jumping. I was back on course with all progressing well.

I corresponded regularly with my old *Yorkshire Post* chosen trio, Edward Tillett, Lilian Rowe and Alfred Willcox. Like Sir Archibald McIndoe who kept in touch with my progress, these more-than-friends constantly urged me to write my wartime story before the actualities of war drew farther and farther away. They were insistent I put on record, as far as truthfully possible and permissible, facts about the unselfishness and loyalty of people who had suffered and died as a result of aiding me. It was true, certain authentic information had come to light about my Dutch helpers, but I lacked any enthusiasm to make a start. I was living in a small flat overlooking a noisy, busy street, close to my newspaper office. The task of serious book-writing was well-nigh out of the question in such circumstances and I used this as an excuse. With so much variety and activity in everyday life and outdoor pursuits, I had little inclination towards revealing a slab of my wartime life, facts stark and disturbing which I considered best untold. Neither was I inspired by any possible literary reward, fame or glory.

Fate threw double sixes in my favour for a reversal of decision when I met Nicholas Monsarrat who was earning his living working for the British Information Office in Johannesburg. We met on occasions at the small Hotel Waverley for a drink or two after business hours, and I learned he was devoting practically all his spare time to writing a novel, destined to be named *The Cruel Sea* and become a world bestseller. Monsarrat was a committed writer bursting with new ideas, new dimensions and insights. We discussed our respective wartime experiences – his in the Royal Navy – and I told him of the pressures from honoured friends to narrate my story, and I would doubtless make a start sometime to placate their urgings. Monsarrat pressed me to begin work on a manuscript as a first priority.

He strenuously advised me to cut adrift from easy pleasures, outdoor activities and time-wasting social rounds until I had finished what he considered my unusually thrilling story. He brought me round to his line of thinking to meet the challenge, and of first importance was to find a writing retreat, if possible where meals were laid on to free myself of domestic demands. I heeded Monsarrat's advice.

A splendid mentor, Alfred Billett, much older than myself, wholeheartedly agreed that I owed it to others to make a start on the book. He introduced me to his close friend, the Secretary of the Johannesburg YMCA. At thirty-two I was not exactly a young man but regulations would be waived to encourage writing after office hours with full freedom. I was allocated a small, secluded room containing bed and wardrobe, and for a modest inclusive charge could take all meals in the communal dining-room. I well recall the desk I improvised below the room's small window by standing two orange boxes upright and bridging them with a fair-sized board. The well-disposed Secretary gave me a special concession to work in the spacious board room at nights where the sound of my typewriter could not disturb others. I plunged into construction of the first draft of the manuscript which demanded patience and self-discipline, especially when tempted to play a round of golf or saddle up my horse at the stables for a long, healthy canter across the highveldt. But I stuck to my guns and routine application after finishing the day's work at the *Star*, and throughout the weekends. Gradually the task became more absorbing as I unravelled my tale. The mixed company of newspaper and sporting friends who had frequently dropped in to see me at the flat, invariably leading off to the nearby pub, fell away and occasioned no distractions. I was particularly pleased that females were not permitted on the premises. I soon settled into the YMCA milieu and found the other boarders refreshing, comradely and respectful of my privacy. I had every reason to return thanks to the high gods for directing me to an ideal place of seclusion for tranquil thinking and writing.

The view from my window offered an enclosed expanse of red tin roofing, and I was intrigued to learn that the famous author, Edgar Wallace, had also lived in a humble room somewhere below that red roofing when he wrote his first book, *The Four Just Men*. Like Monsarrat and myself, he had a war background, having served with the British Army in the Boer War. After discharge in Britain he returned to South Africa where he was working on Johannesburg's morning newspaper, *The Rand Daily Mail*, when he turned all his spare time to book-writing. It was curious the three of us finding our footing in authorship in very similar circumstances in Johannesburg, although at the time I was not a dedicated writer but essentially fulfilling pressing requests to 'Get on with it', and honouring obligations to a few valued friends.

On infrequent occasions I had to break away from YMCA isolation to attend functions directly connected with newspaper business. One such unavoidable commitment took me to a cocktail party at the home of a Countess Ditcham. There I was introduced to a tallish, attractive woman around my own age with a pleasantly modulated voice. Conversation passed off lightly in an orderly procession of thought, and I learned that Miss Nan Forder was employed in a medical capacity by a foremost gold-mining corporation. She had a natural air of pride and grace and I found something intriguing about her. My eyes followed her around the room as she moved from group to group and it was obvious she was very popular.

Since Blondie's tragic death in 1941, I had known no further awakening of romantic love. I was in my thirties, a staunch bachelor, and all too well aware of misguided judgements in the love game, mismatched wartime marriages and ex-prisoners of war swept off their feet by a return to freedom, drink and sex. Too many ex-RAF former acquaintances had rushed into ill-considered wedlock, with many still treading the path to the divorce court. Before taking my leave of the gathering I was again brought face to face with the vivacious Nan Forder, and had no desire to wrench myself away. We chatted amiably, and almost without thinking, an impulsive desire took possession of me to suggest diffidently that she may care to dine with me one evening. She smilingly agreed and thereafter we met frequently until the inevitable happened. I fell in love, no longer dwelling on phantom memories of the WAAF to whom I had been engaged, or a marriage that might have been. Allegiance to independence and a lonely existence seemed to be over, and it came as a happy surprise to mutual friends when we announced we were engaged and soon to marry. This sudden and dramatic turn of events seriously interfered with the book's progress. The manuscript was not finished by a long way, and drafts assembled required rewriting and polishing. Leaving the YMCA I vouched that as soon as possible I would resume work on the project and bring it to final shape.

Nan and I moved into a charming apartment, but the marriage was not destined to survive. After a year it showed signs of withering. The manuscript had been relegated to an old tin trunk where it might have died an unknown death. Not getting down to finishing the narration did weigh on my mind for a time but as months slipped by, belief that it would ever be completed became a fast vanishing hope. Nan and I were two people of professional outlook, long established in determined independence. Accustomed to leading competitive lives, it seemed we were mis-mated, with interests too disparate to make for compatibility. I was vigorously occupied with newspaper assignments and making quite a lot of money in my spare time creating advertising campaigns and handling public relations accounts privately. Indeed, I was remarkably well on my way towards eventually branching out fully into my own business. My devotion to golf was stronger than ever and I spent far too much time out of doors and away from my wife. Tensions grew between us and we decided to separate for a time; after a short break we realized we were irreconcilable and painfully aware the marriage would not last. Nan saw her lawyer for a divorce and I saw mine. Any marriage break-up is an emotional ordeal and returning to bachelor status was a miserable business.

Following hard upon this, in mid-1952 my sister Mary cabled from England that our mother was gravely ill. Given six months' leave from the *Star*, I flew to Britain with all haste but sadly my mother died just a few hours before I reached her bedside. Her death was a disturbing blow, but upon looking back on that urgent flight to England, I am reminded that one can never tell whether bad luck or misfortune may not turn out well in the end, as if in the long term preordained. I was able to be reunited with my old *Yorkshire Post* trio and Sir Archibald McIndoe, and all were a source of help and subtle inspiration. In so many terms I was told to stop wringing my hands and put them to productive use and resume work on the long-awaited and neglected wartime story. I returned to Johannesburg and my job, a revitalized man, having come to terms with myself. The manuscript was retrieved from the tin trunk, again to receive considered attention combined with speed. Completed, it was dispatched forthwith to Sir Archibald who later quipped that when it arrived he had to pay a postage charge of eight shillings and fourpence – an oversight on my part. He promptly found me a literary agent who placed the manuscript with a London publisher. Little did I realize when I dispatched the finished book that it was to prove the luckiest day of my life. The publisher, the late Paul Elek, was ecstatic over my story and hastened to get it into print – Nicholas Monsarrat's *The Cruel Sea* was in print and climbing the bestseller list. Monsarrat had ever been confident that my book would make the grade and before he had left for London he had advised me not to hibernate in Johannesburg, if success surrounded me, in a little nest of ego like a special cat to be stroked while the glory lasted, but to get moving when I would see everything, particularly my failed marriage, in a different light. He too had suffered divorce.

The title I had given my book was *Freedom Wasn't Cheap* but Paul Elek failed to be impressed and urged me to think of something more striking. I racked my brains and sent off various titles but he was not satisfied. I was at a loss. I called on a poet friend, Reginald Youngman, hoping he might come up with magic words. He was occupied on something when I arrived and he asked me to sit down for a moment. I flopped into a chair in his lounge, facing a large glass bowl with a goldfish aimlessly going round in circles. Propped up beside the bowl was a card on which was printed, 'Words, like glass, obscure what they do not make clear.' Reggie had cards like this all over the place but I stared at it glumly, its message not at all cheering. Then luck came to my aid. I gazed at the goldfish in its glass bowl, then my sight shifted just beyond to fix upon a volume of the 'Complete Works of William Shakespeare'. I picked it up, flicked open the pages and paused at the play, *Cymbeline*. My eyes alighted upon the words:

> Boldness be my friend!
> Arm me, audacity, from head to foot!
> Or, like the Parthian, I shall flying fight.

The title of my book stood out like illuminated lettering. I could have kissed that fish! I departed hastily and wrote immediately to Elek. He was jubilant. Many a time I have been complimented on the apt and arresting title, and have readily confessed that the credit lies with the illustrious bard. Indeed, in that one quotation, I had the title for my second book, *Arm Me Audacity*.

# Conclusion

I left South Africa after six years in that country for London, at the age of thirty-seven, a divorced man with fame and riches accumulating. I was honoured at a distinguished reception at the Royal Air Force Club, Piccadilly, where I was received by Lord Tedder and Sir Archibald McIndoe. A surprising number of military, Air Force and other top brass were present, and famous personages such as Sir Frank Whittle, the jet inventor, Neville Duke, holder of the world speed record, and Sir Edmund Hillary, conqueror of Everest. I kept my head, gave a restrained speech and set myself to acclimatizing to sudden trumpets of glory. The dramatic success of *Boldness Be My Friend* rapidly remodelled the whole of my life and means of living. The book was serialized in newspapers and magazines at home and overseas, dramatized in serial form by the British Broadcasting Corporation, and radio rights sold abroad. Seven foreign translations followed and a highly delighted publisher thrust me into an extended lecture tour around Britain. I found eminent people, such as the Duke of Hamilton in Edinburgh, chairing public gatherings I addressed. I travelled almost without ceasing and when the tour came to an end I was exhausted.

The Netherlands Press accorded the book tremendous publicity and Dutch people clamoured for me to visit Holland. I crossed to Amsterdam and returned to the village of Hengelo, close to where the Stirling had crashed, and where Jock Moir and I had been hidden on the farm of Bernard Besselink, until the village schoolmaster, Jan Agterkamp, had organized our transfer into the Dutch underground movement proper. Both men had been executed. I unveiled a bronze plaque engraved in Dutch to the memory of these courageous patriots. I met other members of the 1941 underground group with whom I had lived, survivors from concentration camps. Mona and 'Billy' Leonhardt had suffered greatly but she proudly showed me a certificate from President Eisenhower expressing the gratitude of the American people for gallant service in assisting the escape of Allied soldiers and airmen from the enemy. A similar certificate had been sent to her from Lord Tedder. I was to be presented with a Royal Netherlands decoration, 'De Erkentelijkheidsmedaille', for honour and bravery, and I was proud to receive it in the Hall of Knights at The Hague.

It was a sad but memorable visit. I was also entrusted to deliver to Sir Winston Churchill the silver teaspoons, a gift thirteen years late. This was the gift which Jan Agterkamp had asked me to hand into his safe-keeping so as not to identify Jock and myself in any way with the town of Steenderen should we be captured. I duly delivered the gift to No. 10 Downing Street with a letter from the Burgomaster of Steenderen.

I took up residence in a small suite at the RAF Pathfinders' Club, off Berkeley Square, to be whisked off on more lecture tours. I became weary of having to talk about myself, of being publicized and fêted as a hero. Eating, drinking and ostentation became a bore. I missed the outdoor physical activities I had known in South Africa. I began to lack zest and enthusiasm and wanted to get clear of all obligations. In short, I was damned fed up with being a celebrated author. Existence was becoming shadowy and false. Fan-mail poured in from around the world, including many letters from hero-worshipping females with anything but subtle romantic approaches. Photographs of glamorous and not so exciting females arrived on my desk, and basically it seemed the only interest they had in me was sex and to tuck me away in bed. I regretted a joking answer I gave to a question put to me by a reporter as to what I eventually intended to do. I said I thought I would find a girl who could cook a good Yorkshire pudding, and settle down and have fifteen children. My remarks were printed. Letters arrived from around England stressing their authors' culinary abilities. One writer even sent a sample. It consisted of a cold Yorkshire pudding, a jar of jelly-gravy – and instructions how to heat the blasted mixture.

I had settled in London about six months when I was pressured to make a broadcast to the Polish nation from the London-controlled Radio Free Europe, an American propaganda network. In my talk, which I was coached phonetically to deliver in Polish, I made mention of Mieteck who had played such a vital role in my first escape, and that all the information I could obtain from official sources was that he had escaped to Turkey where he had died of tuberculosis. I had no idea then that he had become a leader of a Polish Intelligence unit on the Polish–Ukraine border, also supplying Russian Intelligence with valuable information. That broadcast lured me into a dangerous post-war adventure. Foreign agents contacted me in London to say all broadcasts to countries behind the Iron Curtain were monitored, also my book had been carefully probed by Soviet security. In brief, I was staggered to be told that Mieteck was alive and that his imprisonment in Russia had been a great mistake. I was informed that if I visited Vienna and from there crossed into the Soviet Occupation Zone, a meeting with the vanished British diplomat, Donald Maclean, was promised, and I would also be able to meet Mieteck whose release was assured.

Driving a powerful British car, I arrived in Vienna which was still under occupation supervised by a four-power authority, the UK, USA, France and Russia. I received accreditation papers and passed into the Soviet Zone, heading for Wiener Neustadt, less than fifteen miles from the Iron Curtain frontier of Hungary. My safe return had been guaranteed, but at the meeting place there was no Mieteck or Maclean, only NKVD agents in Mercedes cars. By now I was convinced that this was a kidnap attempt, a trap and, pretending to follow, I suddenly swung my car round and raced through the winding Austrian mountain passes. It was a ninety-mph chase, until I reached the safety of the British Zone of Austria. The Soviet NKVD crashed. What was intended as a confidential mission unfortunately made headlines. The London *Evening News* carried across its front page, 'Bomber Command Hero in Iron Curtain Riddle'. *The People* newspaper, under a front-page heading, printed, 'Air Hero in Soviet Kidnap Drama'. The episode was then put under security clamps and back in Britain it was considered discreet that I disappear from the scene for a time. Frightening as the episode had been, I was only too relieved that headlines were not declaring my mysterious disappearance in Austria, or that the Soviets were acclaiming me as an enlightened defector joining British colleagues Maclean and Burgess! I readily agreed to leave London and sailed immediately on the *Rangitane* on a round trip to New Zealand where happily I met Winston Yeatman again. Returning to London, I settled down in the Pathfinders' Club and wrote my first novel, *Arm Me Audacity*, basing it in part on that Soviet adventure.

Summing up my situation, and surveying my whole new way of life, I decided to avoid pressures from the media and other sources seeking to probe for more about my life in Hitler's Europe. I was also aware of the feasibility that under stress of drink or mental disregard I might be inveigled into letting my tongue slip. With forethought, or taking the best means at my command – money earned from royalties – I resolved to escape from it all, seeking freedom by travelling and accepting new adventures or whatever came along. Since as long as I could remember, far back into boyhood, I had been imbued with an insatiable appetite for challenging adventure. Now I had the means and opportunity to give full rein to my inclinations for global movement, to convert dreams into reality and make the vast, wonderful world my oyster. At this stage I was presented with an opportunity to undertake a marathon drive, from a thousand miles north of the Arctic Circle, in Norway, then heading at speed through Europe to Gibraltar. Crossing the Mediterranean, I would proceed over the entire length of the African continent to Cape Town, taking in a Sahara crossing and slogging my way through the Congo. If I fulfilled this fast endurance drive I would become the first man to place a car on the 1,000-foot-high cliffs on the North Wall of Europe, overlooking the Arctic Ocean, and the first to drive from there to Cape Town. It would be a Cape Cold to Cape Hot drive, providing all the excitement and challenge dear to my heart. This drive (in a six-cylinder Austin A90 Westminster) through twenty-one countries, covering 17,500 miles, was achieved, but not without narrowly missing losing my life on four occasions. Great publicity resulted for British cars, and this first long-distance drive was the forerunner of others.

In a short time I crossed to America and then on to Canada to attempt a record for Rootes Motors and test the reliability of British cars in traversing the Alaska Highway, the most fearsome highway on the North American continent. This drive of 5,000 miles in four and a half days non-stop, from Vancouver to Fairbanks in Alaska and back, was achieved and another record created, in one of the most savage, romantic and outlandish parts of the world. It gave a tremendous boost to British car sales on the North American continent, capturing public imagination which echoed nationally and internationally. The aftermath of this fast drive led me to a second marriage, ten years after the first. The Alaska Highway accomplishment and the interest aroused in international motoring circles expedited an almost immediate follow-on drive planned across Canada, from Vancouver to Toronto, involving crossing the mighty Rockies, on a rough, newly engineered road. If achieved, the British car would be the first across in 1958.

It seemed driving adventures were now in my blood and I had become addicted to a semi-nomadic life. The story of the sensational British car and its achievements had gone around America and overseas in a whirl of publicity. Rootes Motors in London suggested taking a female co-driver on the Trans-Canada adventure as an ambassadress – it would be a tremendous promotional platform and lend glamour to the record bid. At first I flatly refused to have a female co-driver on such a strenuous and dangerous project, but finally I agreed and 'Billie' Brickman now came to the forefront of events in my life. She was a New Zealander, then living in Canada, trained in radio broadcasting and public relations, but above all a gifted, courageous driver and a woman of adventurous make-up. She handled a car with precision and speed, and I was impressed by her strong self-control, stamina and determination. In her early thirties, Billie, like myself a divorcee, was dark, slender and distinctively attractive.

The small, four-cylinder British Hillman Minx, 'The Peanut' as the Americans and Canadians called it, showed on its mileage clock from Vancouver to Toronto 3,095 miles, for a driving time of fifty-five hours, an average speed of 56.27 mph. Crossing the Rockies on a rib-cracking road was demanding, convincing proof of Billie's quality as a driver, and reliability of the car which won widespread praise. We were persuaded to continue the drive around the forty-eight states of America, and we raced onwards to Miami and westwards towards the Badlands, the great desert regions of Texas,

New Mexico and Arizona, and finally up the West Coast back to Vancouver, at an average 585 miles a day. It certainly resulted in great media coverage and impetus to British car exports which were still trying to recoup after the war. Within a week of returning to Vancouver, Billie and I were compelled to part, she to return to New Zealand while I flew back to Britain to fulfil commitments and write a further book. Eight months later I went out to New Zealand where Billie and I were married in August 1958. The honeymoon was short and sweet, for another adventure was imminent which could not be put aside. Four months after marriage I sailed as British observer–writer with the USA Operation Deepfreeze IV which was an on-going part of the US scientific participation in Antarctica during the International Geophysical Year which began on 1 July 1957. I was accredited to this expedition by the US Navy authorities, with the approval of Rear Admiral George J. Dufek, Commander US Naval Support Force, Antarctica. Dufek held the reputation of being one of the world's top-flight cold weather experts and, doubtless to Soviet chagrin, had been the first man since Britain's immortal Captain Scott and his companions in 1912 to set foot at the South Pole. Dufek had flown there in a jet-assisted take-off plane fitted with skis and had planted his country's flag to establish a permanent US base at the South Pole. Admiral Dufek made it possible for me to visit the huts, now historic shrines, used by the famous expeditions of Scott and Shackleton in the early part of this century – the 'heroic age' of Antarctic exploration.

Billie and I returned to London in due course to settle down. She insisted I resumed serious book-writing as she had no wish to become part of an adventure-packed marriage. However, the marriage was short-lived and ended in divorce, for my nomadic days were not over. I was approached by an important public relations organization in

London, confidentially operating under the aegis of the British Colonial Office. Full independence of Malta from British control was still four years in the future but already there was growing concern on this 'George Cross'* island over proposed British Naval reorganization and economies which it was felt would seriously affect employment in Malta, its economy and political texture. It was proposed to accelerate tourism, turning the island into a fully fledged holiday centre and Mediterranean tourist Mecca. I undertook to become editor and produce a tourist newspaper, the *Malta Sun*, for worldwide circulation among tourist bodies and markets. Billie and I gradually drifted farther and farther apart, discord between us presented itself with ever-increasing frequency. Billie may have been a wonderful co-driver, but married existence in London was driving me up the wall. So there arrived another miserable parting which was to lead to permanent separation and divorce. Once more I returned to solitary living after relinquishing the successfully initiated Malta assignment, and strove to settle down to serious literary work again. I was low-spirited and restless and became ill. What lay before me now? I could not shut my eyes to the fact that I was advancing in years, still rootless and now virtually drained of purpose. I felt completely baffled, destitute of ideas of what to do or where to turn. Admittedly I was equipped with a capacious knowledge of the world, and my travels had brought me into contact with the widest commonality of people. My love of the out-of-doors world with its pageant of nature and freedom suggested leaving Britain for a land which might open out for me new and clear horizons. But where? To return to South Africa, Canada, New Zealand or America

* The highest British award for civilians, conferred on Malta for the heroism of its people under siege from German attack in the Second World War.

would be returning to the past; it seemed Australia might be the answer. I found it impossible to continue book-writing, and abandoned it. I had lived through some tremendous events, risked my life many times over, and I realized that time and circumstances had favoured me in an extraordinary way. I was now forty-seven, with ten published books behind me, which somehow I had managed to write in between my varied travels – for material for factual and fictional books had come to me of its own bidding in the strangest places and in the most unexpected circumstances. It seemed a bitter thing to surrender a literary career and the hope of further achievement, but I had to attune to a new philosophy and hopefully build a new life out of the wreckage. Success had brought me fame, money, good living, pride, flattery, women. My health was worsening and a warning sense sounded an alarm. In my state of mind, I held a strong conviction that literary popularity and money were holding me captive and I would never find sense or real truth in life until I got rid of them, everything, and just cleared out. I was almost at the end of my tether, and in sheer despair I acted decisively and irrevocably. I disposed of a large sum of accumulated royalties and part of the inheritance from my mother to charitable causes. The first edition of *Boldness Be My Friend* had propelled me into a life of nomadic *Wanderlust* and authorship, but now the money I had earned seemed tainted. I had developed a hatred towards my success, an odd belief that there was something malevolent about my first literary effort, about having made money out of describing the sufferings of others. I was completely perplexed, drinking far too heavily, and my will was loosening to make any effort to depart for anywhere. My adventurous roaming days were over but they had given me many memories and much food for thought. My life had been a broad experience of extremes. Years of continuous world-wide travelling, not of a uniform or passive kind, had revealed incredible extremes of geography, nations, people and natural phenomena. The globe's personality I had found gentle, and savage, and like human nature also limitless of knowledge, mystery and magnificence. I did not regret my encounters between outermost terminals, and I knew that power, sequence and the self-expression of all creation stem from extremes. My years of vagabondage had been maintained with the spirit of exploration, with an open, questioning, curious and adventurous mind, a vital foundation in the art of living and writing. I had no regrets. From the first appearance of *Boldness Be My Friend*, nothing on earth had persuaded me to reveal secret facts and undercover details of the life I had endured in Occupied Europe. My first wife and my second knew about my wartime activities only in what had been revealed in that book. Neither of them had the slightest inkling of the psychological reactions and inhibitions which had plagued me since the firing squad episode, that pitting myself against dangers and surviving them after the war had given me an indefinable sense of security and temporary peace.

Little did I realize it when filled with misgivings that the wheel of chance was revolving favourably towards me, and the waves of destiny again actively planning to set me down on the shores of one of the most primitive Stone Age lands in the world, to make new friends and face up to new challenges. I look back on the correlation of events and the causes influencing my life in the years which then lay ahead and will never find a logical answer. It was by chance at this stage that I came into the orbit of Group Captain Leonard Cheshire, VC, DSO, DFC, who had flown in Bomber Command and had read *Boldness Be My Friend* long before I met him. I too had been deeply impressed by what I had learned of Cheshire and his post-war efforts for the relief of suffering. There is no need for me to expound at length upon Cheshire's wonderful work, so nobly complemented by his wife, Sue Ryder. Just briefly, Cheshire was an outstanding RAF flier and made effective contribution to winning the war by his low-level, point-blank bombing of immense strategical consequence. He also flew as British observer on the aircraft carrying the atom bomb to Nagasaki. Witnessing the horrifying fireball in the sky, and man's new manifestation of physical and human destruction, proved a supreme emotional ordeal. As a result of his war experiences, Cheshire embarked on a mission for the relief of suffering and the creation of peace consciousness. In the face of every kind of difficulty and discouragement, he managed to establish a world-wide network of Cheshire Homes for the incurably sick.

Meeting Cheshire and Sue Ryder at their home, I told them I was intending to head for Australia. This was to change my life radically. He immediately showed interest and suggested I might be able to lend a hand to stimulate interest in his project for a home he wished to establish for handicapped native children in Port Moresby, Papua New Guinea. I discovered it was a United Nations Trust Territory administered by Australia and lying just south of the equator and about 100 miles from the northernmost tip of the Australian continent. Cheshire had explored the feasibility for such a home but had met with little encouragement. I agreed to do what I could, and was delighted to align myself with his cause. I stopped solitary drinking and introverted thinking, feeling that the whole of my mental range had been elevated and, by some mysterious propulsion, my old search for adventure reactivated. I was not to know I was heading towards my last close shave with death in the not distant future in the wild Gulf District, close to the West Irian border, in the most desolate, primitive region of Papua New Guinea. Yet, paradoxically, I was also adventuring towards my greatest contentment and fulfilment in life.

Through Cheshire's contacts and my decision to aid his cause, I obtained a position on arrival in Australia as Senior Publications Officer with the Department of Information, Port Moresby, and a two-year contract at a good salary. I spent a final week in Sydney attending the Australian School of Pacific Administration for introductory lectures on the hot, strange and savage conditions in the land to which a group of us newest recruits was going. We were a mixed lot of professional, technical and administrative people. There I met Helen Prouting. She was a lawyer, unmarried and eight years younger than myself. She struck me as a most attractive and agreeable person. Helen was seconded from the Commonwealth Crown Solicitor's Office in Sydney for two years with the Department of Law in Port Moresby. She had volunteered for a limited stint to avoid the rut of things, and because there was an appealing admixture of adventure in her make-up. I found something imaginative and realistic in her outlook which I had rarely met in women. Coupled to an acute intelligence and charm, she had the best kind of humour and a sound sense of proportion.

On arrival in Port Moresby Helen was placed with the Public Solicitor's Office where apparently every one of the two million native population was a potential client. I commenced my publications job, and joined the Cheshire Home steering committee. Within two weeks of arrival I was sent on an acclimatization trip to the Gulf of Papua to acquire some knowledge of the economic, social and political development through which the Australian Government was aiming to bring a fragmented country to eventual unity and self-government. I found myself in a wild area deriving most of its income from crocodile shooting and supposedly only a decade removed from age-old traditions of head-hunting, head-shrinking and cannibalism. The native people who lived in small, isolated villages were predominantly primitive hunters still virtually untouched by modern development. Not far from where I was, in fact just over the West Irian border at Merauke, Michael Rockefeller had swum ashore three years earlier from a drifting raft. It was a depressing region of mangrove and sago swamps and the 25-year-old son of Nelson Rockefeller, multi-millionaire Governor of New York, had disappeared among the fierce Agat tribesmen. Officials were certain from information brought by natives, and with which I was acquainted, that young Rockefeller had reached the shore only to be murdered, and cooked with sago for a cannibal feast.

At a village called Moveave I slightly cut my elbow and within hours I had lost consciousness with a temperature of 104 degrees. I had been struck down by one of the virulent and strange viruses existing in the wild Gulf District. A New Zealander, Bill Barclay, and an Australian companion, Ken Graham, paddled me in a hollowed-out canoe along the Tauri River to a small mission station, run by an Australian nun, Sister Joseph Mary. I was unconscious and delirious for two days and completely exhausted her stock of drugs. A message was eventually got through by native runner to the District Commissioner, and a specially chartered Cessna aircraft was flown to the mission station from Port Moresby. I was taken back to the General Hospital and it was quite a time before my mind cleared. It seemed all things were coming to an end, the isolation, the nothingness of all things. The Devil of Challenge, it seemed, had at last won the vendetta. Reuters News Agency had circulated the story around the world, and the London *Daily Express* flew a journalist to the mission outpost for the story and photographs. This newspaper published a half-page illustration under the heading, 'The Nun who carries a Gun', showing Sister Joseph Mary in white habit, sitting with her rifle at the ready in the prow of a boat with two young

Papuan nurses, using their practised native eye to scan the river banks for the crocodile monsters.

I had cheated death again. Helen came to see me in hospital and I knew without reservation I had found my soul companion, the desired pacifying spirit for my restless roaming nature. Helen and I were married by the District Commissioner in Port Moresby, in some 'Saunders of the River' tradition, in 1966, with a jungle of problems behind me. It was certainly third time lucky, and I settled down to a domestic happiness which I had never known, always enlivened and comforted by Helen's presence. Looking back, it seems my path in life as a result of *Boldness Be My Friend*, and after meeting Leonard Cheshire, had taken a complete new turning. Both had been instrumental in leading me towards Helen. Little more remains to be said apart from the fact that I confided in her fully and she overcame my resistance to book-writing. The manuscript of this present autobiography would many times have been cast into an old tin trunk, like my first manuscript in Johannesburg, but for Helen's encouragement and reasonableness. She revived flagging spirits, and step by step we have persevered. Such are the blessings of an incomparable wife. Without her life would lose much of its meaning and worth.

At the conclusion of our two-year contracts, we did not quit the Territory but, with intermittent holidays in cooler climates, we remained in Papua New Guinea for over nine years. A new Cheshire Home was established for sick and handicapped native children, and in this work Helen helped me immeasurably. Our professional careers prospered. Helen became Deputy Public Solicitor for the Territory while I became Principal Publications Officer for the Department of Information. Our combined work was involved with many intriguing phases in the evolution towards integrated independence of the fragmented indigenous communities in that forbidding and fascinating land. Together we helped in some measure a backward people in their movement towards national identity and ordered advancement. A month after the country achieved self-government on 1 December 1973, we disentangled ourselves from our professional commitments.

Finally, I have many times been asked, if I had the chance to live my life over again would I want to change it? My answer is undubitably no; nonetheless, I very much doubt if I would be blessed with the same incredible luck and opportunities a second time round. And I have frequently been asked, would I again risk my neck as I did during three years in Hitler's Occupied Europe, or resist in the same way if the freedom of Britain and democracy were again threatened by dictatorship? I reply unreservedly, yes! A further question levelled at me is, what is my most ardent wish in today's world of political and ideological unrest, rivalries, despotism and threat? I unhesitatingly state, the liberation of gallant Poland from its bondage and a true return to national independence and freedom. The last note on which to end, is my reply to innumerable enquiries as to my credo on fear and mastery of fear, if not the absence of fear. I quote Sir Winston Churchill: 'Courage is the first of human qualities because it is the quality which guarantees all others . . .'

So ends this book.

# APPENDIX A
# Foreword to the First Edition

I doubt whether those of us who have never had the experience of being a prisoner of war can ever even begin really to understand or appreciate the fantastic other world of the Prison Camp, the Escaping Clubs, the 'Underground'. Yet without some appreciation of that other side, our picture of the war would be dangerously incomplete. Here in this book is the story of three years in that other world; three years in the life of a Royal Air Force Warrant Officer Navigator; a story packed with far more real life thrills than any novelist packed into a best seller thriller.

But this blunt narrative is no mere adventure story. There was little glamour or romance in that other world. Here, through the eyes of this Bomber Command Warrant Officer, we see some of the wonderful heights to which human nature can attain and some of the appalling depths to which it can sink when the gloves are off. We who have not suffered the agonies of occupation do well to be reminded – as we are again and again in this book – of the shining courage and utter unselfishness with which men and women in the occupied countries risked, and only too often sacrificed, their lives to help our men to escape. Equally it is well to be reminded, as we are here reminded with almost brutal frankness, of the purgatory of boredom, squalor and indecency and the hell of Gestapo bestiality and sadism through which our prisoners and many of their helpers passed. Let us not forget the scars those years have left on individuals and on peoples; let us not forget the depths to which an evil creed can lead.

I read this book under the worst conditions, when it was in the form of a rather battered typescript, spotted with typing errors. I could not put it down and I shall not forget it. It is not a 'nice' book – but that other world was not 'nice'. Crude? Perhaps, but, to me it rings true and as Ibsen said, 'A man should never put on his best trousers when he goes out to battle for freedom and truth.'

My advice would be – read; lest we forget.

TEDDER
14 April 1953

## APPENDIX B

# Introduction to the First Edition

Richard Pape, a tough red-headed Sergeant Navigator from York-shire, was shot down and captured in 1941 while returning from a bomber raid over Berlin. Inspired by Douglas Bader whom he met in his first camp, he made up his mind to escape from Germany at all costs. After incredible adventures and severe hardship he did so in 1944 exactly three years after his capture. The method he finally adopted was at least novel.

Shortly after his return to England and following a second crash, he came under my care. At that time, though anxious to fly, he still showed the mental and physical marks of his sufferings in enemy hands. Contact with his own kind, however, did much to restore his health.

Readers will congratulate him on his indomitable courage and his remarkable endurance under the most nerve-racking circumstances. They cannot fail to be impressed by this unvarnished record of his unending fight for freedom.

ARCHIBALD MCINDOE
East Grinstead
8 April 1953

# MAPS

# ROUTES TAKEN BY PAPE AS A POW

ESCAPE ROUTE
PRISONER ROUTE
ROUTE TO
AND FROM
BERCHTESGADEN

HOLLAND
AMSTERDAM
③
⑤ LEYDEN
④ LAREN
② ZUTPHEN
① HENGELO

HAGUE

NORTH

GERMANY

LEIPZIG

FRANKFURT

SALZBU

BERCHTESGADEN

MA
PO

A

1 Crashed near Hengelo
2-4 Joined and worked for
Dutch Underground movement
5 Captured on night we were
due to be taken off by British
submarine
6 Stalag VIII B
7 Escaped from coal mine with
Mieteck
8 Cared for by Nuns
9 Recaptured in German Officers' mess
10 In farm camp here
11 Escaped from farm
12 Go to meet underground helper
who was arrested two days
before my arrival
13 Broke into home for food and
attacked man when discovered
14 Recaptured
15 Stalag Luft VI: Feigned incurable
disease

MILES 0 20 40 60 80 100 120 140

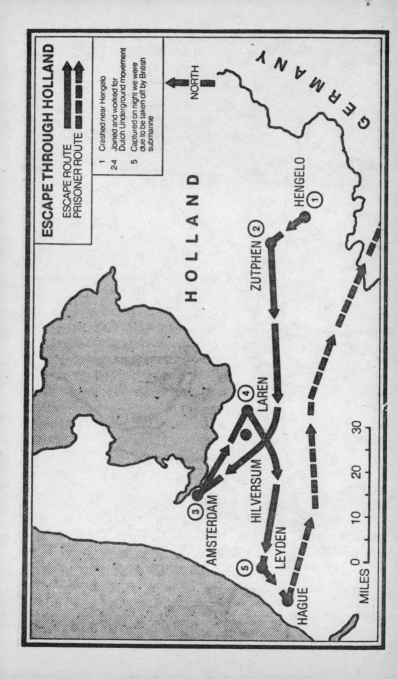

NORTH

GERMANY

DRESDEN

BRESLAU

VIII B

PRAGUE

C Z E C H O S L O V A K I A

BRÜNN

PUPPING

MUNICH

VIENNA

SALZBURG

KAISERSTEINBRUCH

BERCHTESGADEN

H U N G A R Y

MARKT PONGAU

AUSTRIA

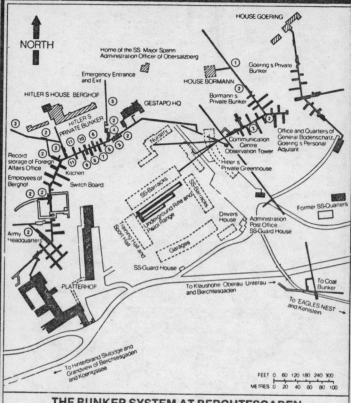

NORTH

HOUSE GOERING

Home of the SS Major Spann
Administration Officer of Obersalzberg

Goering's Private
Bunker

Emergency Entrance
and Exit

HOUSE BORMANN

HITLER'S HOUSE BERGHOF

Bormann's
Private Bunker

GESTAPO HQ

HITLER'S
PRIVATE BUNKER

Nursery

Office and Quarters of
General Bodenschatz,
Goering's Personal
Adjutant

Communication
Centre
Observation Tower

Record
storage of Foreign
Affairs Office

Hitler's
Private Greenhouse

Kitchen

Employees of
Berghof

Switch Board

SS-Barracks

SS-Barracks

Former SS-Quarters

Underground Rifle and
Pistol Range

Army
Headquarters

Drivers
House

Administration
Post Office
SS-Guard House

Garages

PLATTERHOF

SS-Guard House

To Klaushohe Oberau Unterau
and Berchtesgaden

To Coal
Bunker

To 'EAGLES NEST'
and Kehlstein

To Hinterbrand Skilodge and
Grandview of Berchtesgaden
and Koenigssee

FEET 0 60 120 180 240 300
METRES 0 20 40 60 80 100

# THE BUNKER SYSTEM AT BERCHTESGADEN, ILLUSTRATING ORIGINAL AND PRESENT-DAY LAYOUT

UNDERGROUND FACILITIES
Average depth 100 feet in rock

1 Way to the Administration and
Bormann-Bunker
2 Shelter of the Machine-Guns
3 Heating and Fresh Air Ventilation
Shaft
4 Dog Kennels
5 Toilets and Bathroom for
Private Guard
6 Private Guard
7 Dining Room
8 Hitler's Private Living Quarters
9 Quarters of Dr. Morell,
Hitler's Personal Doctor
10 Eva Braun's Private Living
Quarters
11 Guest Rooms

 EXISTING BUILDINGS

 DESTROYED BUILDINGS

 HISTORICAL

 EXISTING UNDERGROUND
FACILITIES

 PROJECTED OR DESTROYED
UNDERGROUND FACILITIES

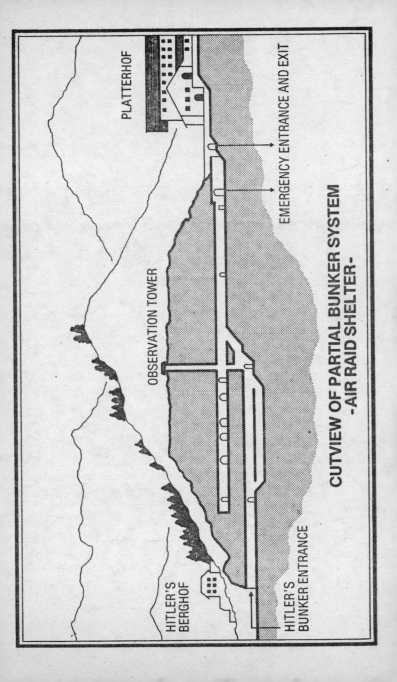

CUTVIEW OF PARTIAL BUNKER SYSTEM
-AIR RAID SHELTER-

PLATTERHOF

EMERGENCY ENTRANCE AND EXIT

OBSERVATION TOWER

HITLER'S BERGHOF

HITLER'S BUNKER ENTRANCE